Basic Engineering Thermodynamics

Basic Engineering Thermodynamics

M. W. Zemansky, Ph.D.

The City College of the
City University of New York

H. C. Van Ness, D. Eng.
Professor of Chemical Engineering
Rensselaer Polytechnic Institute

McGraw-Hill Book Company
New York/St. Louis
San Francisco
Toronto
London
Sydney

Basic Engineering Thermodynamics

Copyright © 1966 by McGraw-Hill, Inc.
All Rights Reserved. Printed in the
United States of America. This book, or
parts thereof, may not be reproduced in
any form without permission of the
publishers. *Library of Congress Catalog
Card Number* 65-28596

72805

234567890 M P 732106987

Preface

It has been our purpose to prepare a textbook for an initial, one-semester course in thermodynamics for engineers of any discipline. Such a course must stress the fundamental principles of thermodynamics, but at the same time its scope must serve to prepare students for a variety of second courses in which the principles are applied to different kinds of systems. Thus, while paying ample attention to simple fluid systems, we have also included careful treatments of solid systems under stress, surfaces, cells, and electric and magnetic systems. Specialized applications, however, are left to later courses.

We have drawn very heavily upon Zemansky's "Heat and Thermodynamics," which has had wide acceptance for some thirty years as an introductory text for students in both science and engineering. The present work may reasonably be viewed as an engineering edition of that work, specifically designed for use in the "engineering science" portion of engineering curricula.

The first fourteen chapters are devoted to classical thermodynamics, which makes no appeal to the atomistic nature of matter. The final chapter presents an introduction to statistical thermodynamics, which is based on atomic and quantum theory. Its purpose is to provide a deeper insight into the laws of thermodynamics through consideration of the microscopic behavior of material systems.

M. W. Zemansky
H. C. Van Ness

Contents

Capital Italics

A	Helmholtz function, area, first virial coefficient
B	Second virial coefficient
C	Heat capacity, third virial coefficient, capacitance, Curie constant
D	Fourth virial coefficient
E	Young's modulus, unavailable energy, energy
F	Faraday constant, force, fluid friction
G	Gibbs function
H	Enthalpy
I	Current
K	Dielectric coefficient, equilibrium constant
L	Length
M	Molecular weight
N	Number of particles
N_0	Avogadro's number
P	Total pressure, probability
Q	Heat
R	Universal gas constant, electric resistance
S	Entropy
T	Absolute temperature
U	Internal energy
V	Volume
W	Work

X Generalized force

Z Compressibility factor, partition function

Lower-case Italics

a Acceleration

c Velocity of sound

d Exact differential sign

e Electromotive force, base of natural logarithms

g Local acceleration of gravity, degeneracy

g_c Dimensional constant

h Planck's constant

j Valence

k Isothermal compressibility, Boltzmann's constant

k_S Adiabatic compressibility

l Length

m Mass

n Number of moles

p Partial pressure

q Electric charge

r Radius

t Celsius or Fahrenheit temperature

u Velocity

v Potential difference

x Mole fraction, quality, generalized displacement

y Mole fraction, fraction liquefied

z Elevation above datum level

Script Capitals

$\mathscr{B}$ Magnetic induction

$\mathscr{E}$ Electric field intensity

$\mathscr{H}$ Magnetic field intensity

$\mathscr{M}$ Magnetization

$\mathscr{P}$ Polarization

Special Symbols

đ   Inexact differential sign

ln   Natural logarithm

T^* Magnetic temperature

$\langle \ \rangle$ Average-value sign

$|\ \ |$ Absolute-value sign

$\cdot$ Time-derivative sign

Greek Letters

α Linear expansivity

β Volume expansivity

γ Ratio of heat capacities, surface tension
δ Linear compressibility
Δ Finite-difference sign
ϵ Strain, permittivity, degree of reaction
ϵ_0 Permittivity of a vacuum
η Efficiency
θ Empiric temperature
μ Joule-Kelvin coefficient
μ_0 Constant
ν Stoichiometric coefficient
Π Continuous-product sign
ρ Density
Σ Summation sign
σ Stress, deviation
τ Time

Chapter 1/
Temperature

1.1/ Macroscopic Point of View

The application of scientific principles to the solution of any real problem must necessarily start with a separation of a restricted region of
space or a finite portion of matter from its surroundings. The portion
which is set aside (in the imagination) and on which attention is focused
is called the *system*, and everything outside the system which has a
direct bearing on its behavior is known as the *surroundings*. When a
system has been chosen, the next step is to describe it in terms of quantities that will be helpful in discussing the behavior of the system or its
interactions with the surroundings, or both. There are in general two
points of view that may be adopted, the *macroscopic* and the *microscopic*.
Let us take as a system the contents of a cylinder of an automobile
engine. A chemical analysis would show a mixture of hydrocarbons
and air before explosion, and after the mixture had been ignited there
would be combustion products describable in terms of certain chemical
compounds. A statement of the relative amounts of these substances
is a description of the *composition* of the system. At any moment, the
system whose composition has just been described occupies a certain
volume, depending on the position of the piston. The volume can be
easily measured and, in the laboratory, is recorded automatically by
means of an appliance coupled to the piston. Another quantity that
is indispensable in the description of our system is the *pressure* of the

1

gases in the cylinder. After explosion this pressure is large; after exhaust it is small. In the laboratory, a pressure gauge may be used to measure the changes of pressure and to make an automatic record as the engine operates. Finally, there is one more quantity without which we should have no adequate idea of the operation of the engine: the *temperature*. As we shall see, in many instances, it can be measured just as simply as the other quantities.

We have described the materials in a cylinder of an automobile engine by specifying four quantities: composition, volume, pressure, and temperature. These quantities refer to the gross characteristics, or large-scale properties, of the system and provide a *macroscopic description*. They are therefore called *macroscopic coordinates*. The quantities that must be specified to provide a macroscopic description of other systems are, of course, different; but macroscopic coordinates in general have the following characteristics in common:

1. They involve no special assumptions concerning the structure of matter.
2. Only a few coordinates are needed for a macroscopic description.
3. They are suggested more or less directly by our sense perceptions.
4. They can in general be directly measured.

In short, a macroscopic description of a system involves the specification of a *few fundamental measurable properties* of a system. Although the macroscopic point of view is the one adopted in thermodynamics, the student should understand that the microscopic point of view is of great value and that it may serve to provide a deeper insight into the principles of thermodynamics. This point of view is taken in the branch of science called *statistical mechanics*. Since we shall return later to this subject, it seems at this point worthwhile to indicate the distinction between the two points of view. Let us give a simple microscopic description of a gas in a containing vessel.

1.2/ Microscopic Point of View

We shall assume that a gas consists of an enormous number N of particles called molecules, all having the same mass and each moving with a velocity independent of the others. The position of any molecule is specified by the three cartesian coordinates x, y, and z, and the velocity by the three components v_x, v_y, and v_z. Therefore, to describe the position and velocity of a molecule, six numbers are required. A microscopic description of the state of the gas consists of the specification of these six numbers for each of the N molecules.

It is not necessary to pursue the matter further to understand that a microscopic description involves the following characteristics:

1. Assumptions are made concerning the structure of matter; e.g., the existence of molecules is assumed.
2. Many quantities must be specified.
3. The quantities specified are not suggested by our sense perceptions.
4. These quantities cannot be measured.

1.3/ Macroscopic versus Microscopic

Although it might seem that the two points of view are hopelessly different and incompatible, there is, nevertheless, a relation between them, and when both points of view are applied to the same system, they must lead to the same conclusions. The relation between the two points of view lies in the fact that the few directly measurable properties whose specification constitutes the macroscopic description are really averages over a period of time of a large number of microscopic characteristics. For example, the macroscopic quantity pressure is the average rate of change of momentum due to all the molecular collisions made on a unit of area. Pressure, however, is a property that is perceived by our senses. We feel the effects of pressure. Pressure was experienced, measured, and used long before scientists and engineers had reason to believe in the existence of molecular impacts. If molecular theory is changed or even discarded at some time in the future, the concept of pressure will still remain and will still mean the same thing to all normal human beings. Herein lies an important distinction between the macroscopic and microscopic points of view. The few measurable macroscopic properties are as sure as our senses. They will remain unchanged as long as our senses remain the same. The microscopic point of view, however, goes much further than our senses. It postulates the existence of molecules, their motion, collisions, etc. It is constantly being changed, and we can never be sure that the assumptions are justified until we have compared some deduction made on the basis of these assumptions with a similar deduction based on observed macroscopic behavior.

1.4/ Scope of Thermodynamics

It has been emphasized that a description of the gross characteristics of a system by means of a few of its measurable properties, suggested more or less directly by our sense perceptions, constitutes a macroscopic description. Such descriptions are the starting point of all investigations in all branches of science and engineering. For example, in dealing with the mechanics of a rigid body, the macroscopic point of view is adopted in that only the external aspects of the rigid body are considered. The position of its center of mass is specified with reference to coordinate axes at a particular time. Position and time and a combination of both, such as velocity, represent some of the macroscopic quantities used in mechanics, and are called *mechanical coordinates*. The mechanical coordinates serve to determine the potential and the kinetic energy of the rigid body with reference to the coordinate axes, i.e., the kinetic and the potential energy of the body as a whole. These two types of energy constitute the *external*, or *mechanical*, *energy* of the rigid body. It is the purpose of mechanics to find such relations between the position coordinates and the time as are consistent with Newton's laws of motion.

In thermodynamics, however, attention is directed to the *interior* of a system. A macroscopic point of view is nevertheless adopted, but only those macroscopic quantities are considered which have a bearing on the internal state of a system. It is the function of experiment to determine the quantities that are necessary and sufficient for such a purpose. *Macroscopic quantities having a bearing on the internal state of a system are called thermodynamic coordinates.* Specification of a sufficient number of such coordinates serves to determine the internal state of a system, and in particular to determine its *internal energy*. A system that may be described in terms of thermodynamic coordinates is called a *thermodynamic system*. It is the purpose of thermodynamics to find general relations connecting the internal energy and other internal properties of a system with the thermodynamic coordinates and to relate changes in the thermodynamic state of a system to its interactions with its surroundings. The unifying principles with which all such considerations must be consistent are known as the laws of thermodynamics.

A wide variety of thermodynamic systems is of interest. A pure vapor such as steam constitutes the working medium of a power plant. A reacting mixture of gasoline and air powers an automotive engine. A vaporizing liquid such as ammonia provides refrigeration. The expanding gases in a nozzle propel a rocket. Other examples include the stressed members of structures, the surface region of an emulsion, a fuel cell for the generation of electricity, and thermoelectric devices.

1.5/ Thermal Equilibrium

We have seen that a macroscopic description of a gaseous mixture may be given by specifying such quantities as the composition, the mass, the pressure, and the volume. Experiment shows that for a given composition and for a constant mass many different values of pressure and volume are possible. If the pressure is kept constant, the volume may vary over a wide range of values, and vice versa. In other words, the pressure and the volume are independent coordinates. Similarly, experiment shows that for a wire of constant mass the tension and the length are independent coordinates, whereas in the case of a surface film, the surface tension and the area may be varied independently.

Some systems that, at first sight, seem quite complicated, such as an electric cell with two different electrodes and an electrolyte, may still be described with the aid of only two independent coordinates. On the other hand, some systems composed of a number of homogeneous parts require the specification of two independent coordinates for each homogeneous part. The essential role of experiment in determining the number and nature of the independent variables is particularly to be noted. Details of various thermodynamic systems and their thermodynamic coordinates will be given in Chap. 2. For the present, to simplify our discussion, we shall deal only with systems of constant mass and composition, each requiring *only one pair* of independent coordinates for its description. This involves no essential loss of generality and results in a considerable saving of words. In referring to any nonspecified system, we shall use the symbols Y and X for the pair of independent coordinates.

A state of a system in which Y and X have definite values which remain constant so long as the external conditions are unchanged is called an *equilibrium* state. Experiment shows that the existence of an equilibrium state in one system depends on the proximity of other systems and on the nature of the wall separating them. Walls are said to be either adiabatic or diathermic. If a wall is *adiabatic* (see Fig. 1.1a), a state Y, X for system A and Y', X' for system B may coexist as equilibrium states for *any* attainable values of the four quantities, provided only that the wall is able to withstand the stress associated with the difference between the two sets of coordinates. Thick layers of wood, asbestos, felt, etc., are good experimental approximations to adiabatic walls. If the two systems are separated by a *diathermic* wall (see Fig.

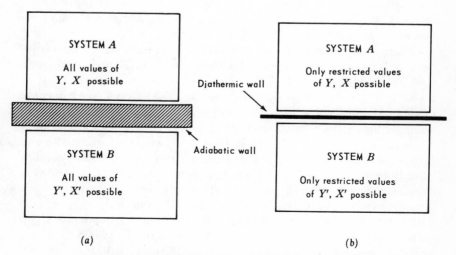

(a)

(b)

Fig. 1.1 **Properties of adiabatic and diathermic walls.**

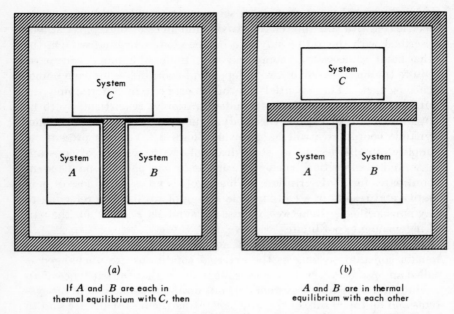

(a)

If A and B are each in
thermal equilibrium with C, then

(b)

A and B are in thermal
equilibrium with each other

Fig. 1.2 The zeroth law of thermodynamics. (Adiabatic walls are designated by cross shading; diathermic walls, by heavy lines.)

1.1b), the values of Y, X and Y', X' will change spontaneously until an equilibrium state of the combined system is attained. The two systems are then said to be in *thermal equilibrium* with each other. The commonest diathermic wall is a thin metallic sheet. *Thermal equilibrium is the state achieved by two (or more) systems, characterized by restricted values of the coordinates of the systems, after they have been in communication with one another through a diathermic wall.*

Imagine two systems A and B separated from each other by an adiabatic wall but each in contact with a third system C through diathermic walls, the whole assembly being surrounded by an adiabatic wall as shown in Fig. 1.2a. Experiment shows that the two systems will come to thermal equilibrium with the third and that no further change will occur if the adiabatic wall separating A and B is then replaced by a diathermic wall (Fig. 1.2b). If, instead of allowing both systems A and B to come to equilibrium with C at the same time, we first have equilibrium between A and C and then equilibrium between B and C (the state of system C being the same in both cases), then, when A and B are brought into communication through a diathermic wall, they will be found to be in thermal equilibrium. We shall use the expression "two systems are in thermal equilibrium" to mean that the two systems are in states such that, if the two *were* connected through a diathermic wall, the combined system *would be* in thermal equilibrium.

These experimental facts may then be stated concisely in the following form: *Two systems in thermal equilibrium with a third are in thermal equilibrium with each other.* Following R. H. Fowler, we shall call this postulate the *zeroth law of thermodynamics*.

1.6/ Temperature Concept

Consider a system A in the state Y_1, X_1 in thermal equilibrium with a system B in the state Y_1', X_1'. If system A is removed and its state changed, there will be found another state Y_2, X_2 in which it is in thermal equilibrium with the *original* state Y_1', X_1' of system B. Experiment shows that there exists a whole set of states Y_1, X_1; Y_2, X_2; Y_3, X_3; . . . every one of which is in thermal equilibrium with this *same* state Y_1', X_1' of system B and which, by the zeroth law, are in thermal equilibrium with one another. We shall suppose that *all* such states, when plotted on a YX diagram, lie on a curve such as I in Fig. 1.3, which we shall call an *isotherm.* *An isotherm is the locus of all points representing states at which a system is in thermal equilibrium with one state of another system.* We make no assumption as to the continuity of the isotherm, although experiments on simple systems indicate usually that at least a portion of an isotherm is a continuous curve.

Similarly, with regard to system B, we find a set of states Y_1', X_1'; Y_2', X_2'; . . . all of which are in thermal equilibrium with one state (Y_1, X_1) of system A, and therefore in thermal equilibrium with one another. These states are plotted on the $Y'X'$ diagram of Fig. 1.3 and lie on the isotherm I'. From the zeroth law, it follows that all the states on isotherm I of system A are in thermal equilibrium with all the states on isotherm I' of system B. We shall call curves I and I' *corresponding isotherms* of the two systems.

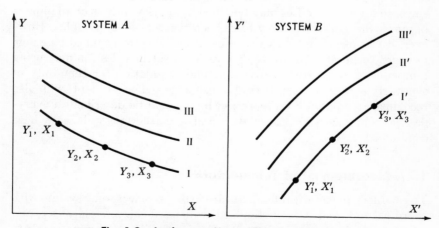

Fig. 1.3 Isotherms of two different systems.

If the experiments outlined above are repeated with different starting conditions, another set of states of system A lying on curve II may be found, every one of which is in thermal equilibrium with every state of system B lying on curve II'. In this way, a family of isotherms, I, II, III, etc., of system A and a corresponding family I', II', III', etc., of system B may be found. Furthermore, by repeated applications of the zeroth law, corresponding isotherms of still other systems C, D, etc., may be obtained.

All states of corresponding isotherms of all systems have something in common, namely, that they are in thermal equilibrium with one another. The systems themselves, in these states, may be said to possess a property that ensures their being in thermal equilibrium with one another. We call this property *temperature*. *The temperature of a system is a property that determines whether or not a system is in thermal equilibrium with other systems.*

The temperature of all systems in thermal equilibrium may be represented by a number. The establishment of a temperature scale is merely the adoption of a set of rules for assigning one number to one set of corresponding isotherms and a different number to a different set of corresponding isotherms. Once this is done, the necessary and sufficient condition for thermal equilibrium between two systems is that they have the same temperature. Also, when the temperatures are different, we may be sure that the systems are not in thermal equilibrium.

The preceding operational treatment of the concept of temperature merely expresses the fundamental idea that the temperature of a system is a property which eventually attains the same value as that of other systems when all these systems are put in contact or separated by thin metallic walls within an enclosure of thick asbestos walls. The student will recognize that this concept is identical with the everyday idea of temperature as a measure of the hotness or coldness of a system, since, so far as our senses may be relied upon, the hotness of all objects becomes the same after they have been together long enough. However, it was necessary to express this simple idea in technical language in order to be able to establish a rational set of rules for measuring temperature and also to provide a solid foundation for the study of thermodynamics and statistical mechanics. The student will also recognize an adiabatic wall as one which would be described in everyday language as a heat insulator, and a diathermic wall, as a heat conductor.

1.7/ Measurement of Temperature

To establish an empirical temperature scale, we select some system with coordinates Y and X as a standard, which we call a *thermometer*, and adopt a set of rules for assigning a numerical value to the temperature

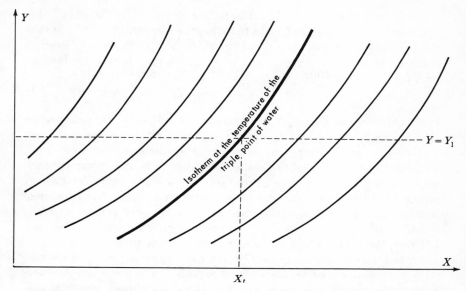

Fig. 1.4   Setting up a temperature scale involves the assignment of numerical values to the isotherms of an arbitrarily chosen standard system, or thermometer.

associated with each of its isotherms.   To every other system in thermal equilibrium with the thermometer, we assign the same number for the temperature.   The simplest procedure is to choose any convenient path in the YX plane such as that shown in Fig. 1.4 by the dashed line $Y = Y_1$ which intersects the isotherms at points each of which has the same Y coordinate but a different X coordinate.   The temperature associated with each isotherm is then taken to be a convenient function of the X at this intersection point.   The coordinate X is called the *thermometric property*, and the form of the *thermometric function* $\theta(X)$ determines the temperature scale.   There are five important kinds of thermometer, each with its own thermometric property, as shown in Table 1.1.

Table 1.1/ Thermometers and Thermometric Properties

Thermometer	Thermometric property	Symbol
Gas kept at constant volume	Pressure	P
Gas kept at constant pressure	Volume	V
Electric resistor (under constant pressure and tension)	Electric resistance	R
Thermocouple (under constant pressure and tension)	Thermal emf	e
Liquid column in a glass capillary	Length	L

Let X stand for any one of the thermometric properties listed in Table 1.1, and let us decide arbitrarily to define the temperature scale so that the temperature θ is directly proportional to X. Thus the temperature common to the thermometer *and to all systems in thermal equilibrium with it* is given by

$$\theta = aX \qquad \text{const } Y. \tag{1.1}$$

It should be noted that *different* temperature scales usually result when this arbitrary relation is applied to different kinds of thermometers and even when it is applied to different systems of the same kind. Thus one must ultimately select, either arbitrarily or in some rational way, one kind of thermometer and one particular system (or type of system) to serve as the standard thermometric device. But regardless of what standard is chosen, one must clearly have some rule by which to establish the value of a in Eq. (1.1) so as to yield a numerical relation between the temperature θ and the thermometric property X.

Equation (1.1) applies generally to a thermometer placed in contact with a system whose temperature θ is to be measured. If the thermometer is placed in contact with an arbitrarily chosen standard system in an easily reproducible state where the temperature is θ_t, then

$$\theta_t = aX_t. \tag{1.2}$$

An easily reproducible state of an arbitrarily chosen standard system is called a fixed point. Since 1954 only one fixed point has been in use, the *triple point of water*, the state of pure water existing as an equilibrium mixture of ice, liquid, and vapor. The temperature at which this state exists is arbitrarily assigned the value of 273.16 degrees Kelvin, abbreviated 273.16°K. (The reason for the use of Kelvin's name will become clear later.) Equation (1.2) solved for a now becomes†

$$a = \frac{273.16°}{X_t}. \tag{1.3}$$

The subscript t is used to identify the property value X_t explicitly with the triple-point temperature. Equation (1.1) now becomes

$$\theta = \left(\frac{273.16°}{X_t}\right) X \qquad \text{const } Y. \tag{1.4}$$

The temperature of the triple point of water is the *standard fixed point* of thermometry. To achieve the triple point, water of the highest purity is distilled into a vessel, depicted schematically in Fig. 1.5.

---

† Prior to 1954 the method employed to determine a was based on the use of two fixed points, the ice point and steam point of water. The present method is both simpler and more precise. The reason for the choice of the number 273.16 is that it makes the new temperature scale agree as closely as possible with the old.

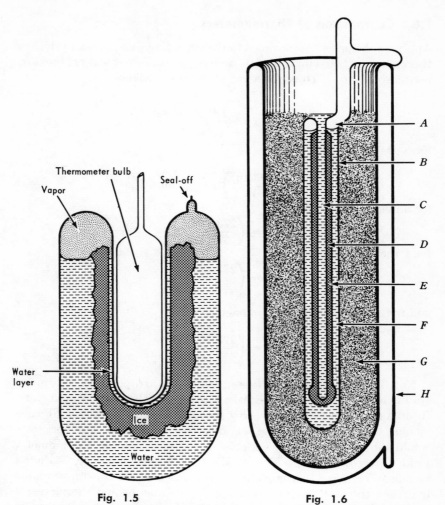

Fig. 1.5

Fig. 1.6

Fig. 1.5 Triple-point cell, with a thermometer in the well, which melts a thin layer of ice nearby.

Fig. 1.6 Diagram of the NBS triple-point cell (B, D) in use in an ice bath (G) within a Dewar flask (H). A, water vapor; C, thermometer well; E, ice mantle; F, liquid water.

When all air has been removed, the vessel is sealed off.   With the aid of a freezing mixture in the inner well, a layer of ice is formed around the well.   When the freezing mixture is replaced by a thermometer bulb, a thin layer of ice is melted nearby, as shown in Fig. 1.5.   So long as the solid, liquid, and vapor phases coexist in equilibrium, the system is at the triple point.   The actual shape of the apparatus used by the U.S. National Bureau of Standards is shown in Fig. 1.6.

1.8/ **Comparison of Thermometers**

Applying the principles outlined in the preceding paragraphs to the five thermometers listed in Table 1.1, we have five different ways of measuring temperature. Thus, for a gas at constant volume,

$$\theta_P = \left(\frac{273.16°}{P_t}\right) P \qquad \text{const } V;$$

for a gas at constant pressure,

$$\theta_V = \left(\frac{273.16°}{V_t}\right) V \qquad \text{const } P;$$

for an electric resistor,

$$\theta_R = \left(\frac{273.16°}{R_t}\right) R;$$

for a thermocouple,

$$\theta_e = \left(\frac{273.16°}{e_t}\right) e;$$

and for a liquid-in-glass thermometer,

$$\theta_L = \left(\frac{273.16°}{L_t}\right) L.$$

Now imagine a series of tests in which the temperature of a given system is measured simultaneously with each of the five thermometers. Results of such a test would show that there is considerable difference among the readings of the various thermometers. Further tests would show that different varieties of the same kind of thermometer yield different results. The smallest variation, however, is found among different gas thermometers. In particular, the constant-volume hydrogen thermometer and the constant-volume helium thermometer agree more closely than the others. For this reason a gas is chosen as the standard thermometric substance.

1.9/ **Gas Thermometer**

A schematic diagram of a constant-volume gas thermometer is shown in Fig. 1.7. The materials, construction, and dimensions differ in the various bureaus and institutes throughout the world where these instruments are used, and depend on the nature of the gas and the temperature range for which the thermometer is intended. The gas is contained in the bulb B, which communicates with the mercury column M through a capillary. The volume of the gas is kept constant by adjusting the height of the mercury column M until the mercury level

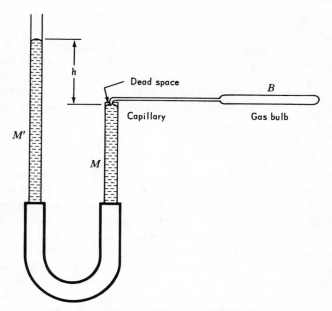

Fig. 1.7   Constant-volume gas thermometer.

just touches the tip of the projection of the capillary into the space above M, known as the *dead space*, or *nuisance volume*.   The mercury column M is adjusted by raising or lowering the tube M'.   The difference in height h between the two mercury columns M and M' is measured when the bulb is surrounded by the system whose temperature is to be measured and when it is surrounded by water at the triple point.   It is clear that the pressure of the gas under any conditions is given by

$$P = \text{atmospheric pressure} \pm h,$$

the plus sign to be used when the top of M' is above the top of M.

The various values of the pressure must be corrected to take account of the following sources of error:

1. The gas present in the dead space (and in any other nuisance volumes) is at a temperature different from that in the bulb.

2. The gas in the capillary connecting the bulb with the manometer has a temperature gradient; i.e., it is not at a uniform temperature.

3. The bulb, capillary, and nuisance volumes undergo changes of volume when the temperature and pressure change.

4. If the diameter of the capillary is comparable with the mean free path of the molecules of the gas, a pressure gradient exists in the capillary (Knudsen effect).

5. Some gas is adsorbed on the walls of the bulb and capillary; the lower the temperature, the greater the adsorption.

6. There are effects due to temperature and compressibility of the mercury in the manometer.

Some of these sources of error may be eliminated by proper design of the gas thermometer. Others are taken into account by elaborate calculations. For the present, let us assume that the corrections have been made and that the temperature is calculated from the equation

$$\theta = 273.16° \frac{P}{P_t} \qquad \text{const } V.$$

In this discussion nothing has been said and nothing need be said regarding the physical reality or attainability of the state of a gas for which $\theta = 0$, $P = 0$. We have simply chosen to fix our temperature scale so that θ is directly proportional to P for a gas at constant volume throughout whatever range the gas actually exists. Clearly, our definition is still incomplete, for we have not specified the gas to be used or the amount of gas to be confined in a given volume when pressure measurements are made. This is taken up in the next section.

The constant-volume gas thermometer is superior to the constant-pressure instrument with regard to simplicity of construction, ease of operation, and reliability of correction, and therefore the constant-volume thermometer is used almost exclusively in present-day work.

1.10/ Ideal-gas Temperature

Suppose that an amount of gas is introduced into the bulb of a constant-volume gas thermometer so that the pressure P_t, when the bulb is surrounded by water at its triple point, is equal to 1,000 mm Hg. Keeping the volume V constant, suppose the following procedures are carried out:

1. Surrounding the bulb with steam condensing at 1 atm pressure, determine the gas pressure P and calculate

$$\theta = 273.16° \frac{P}{1,000}.$$

2. Remove some of the gas so that P_t has a smaller value, say, 500 mm Hg. Determine the new value of P and calculate a new value

$$\theta = 273.16° \frac{P}{500}.$$

3. Continue reducing the amount of gas in the bulb so that P_t and P have smaller and smaller values, P_t having values of, say, 250 mm Hg, 100 mm Hg, etc. At *each* value of P_t, calculate the corresponding θ.

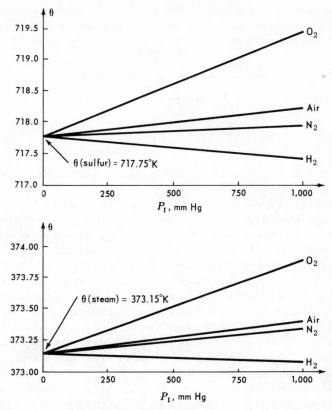

Fig. 1.8 Readings of a constant-volume gas thermometer for the temperature of condensing steam and for that of condensing sulfur when different gases are used at various values of P_t.

4. Plot θ against P_t and extrapolate the resulting curve to the axis where $P_t = 0$. Read from the graph

$$\lim_{P_t \to 0} \theta.$$

The results of a series of tests of this sort are plotted in Fig. 1.8 for four different gases in order to measure θ not only of condensing steam but also of condensing sulfur. The graph conveys the information that, although the readings of a constant-volume gas thermometer depend upon the nature of the gas at ordinary values of P_t, *all gases indicate the same temperature as P_t is lowered and made to approach zero.*

A similar series of tests may be made with a constant-pressure gas thermometer. The constant pressure P may first be taken to be 1,000 mm Hg, then 500 mm Hg, etc., and at each value of P, the corresponding value of θ may be calculated. Again, experiment shows that all gases indicate the same value of θ as P approaches zero.

We therefore define the *ideal-gas temperature* T by either of the two equations

$$
T = \begin{cases} 273.16° \lim\limits_{P_t \to 0} \dfrac{P}{P_t} & \text{const } V, \\[2ex] 273.16° \lim\limits_{P \to 0} \dfrac{V}{V_t} & \text{const } P, \end{cases}
$$

where θ has been replaced by T to denote this particular temperature scale.

Although the ideal-gas temperature scale is independent of the properties of any one particular gas, it still depends on the properties of gases in general. To measure a low temperature, a gas must be used at that low temperature. The lowest ideal-gas temperature that can be measured with a gas thermometer is about 1°K, provided low-pressure helium is used. *The temperature $T = 0$ remains as yet undefined.*

In Chap. 8 the Kelvin temperature scale, which is independent of the properties of any particular substance, will be developed. It will be shown that, in the temperature region in which a gas thermometer may be used, the ideal-gas scale and the Kelvin scale are identical. In anticipation of this result we write °K after an ideal-gas temperature. It will also be shown in Chap. 8 how the absolute zero of temperature is defined on the Kelvin scale. Until then, the phrase "absolute zero" will have no meaning. It should be remarked that the statement, found in so many textbooks of elementary physics, that, at the temperature $T = 0$, all molecular activity ceases is entirely erroneous. First, such a statement involves an assumption connecting the purely macroscopic concept of temperature and the microscopic concept of molecular motion. If we want our theory to be general, this is precisely the sort of assumption that must be avoided. Second, when it is necessary in statistical mechanics to correlate temperature to molecular activity, it is found that classical statistical mechanics must be modified with the aid of quantum mechanics and that, when this modification is carried out, the molecules of a substance at absolute zero have a *finite* amount of kinetic energy, known as the zero-point energy.

1.11/ Celsius Temperature Scale

The Celsius temperature scale employs a degree of the same magnitude as that of the ideal-gas scale, but its zero point is shifted so that *the Celsius temperature of the triple point of water is 0.01 degree Celsius,* abbreviated 0.01°C.   Thus, if t denotes the Celsius temperature,

$$t = T - 273.15°.$$

Thus the Celsius temperature t_S at which steam condenses at 1 atm pressure is

$$t_S = T_S - 273.15°,$$

and reading θ_S (now T_S) from Fig. 1.8,

$$t_S = 373.15° - 273.15°,$$
or $$t_S = 100.00°C.$$

Similar measurements for the ice point show this temperature on the Celsius scale to be 0.00°C.   It should be noted, however, that these two temperatures are subject to the experimental uncertainty attending the determination of intercepts by extrapolation as illustrated in Fig. 1.8. The only Celsius temperature which is fixed *by definition* is that of the triple point.

Helium is the most useful gas for thermometric purposes for two reasons.   At high temperatures helium does not diffuse through platinum, whereas hydrogen does.   Furthermore, helium becomes a liquid at a temperature lower than any other gas, and therefore a helium thermometer may be used to measure temperatures lower than those which can be measured with any other gas thermometer.   The accurate measurement of an ideal gas or Celsius temperature requires months of painstaking laboratory work and mathematical computation and, when completed, is an international event.   This work is published in a physical journal, and the temperatures of such fixed points as the normal boiling points and normal melting points of selected materials are listed in tables of physical constants.

1.12/ Temperature Scales before 1954

The temperature scales in use before 1954 required for their specification two fixed points, the ice point and the steam point.   The primary difficulty with this procedure was that these fixed points proved to be not so easily reproduced.   Measurements made with the greatest care in laboratories around the world failed to agree to the extent considered desirable.   Moreover, it gradually became evident in the years preceding 1954 that the triple point of water was reproducible with great precision and that it alone would suffice to define the ideal-gas temperature scale.

The idea of defining a temperature scale with the aid of only one fixed point with an arbitrary choice of a *universal constant* for the temperature at this point was first suggested by Lord Kelvin in 1854, but it was not regarded as expedient at the time. The idea was revived in 1939 by W. F. Giauque, professor of chemistry at the University of California, and supported most vigorously by the physicists and chemists engaged in research throughout the world.

In May, 1948, the Advisory Committee on Thermometry of the International Committee on Weights and Measures chose the value 273.15°K for the ice point (273.16°K for the triple point of water) for consideration by the International Union of Physicists. The Union, at its meeting in July, 1948, made the definite and positive recommendation that the Giauque proposal be adopted to replace the old scale. When the International Committee on Weights and Measures met in October, 1948, to consider this recommendation, it was felt that the advisory committee should study the matter further and report at the next meeting in 1954.

At the Tenth Conference on Weights and Measures in Paris during the summer of 1954, the Giauque proposal was passed. As we have seen, the single fixed point was chosen to be the triple point of water, which was set arbitrarily at the value 273.16°K. The Celsius scale was defined at the same time. This scale was formerly referred to in many parts of the world, including the United States, as the centigrade scale.

1.13/ Electric-resistance Thermometry

Very accurate temperature measurements are possible with carefully calibrated resistance thermometers. The platinum resistance thermometer serves as a secondary temperature standard over a wide temperature range in laboratories throughout the world. It is a delicate instrument, made of a long fine wire, usually wound on a thin frame in such a way as to avoid appreciable changes in stress with temperature change.

It is customary to measure the resistance by maintaining a known constant current in the thermometer and measuring the potential difference across it with the aid of a very sensitive potentiometer. A typical circuit is shown in Fig. 1.9. The current is held constant by adjusting a rheostat so that the potential difference across a standard resistor in series with the thermometer, as observed with a monitoring potentiometer, remains constant.

The platinum resistance thermometer may be used for very accurate work within the range of −200 to 1200°C. It is rather slow, however, because of the mass of metal that must come to thermal equilibrium. The calibration of the instrument involves the measurement of its resistance R at various known temperatures and the representation of the results by an empirical formula. In a restricted range, the following

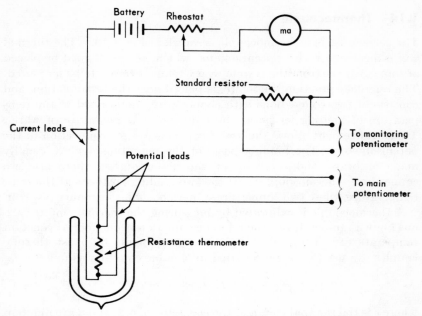

Fig. 1.9 Circuit for measuring the resistance of a resistance thermometer through which a constant current is maintained.

quadratic equation is often used:

$$R = R_0(1 + At + Bt^2),$$

where A and B are constants, and R_0 is the resistance of the platinum wire when it is surrounded by melting ice, or better, placed in a triple-point cell.

It should be noted that once the ideal-gas scale is adopted as the standard temperature scale, the relation between resistance and temperature is not linear. This is true also of other thermometric properties. Earlier in this chapter we noted the possibility of defining linear temperature scales based on several thermometric properties. However, once a particular property is chosen to provide a linear scale, the others will in general not be linear. Moreover, the resistance of different materials varies in different ways with temperature, and purity of material is important. This problem does not arise in gas thermometry when limiting values such as $P \rightarrow 0$ are used.

The thermistor, a resistance thermometer made of a semiconductor, has now come into widespread use. Its resistance *decreases* rapidly with increasing temperature, and when placed in a Wheatstone-bridge circuit, it can be used as a very sensitive thermometer. Thermistors are available in many shapes and sizes, and are thus suitable for a great variety of applications.

1.14/ Thermocouple

The correct use of a thermocouple is shown in Fig. 1.10. The thermal emf is measured with a potentiometer, which, as a rule, must be placed at some distance from the system whose temperature is to be measured. The reference junction, therefore, is placed near the test junction, and consists of two connections with copper wire, maintained at the temperature of melting ice or at the triple-point temperature of water. This arrangement allows the use of copper wires for connection to the potentiometer. The binding posts of the potentiometer are usually made of brass, and therefore at the potentiometer there are two copper-brass thermocouples. If the two binding posts are at the same temperature, these two copper-brass thermocouples introduce no error.

A thermocouple is calibrated by measuring the thermal emf at various known temperatures, the reference junction being kept at constant temperature. The results of such measurements on most thermocouples can usually be represented by a cubic equation as follows:

$$e = a + bt + ct^2 + dt^3,$$

where e is the thermal emf, and the constants a, b, c, and d are different for each thermocouple. Within a restricted range of temperature, a quadratic equation is often sufficient. The range of a thermocouple depends upon the materials of which it is composed. A platinum–platinum-rhodium couple has a range of 0 to 1600°C. The advantage of a thermocouple is that it comes to thermal equilibrium with the system whose temperature is to be measured quite rapidly, because its mass is small. It therefore follows temperature changes easily.

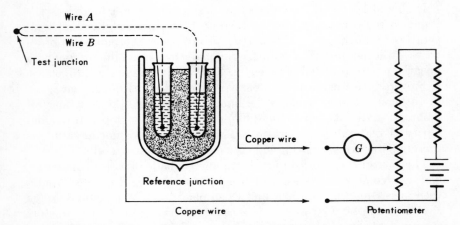

Fig. 1.10 Thermocouple of wires A and B with a reference junction consisting of two junctions with copper, connected to a potentiometer.

1.15/ International Practical Temperature Scale

At the meeting of the Seventh General Conference of Weights and Measures in 1927, at which 31 nations were represented, an international temperature scale was adopted, not to replace the Celsius or ideal-gas scales, but to provide a scale that could be easily and rapidly used to calibrate scientific and industrial instruments. Slight refinements were incorporated into the scale in revisions adopted in 1948, 1954, and 1960. The international practical scale agrees with the Celsius scale at the defining fixed points listed in Table 1.2. Values are also available for 22 secondary reference points. At temperatures between these fixed points the departure from the Celsius scale is small enough to be neglected in most practical work. The temperature interval from the oxygen point to the gold point is divided into three main parts, as follows:

1. From 0 to 660°C

A platinum resistance thermometer with a platinum wire whose diameter must lie between the limits 0.05 and 0.20 mm is used, and the temperature is given by the formula

$$R = R_0(1 + At + Bt^2),$$

where the constants R_0, A, and B are determined by measurements at the ice point, steam point, and sulfur point.

2. From —190 to 0°C

The same platinum resistance thermometer is used, and the temperature is given by the formula

$$R = R_0[1 + At + Bt^2 + C(t - 100)t^3].$$

R_0, A, and B are the same as before, and C is determined from one measurement at the oxygen point.

Table 1.2/ Defining Fixed Points for the International Practical Temperature Scale†

	Temp., °C
Normal boiling point of oxygen	−182.97
Triple point of water (standard)	+ 0.01
Normal boiling point of water	100.00
Normal boiling point of sulfur	444.6
(Normal melting point of zinc—suggested as an alternative to the sulfur point)	419.505
Normal melting point of silver	960.8
Normal melting point of gold	1063

† As given by H. F. Stimson, *J. Res. Natl. Bur. Std.*, 65A:140 (1961).

3. From 660 to 1063°C

A thermocouple, one wire of which is made of platinum and other made of an alloy of 90 percent platinum and 10 percent rhodium, is maintained with one junction at 0°C. The diameter of each wire must lie between 0.35 and 0.65 mm. The temperature is given by the formula

$$e = a + bt + ct^2,$$

where a, b, and c are determined from measurements at the antimony point, silver point, and gold point.

For temperatures higher than the gold point, an optical method is used. The intensity of the radiation of any convenient wavelength is compared with the intensity of radiation of the same wavelength emitted by a blackbody at the gold point. The temperature is then calculated with the aid of Planck's radiation law.

1.16/ The Rankine and Fahrenheit Scales

The temperature scales most commonly used by engineers are based on a degree five-ninths the size of the Kelvin and Celsius degree. By definition, the Rankine scale is given by

$$T°R = 1.8(T°K).$$

The Fahrenheit scale is defined in relation to the Rankine scale by the equation

$$t°F = T°R - 459.67.$$

Thus, at the ice point, where the Kelvin temperature is 273.15, the Rankine temperature is $(1.8)(273.15) = 491.67$. Hence the Fahrenheit temperature is

$$491.67 - 459.67 = 32.00°F.$$

Similarly, at the steam point, the Rankine temperature is

$$(1.8)(373.15) = 671.67,$$

and the Fahrenheit temperature is

$$671.67 - 459.67 = 212.00°F.$$

The Fahrenheit temperature is related to the Celsius temperature by

$$t°F = 1.8(t°C) + 32.00.$$

Problems

1.1 The limiting value of the ratio of the pressures of a gas at the steam point and at the triple point of water when the gas is kept at constant volume is found to be 1.36605.   What is the ideal-gas temperature of the steam point?

1.2   The resistance of a platinum wire is found to be 11.000 ohms at the ice point, 15.247 ohms at the steam point, and 28.887 ohms at the sulfur point.   Find the constants A and B in the equation

$$R = R_0(1 + At + Bt^2),$$

and plot R against t in the range from 0 to 660°C.

1.3   When the reference junction of a thermocouple is kept at the ice point and the test junction is at the Celsius temperature t, the emf e of the thermocouple is given by the equation

$$e = \alpha t + \beta t^2,$$

where $\alpha = 0.20$ mv/°C, and $\beta = -5.0 \times 10^{-4}$ mv/°C².

(a)   Compute the emf when $t = -100, 200, 400,$ and 500°C, and draw a graph of e against t in this range.

(b)   Suppose the emf e is taken as a thermometric property and that a temperature scale t^* is defined by the linear equation

$$t^* = ae + b$$

and that $t^* = 0$ at the ice point and $t^* = 100°$ at the steam point. Find the numerical values of a and b, and draw a graph of e against t^*.

(c)   Find the values of t^* when $t = -100, 200, 400,$ and 500°C, and draw a graph of t^* against t.

(d)   Compare the Celsius scale with the t^* scale.

1.4   It will be shown in Chap. 5 that, for the same number of moles of gas at the same temperature,

$$\lim_{P \to 0} (PV) = \text{a universal constant}$$

for all gases.   Show how this fact may be used to set up a temperature scale:

(a)   Using the triple point of water as the only fixed point.

(b)   Using both the ice point and the steam point as fixed points.

1.5   When the ice point and the steam point are chosen as fixed points with 100 degrees between them, the ideal-gas temperature of the ice point may be written

$$T_i = \frac{100}{r_s - 1},$$

where $r_s = \lim (P_s/P_i)$ at const V.

(a)   Show that the fractional error in T_i produced by an error in r_s is very nearly 3.73 times the fractional error in r_s, or

$$\frac{dT_i}{T_i} = 3.73 \frac{dr_s}{r_s}.$$

Any ideal-gas temperature may be written

$$T = T_i r,$$

where $r = \lim (P/P_i)$ at const V.

(b) Show that the fractional error in T is

$$\frac{dT}{T} = \frac{dr}{r} + 3.73 \frac{dr_s}{r_s}.$$

(c) Now that there is only one fixed point at which the ideal-gas temperature is a universal constant, show that the fractional error in T is

$$\frac{dT}{T} = \frac{dr}{r},$$

where $r = \lim (P/P_t)$ at const V.

Chapter 2/
Thermodynamic Systems

2.1/ Thermodynamic Equilibrium

Suppose that experiments have been performed on a thermodynamic system and that the coordinates necessary and sufficient for a macroscopic description have been determined. When these coordinates change in any way whatsoever, either spontaneously or by virtue of outside influence, the system is said to undergo a *change of state*.† When a system is not influenced in any way by its surroundings, it is said to be isolated. In practical applications of thermodynamics, isolated systems are of little importance. We usually have to deal with a system that is influenced in some way by its surroundings. In general, the surroundings may exert forces on the system or provide contact between the system and a body at some definite temperature. When the state of a system changes, interactions usually take place between the system and its surroundings.

When there is no unbalanced force in the interior of a system and also none between a system and its surroundings, the system is said to be in a state of *mechanical equilibrium*. When these conditions are not satisfied, either the system alone or both the system and its surroundings

---

† This must not be confused with the terminology of elementary physics, where the expression "change of state" is often used to signify a transition from solid to liquid or liquid to gas, etc. Such a change in the language of thermodynamics is called a "change of phase."

will undergo a change of state, which will cease only when mechanical equilibrium is restored.

When a system in mechanical equilibrium does not tend to undergo a spontaneous change of internal structure, such as a chemical reaction, or a transfer of matter from one part of the system to another, such as diffusion or solution, however slow, it is said to be in a state of *chemical equilibrium.* A system not in chemical equilibrium undergoes a change of state that, in some cases, is exceedingly slow. The change ceases when chemical equilibrium is reached.

Thermal equilibrium exists where there is no spontaneous change in the coordinates of a system in mechanical and chemical equilibrium when it is separated from its surroundings by a diathermic wall. In thermal equilibrium, all parts of a system are at the same temperature, and this temperature is the same as that of the surroundings. When these conditions are not satisfied, a change of state will take place until thermal equilibrium is reached.

When the conditions for all three types of equilibrium are satisfied, the system is said to be in a state of *thermodynamic equilibrium;* in this condition, it is apparent that there will be no tendency whatever for any change of state of either the system or the surroundings to occur. *States of thermodynamic equilibrium can be described in terms of macroscopic coordinates that do not involve the time, i.e., in terms of thermodynamic coordinates.* Thermodynamics does not attempt to deal with any problem involving the rate at which a process takes place. The investigation of such problems is carried out in other branches of science and engineering, such as fluid mechanics, transport phenomena, and chemical kinetics.

When the conditions for any one of the three types of equilibrium that constitute thermodynamic equilibrium are not satisfied, the system is said to be in a *nonequilibrium state.* Thus, when there is an unbalanced force in the interior of a system or between a system and its surroundings, the following phenomena may take place: acceleration, turbulence, eddies, waves, etc. While such phenomena are in progress, a system passes through nonequilibrium states. If an attempt is made to give a macroscopic description of any one of these nonequilibrium states, it is found that the pressure varies from one part of a system to another. There is no single pressure that refers to the system as a whole. Similarly, in the case of a system at a different temperature from its surroundings, a nonuniform temperature distribution is set up and there is no single temperature that refers to the system as a whole. We therefore conclude that *when the conditions for mechanical and thermal equilibrium are not satisfied, the states traversed by a system cannot be described in terms of thermodynamic coordinates referring to the system as a whole.*

It must not be concluded, however, that we are entirely helpless in dealing with such nonequilibrium states. If we divide the system into a large number of small mass elements, then thermodynamic coordinates may be found in terms of which a macroscopic description of each mass element may be approximated. There are also special methods for dealing with systems in mechanical and thermal equilibrium, but not in chemical equilibrium. At present we shall deal exclusively with systems in thermodynamic equilibrium.

2.2/ Equation of State

Imagine for the sake of simplicity a constant mass of gas in a vessel so equipped that the pressure, volume, and temperature may be easily measured. If we fix the volume at some arbitrary value and cause the temperature to assume an arbitrarily chosen value, we shall not be able to vary the pressure at all. Once V and T are chosen by us, the value of P at equilibrium is determined by nature. Similarly, if P and T are chosen arbitrarily, the value of V at equilibrium is fixed. That is, of the three thermodynamic coordinates P, V, and T, only two are independent variables. This implies that there exists an equation of equilibrium which connects the thermodynamic coordinates and which robs one of them of its independence. Such an equation is called an *equation of state*. Every thermodynamic system has its own equation of state, although in some cases the relation may be so complicated that it cannot be expressed in terms of simple mathematical functions.

An equation of state expresses the individual peculiarities of one system in contradistinction to another, and must therefore be determined either by experiment or by molecular theory. A general theory like thermodynamics, based on general laws of nature, is incapable of expressing the behavior of one material as opposed to another. An equation of state is therefore not a theoretical deduction from thermodynamics, but is usually an experimental addition to thermodynamics. It expresses the results of experiments in which the thermodynamic coordinates of a system were measured as accurately as possible, within a limited range of values. An equation of state is therefore only as accurate as the experiments that led to its formulation and holds only within the range of values measured. As soon as this range is exceeded, a different form of equation of state may be valid.

For example, a system consisting of exactly 1 mole of gas (1 gram mole = M grams, or 1 pound mole = M pounds, where M is the molecular weight) and at low pressure has the equation of state

$$PV = RT,$$

where R is a constant, and the V indicates molar volume. At higher pressures, its equation of state is more complicated, and is often represented by

$$\frac{PV}{RT} = 1 + \frac{B(T)}{V} + \frac{C(T)}{V^2} + \cdots,$$

where R is a constant, and $B(T)$ and $C(T)$ are functions of T. As far as thermodynamics is concerned, the important thing is that an equation of state exists, not whether we can write it down mathematically.

It is obvious that no equation of state exists for the states traversed by a system which is not in mechanical and thermal equilibrium, since such states cannot be described in terms of thermodynamic coordinates referring to the system as a whole. For example, if a gas in a cylinder were to expand and to impart to a piston an accelerated motion, the gas might have, at any moment, a definite volume and temperature, but the corresponding pressure could not be calculated from an equation of state. The pressure would not be a thermodynamic coordinate because it would not only depend on the velocity and the acceleration of the piston but would also perhaps vary from point to point.

The example of a gas at equilibrium is a special case of a general class of systems which can be described in terms of the three thermodynamic coordinates P, V, and T. The next section is devoted to a consideration of such systems. There are many other types of systems which may be described at least to a first approximation by means of three thermodynamic coordinates, which may be given the generalized designations X, Y, and Z. It is characteristic of such systems that an equation of state exists which connects the three coordinates. Such "XYZ systems" will be called *simple systems*. PVT systems represent an important type of simple system. Another type is represented by structural members in tension or compression; yet another, by surfaces. These and others will be considered later in this chapter and in subsequent chapters.

2.3/ PVT Systems

Any isotropic system of constant mass and constant composition that exerts on the surroundings a uniform hydrostatic pressure, in the absence of surface, gravitational, electrical, and magnetic effects, we shall call a *PVT system*. *PVT* systems are divided into the following categories:

1. *A pure substance*, which is one chemical constituent in the form of a solid, a liquid, or a gas.

2. *A homogeneous mixture of different constituents*, such as a mixture of gases, a mixture of liquids, or a solid solution.

Experiment shows that the states of equilibrium† of a *PVT* system can be described with the aid of three coordinates, namely, the pressure

---

† In the remainder of this book the word "equilibrium," unmodified by any adjective, will refer to thermodynamic equilibrium.

P exerted by the system on the surroundings, the volume V, and the absolute temperature T.

Every PVT system has an equation of state expressing a relation among these three coordinates that is valid for states of equilibrium only. If the system undergoes a small change of state whereby it passes from an initial state of equilibrium to another state of equilibrium very near the initial one, then all three coordinates, in general, undergo slight changes. If the change of, say, V is very small in comparison with V and very large in comparison with the space occupied by a few molecules, this change of V may be written as a differential dV. If V were a geometrical quantity referring to the volume of space, dV could be used to denote a portion of that space arbitrarily small. Since, however, V is a macroscopic coordinate denoting the volume of *matter*, then, for dV to have a meaning, it must be large enough to include enough molecules to warrant the use of the macroscopic point of view.

Similarly, if the change of P is very small in comparison with P and very large in comparison with molecular fluctuations, it also may be represented by the differential dP. *Every infinitesimal in thermodynamics must satisfy the requirement that it represents a change in a quantity which is small with respect to the quantity itself and large in comparison with the effect produced by the behavior of a few molecules.* The reason for this is that thermodynamic coordinates such as volume, pressure, and temperature have no meaning when applied to a few molecules. This is another way of saying that thermodynamic coordinates are macroscopic coordinates.

We may imagine the equation of state solved for any coordinate in terms of the other two. Thus

$$V = \text{function of } (T,P).$$

An infinitesimal change from one state of equilibrium to another state of equilibrium involves a dV, a dT, and a dP, all of which we shall assume satisfy the condition laid down in the previous paragraph. A fundamental theorem in partial differential calculus enables us to write

$$dV = \left(\frac{\partial V}{\partial T}\right)_P dT + \left(\frac{\partial V}{\partial P}\right)_T dP,$$

where each partial derivative is itself a function of T and P. Both the above partial derivatives have an important physical meaning. The student will remember from elementary physics a quantity called the average coefficient of volume expansion, or volume expansivity. This was defined as

$$\text{Average volume expansion} = \frac{\text{change of volume per unit volume}}{\text{change of temperature}}$$

and referred to conditions under which the pressure was constant. If the change of temperature is made smaller and smaller until it becomes infinitesimal, the change in volume also becomes infinitesimal and we have what is known as the instantaneous volume expansivity, or just volume expansivity, which is denoted by β. Thus

$$\beta = \frac{1}{V}\left(\frac{\partial V}{\partial T}\right)_P.$$

A similar quantity called the *isothermal compressibility*, denoted by k, shows the influence of pressure on volume at constant temperature. Thus

$$k = -\frac{1}{V}\left(\frac{\partial V}{\partial P}\right)_T.$$

Since a positive change (increase) of pressure produces a negative change (decrease) of volume, the minus sign is introduced to make the isothermal compressibility a positive number.

Both β and k are properties and, like volume, are functions of T and P. Numerical values of β and k obtained by experiment are often tabulated for liquids and solids in compilations of data. It is often found that they vary only slowly with T and P, and are therefore sometimes treated as though constant.

If the equation of state is solved for P, then

$$P = \text{function of } (T,V)$$

and

$$dP = \left(\frac{\partial P}{\partial T}\right)_V dT + \left(\frac{\partial P}{\partial V}\right)_T dV.$$

Finally, if T is imagined as a function of P and V,

$$dT = \left(\frac{\partial T}{\partial P}\right)_V dP + \left(\frac{\partial T}{\partial V}\right)_P dV.$$

In all the above equations the system was assumed to undergo an infinitesimal change from an initial state of equilibrium to another. This enabled us to use an equation of equilibrium (equation of state) and to solve it for any coordinate in terms of the other two. The differentials dP, dV, and dT therefore are differentials of actual functions, and are called *exact differentials*. If dz is an exact differential of a function of, say, x and y, then dz may be written

$$dz = \left(\frac{\partial z}{\partial x}\right)_y dx + \left(\frac{\partial z}{\partial y}\right)_x dy.$$

An infinitesimal that is not the differential of an actual function is called an *inexact differential*, and cannot be expressed by an equation of the above type.   There are other distinctions between exact and inexact differentials that will be made clear later.

2.4/ Mathematical Theorems

Two simple theorems in partial differential calculus are used very often in this subject.   The proofs are as follows: Suppose there is a relation among the three coordinates x, y, and z; thus

$$f(x,y,z) = 0.$$

Then x can be imagined as a function of y and z, and

$$dx = \left(\frac{\partial x}{\partial y}\right)_z dy + \left(\frac{\partial x}{\partial z}\right)_y dz.$$

Also, y can be imagined as a function of x and z, and

$$dy = \left(\frac{\partial y}{\partial x}\right)_z dx + \left(\frac{\partial y}{\partial z}\right)_x dz.$$

Substituting the second equation into the first, we have

$$dx = \left(\frac{\partial x}{\partial y}\right)_z \left[\left(\frac{\partial y}{\partial x}\right)_z dx + \left(\frac{\partial y}{\partial z}\right)_x dz\right] + \left(\frac{\partial x}{\partial z}\right)_y dz,$$

or $$dx = \left(\frac{\partial x}{\partial y}\right)_z \left(\frac{\partial y}{\partial x}\right)_z dx + \left[\left(\frac{\partial x}{\partial y}\right)_z \left(\frac{\partial y}{\partial z}\right)_x + \left(\frac{\partial x}{\partial z}\right)_y\right] dz.$$

Now, of the three coordinates, only two are independent.   Choosing x and z as the independent coordinates, the above equation must be true for all sets of values of dx and dz.   Thus, if $dz = 0$ and $dx \neq 0$, it follows that

$$\left(\frac{\partial x}{\partial y}\right)_z \left(\frac{\partial y}{\partial x}\right)_z = 1,$$

or

$$\boxed{\left(\frac{\partial x}{\partial y}\right)_z = \frac{1}{(\partial y/\partial x)_z}.}$$

(2.1)

If $dx = 0$ and $dz \neq 0$, it follows that

$$\left(\frac{\partial x}{\partial y}\right)_z \left(\frac{\partial y}{\partial z}\right)_x + \left(\frac{\partial x}{\partial z}\right)_y = 0,$$

$$\boxed{\begin{array}{c}\left(\frac{\partial x}{\partial y}\right)_z \left(\frac{\partial y}{\partial z}\right)_x = -\left(\frac{\partial x}{\partial z}\right)_y, \\[2mm] \left(\frac{\partial x}{\partial y}\right)_z \left(\frac{\partial y}{\partial z}\right)_x \left(\frac{\partial z}{\partial x}\right)_y = -1.\end{array}}$$

(2.2)

In the case of a PVT system, the second theorem yields the result

$$\left(\frac{\partial P}{\partial V}\right)_T \left(\frac{\partial V}{\partial T}\right)_P = -\left(\frac{\partial P}{\partial T}\right)_V.$$

The volume expansivity β and the isothermal compressibility k were defined as

$$\beta = \frac{1}{V}\left(\frac{\partial V}{\partial T}\right)_P \quad \text{and} \quad k = -\frac{1}{V}\left(\frac{\partial V}{\partial P}\right)_T,$$

and therefore

$$\left(\frac{\partial P}{\partial T}\right)_V = \frac{\beta}{k}.$$

An infinitesimal change in pressure may now be expressed in terms of these physical quantities. Thus

$$dP = \left(\frac{\partial P}{\partial T}\right)_V dT + \left(\frac{\partial P}{\partial V}\right)_T dV$$

$$= \frac{\beta}{k} dT - \frac{1}{kV} dV.$$

At constant volume,

$$dP = \frac{\beta}{k} dT.$$

If we cause the temperature to change a finite amount from T_1 to T_2 at constant volume, the pressure will change from P_1 to P_2, where the subscripts 1 and 2 denote the initial and final states, respectively. Upon integrating between these two states, we get

$$P_2 - P_1 = \int_{T_1}^{T_2} \frac{\beta}{k} dT.$$

The right-hand member can be integrated if we know the way in which β and k vary with T at constant volume. If the temperature range $T_2 - T_1$ is small, very little error is introduced by assuming that both are constant. With these assumptions we get

$$P_2 - P_1 = \frac{\beta}{k}(T_2 - T_1),$$

from which the final pressure may be calculated. For example, consider the following problem: A mass of mercury at a pressure of 1 atm and a temperature of 0°C is kept at constant volume. If the temperature is raised to 10°C, what will be the final pressure? From tables of physical constants, β and k of mercury remain practically constant within the temperature range of 0 to 10°C and have the values

$$\beta = 181 \times 10^{-6} \text{ °C}^{-1},$$
$$k = 4.04 \times 10^{-6} \text{ atm}^{-1};$$

whence

$$P_2 - P_1 = \frac{181 \times 10^{-6} \ °C^{-1}}{4.04 \times 10^{-6} \ atm^{-1}} \times 10°C$$
$$= 449 \ atm$$

and
$$P_2 = 449 + 1 = 450 \ atm.$$

2.5/ Engineering Units

The same fundamental quantities needed in the science of mechanics, i.e., length, time, and mass (or length, time, and force), are used in thermodynamics, with the addition of a fourth, the temperature. The primary standard units for these fundamental quantities have been arbitrarily defined through international agreement, and other convenient units are defined as fractions or multiples of the standard units. As we have already seen, the primary standard unit of temperature is the Kelvin degree. The Celsius, Fahrenheit, and Rankine degrees are all defined in terms of the Kelvin degree.

The primary standard of length is the wavelength of orange-red light from krypton-86 atoms. A commonly used unit of length is called one *meter*, and is defined to be 1,650,763.73 standard wavelengths. The primary standard of time is the tropical year 1900, and the commonest unit of time, one *second*, is defined to be 1/31,556,925.9747 of the standard. The primary standard of mass is the mass of a platinum-iridium cylinder preserved at the International Bureau of Weights and Measures in Sèvres, France. The mass of this standard is often used as a unit, and is called one *kilogram*. When one uses these units of length, mass, and time, one speaks of the mks system of units. The centimeter-gram-second, or cgs, system of units is also commonly employed by scientists.

Engineers in the English-speaking world use an English system of units based upon the pound, the foot, and the second. Nevertheless, they must have a familiarity with scientific units, for data are often available only in such units. Facility in conversion from one system of units to another is essential.

The dual role played by the pound in the English system of units to designate both force and mass leads to an unfortunate ambiguity. Since force and mass are different concepts, the pound *force* must be carefully distinguished from the pound *mass*. In this book the mass unit will be designated by lb_m and the force unit by lb_f.

Force and mass are related by Newton's second law of motion, which states that the net force on a body is proportional to its mass and acceleration. Most systems of units are contrived to make the proportionality constant unity. Thus we normally write

$$F = ma.$$

In the mks system, the unit of force is the newton, defined as that force necessary to accelerate a one-kilogram mass one meter per second per second. Thus

$$1 \text{ newton} = (1 \text{ kilogram}) \left(1 \frac{\text{meter}}{\text{second}^2}\right).$$

The newton is clearly not an independent unit, but represents the composite unit kilogram-meter/second². The dyne is similarly related to the gram, centimeter, and second.

In the English system of units the pound *force* is defined independently of Newton's law as that force which accelerates one pound *mass* 32.174 feet per second per second. Substitution into the expression $F = ma$ gives

$$1 \text{ lb}_f = (1 \text{ lb}_m)(32.174 \text{ ft/sec}^2),$$

which is clearly incorrect. This difficulty is resolved by including a proportionality constant in Newton's law:

$$F = \left(\frac{1}{g_c}\right) ma,$$

where the proportionality constant is written $1/g_c$. It is easily seen that the constant g_c has a value of 32.174 and units of pound *mass* per pound *force* times feet per second per second $[(\text{lb}_m/\text{lb}_f)(\text{ft/sec}^2)]$. Hence, if one uses the pound *force* as the unit of force and the pound *mass* as the unit of mass, then Newton's law must include this dimensional proportionality constant. This constant will also appear in numerous other formulas derived from Newton's law.

Two alternative English systems of units are also in use which solve the problem in a different way. If we write Newton's law as

$$F \text{ in lb}_f = \left(\frac{m \text{ in lb}_m}{32.174}\right) (a \text{ in ft/sec}^2),$$

we see that a new mass unit could be defined which would be 32.174 times the pound mass. This unit is called the slug, and

$$1 \text{ slug} = 32.174 \text{ lb}_m.$$

When force is given in pounds *force* and mass in slugs, Newton's law again becomes $F = ma$:

$$F \text{ in lb}_f = (m \text{ in slugs})(a \text{ in ft/sec}^2).$$

The other alternative is to write Newton's law as

$$(F \text{ in lb}_f)(32.174) = (m \text{ in lb}_m)(a \text{ in ft/sec}^2).$$

From this we see that a new force unit may be defined which is smaller than the pound *force* by a factor of 32.174. This unit is called the poundal, and

$$1 \text{ lb}_f = 32.174 \text{ poundals.}$$

When force is given in poundals and mass in pounds *mass*, Newton's law is again written $F = ma$:

$$F \text{ in poundals } = (m \text{ in lb}_m)(a \text{ in ft/sec}^2).$$

In summary, three systems of English units are in use by engineers. They are known by various names; those given in Table 2.1 are as suitable as any.

The English absolute system is analogous to the metric systems of units, the poundal being a derived unit like the Newton and dyne. Thus the poundal represents the composite unit pounds *mass*-foot per second per second ($\text{lb}_m \cdot \text{ft/sec}^2$).

In the English gravitational system the mass unit is the derived quantity and represents the composite unit pounds *force*-second squared per foot ($\text{lb}_f \cdot \text{sec}^2/\text{ft}$).

The English engineering system recognizes the fact that in English-speaking countries mass is measured in pounds *mass* and force in pounds *force*. Although the layman takes no note of the difference, the engineer must always know whether he is dealing with mass or force. This system has the disadvantage of introducing the dimensional constant g_c, the location of which in numerous formulas must be remembered. On the other hand, the inclusion of g_c in the various formulas makes them valid for any self-consistent set of units whatever, for g_c may always be set equal to unity whenever a system of units is employed which does not require it. For this reason the formulas of this book are written with g_c included wherever appropriate. In using either the English absolute or English gravitational system of units, one must always remember to convert either pounds *force* to poundals or pounds *mass* to slugs, depending upon which system is employed.

All this suggests that engineers ought either settle upon one system of English units or, better, adopt the mks system once and for all. This is

Table 2.1 / English Engineering Units

	English absolute system	English gravitational system	English engineering system
Force	poundal ($\text{lb}_m \cdot \text{ft/sec}^2$)	lb_f	lb_f
Mass	lb_m	slug ($\text{lb}_f \cdot \text{sec}^2/\text{ft}$)	lb_m
Length	ft	ft	ft
Time	sec	sec	sec
Form of Newton's law	$F = ma$	$F = ma$	$F = \dfrac{ma}{g_c}$

widely accepted as being desirable, but the prospect for its accomplishment is as dim as ever. The engineer must therefore continue to struggle with his systems of units and their conversion.

Since thermodynamics deals primarily with energy and its transformations, the units of energy are of particular importance. The primary units of energy in scientific work are the dyne-centimeter, or erg, and the newton-meter, or joule. In the English system the basic energy units are the foot-pound *force* and the foot-poundal, the latter being rarely used. Many other energy units are in common use. It seems best, however, to defer discussion of them until the first law of thermodynamics is considered (Chap. 4). A list of commonly used conversion factors is given in Appendix A.

2.6/ Bars in Tension and Compression

Structural members in tension and compression usually exist under conditions of atmospheric pressure. Furthermore, their volume changes are quite negligible. For most practical purposes, it is not necessary to include pressure and volume as thermodynamic coordinates. A sufficiently complete thermodynamic description of bars in tension or compression is given in terms of just three coordinates:

1. The stress in the member σ, defined as the load per unit of cross-sectional area, and usually measured in $lb_f/in.^2$ Stress is taken as $+$ for tension and $-$ for compression.
2. The length of the member L would be an appropriate coordinate, but this is usually replaced by the strain ϵ. By definition,

$$d\epsilon = \frac{dL}{L}.$$

It is seen that $d\epsilon$ is positive for tension and negative for compression.
3. The ideal-gas temperature T.

States of thermodynamic equilibrium are connected by an equation of state, which frequently is by no means simple. In the absence of a specific equation, we can still write a functional relationship connecting the thermodynamic coordinates, in this instance,

$$\epsilon = \epsilon(T,\sigma).$$

From this we have immediately, for a bar which undergoes an infinitesimal change from one equilibrium state to another,

$$d\epsilon = \left(\frac{\partial \epsilon}{\partial T}\right)_\sigma dT + \left(\frac{\partial \epsilon}{\partial \sigma}\right)_T d\sigma,$$

where both partial derivatives represent important physical quantities.

The first is called the linear expansivity, or coefficient of linear (thermal) expansion,

$$\alpha = \left(\frac{\partial \epsilon}{\partial T}\right)_\sigma,$$

and the second is the reciprocal of Young's modulus E, where

$$E = \left(\frac{\partial \sigma}{\partial \epsilon}\right)_T.$$

Thus we may write

$$d\epsilon = \alpha \, dT + \frac{1}{E} \, d\sigma.$$

If ϵ is constant, this equation becomes

$$\left(\frac{\partial \sigma}{\partial T}\right)_\epsilon = -\alpha E,$$

a result also obtained from Eq. (2.2).

Experimental measurements of α show it to be nearly independent of σ and to be a weak function of T. Thus, for small temperature changes, it may be regarded as essentially constant. Its units are reciprocal degrees. Young's modulus E is found to be independent of σ provided the proportional limit of the material is not exceeded. This is equivalent to saying that Hooke's law is valid, that is, $\sigma = E\epsilon$, at constant temperature. E is weakly dependent on temperature, but for a small temperature change it may safely be taken as constant. For metals, α and E are both usually positive. For rubber and rubberlike materials, α is negative, though E is positive.

2.7 / Surfaces

The surfaces of liquids and solids have properties which are distinctly different from the bulk properties of the underlying material. The simplest experimental demonstration of the influence of surfaces is given by a film of liquid (usually a soap solution) formed on a wire frame as shown in Fig. 2.1.

This film consists of two surfaces and a layer of liquid of small but finite thickness between them. It is found that a force F applied to the movable wire of the frame is necessary to hold the film in equilibrium. It is further observed that the force F is directly proportional to the length of the wire l, but that it is independent of x, and therefore is independent of the film thickness. This leads immediately to the conclusion that the origin of the force F is in the surfaces of the film and not in its interior. Thus the applied force F is a direct measure of the surface tension of the two surfaces which confine the bulk of the film:

$$\gamma = \frac{F}{2l}.$$

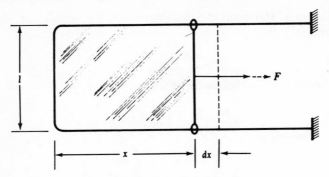

Fig. 2.1   Liquid film formed on a wire.

The *surface tension* by definition is the force attributed to the surface acting perpendicular to any boundary, real or imaginary, per unit length of boundary.   It is usually expressed in dynes per centimeter.

When the film of Fig. 2.1 is extended, material moves from the bulk of the liquid to the surfaces so as to form additional surface.   The film does not *stretch* in the usual sense of the word.   Only when the film is extended sufficiently to decrease its thickness to the point where no interior remains, so that it consists of just the two surfaces but a few molecules thick, does the film tend to stretch, and then it ruptures.

There is no sharp line of demarcation between a surface region (which is what is meant by *surface*) and the bulk of the underlying liquid.   By its very nature the surface cannot exist separately.   Thus liquid surfaces cannot be considered without including the accompanying liquid as part of the system.   We merely attribute to the surface that part of a "total system property" which results from the abnormality of a surface region.   For a pure liquid, the surface tension and the influence of the surface on the properties of the entire system are found to depend solely on temperature.   A number of empirical equations have been proposed to express γ as a function of T.

The phenomenon of capillarity depends upon the existence of surface tension in liquids, and certain properties of small drops and bubbles are significantly affected by their surfaces.   One cannot proceed very far with a study of this topic without finding it to be exceedingly complex. We do not pretend here to give more than the most elementary introduction.   For our purposes it is appropriate to treat a surface as a simple system characterized by the three coordinates surface tension γ, surface area A, and temperature T.

2.8/ Reversible Cell

There are several common types of reversible cell, but all consist of one or more electrolytes in which two electrodes are immersed.   The

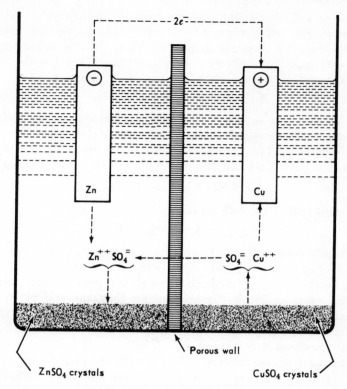

Fig. 2.2   The Daniell cell.

electromotive force of the cell depends on the nature of the materials, on the concentrations of the electrolytes, and on the temperature. The Daniell cell, which is representative of one type of reversible cell, is shown schematically in Fig. 2.2.   A zinc electrode immersed in a saturated $ZnSO_4$ solution is separated by a porous wall from a copper electrode immersed in a saturated solution of $CuSO_4$.   The cell is conventionally represented as

$$Zn|ZnSO_4(sat)\|CuSO_4(sat)|Cu,$$

where the single | indicates a phase boundary, and the double ‖ indicates the division of the cell into two half-cells.

Experiment shows that the copper electrode is positive with respect to the zinc.   Thus, if the electrodes of Fig. 2.2 are connected externally by a purely resistive circuit, the current in the external circuit may be described conventionally as a transfer of positive electricity from the copper to the zinc electrode.   The electrons flow in the opposite direction as indicated in Fig. 2.2.   The convention adopted for representation of cells, either pictorially or symbolically, is to place the negative electrode on the left and the positive electrode on the right. When so represented, the emf of the cell is conventionally regarded as positive.

The changes which occur in the cell when the electrodes are connected externally by a purely resistive circuit are represented by the chemical equation

$$Zn + CuSO_4 \rightarrow Cu + ZnSO_4.$$

Thus zinc goes into solution, zinc sulfate is formed, copper sulfate is used up, and copper is deposited on the positive electrode. The reaction may be divided into two half-reactions, one occurring in each half of the cell. In the left half of the Daniell cell the half-cell reaction is

$$Zn + SO_4^= \rightarrow ZnSO_4 + 2e^-.$$

In the right half of the cell, we have

$$CuSO_4 + 2e^- \rightarrow Cu + SO_4^=.$$

The sum of these two half-cell reactions gives the overall reaction of the cell.

Suppose that the cell is connected to a potentiometer whose potential difference opposes but is slightly smaller than the emf of the cell. Under these conditions the changes described above occur very slowly. If the imposed potential difference is slightly larger than the emf of the cell, the transfer of electricity in the cell will be reversed and the chemical changes will proceed slowly in the opposite direction. The essential feature of a reversible cell is that the chemical changes accompanying the transfer of electricity in one direction take place to the same extent in the reverse direction when the same quantity of electricity is transferred in the reverse direction. Furthermore, according to one of Faraday's laws of electrolysis, the simultaneous solution of one gram mole of zinc and deposition of one gram mole of copper, or the reverse, are accompanied by the transfer of exactly jF coul of electricity, where j is the valence and F is Faraday's constant, 96,500 coul.

We may therefore define a quantity q, called the *charge* of the cell, as a number whose absolute magnitude is of no consequence but whose change is numerically equal to the quantity of electricity that is transferred during the chemical reaction. Thus, if dn moles of material react, the charge of the cell changes by an amount dq, where

$$dq = -jF \, dn.$$

The minus sign arises because we adopt the convention that dn is positive when the chemical reaction proceeds in the forward direction, corresponding to *discharge* of the cell, and negative when the chemical reaction is reversed so as to *charge* the cell. For a finite change,

$$q_2 - q_1 = -jFn,$$

where the same sign convention applies to n as to dn.

Table 2.2/ Intensive and Extensive Quantities

System	Intensive coordinate	Extensive coordinate
PVT system	Pressure P	Volume V
Stressed bar	Stress σ	Strain ϵL
Surface	Surface tension γ	Area A
Electric cell	Emf e	Charge q

Now, if we limit ourselves to reversible cells in which no gases are liberated and which operate at constant pressure (usually atmospheric), we may ignore the pressure and volume and consider the cell a simple system characterized by the following three coordinates:

1. The emf of the cell e in volts.
2. The charge q in coulombs.
3. The ideal-gas temperature T.

A reversible cell is in equilibrium *only* when it is connected to a potentiometer and the circuit is adjusted until there is no current. The emf of the cell is then balanced, and the cell is in mechanical and chemical equilibrium. When thermal equilibrium is also established, the cell is in thermodynamic equilibrium. The states of thermodynamic equilibrium of a reversible cell are connected by an equation of state among the coordinates e, q, and T.

2.9/ Intensive and Extensive Quantities

Imagine a system in equilibrium to be divided into two equal parts, each with equal mass. Those properties of each half of the system which remain the same are said to be *intensive*. Those which are halved are called *extensive*. The intensive coordinates of a system, such as temperature and pressure, are independent of the mass; the extensive coordinates are proportional to the mass.

The thermodynamic coordinates for the four types of simple system that have been introduced in this chapter are listed in Table 2.2.

Problems

2.1   A mass of mercury at 40°F and 1 atm is heated to 50°F and its volume is held constant. What is the final pressure? Assume β and k constant at the values 1.0×10^{-4} °R^{-1} and 3.9×10^{-4} atm^{-1}.

2.2   Making use of the fact that

$$\frac{\partial^2 V}{\partial T\, \partial P} = \frac{\partial^2 V}{\partial P\, \partial T},$$

prove that

$$\left(\frac{\partial \beta}{\partial P}\right)_T = -\left(\frac{\partial k}{\partial T}\right)_P.$$

2.3 For water at 80°F, $k = 4.5 \times 10^{-5}$ atm^{-1}. To what pressure (in atmospheres) must water be compressed at 80°F to change its density by 1 percent? Assume k to be independent of P.

2.4 A hypothetical substance has the following volume expansivity and isothermal compressibility:

$$\beta = \frac{3aT^3}{V}, \qquad k = \frac{b}{V},$$

where a and b are constants. Find the equation of state.

2.5 The volume expansivity and the isothermal compressibility of a certain gas are

$$\beta = \frac{nR}{PV}, \qquad k = \frac{1}{P} + \frac{a}{V},$$

where n, R, and a are constants. Find the equation of state.

2.6 Express the volume expansivity and the isothermal compressibility in terms of the density ρ and its partial derivatives.

2.7 Is the pound *force*, which is defined in terms of its effect on a pound *mass*, independent of the acceleration of gravity; e.g., is it the same on the moon as on the earth?

2.8 An instrument to measure the acceleration of gravity on Mars is constructed of a spring from which is suspended a mass of 0.53 lb$_m$. At a place on earth where the local acceleration of gravity is 32.16 ft/sec^2, the spring extends 0.24 in. When the instrument package is landed on Mars, it radios back the information that the spring is extended 0.08 in. What is the Martian acceleration of gravity?

2.9 A group of scientists have landed on the moon, and they would like to determine the mass of several unusual rocks. They have a spring scale calibrated to read pounds *mass* at a location where the local acceleration of gravity is 32.2 ft/sec^2. One of the moon rocks gives a reading of 25 on the scale. What is its mass? What is its weight on the moon? The value of g on the surface of the moon is 5.47 ft/sec^2.

2.10 The equation of state of an ideal elastic substance under tension is

$$\sigma = KT\left(\lambda - \frac{1}{\lambda^2}\right),$$

where σ = nominal stress (force divided by the no-load area),
$\quad K$ = a constant,
$\quad \lambda$ = extension ratio, defined by $\lambda = L/L_0$, where L_0 (the no-load value of L) is a function of temperature only.

(a) Show that the isothermal Young's modulus is given by

$$E = \lambda \left(\frac{\partial \sigma}{\partial \lambda}\right)_T = \sigma + \frac{3KT}{\lambda^2}.$$

(b) Show that the isothermal Young's modulus at zero tension is given by

$$E_0 = 3KT.$$

(c) Show that the linear expansivity is given by

$$\alpha = \alpha_0 - \frac{\sigma}{ET},$$

where α_0 is the value of α at zero tension, or

$$\alpha_0 = \left(\frac{\partial \epsilon}{\partial T}\right)_{\sigma=0}.$$

(d) Assume the following values for a sample of rubber: $T = 500°R$, $K = 0.15 \text{ lb}_f/\text{in.}^2 \cdot °R$, and $\alpha_0 = 3 \times 10^{-4} °R^{-1}$. Calculate σ, E, and α for the following values of λ: 0.5, 1.0, 1.5, 2.0. Show on a graph how σ, E, and α depend on λ.

2.11 (a) A steel rod 0.5 in.^{2} in cross-sectional area, under a tensile stress of 8,000 lb$_f$/in.^{2} at 80°F, is held between two fixed supports 10 ft apart. If the temperature falls to 20°F, what is the tensile stress in the rod? Take $E = 30.0 \times 10^6 \text{ lb}_f/\text{in.}^2$ and $\alpha = 6.5 \times 10^{-6} °F^{-1}$.

(b) If, in addition, the supports approach each other by 0.02 in., what is the final tensile stress in the rod?

2.12 Show that if Young's modulus E is independent of temperature, the linear expansivity α is independent of stress.

2.13 For a PVT system we wrote in Sec. 2.3

$$V = V(T,P),$$

and for a stressed bar we wrote in Sec. 2.6

$$\epsilon = \epsilon(T,\sigma).$$

In Secs. 2.7 and 2.8 on surfaces and reversible cells, we did *not* write

$$A = A(\gamma,T), \qquad q = q(e,T).$$

Why not? How are these systems different?

Chapter 3/
Work

3.1/ Work

In the study of mechanics, one learns to draw a free-body diagram of the system under study and to show all the external forces acting *on* the system. If the system moves, each such force is said to do work equal in amount to the product of the displacement of its point of application ds and the component of the force in the direction of the displacement F_s. In mechanics, we regard work as positive when F_s and ds have the same sign, and refer to such work as being done *on* the system and increasing its energy. When F_s and ds are of opposite sign, the work is negative, and work is done *by* the system, decreasing its energy.

The definition of work is, of course, the same in thermodynamics as in mechanics. However, the point of view is different. It has become customary to regard work done *by* the system as positive and work done *on* the system as negative. Thus the sign convention in thermodynamics is opposite to that of mechanics when considered with respect to whether it is done *on* or *by* the system. With respect to forces and displacements, however, the two sign conventions can be made to agree if in thermodynamics we draw a free-body diagram of the system which shows not the external forces acting *on* the system, but rather the forces which are exerted *by* the system on its surroundings. Each such force then does positive work if its sign is the same as that of its displacement, and does negative work if the signs are opposite.

It is important to note that the only forces considered in the fore-going discussion are those exerted by the system on its surroundings. The work done by these forces is called *external work*. Thus a gas confined in a cylinder and at uniform pressure, while expanding and imparting motion to a piston, does external work on its surroundings. The work done, however, by one part of a system on another part is called *internal work*. The interactions of molecules or electrons on one another constitute internal work.

Internal work has no place in thermodynamics. Only the work that involves an interaction between a system and its surroundings is significant. When a system does external work, the changes that take place can be described by means of macroscopic quantities referring to the system as a whole, in which case the changes may be imagined to result from, or to cause in the surroundings, the raising or lowering of a suspended body in a gravitational field (loosely called a "weight"), the winding or unwinding of a spring, or in general, the alteration of the position or configuration of some external mechanical device. This may be regarded as the ultimate criterion as to whether external work is done or not. It will often be found convenient throughout this book to describe the performance of external work in terms of or in conjunction with the operation of a mechanical device such as a system of suspended weights. *Unless otherwise indicated, the word "work," unmodified by any adjective, will mean external work.*

A few examples will be found helpful. If an electric cell is on open circuit, changes that take place in the cell (such as diffusion) are not accompanied by the performance of work. If, however, the cell is connected to an external circuit through which electricity is transferred, the current may be imagined to produce rotation of the armature of a motor, thereby lifting a weight or winding a spring. Therefore, *for an electric cell to do work, it must be connected to an external circuit*. As another example, consider a magnet far removed from any external electric conductor. A change of magnetization within the magnet is not accompanied by the performance of work. If, however, the magnet undergoes a change of magnetization while it is surrounded by an electric conductor, eddy currents are set up in the conductor, constituting an external transfer of electricity. Hence, *for a magnetic system to do work, it must interact with an electric conductor or with other magnets.*

3.2/ Quasi-static Process

A system in thermodynamic equilibrium satisfies the following stringent requirements:

1. Mechanical Equilibrium
The external forces on the system as a whole and the forces on every element of the system are in balance.

2. Thermal Equilibrium

The temperature is uniform throughout the system and is the same as that of the surroundings.

3. Chemical Equilibrium

The internal structure and chemical composition remain constant.

Once a system is in thermodynamic equilibrium and the surroundings are kept unchanged, *no* motion will take place and *no* work will be done. If, however, the sum of the external forces is changed so that there is a finite unbalanced force acting on the system, then the condition for mechanical equilibrium is no longer satisfied and the following situations may arise:

1. Forces within the system may no longer be uniform throughout the system, and as a result, turbulence, waves, etc., may be set up. Also, the system as a whole may execute some sort of accelerated motion.
2. As a result of this turbulence, acceleration, etc., a nonuniform temperature distribution may be brought about, as well as a finite difference of temperature between the system and its surroundings.
3. The sudden change in the forces and in the temperature may produce a state that does not correspond to chemical equilibrium, and a chemical change may proceed at a finite rate.

It is clear from the foregoing considerations that a finite unbalanced force causes the system to pass through nonequilibrium states. If it is desired during a process to describe every state of a system by means of thermodynamic coordinates referring to the system as a whole, the process must *not* be brought about by a finite unbalanced force. We are led, therefore, to conceive of an ideal situation in which the external forces acting on a system are varied only slightly so that the unbalanced force is infinitesimal. A process performed in this ideal way is said to be *quasi-static*. *During a quasi-static process, the system is at all times infinitesimally near a state of thermodynamic equilibrium*, and also the states through which the system passes can be described by means of thermodynamic coordinates referring to the system as a whole. An equation of state is valid, therefore, for all these states. A quasi-static process is an idealization that is applicable to all thermodynamic systems, including electrical and magnetic systems. The conditions for such a process can never be rigorously satisfied in the laboratory, but they can be approached to almost any desired degree. In the next few articles it will be seen how approximately quasi-static processes may be performed by a variety of systems.

3.3/ Work in Changing the Volume of a *PVT* System

Imagine any *PVT* system contained in a cylinder equipped with a movable piston on which the system and the surroundings may act. Suppose that the cylinder has a cross-sectional area A and that the pressure exerted by the system at the piston face is P. The force on the piston is therefore PA. If the piston moves out an infinitesimal distance dx, the system performs an infinitesimal amount of work dW (the differential sign with the line drawn through it will be explained later) equal to

$$dW = PA \, dx.$$

But

$$A \, dx = dV;$$

hence

$$\boxed{dW = P \, dV.}$$

Now suppose the piston is caused to move a finite amount so that the volume changes from V_1 to V_2, and let the symbol P stand for the pressure at any moment on the piston face. The amount of work W done by the system will evidently be

$$W = \int_{V_1}^{V_2} P \, dV.$$

If the motion of the piston is produced by a finite difference between the pressure exerted by the system and the external pressure, or in other words, if the piston moves with accelerated motion, both P and V are functions of quantities involving the time. The integration of the above equation therefore becomes a problem in fluid mechanics. If, however, the change in volume is performed quasi-statically, P is at all times a thermodynamic coordinate and can be expressed as a function of T and V by means of an equation of state. The evaluation of the integral can then be accomplished once the behavior of T is specified, because then P can be expressed as a function of V only. If P is expressed as a function of V, the *path* of integration is defined. Along a particular quasi-static path R, the work done by a system in going from a volume V_1 to a larger volume V_2 is

$$W_{1 \to 2} = {}_R\!\int_{V_1}^{V_2} P \, dV,$$

whereas from 2 to 1, along the same path but in the opposite direction, the work absorbed by the system is

$$W_{2 \to 1} = {}_R\!\int_{V_2}^{V_1} P \, dV.$$

When the path R is quasi-static,

$$W_{1 \to 2} = -W_{2 \to 1}.$$

Sufficient approximation to a quasi-static process may be achieved in practice by having the external pressure differ from that exerted by the system by only a small finite amount. The usual engineering unit of pressure is the pound *force* per square inch, or the psi. Absolute pressure must be employed, and this is often stated explicitly as pounds *force* per square inch absolute, or psia. Pressure gauges normally indicate the difference between absolute pressure and atmospheric pressure, and the gauge reading is given as pounds *force* per square inch gauge, or psig. Atmospheric pressure must be added to gauge pressure to convert to absolute pressure. Since volume is usually given in cubic feet, the absolute pressure in psia is divided by 144 in.^{2}/ft^2 to convert pressure to pounds *force* per square foot (lb$_f$/ft^2). The resulting unit of work is then the foot-pound *force* (ft · lb$_f$).

3.4/ PV Diagram

As the volume of a PVT system changes by virtue of the motion of a piston in a cylinder, the position of the piston at any moment is proportional to the volume. A pen whose motion along the X axis of a diagram follows exactly the motion of the piston will trace out a line every point of which represents an instantaneous value of the volume. If, at the same time, this pen is given a motion along the Y axis such that the Y coordinate is proportional to the pressure, then the pressure and volume changes of the system during expansion or compression are indicated simultaneously on the same diagram. Such a device is called an *indicator*. The diagram in which pressure is plotted along the Y axis and volume along the X axis is called an *indicator diagram*, or PV *diagram*.

In Fig. 3.1a, the pressure and volume changes of a gas during expansion are indicated by curve I. The $\int P\,dV$ for this process is evidently

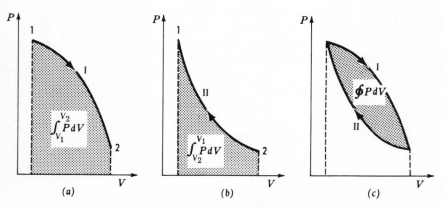

Fig. 3.1 PV **diagram.** (*a*) **Curve I, expansion;** (*b*) **curve II, compression;** (*c*) **curves I and II together constitute a cycle.**

the shaded area under curve I. Similarly, for a compression, the work absorbed by the gas is represented by the shaded area under curve II in Fig. 3.1b. In conformity with the sign convention for work, the area under curve I is regarded as positive and that under curve II as negative. In Fig. 3.1c, curves I and II are drawn together so that they constitute a series of processes whereby the gas is brought back to its initial state. Such a series of processes, represented by a closed figure, is called a *cycle*. The area within the closed figure is obviously the difference between the areas under curves I and II and therefore represents the *net* work done in the cycle. It should be noticed that the cycle is traversed in such a direction that the net work is positive. If the direction were reversed, the net work would be negative.

Indicator diagrams of the processes taking place in the cylinder of an air compressor or an internal-combustion engine are extremely valuable in providing information as to the work delivered at the piston face. The area within a closed curve is usually measured with a planimeter.

3.5/ Work Depends on the Path

On the PV diagram depicted in Fig. 3.2, an initial equilibrium state 1 (characterized by the coordinates P_1, V_1, T_1) and a final equilibrium state 2 (coordinates P_2, V_2, T_2) of a PVT system are represented by the two points 1 and 2. There are many ways in which the system may be taken from 1 to 2. For example, the pressure may be kept constant from 1 to a (*isobaric process*) and then the volume kept constant from a to 2 (*isochoric process*), in which case the work done is equal to the area under the line 1a. Another possibility is the path 1b2, in which case the work is the area under the line b2. The series of short isobarics and

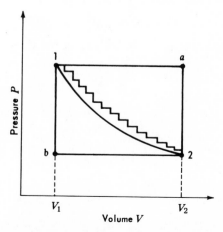

Fig. 3.2 Work depends on the path.

isochorics from 1 to 2 and the continuous curve from 1 to 2 represent other possibilities in each of which the work done is different. We can see, therefore, that *the work done by a system depends not only on the initial and final states, but also on the intermediate states, i.e., on the path.* This is merely another way of saying that, for a quasi-static process, the expression

$$W = \int_{V_1}^{V_2} P \, dV$$

cannot be integrated until P is specified as a function of V.

The expression $P \, dV$ is an infinitesimal amount of work, and has been represented by the symbol $đW$. There is, however, an important distinction between an infinitesimal amount of work and the other infinitesimals we have considered up to now. An infinitesimal amount of work is an *inexact differential;* i.e., it is *not* the differential of an actual function of the thermodynamic coordinates. There is no function of the thermodynamic coordinates representing the work in a body. The phrase "work in a body" has no meaning. To indicate that an infinitesimal amount of work is *not* a mathematical differential of a function W and to emphasize at all times that it is an inexact differential, a line is drawn through the differential sign thus: $đW$.

3.6/ Calculation of ∫P dV for Quasi-static Processes

The preceding ideas will be clarified by the following examples:

1. Quasi-static Isothermal Expansion or Compression of an Ideal Gas

$$W = \int_{V_1}^{V_2} P \, dV;$$

but an ideal gas is one whose equation of state is

$$PV = nRT,$$

where n and R are constants. Substituting for P, we get

$$W = \int_{V_1}^{V_2} \frac{nRT}{V} \, dV,$$

and since T is also constant,

$$W = nRT \int_{V_1}^{V_2} \frac{dV}{V}$$
$$= nRT \ln \frac{V_2}{V_1},$$

where the symbol ln denotes the natural, or Napierian, logarithm. At constant temperature $P_1 V_1 = P_2 V_2$, or

$$\frac{V_2}{V_1} = \frac{P_1}{P_2}.$$

Substitution in the last equation above gives an alternative expression for the work:

$$W = nRT \ln \frac{P_1}{P_2}.$$

As an illustration consider the compression of 2 lb moles of an ideal gas from 23.2 to 45.8 psig at a constant temperature of 80°F:

$n = 2$ lb moles,
$R = 1{,}545$ ft $\cdot$ lb$_f$/lb mole $\cdot$ °R   (see p. 91),
$T = 80 + 460 = 540$°R   (three significant figures),
$P_1 = 23.2 + 14.7 = 37.9$ psia $\}$ where standard atmospheric pressure
$P_2 = 45.8 + 14.7 = 60.5$ psia $\int$ of 14.7 psi is assumed,

$$W = (2)(1{,}545)(540) \ln \frac{37.9}{60.5} \text{ ft} \cdot \text{lb}_f$$

$$= -782{,}000 \text{ ft} \cdot \text{lb}_f.$$

The minus sign indicates that work is done on the gas.

2. Quasi-static Isothermal Increase of Pressure on a Solid

Suppose the pressure on 10 lb$_m$ of solid copper is increased quasi-statically and isothermally at 0°C from 0 to 1,000 atm.   The work is calculated as follows:

$$W = \int P \, dV,$$

$$dV = \left(\frac{\partial V}{\partial P} \right)_T dP + \left(\frac{\partial V}{\partial T} \right)_P dT.$$

Since the isothermal compressibility is

$$k = -\frac{1}{V} \left(\frac{\partial V}{\partial P} \right)_T,$$

we have, at constant temperature,

$$dV = -kV \, dP.$$

Substituting for dV,

$$W = - \int_{P_1}^{P_2} kVP \, dP.$$

Now the changes in V and k at constant temperature are so small that they may be neglected.   Hence

$$W = -\frac{kV}{2} (P_2{}^2 - P_1{}^2).$$

Since the volume is equal to the mass m divided by the density ρ,

$$W = -\frac{km}{2\rho} (P_2{}^2 - P_1{}^2).$$

For copper at 0°C:

$\rho = 556 \text{ lb}_m/\text{ft}^3,$
$k = 0.774 \times 10^{-6} \text{ atm}^{-1},$
$m = 10 \text{ lb}_m,$
$P_1 = 0,$
$P_2 = 1,000 \text{ atm.}$

Hence $W = -\dfrac{(0.774 \times 10^{-6})(10)(1,000)^2}{(2)(556)}$
$= -0.00696 \text{ atm} \cdot \text{ft}^3,$
or $W = -(0.00696 \text{ atm} \cdot \text{ft}^3)[14.7 \ (\text{lb}_f/\text{in.}^2)/(\text{atm})](144 \text{ in.}^2/\text{ft}^2)$
$= -14.7 \text{ ft} \cdot \text{lb}_f.$

The minus sign indicates that work is done on the copper.

3.7/ Work in Straining a Bar

If the length of a bar in tension or compression is changed from L to $L + dL$, the infinitesimal amount of work done is equal to

$$\text{d}W = -F \, dL,$$

where F is the total axial load on the bar.   For tension, F is taken as $+$, and for compression, as $-$, in agreement with the convention first adopted in Sec. 2.6.   The student should satisfy himself of the necessity of including the minus sign in the above equation.

Since $F = \sigma A$, where σ is stress and A is cross-sectional area, and $dL = L \, d\epsilon$,

$$\text{d}W = -\sigma A L \, d\epsilon.$$

The product AL is the volume of the bar V.   Hence

$$\text{d}W = -V\sigma \, d\epsilon,$$

or on the basis of a unit volume,

$$\frac{\text{d}W}{V} = -\sigma \, d\epsilon.$$

If σ is measured in $\text{lb}_f/\text{in.}^2$ and ϵ in in./in., the work is given in in. $\cdot \text{lb}_f/\text{in.}^3$ This may be converted to $\text{ft} \cdot \text{lb}_f/\text{ft}^3$ by multiplying by 144 in.^{2}/ft^2.

For a finite change in strain,

$$W = -\int_{\epsilon_1}^{\epsilon_2} \sigma \, d\epsilon \qquad \text{unit volume,}$$

where σ indicates the instantaneous value of the stress at the particular value of ϵ existing during the straining process.   If the bar undergoes

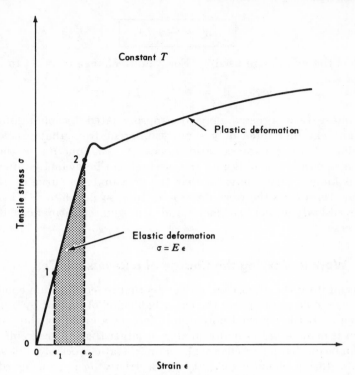

Fig. 3.3   Conventional stress-strain diagram.

any kind of accelerated motion, the integral cannot be evaluated in terms of thermodynamic coordinates referring to the bar as a whole. If, however, the external load is applied slowly, the process is, for all practical purposes, quasi-static and an equation of state may be used to relate σ and ϵ so that the required integration may be carried out.

A typical stress-strain diagram for low-carbon steel in tension is shown in Fig. 3.3.   The work done per unit volume of a bar stressed in tension from state 1 to state 2 is represented by the area under the curve between points 1 and 2.   In this case (constant T) the curve is a straight line, representative of Hooke's law.

3.8/ Work in Changing the Area of a Surface

Consider a double surface with liquid in between stretched across a wire framework one side of which is movable, as in Fig. 2.1.   As shown in Sec. 2.7, the force exerted by both films is $2\gamma l$.   For an infinitesimal displacement dx, the work is

$$dW = -2\gamma l\,dx.$$

But
$$2l\,dx = dA.$$

Hence

$$\dW = -\gamma \, dA.$$

(Why is the minus sign used?)   For a finite change from A_1 to A_2,

$$W = -\int_{A_1}^{A_2} \gamma \, dA.$$

A quasi-static process may be approximated by maintaining a constant external force only slightly different from that exerted by the film.   During a quasi-static process, γ is a function of thermodynamic coordinates only and the integral can be evaluated once the path is known.   It is obvious that the area under a curve on an γA diagram represents the work done on or by a surface film.   When γ is expressed in dynes per centimeter and A in square centimeters, W will be in ergs.

3.9/ Work in Varying the Charge of a Reversible Cell

We recall from the discussion of Sec. 2.8 that an equilibrium condition for a reversible cell requires the exact balancing of its emf by a potentiometer.   If the external potential difference applied by the potentiometer is made infinitesimally smaller or larger than the cell emf e, the cell can be discharged or charged by a quasi-static process.   For such a process, during which a quantity of electricity dq is transferred, the work is given by

$$\dW = -e \, dq.$$

Since q represents the *charge* of the cell, dq is positive when the cell is being charged and negative when the cell is discharging.   Thus the minus sign is required to make $\dW$ positive for discharge of the cell (work done *by* the cell) and negative for charging the cell (work done *on* the cell).

It was shown in Sec. 2.8 that

$$dq = -jF \, dn.$$

Hence
$$\dW = ejF \, dn,$$

where jF is the charge transferred per mole of reacting material, and dn is the moles of material reacted.   By convention dn is taken as positive for discharging and as negative for charging.   For a finite change,

$$W = jF \int_0^n e \, dn.$$

For the quasi-static reaction of n moles of material in a reversible cell at constant e, we may integrate to get

$$W = ejFn.$$

The emf of a Daniell cell is a function of temperature only. The reason for this is that the electrolytes exist in contact with excess crystals and are therefore saturated solutions of constant concentration so long as the temperature is constant. Thus a finite amount of reaction can easily be obtained at constant e. This is not the case for all cells. However, one can always imagine a cell of infinite size for which a finite reaction and alteration of charge would not change the emf. The only measurement necessary to allow the calculation of the work that *would* occur in a quasi-static process for a cell is its emf, and this can readily be made with a cell of finite size and a potentiometer.

3.10/ Work in Changing the Polarization of a Dielectric in a Parallel-plate Capacitor

Consider a capacitor consisting of two parallel conducting plates of area A, whose linear dimensions are large compared with their separation l, filled with an isotropic solid or fluid dielectric. If a potential difference v is established across the plates, one plate is given a charge $+q$ and the other $-q$. If the charge of the capacitor is changed by an amount dq, the work done is

$$\mathrm{d}W = -v \, dq,$$

the minus sign indicating that an increase of charge (positive dq) requires work done *on* the capacitor. Work supplied by an outside source accomplishes two objectives: (1) an increase in the electric field $\mathcal{E}$ in the space between the two plates and (2) an increase in the polarization of the dielectric. We therefore seek to find the contribution of each of these terms to the total work $-v \, dq$.

If $\mathcal{E}$ is the electric intensity in the dielectric, then the potential difference between the capacitor plates v is equal to

$$v = \mathcal{E}l.$$

Also, $q = Cv$, where C is the capacitance, which for a parallel-plate capacitor is given by

$$C = \frac{\epsilon A}{l},$$

with ϵ equal to the permittivity of the dielectric. Therefore

$$q = A\epsilon\mathcal{E}.$$

It is shown in physics texts that, for a parallel-plate capacitor,

$$\epsilon\mathcal{E} = \epsilon_0\mathcal{E} + \mathcal{P},$$

where $\mathcal{P}$ is the polarization of the dielectric or its dipole moment per unit volume, and ϵ_0 is a constant, also known as the permittivity of a vacuum. Note that the ratio $\epsilon/\epsilon_0 = K$ is the dielectric coefficient.

Combination of the last two equations gives

$$q = A(\epsilon_0 \mathcal{E} + \mathcal{P})$$

and
$$dq = A(\epsilon_0\, d\mathcal{E} + d\mathcal{P}).$$

Substitution in the equation for work gives

$$\mathrm{d}W = -v\, dq = -\mathcal{E}l\, dq = -\mathcal{E}lA(\epsilon_0\, d\mathcal{E} + d\mathcal{P}).$$

Since $lA = V$, the volume of the capacitor,

$$\mathrm{d}W = -V(\epsilon_0 \mathcal{E}\, d\mathcal{E} + \mathcal{E}\, d\mathcal{P}).$$

The first term of this equation represents the work required to increase the field by an amount $d\mathcal{E}$, and the second, the work to increase the polarization of the dielectric by $d\mathcal{P}$. If a vacuum existed between the plates, the first term would be unchanged. The second term would be zero, however, because $\mathcal{P}$ is a property of the dielectric. Thus the work done *by the dielectric* is

$$\mathrm{d}W = -V\mathcal{E}\, d\mathcal{P},$$

or for a unit volume,

$$\boxed{\frac{\mathrm{d}W}{V} = -\mathcal{E}\, d\mathcal{P}.}$$

The mks units of $\mathcal{E}$ are newtons per coulomb (newtons/coul), and the units of $\mathcal{P}$ are coulombs per square meter (coul/m^2). Hence the work is expressed in newton-meters per cubic meter (newton $\cdot$ m/m^3), or in joules per cubic meter (joules/m^3).

The thermodynamic coordinates of a dielectric are evidently $\mathcal{E}$, $\mathcal{P}$, and T. A typical equation of state used to relate these coordinates is

$$\mathcal{P} = \left(a + \frac{b}{T}\right)\mathcal{E},$$

where a and b are constants. Although our derivation has been specific for the case of a dielectric in a parallel-plate capacitor, the result is general for a dielectric in a field of uniform electric intensity. This condition is satisfied in many problems of interest.

3.11/ Work in Changing the Magnetization of a Magnetic Solid

Consider a sample of magnetic material in the form of a ring of cross-sectional area A and of mean circumference L. Suppose an insulated wire is wound on top of the sample, forming a toroidal winding of N

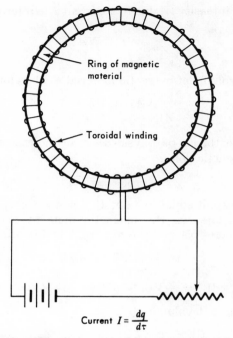

Fig. 3.4   Changing the magnetization of a magnetic solid.

closely spaced turns, as shown in Fig. 3.4.   A current may be maintained
in the winding by a battery, and by moving the sliding contactor of a
rheostat, this current may be changed.

The effect of a current in the winding is to set up a magnetic field
with magnetic induction $\mathcal{B}$.   Suppose the current is changed and, in
time $d\tau$, the magnetic induction changes by an amount $d\mathcal{B}$.   Then, by
Faraday's principle of electromagnetic induction, there is induced in the
winding a back emf e, where

$$e = -NA \frac{d\mathcal{B}}{d\tau}.$$

During the time interval $d\tau$, a quantity of electricity dq is transferred
in the circuit, and the work done by the system to maintain the current
is

$$
\begin{aligned}
đW &= e\,dq \\
&= -NA \frac{d\mathcal{B}}{d\tau}\,dq \\
&= -NA \frac{dq}{d\tau}\,d\mathcal{B} \\
&= -NAI\,d\mathcal{B},
\end{aligned}
$$

where I, equal to $dq/d\tau$, is the momentary value of the current.

The magnetic intensity $\mathscr{H}$ due to a current I in a toroidal winding is given by

$$\mathscr{H} = \frac{NI}{L} = \frac{NAI}{V},$$

where V is the volume of magnetic material. Therefore

$$NAI = V\mathscr{H}$$

and

$$\dW = -V\mathscr{H}\,d\mathscr{B}.$$

It is shown in textbooks on physics that, in the case of a ring where there are no magnetic poles,

$$\mathscr{B} = \mu_0(\mathscr{H} + \mathscr{M})$$

where μ_0 is a constant equal to $4\pi \times 10^{-7}$ newton/amp^2, and $\mathscr{M}$ is the *magnetization*, defined as the magnetic moment per unit volume, measured in amperes per meter (amp/m). Differentiation gives

$$d\mathscr{B} = \mu_0(d\mathscr{H} + d\mathscr{M}).$$

Therefore

$$\dW = -\mathscr{H}V\mu_0(d\mathscr{H} + d\mathscr{M}),$$

or

$$\dW = -V(\mu_0\mathscr{H}\,d\mathscr{H} + \mu_0\mathscr{H}\,d\mathscr{M}).$$

On the basis of a unit volume,

$$\frac{\dW}{V} = -\mu_0\mathscr{H}\,d\mathscr{H} - \mu_0\mathscr{H}\,d\mathscr{M}.$$

If no material were present within the toroidal winding, $\mathscr{M}$ would be zero, $\mathscr{B}$ would equal $\mu_0\mathscr{H}$, and

$$\frac{\dW}{V} = -\mu_0\mathscr{H}\,d\mathscr{H} \qquad \text{vacuum only.}$$

This is the work necessary to increase the magnetic field in a unit volume *of empty space* by an amount $d\mathscr{H}$. The second term, $-\mu_0\mathscr{H}\,d\mathscr{M}$, is the work done in increasing the magnetization of the material by an amount $d\mathscr{M}$. We shall be concerned in this book with changes of temperature, energy, etc., of the material only, brought about by work done on or by the material. Consequently, for the purpose of this book, the work per unit volume is

$$\boxed{\frac{\dW}{V} = -\mu_0\mathscr{H}\,d\mathscr{M}.}$$

The minus sign merely provides that an increase of magnetization (positive $d\mathscr{M}$) involves negative work; i.e., work is done *on* the magnetic material taken as the system. Both $\mathscr{H}$ and $\mathscr{M}$ are measured in units of amp/m. Since μ_0 is given in newtons/amp^2, the work is expressed in newton $\cdot$ m/m^3, or in joules/m^3. If the magnetization is caused to change a finite amount from $\mathcal{M}_1$ to $\mathcal{M}_2$, the work is given by

$$\frac{W}{V} = -\mu_0 \int_{\mathcal{M}_1}^{\mathcal{M}_2} \mathcal{H}\, d\mathcal{M}.$$

Modern experiments on paramagnetic materials are usually performed on samples in the form of cylinders or ellipsoids, not toroids. In these cases, the $\mathcal{H}$ field inside the material is somewhat smaller than the $\mathcal{H}$ field generated by the electric current in the surrounding winding because of the reverse field (demagnetizing field) set up by magnetic poles which form on the surfaces of the samples. In longitudinal magnetic fields, the demagnetizing effect may either be rendered negligible by using cylinders whose length is much larger than the diameter or corrected for in a simple way. In transverse magnetic fields, a correction factor must be applied. We shall limit ourselves to toroids or to long thin cylinders in longitudinal fields where the internal and external $\mathcal{H}$ fields are the same.

Most experiments on magnetic materials are performed at constant atmospheric pressure and involve only minute volume changes. Consequently, we may ignore the pressure and the volume and describe a magnetic material through the use of just three thermodynamic coordinates: the magnetic intensity $\mathcal{H}$, the magnetization $\mathcal{M}$, and the temperature T. This is not true for ferromagnetic materials, however, for they are subject to hysteresis. The state of such a material therefore depends not only on $\mathcal{H}$, $\mathcal{M}$, and T, but also on its past history. The equilibrium states of diamagnetic and paramagnetic materials can be represented by an equation of state among these coordinates. For example, paramagnetic materials are often satisfactorily described by the *Curie equation*

$$\mathcal{M} = C\frac{\mathcal{H}}{T},$$

where C is the *Curie constant*, and is measured in degrees. Changes in magnetization in any actual case are accomplished very nearly quasi-statically, and therefore an equation of state may be used in the integration of the expression for work. Alternatively, an $\mathcal{H}\mathcal{M}$ diagram may be constructed, in which case the area under the curve is proportional to the work done.

3.12/ Summary

The results of this chapter are summarized in Table 3.1. It will be noticed that each expression for work is the product of an intensive and an extensive quantity.

We have seen that a work diagram is obtained if any one of the intensive coordinates is plotted against its corresponding extensive coordi-

Table 3.1/ Work in Simple Systems

System	Intensive quantity (generalized force) with typical units	Extensive quantity (generalized displacement) with typical units	Work with typical units
PVT system	P, lb$_f$/ft^2	V, ft^3	$W = \int P \, dV$, ft · lb$_f$
Stressed bar	σ, lb$_f$/in.^{2}	ϵ, in./in.	$W/V = -\int \sigma \, d\epsilon$, in. · lb$_f$/in.^{3}
Surface	γ, dynes/cm	A, cm^2	$W = -\int \gamma \, dA$, ergs
Reversible cell	e, volts	q, coul	$W = -\int e \, dq$, joules
Dielectric	$\mathcal{E}$, newtons/coul	$\mathcal{P}$, coul/m^2	$W/V = -\int \mathcal{E} \, d\mathcal{P}$, joules/m^3
Magnetic material	$\mathcal{H}$, amp/m	$\mathcal{M}$, amp/m	$W/V = -\mu_0 \int \mathcal{H} \, d\mathcal{M}$, joules/m^3

nate. There are, therefore, as many work diagrams as there are systems. It is desirable at times, for the sake of argument, to refer to a work diagram that does not pertain to one system in particular, but represents the behavior of any system. If we designate the intensive quantities P, σ, γ, e, $\mathcal{E}$, and $\mathcal{H}$ as *generalized forces* and their corresponding extensive quantities V, ϵ, A, q, $\mathcal{P}$, and $\mathcal{M}$ as *generalized displacements*, we may represent the work done by any system on a *generalized work diagram* by plotting the generalized force X against the generalized displacement x. Conclusions based upon such a diagram will hold for any system.

Problems

3.1 (a) Steam is admitted to the cylinder of a steam engine at a constant pressure of 300 psia. The bore of the cylinder is 8 in., and the stroke of the piston is 12 in. How much work is done per stroke?

(b) If 10 lb$_m$ of water is evaporated at atmospheric pressure until a volume of 288.5 ft^3 is occupied, how much work is done?

3.2 A thin-walled metal bomb of volume V_B contains n moles of gas at high pressure. Connected to the bomb is a capillary tube and stopcock. When the stopcock is opened slightly, the gas leaks slowly into a cylinder equipped with a nonleaking, frictionless piston where the pressure remains constant at the atmospheric value P_0.

(a) Show that, after as much gas as possible has leaked out, an amount of work.

$$W = P_0(nV_0 - V_B)$$

has been done, where V_0 is the molar volume of the gas at atmospheric pressure and temperature.

(b) How much work would be done if the gas leaked directly into the atmosphere?

3.3 Calculate the work done by 1 mole of a gas during a quasi-static, isothermal expansion from an initial volume V_1 to a final volume V_2 when the equation of state is

$$P(V - b) = RT,$$

where b and R are constants.

3.4 Compute the quasi-static work done in compressing 1 ft^3 of mercury at a constant temperature of 32°F from a pressure of 1 atm to a pressure of 3,000 atm. The isothermal compressibility of mercury at 32°F is given as a function of pressure by

$$k = 3.9 \times 10^{-6} - 0.1 \times 10^{-9} \, P$$

where P is in atm, and k is in atm^{-1}. Justify any assumption you make.

3.5 (a) The tensile stress in a metal bar is increased quasi-statically and isothermally from σ_1 to σ_2. If the volume of the bar and Young's modulus remain essentially constant, show that the work is given by

$$W = -\frac{V}{2E} (\sigma_2^2 - \sigma_1^2).$$

(b) The tensile stress in a steel bar 10 ft long and 1 in.^{2} in area is increased quasi-statically and isothermally from 10,000 to 40,000 lb$_f$/in.^{2} What is the work in ft · lb$_f$? $E = 30.0 \times 10^6$ lb$_f$/in.^{2} for steel.

3.6 The equation of state for an ideal elastic substance is

$$\sigma = \frac{A_0}{A} KT \left(\lambda - \frac{1}{\lambda^2} \right),$$

where K is a constant, λ is the extension ratio L/L_0, and the ratio of no-load area to area of the stressed specimen A_0/A converts the stress σ from the nominal value (based on the no-load area) to the actual value. L_0 is the no-load length and is a function of temperature only.

(a) Using the formula for work in the form

$$dW = -V\sigma \, d\epsilon,$$

show that

$$\frac{dW}{V_0} = -KT \left(\lambda - \frac{1}{\lambda^2} \right) d\lambda$$

for isothermal, quasi-static extension or compression.

(b) For a sample of rubber, $L_0 = 1$ ft and $A_0 = 0.1$ in.^{2}, and for which $K = 0.15$ lb$_f$/in.$^2 \cdot$ °R at 500°R, calculate W for elongation of the sample from $L = L_0$ to $L = 2L_0$.

3.7 Show that the work per unit volume done during a quasi-static isothermal change of state of a paramagnetic substance obeying Curie's equation is given by

$$W = -\frac{\mu_0 T}{2C} (\mathcal{M}_2{}^2 - \mathcal{M}_1{}^2)$$
$$= -\frac{\mu_0 C}{2T} (\mathcal{H}_2{}^2 - \mathcal{H}_1{}^2).$$

3.8 Show that the work of magnetization per unit volume in empty space is $\mu_0 \mathcal{H}^2 / 2$.

3.9 A paramagnetic substance occupying a volume of 200 cm³ is maintained at constant temperature. A magnetic field is increased quasi-statically and isothermally from 0 to 1.2×10^6 amp/m. Assuming Curie's equation to hold and the Curie constant to be 0.163°K:

(a) How much work would be required if no material were present?

(b) How much work is done to change the magnetization of the material when the temperature is 300°K, and when it is 1°K?

(c) How much work is done by the agent supplying the magnetic field at each temperature?

3.10 If the equation of state for a dielectric is

$$\mathcal{P} = \left(a + \frac{b}{T}\right)\mathcal{E},$$

where a and b are constants, show that the work of increasing the electric field intensity from $\mathcal{E}_1$ to $\mathcal{E}_2$ is given by

$$W = -\left(a + \frac{b}{T}\right)\frac{\mathcal{E}_2{}^2 - \mathcal{E}_1{}^2}{2}.$$

3.11 Show that the net work for blowing a spherical "soap bubble" of radius r in an isothermal, quasi-static process in the atmosphere is given by

$$W = -16\pi\gamma r^2.$$

Chapter 4/
The First Law of Thermodynamics

4.1 / Work and Heat

It was shown in Chap. 3 how a system could be changed from an initial to a final state by means of a quasi-static process and how the work done during the process could be calculated. There are other means, however, of changing the state of a system that do not necessarily involve the performance of a quasi-static process. Consider, for example, the four situations depicted in Fig. 4.1. In (a) the system is a composite one, consisting of some water and a paddle wheel, which is caused to rotate and churn the water by means of a falling weight. In (b) both the water and the resistor constitute the system, the electric current in the resistor being maintained by a generator turned by means of a falling weight. In both cases the state of the system is caused to change, and since the agency for changing the state of the system is a falling weight, both processes involve the performance of work.

In (c) and (d), however, the situation is quite different. The system in both cases is some water in a diathermic container. In (c) the system is in contact with the burning gases from a bunsen burner, i.e., with another body at a higher temperature, whereas in (d) the system is near but not in contact with an electric lamp whose temperature is much higher than that of the water. In both cases the state of the system is caused to change, but in neither case can the agency for the change be described by mechanical means.

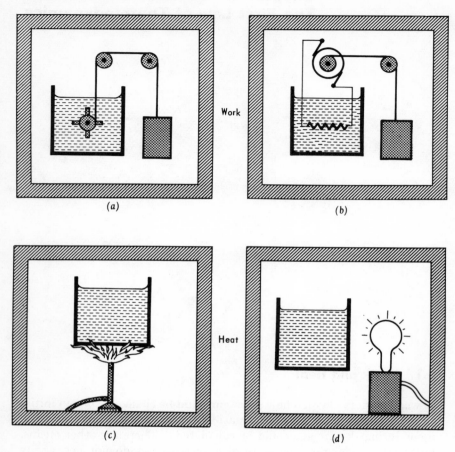

Work

Heat

Fig. 4.1   Distinction between work and heat.

What happens when two systems at different temperatures are placed together is one of the most familiar experiences of mankind. It is well known that the final temperature reached by both systems is intermediate between the two starting temperatures. Up to the beginning of the nineteenth century, such phenomena, which constitute the subject of *calorimetry*, were explained by postulating the existence of a substance, caloric, or heat, in every body. It was believed that a body at a high temperature contained much caloric and one at a low temperature only a little. When the two bodies were put together, the body rich in caloric lost some to the other, and thus the final temperature was intermediate.† Although today we know that heat is not a substance whose total amount remains constant, nevertheless we ascribe the

† An interesting pertinent article is one by S. C. Brown, The Caloric Theory of Heat, *Am. J. Phys.*, **18**:367 (1950).

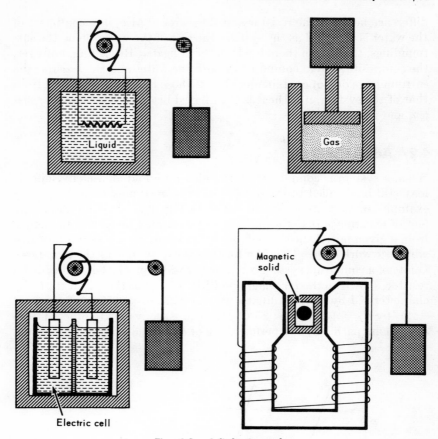

Fig. 4.2   Adiabatic work.

changes that take place in Fig. 4.1c and d to the transfer of "something" from the body at the higher temperature to the one at the lower, and this "something" we call heat.   We therefore adopt as a *calorimetric* definition of heat *that which is transferred between a system and its surroundings by virtue of a temperature difference only.*   Whether heat is a substance or a form of energy cannot be decided yet, but it will appear later that it is a form of energy.   It is obvious that an adiabatic wall is one which is impervious to heat (heat insulator) and that a diathermic wall is a heat conductor.

It is important to observe that the decision as to whether a particular change of state involves the performance of work or the transfer of heat requires first an unequivocal answer to the questions: What is the system, and what are the surroundings?   For example, in Fig. 4.1b, if the resistor is regarded as the system and the water as the surroundings, there is a transfer of heat from the resistor by virtue of the temperature difference between the resistor and the water. Also, if a small part of the water is regarded as the system, the rest of the water being the surroundings, then again there is a transfer of heat. Regarding, however, the composite system composed of both the water and the resistor, the surroundings do not contain any object whose temperature differs from that of the system, if no heat is transferred between *this composite system* and its surroundings.

4.2/ Adiabatic Work

When a system is completely surrounded by an adiabatic envelope, it may still be coupled to the outside so that work may be done. Four examples of *adiabatic work* are shown in Fig. 4.2. It is an important fact of experience that the state of a system may be caused to change from a given initial state to a suitable final state by the performance of adiabatic work *only*. Consider for the sake of simplicity the two states i and f of a composite system composed of water in which is embedded a resistor, shown on the PV diagram of Fig. 4.3. Let the initial state i be characterized by the coordinates $P_i = 1$ atm, $t_i = 20°C$, and the final state f by $P_f = 1$ atm, $t_f = 25°C$. To cause the system to proceed from i to f along path I by the performance of adiabatic work only, it would

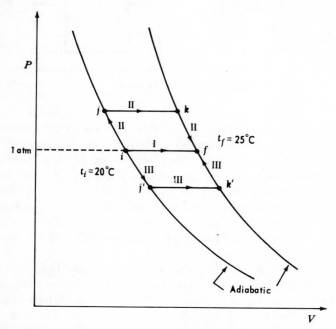

Fig. 4.3   Changing the state of a system from i to f along three different adiabatic paths.

be necessary merely to surround the water with an adiabatic envelope, keep the water at atmospheric pressure, and maintain a current in the resistor for a suitable interval of time.

But path I is not the only path by which the system may be changed from i to f by the performance of adiabatic work only. We might compress the water adiabatically from i to j, then use a current in the resistor from j to k, and then expand from k to f, the whole series of processes being designated by path II. Or we might make use of a similar adiabatic path III. There are an infinite number of paths by which a system may be transferred from an initial state to a final state by the performance of adiabatic work only. Although accurate measurements of adiabatic work along different paths between the same two states have never been made, nevertheless, indirect experiments indicate that the adiabatic work is the same along all such paths. The generalization of this result is known as the *first law of thermodynamics*, namely:

If a system is caused to change from an initial state to a final state by adiabatic means only, the work done is the same for all adiabatic paths connecting the two states.

Whenever a quantity is found to depend only on the initial and final states and not on the path connecting them, an important conclusion can be drawn. The student will recall from mechanics that, in moving an object from a point 1 in a gravitational field to another point 2, in the absence of friction the work done depends only on the positions of the two points and not on the path through which the body was moved. It was concluded from this that there exists a function of the space coordinates of the body whose final value minus its initial value is equal to the work done. This function was called the potential-energy function. Similarly, the work done in moving a quantity of electricity from one point in an electrostatic field to another is also independent of the path and is therefore also expressible as the value of a function (the electric-potential function) at the final state minus its value at the initial state. It therefore follows from the first law of thermodynamics that there exists a function of the coordinates of a thermodynamic system whose value at the final state minus its value at the initial state is equal to the adiabatic work in going from one state to the other. This function is known as the *internal-energy function*.

Denoting the internal-energy function by U, we have

$$-W_{1\rightarrow2} \text{ (adiabatic)} = U_2 - U_1,$$

where the minus sign is introduced so that, when work is done *on* a system, U_2 will be greater than U_1. It is found by experiment that it is not always possible to take a system from an initial state 1 to *any* state 2 by the performance of adiabatic work alone. It will be clear later, however, when entropy is discussed, that if state 2 cannot be reached in this way, it is *always* possible to go from 2 to 1 by adiabatic means, in which case the change in internal energy from state 1 to state 2, instead of being $-W_{1\to2}$, is $+W_{2\to1}$.

4.3/ Internal-energy Function

The physical interpretation of the difference $U_2 - U_1$ is the increase in energy of the system. The equality, therefore, of the increase of energy and the adiabatic work expresses the principle of the conservation of energy. It should be emphasized, however, that the equation expresses more than the principle of the conservation of energy. It states that there exists an energy function, the difference between two values of which is the energy change of the system.

The internal energy is a function of as many thermodynamic coordinates as are necessary to specify the state of a system. The equilibrium states of a PVT system, for example, describable by means of three thermodynamic coordinates P, V, and T, are completely determined by only two, since the third is fixed by the equation of state. Therefore the internal energy may be thought of as a function of only two (any two) of the thermodynamic coordinates. This is true for each of the simple systems described in Chap. 2. It is not always possible to write this function in simple mathematical form. Very often the exact form of the function is unknown. It must be understood, however, that it is not necessary to know actually what the internal-energy function is, so long as we can be sure that such a function exists.

If the coordinates characterizing the two states differ from each other only infinitesimally, the change of internal energy is dU, where dU is an exact differential, since it is the differential of an actual function. In the case of a PVT system, if U is regarded as a function of T and V, then

$$dU = \left(\frac{\partial U}{\partial T}\right)_V dT + \left(\frac{\partial U}{\partial V}\right)_T dV,$$

or, regarding U as a function of T and P,

$$dU = \left(\frac{\partial U}{\partial T}\right)_P dT + \left(\frac{\partial U}{\partial P}\right)_T dP.$$

The student should realize that the two partial derivatives $(\partial U/\partial T)_V$ and $(\partial U/\partial T)_P$ are not equal. They are different mathematically and also have a different physical meaning.

4.4/ Mathematical Formulation of the First Law

We have been considering up to now processes wherein a system undergoes a change of state through the performance of adiabatic work only.

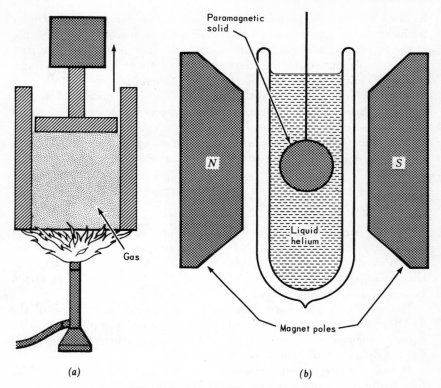

Fig. 4.4   Nonadiabatic processes.

Such experiments must be performed in order to measure the change in the energy function of a system, but they are not the usual processes that are carried out in the laboratory. In Fig. 4.4 are depicted two examples of processes involving changes of state that take place non-adiabatically. In (a) a gas is in contact with a bunsen flame whose temperature is higher than that of the gas and at the same time is allowed to expand. In (b) the magnetization of a paramagnetic solid is increased while it is in contact with liquid helium, the temperature of which is lower than that of the solid. As a matter of fact, some of the helium boils away during the magnetization.

Let us now imagine two different experiments performed on the same system. In one we measure the adiabatic work necessary to change the state of the system from 1 to 2. This is $U_2 - U_1$. In the other we cause the system to undergo the *same* change of state, but nonadiabatically, and measure the work done. The result of all such experiments is that the nonadiabatic work is *not* equal to $U_2 - U_1$. In order that this result may be consistent with the principle of the conservation of energy, we are forced to conclude that energy has been transferred by means *other than* the performance of work. This energy, whose transfer between the system and its surroundings is required by the principle of the conservation of energy, and which has taken place only by virtue of the temperature difference between the system and its surroundings, is what we have previously called heat. We therefore give the following as our thermodynamic definition of heat: *When a system whose surroundings are at a different temperature undergoes a process during which work may be done by the system, the energy transferred by nonmechanical means, equal to the sum of the internal-energy change and the work done, is called heat.* Denoting this sum by Q, we have

$$Q = U_2 - U_1 + W,$$

or

$$\boxed{\Delta U = Q - W,}$$

where the convention has been adopted that heat is positive when it enters a system and negative when it leaves (just the opposite of the sign convention for work). Note that these sign conventions apply to the *numerical values* substituted for Q and W. The preceding equation is known as the *mathematical formulation of the first law*.

It should be emphasized that the mathematical formulation of the first law contains three related ideas: (1) the existence of an internal-energy function, (2) the principle of the conservation of energy, and (3) the definition of heat as *energy* in transit.

It was many years before it was understood that heat is energy. The first really conclusive evidence that heat could not be a substance was given by Benjamin Thompson, an American from Woburn, Mass., who later became Count Rumford of Bavaria. Rumford, in 1798, observed the temperature rise of the brass chips produced during the boring of cannon and concluded that the work of boring was responsible for the flow of heat. One year later, Sir Humphry Davy tried to show that two pieces of ice could be melted by rubbing them together. His idea was to show that heat is a manifestation of energy, but his experiment was highly inconclusive.

The idea that heat is a form of energy was put forward by Séguin, a French engineer, in 1839, and by Mayer, a German physician, in 1842, but no conclusive experiments were performed by either. It remained for Joule,† an independent investigator with a private laboratory, in the period from 1840 to 1849, to convince the world by performing a series of admirable experiments on the relation between heat and work and to establish once and for all the equivalence of these two quantities. Von Helmholtz, originally a surgeon in the Prussian army, recognized the epoch-making importance of Joule's work, and wrote a brilliant paper in 1847, applying Joule's ideas to the sciences of physical chemistry and physiology.

† The diphthong "ou" is pronounced like that in coulomb.

4.5 / Concept of Heat

Heat is energy in transit. It flows from one point to another. When the flow has ceased, there is no longer any occasion to use the word heat. It would be just as incorrect to refer to the "heat in a body" as it would be to speak about the "work in a body." The performance of work and the flow of heat are methods whereby the internal energy of a system is changed. It is impossible to separate or divide the internal energy into a mechanical and a thermal part.

We have seen that, in general, i.e., for nonadiabatic processes, the work done on or by a system is not a function of the coordinates of the system, but depends on the path by which the system was brought from the initial to the final state. Exactly the same is true of the heat transferred to or from a system. Q is not a function of the thermodynamic coordinates, but depends on the path. An infinitesimal amount of heat, therefore, is an inexact differential, and is represented by the symbol dQ.

To quote from Slater's "Introduction to Chemical Physics":

At first sight, it seems too bad that $\int dQ$ is not independent of the path, for some such quantity would be useful. It would be pleasant to be able to say, in a given state of the system, that the system had so and so much heat energy. Starting from the absolute zero of temperature, where we could say that the heat energy was zero, we could heat the body up to the state we were interested in, find $\int dQ$ from absolute zero up to this state, and call that the heat energy. But the stubborn fact remains that we should get different answers if we heated it up in different ways. For instance, we might heat it at an arbitrary constant pressure until we reached the desired temperature, then adjust the pressure at constant temperature to the desired value; or we might raise it first to the desired pressure, then heat it at that pressure to the final temperature; or many other equally simple processes. Each would give a different answer, as we can easily verify. There is nothing to do about it.

Imagine a system A in thermal contact with a system B, the two systems being surrounded by adiabatic walls. For system A alone,

$$U_2 - U_1 = Q - W,$$

and for system B alone,

$$U_2' - U_1' = Q' - W'.$$

Adding, we get

$$U_2 + U_2' - (U_1 + U_1') = Q + Q' - (W + W').$$

Since $(U_2 + U_2') - (U_1 + U_1')$ is the change in energy of the composite system and $W + W'$ is the work done by the composite system, it follows that $Q + Q'$ is the heat transferred by the composite system. Since the composite system is surrounded by adiabatic walls,

$$Q + Q' = 0 \quad \text{and} \quad Q = -Q'.$$

In other words, *under adiabatic conditions, the heat lost (or gained) by system A is equal to the heat gained (or lost) by system B.*

4.6/ Differential Form of the First Law

A process involving only infinitesimal changes in the thermodynamic coordinates of a system is known as an infinitesimal process. For such a process the first law becomes

$$\boxed{dU = \dbar Q - \dbar W.}$$

If the infinitesimal process is quasi-static, dU and $\dbar W$ can be expressed in terms of thermodynamic coordinates only. An infinitesimal quasi-static process is one in which the system passes from an initial equilibrium state to a neighboring equilibrium state.

For an infinitesimal quasi-static process of a PVT system, the first law becomes

$$dU = \dbar Q - P \, dV,$$

where U is a function of any two of the three thermodynamic coordinates, and P is, of course, a function of V and T. A similar equation may be written for each of the other simple systems, as shown in Table 4.1.

In the case of more complicated systems, it is merely necessary to replace $\dbar W$ in the first law by two or more expressions. For example, the operation of a reversible cell in which gases are liberated may involve

Table 4.1/ The First Law for Simple Systems

System	First law	U is a function of only two of:
PVT system	$dU = \dbar Q - P \, dV$	P, V, T
Stressed bar	$dU = \dbar Q + \sigma \, d\epsilon$	σ, ϵ, T
Surface	$dU = \dbar Q + \gamma \, dA$	γ, A, T
Reversible cell	$dU = \dbar Q + e \, dq$	e, q, T
Dielectric	$dU = \dbar Q + \mathcal{E} \, d\mathcal{P}$	$\mathcal{E}, \mathcal{P}, T$
Magnetic material	$dU = \dbar Q + \mu_0 \mathcal{H} \, d\mathcal{M}$	$\mathcal{H}, \mathcal{M}, T$

work in changing not only its charge but also its volume.   Hence

$$dU = dQ - P\,dV + e\,dq,$$

and U is a function of three of P, V, T, e, q.   In the case of a magnetic gas,

$$dU = dQ - P\,dV + \mu_0 \mathcal{H}\,d\mathcal{M},$$

and U is a function of three of P, V, T, $\mathcal{H}$, $\mathcal{M}$.   In the case of a liquid and its surface,

$$dU = dQ - P\,dV + \gamma\,dA,$$

and U is a function of three of P, V, T, γ, A.

4.7 / Units of Heat.   Joule's Experiments

The thermodynamic definition of heat given in Art. 4.4 makes it obvious that heat and work are forms of energy.   It is evident, therefore, that the basic unit of heat should be the same as that for work.   However, this simple idea was not given formal recognition until the ninth General Conference on Weights and Measures, meeting in Paris in 1948, adopted a resolution recognizing the absolute joule as the unit of heat. This international group, recognized as the ultimate authority on scientific standards and measures, refused to recognize any secondary unit of heat.   The reason that earlier action was not taken on so fundamental a matter is that the calorimetric definition of heat (Sec. 4.1) is deeply rooted in the foundations of science.   Furthermore, it preceded the thermodynamic definition.

In general, when heat enters a system, a change of state occurs, involving a change in some or all of the thermodynamic coordinates.   A definite change under specified conditions in any one convenient coordinate of an easily reproduced system may serve to indicate the absorption of a standard amount of heat.   Thus it is not surprising that the unit of heat was early tied to the properties of water.   For many years the unit of heat was taken to be the *calorie*, defined as that amount of heat whose absorption by one gram of water at constant atmospheric pressure is accompanied by a temperature rise from 14.5 to 15.5°C.   Similarly, the *British thermal unit* (Btu) was long defined as that quantity of heat which produces a rise in temperature from 63 to 64°F in one pound *mass* of water.

When the unit of heat is defined in this way, independent of the unit of work, the question arises as to the value of the conversion factor between the unit of heat and the unit of work, both of which are energy units.   To be specific, how many joules are equivalent to one calorie? This can be determined only by experiment, and the obvious experiment is to measure the amount of work which must be done on a unit mass of water to raise its temperature 1 degree. The results of such experiments yield values of a dimensionless conversion factor J, known as the *mechanical equivalent of heat*.

The mechanical equivalent of heat was first measured by James P. Joule, initially in 1840 and many times later in the following years. In his first method, an electric generator was rotated by a known amount of mechanical energy, and the resulting electric energy was supplied to a known mass of water, causing a measured rise of temperature. This method was then replaced by the method most often associated with Joule, namely, that in which a mass of water is churned by paddle wheels set in rotation by a series of falling weights. A short while after the British Association set up the practical electrical units, Joule redetermined the mechanical equivalent of heat by measuring the temperature rise of water surrounding an electric resistor through which a known current was flowing. His result differed so much from his previous, purely mechanical measurement that he was led to repeat with greater accuracy the experiment with the paddle wheels. Confirming his previous measurement, he concluded that the British Association standard of resistance was at fault.

The best value obtained by Joule in all these experiments was 772.5 ft · lb$_f$/Btu, or 4.155 joules/cal. In evaluating his work, it is important to bear in mind that Joule did not have at his disposal the accurately standardized thermometers which exist today; nor was he able to make such reliable corrections of heat losses as are possible now. In spite of this, his final result differs from the present accepted value by less than 1 percent. The work of Joule must be regarded as a most remarkable series of pioneer experiments, in respect not only to the skill and care exercised, but to the influence these experiments had in convincing scientists throughout the world of the correctness of the mechanical theory of heat.

4.8/ Later Measurements of J

Measurements such as Joule's, dealing with direct or indirect measurements of heat, represent a branch of experimental science known as *calorimetry*. A container or system of vessels in which either a transfer of heat takes place or effects are produced that are equivalent to a flow of heat is called a *calorimeter*. Accurate measurement of controlled quantities of heat is an extraordinarily difficult experimental task. During the century following Joule's first measurements, a number of notable investigations were undertaken to establish with reasonable certainty the value of the mechanical equivalent of heat. Several are described here to indicate the care and precision necessary in such work and to indicate the diversity in design of calorimeters which have been used.

1. Experiments of Rowland, 1879

While professor of physics at Johns Hopkins University in Baltimore, Henry A. Rowland engaged in an elaborate and painstaking research on the determination of J that, to this day, remains a model of careful and accurate experimentation.   Rowland suspended a large calorimeter on a wire and caused the water in the calorimeter to be churned by a series of perforated paddle wheels set in rotation by a steam engine. A countertorque was applied to the calorimeter to keep it from rotating; by multiplying this torque by the angle of rotation of the paddle wheels, the work delivered to the water was obtained.   The temperature of the water was measured at regular intervals with the aid of mercury thermometers calibrated with reference to an air thermometer.   In this way, Rowland was able to measure the work corresponding to a 1-degree temperature rise, not only at 15°C, but also at a number of other temperatures.   His value of J was 4.189 joules/cal.

So confident was Rowland of the accuracy of his results that he wrote, "Between the limits of 15°C and 25°C, I feel almost certain that no subsequent experiments will change my values so much as 2 parts in 1000."   Twenty years later, when the constant-volume hydrogen thermometer was adopted as a world standard, William S. Day, with Rowland's permission and advice, compared Rowland's mercury thermometers with the hydrogen standard and recomputed J, which became 4.188 joules/cal.   That Rowland's statement was no idle boast is substantiated by the fact that his value differs from the accepted value today by only 2 parts in 4,000!   Commenting on the agreement between Rowland's value of J and their own value of 4.186 (see heading 4, next page) determined at the National Bureau of Standards in 1939, Osborne, Stimson, and Ginnings stated, "It is possible that Rowland's remarkable agreement with NBS 1939 is accidental, but it is more likely to be due to the extreme care that Rowland exercised."

2. Experiments of Reynolds and Moorby, 1897

Osborne Reynolds and W. H. Moorby carried out experiments on an engineering scale, and in this sense their work is unique.   Their apparatus consisted of a hydraulic brake driven by a steam engine, which provided a power input as large as 65 hp.   The value obtained for J of 4.1832 joules/cal is in close enough agreement with values obtained by painstaking laboratory experiments so that their work is recognized as the classic contribution of engineering to this subject.

3. Experiments of H. L. Callendar and H. T. Barnes, 1899

These physicists employed what is known as a *continuous-flow method*. An electric current was maintained in a resistance wire placed along the axis of a narrow glass tube through which a constant stream of water was caused to flow.   The inlet and outlet temperatures of the water were measured with platinum resistance thermometers, and fairly good thermal insulation was achieved by evacuating the space around the central tube. The flow of water and the strength of the electric current were chosen so that the rise of temperature of the water was only a few degrees. To make a correction for the small loss of energy due to the flow of heat from the water to its cooler surroundings, two separate experiments were performed, each with a different flow of water and a different electric current but with the same change in temperature. In both experiments the heat loss was the same and could be eliminated from the equations.

The potential difference v in volts and the electric current I in amperes were measured, the product vI representing the number of joules of electric energy supplied per second. If m gm of water flows through the calorimeter in τ sec, then

$$\text{Energy supplied to 1 gm of water} = \frac{vI\tau}{m}.$$

This quantity was determined for various temperature intervals starting at a number of different initial temperatures. The value of the above ratio corresponding to a rise of temperature from 14.5 to 15.5°C, corrected for heat loss, gave the desired mechanical equivalent of heat. The value found was 4.182 joules/cal. The advantage of this method lies in the fact that, once a steady state is reached, no change of temperature occurs in any part of the apparatus and therefore no correction need be made to allow for the energy supplied to the glass tube, to the resistance wire, etc. It is also not necessary to allow for a lag in the reading of the thermometers.

4. Experiments of Osborne, Stimson, and Ginnings, 1939

During the 1920s and 1930s, important refinements were made in the fundamental thermometric and electrical standards that made it advisable to undertake a redetermination of the mechanical equivalent of heat. First, the international temperature scale was developed and adopted, thus ensuring that the readings of a platinum resistance thermometer were in agreement with those of the ideal-gas scale; second, by means of very accurate dynamical measurements on electric circuits, it was possible to convert *international joules* (based upon the Weston-cell standard of emf and the manganin-resistance standard) to *absolute joules* (based upon the standard meter, kilogram, and second), with the result that

$$1 \text{ international joule} = 1.000165 \text{ abs joules}.$$

Therefore, with all the tremendous resources of the National Bureau of Standards at their disposal, Osborne, Stimson, and Ginnings undertook in 1939 to determine the amount of work needed to increase the

Table 4.2/ Values of the Mechanical Equivalent of Heat

Experimenters	Date	J, joules/cal
Joule	1850	4.155
Rowland	1879	4.188
Reynolds and Moorby	1897	4.183
Callendar and Barnes	1899	4.182
Osborne, Stimson, and Ginnings	1939	4.1858

temperature of 1 gm of water 1°C at temperatures over the entire range of 0 to 100°C. They used the simple electrical method of supplying energy electrically and noting the accompanying rise of temperature of a large mass of water. Measurements of potential difference and current were referred directly to NBS standards; temperature was measured on the international scale; and particular attention was paid to the shielding of the apparatus. As part of their results they obtained a value of J equal to 4.1858 joules/cal. A chronological list of the values of the mechanical equivalent of heat is given in Table 4.2.

4.9/ Present Definition of Heat Units

It is clear from the results of the experiments described in the preceding article that the mechanical equivalent of heat, and hence the quantity of energy, represented by the calorie (or Btu) as defined in Sec. 4.7 can never be established with absolute certainty. It is subject to change with each new experiment and with each refinement of the temperature scale. As calorimetric techniques improved, this deficiency in the exactness of definition of the calorie and Btu became more and more apparent. It is for this reason that the General Conference on Weights and Measures of 1948 refused to recognize any unit other than the joule as the unit of heat.

With the joule as the unit of heat, the "mechanical equivalent of heat" no longer is a meaningful term. The units of heat, work, and energy are all the same, and one merely must be sure that the same unit is used for each term in any expression of the first law, such as $\Delta U = Q - W$. This is not to say, however, that units called the calorie and the Btu have passed out of use, desirable as that might be. Instead they are now used as units of energy and *defined* by common consent as a multiple of the absolute joule (newton-meter). Unfortunately, two different calories are in use. They are the International Steam Table calorie, or I.T. calorie, used for the preparation of steam tables, and the thermochemical calorie, used to report thermochemical data.   The primary conversion factors are as follows:

$$1 \text{ I.T. cal} = 4.1867 \text{ abs joules,}$$
$$1 \text{ thermochemical cal} = 4.1840 \text{ abs joules,}$$
$$1 \text{ Btu} = 1{,}055.04 \text{ abs joules.}$$

The Btu has been defined so that

$$1 \text{ Btu/lb}_m = 1.8 \text{ I.T. cal/gm.}$$

In relation to the foot-pound *force*, the Btu is given as

$$1 \text{ Btu} = 778.156 \text{ ft} \cdot \text{lb}_f,$$

and in relation to the two defined calories, as

$$1 \text{ Btu} = 251.996 \text{ I.T. cal}$$
$$= 252.161 \text{ thermochemical cal.}$$

Other conversion factors for energy units are tabulated in Appendix A.

Since the two defined calories differ by less than one part per thousand, it is not necessary in most engineering work to distinguish between them.   Hence we shall often simply refer to the calorie and make frequent use of the following approximate conversion factors:

$$1 \text{ Btu} = 252 \text{ cal} = 778 \text{ ft} \cdot \text{lb}_f.$$

4.10/ Heat Capacity

When heat is absorbed by a system, a change of temperature may or may not take place, depending on the process.   If a system undergoes a change of temperature from T_1 to T_2 during the transfer of Q units of heat, the *average heat capacity* of the system is defined as the ratio

$$\text{Average heat capacity} = \frac{Q}{T_2 - T_1}.$$

As both Q and $T_2 - T_1$ get smaller, this ratio approaches the *instantaneous heat capacity*, or heat capacity C, thus:

$$C = \lim_{T_2 \to T_1} \frac{Q}{T_2 - T_1},$$

$$\boxed{C = \frac{dQ}{dT}.}$$

The heat capacity may be negative, zero, positive, or infinite, depending on the process the system undergoes during the heat transfer.   It has a definite value only for a definite process.   In the case of a PVT

system, the ratio $đQ/dT$ has a unique value when the pressure is kept constant. Under these conditions, C is called the *heat capacity at constant pressure*, and is denoted by the symbol C_P, where

$$C_P = \left(\frac{đQ}{dT}\right)_P.$$

In general, C_P is a function of P and T. Similarly, the heat capacity at constant volume is

$$C_V = \left(\frac{đQ}{dT}\right)_V$$

and depends on both V and T. In general, C_P and C_V are different. Both will be discussed thoroughly throughout the book. Each system has its own heat capacities, as shown in Table 4.3.

Each heat capacity is a function of two variables. Within a small range of variation of these coordinates, however, the heat capacity may be regarded as practically constant. Very often, one heat capacity can be set equal to another without much error. Thus the $C_{\mathcal{H}}$ of a paramagnetic solid is at times very nearly equal to C_P.

The measurements made by Osborne, Stimson, and Ginnings of the energy necessary to raise the temperature of 1 gm of water 1°C at various temperatures yielded values of heat capacity at constant P in joules/gm · °C. In 1948 the General Conference on Weights and Measures placed heavy emphasis on these measurements in preparing a table of heat capacities of water from 0 to 100°C. This table was accepted by the conference and published as the most probable values as of that time. Table 4.4 lists some of these values. It is seen that the variation of the heat capacity of water with temperature is slight, and consequently it can often be neglected in practical problems.

Table 4.3

System	Heat capacity	Symbol
PVT system	Heat capacity at constant pressure	C_P
	Heat capacity at constant volume	C_V
Stressed bar	Heat capacity at constant stress	C_σ
	Heat capacity at constant strain	C_ϵ
Surface	Heat capacity at constant surface tension	C_γ
	Heat capacity at constant area	C_A
Reversible cell	Heat capacity at constant emf	C_e
	Heat capacity at constant charge	C_q
Dielectric system	Heat capacity at constant field	$C_{\mathcal{E}}$
	Heat capacity at constant polarization	$C_{\mathcal{P}}$
Magnetic system	Heat capacity at constant field	$C_{\mathcal{H}}$
	Heat capacity at constant magnetization	C_m

Table 4.4/ Heat Capacities of Water, C_P

Temp., °C	Abs joules gm · °C	Temp., °C	Abs joules gm · °C
0	4.2174	40	4.1783
5	4.2019	45	4.1792
10	4.1919	50	4.1804
15	4.1855	60	4.1841
20	4.1816	70	4.1893
25	4.1793	80	4.1961
30	4.1782	90	4.2048
35	4.1779	100	4.2156

4.11/ Quasi-static Flow of Heat.   Heat Reservoir

It was shown in Chap. 3 that a process caused by a finite unbalanced force is attended by phenomena such as turbulence and acceleration which cannot be handled by means of thermodynamic coordinates that refer to the system as a whole.   A similar situation exists when there is a finite difference between the temperature of a system and that of its surroundings.   A nonuniform temperature distribution is set up in the system, and the calculation of this distribution and its variation with time is in most cases an elaborate mathematical problem.   During a quasi-static process, however, the difference between the temperature of a system and that of its surroundings is infinitesimal.   As a result, the temperature of the system is at any moment uniform throughout, and its changes are infinitely slow.   The flow of heat is also infinitely slow, and may be calculated in a simple manner in terms of thermodynamic coordinates referring to the system as a whole.

Suppose that a system is in good thermal contact with a body of extremely large mass and that a quasi-static process is performed.   A finite amount of heat that flows during this process will not bring about an appreciable change in the temperature of the surrounding body if the mass is large enough.   For example, a cake of ice of ordinary size, thrown into the ocean, will not produce a drop in temperature of the ocean.   No ordinary flow of heat into the outside air will produce a rise of temperature of the air.   The ocean and the outside air are approximate examples of an ideal body called a heat reservoir.   *A heat reservoir is a body of such a large mass that it may absorb or reject an unlimited quantity of heat without suffering an appreciable change in temperature or in any other thermodynamic coordinate.*   It is not to be understood that there is no change in the thermodynamic coordinates of a heat reservoir when a finite amount of heat flows in or out.   There is a change, but an extremely small one, too small to be measured.

Any quasi-static process of a system in contact with a heat reservoir is bound to be isothermal.   To describe a quasi-static flow of heat involving a change of temperature, one could conceive of a system placed in contact successively with a series of reservoirs. Thus, if we imagine a series of reservoirs ranging in temperature from T_1 to T_2 placed successively in contact with a system at constant pressure of heat capacity C_P, in such a way that the difference in temperature between the system and the reservoir with which it is in contact is infinitesimal, the flow of heat will be quasi-static, and can be calculated as follows: By definition,

$$C_P = \left(\frac{dQ}{dT} \right)_P,$$

and therefore

$$Q = \int_{T_1}^{T_2} C_P \, dT.$$

For example, the heat that is absorbed by a gram of water from a series of reservoirs varying in temperature from T_1 to T_2 during a quasi-static isobaric process is given by this equation, and if C_P is assumed to remain practically constant,

$$Q = C_P(T_2 - T_1).$$

For a quasi-static isochoric process,

$$Q = \int_{T_1}^{T_2} C_V \, dT.$$

Similar considerations hold for other systems and other quasi-static processes.

4.12/ Notation

In this and earlier chapters we have not always stated specifically the amount of material in the system to which our symbols refer. For example, the first law as written for an infinitesimal quasi-static process of a PVT system was given as

$$dU = dQ - P \, dV.$$

In this equation U, Q, and V are extensive quantities, dependent upon the amount of the constant-mass system under consideration. The first-law equation as written could apply to a system of any amount, where U, Q, and V would represent total quantities for the entire system. However, we shall hereafter adopt a different policy with respect to the thermodynamic properties, such as U and V, and let the capital-letter symbols represent properties of a unit mass or a mole of the material making up the system. If we wish to deal with a system of m gm or m lb$_m$ or a system of n moles, we shall express the amount of material explicitly by writing mU or nU, mV or nV, etc. Thus, for a PVT system of n moles, the first law becomes, for a quasi-static process,

$$d(nU) = dQ - P \, d(nV),$$

where Q always represents the total heat transferred to the entire system, whatever its amount. The work W is treated in the same way as Q.

For simple systems other than PVT systems one must take account of the basic definitions of the quantities involved. For example, the polarization $\mathcal{P}$ of a dielectric is by definition the electric dipole moment per unit volume. Hence, if U and V represent the internal energy and volume per unit mass, the first law for a dielectric would have to be written

$$dU = đQ + \mathcal{E}V \, d\mathcal{P}.$$

For a mass m, we should then write

$$d(mU) = đQ + \mathcal{E}(mV) \, d\mathcal{P}.$$

The quantities U and V could just as readily refer to 1 mole (molar quantities), in which case the equation appropriate to n moles would be

$$d(nU) = đQ + \mathcal{E}(nV) \, d\mathcal{P}.$$

In the case of a liquid and its surface, the first law could be written

$$d(nU) = đQ - P \, d(nV) + \gamma \, dA,$$

where U and V are molar quantities, and Q and A refer to the entire system.

The symbol C for heat capacity will always mean either the molar heat capacity or the specific heat capacity (abbreviated "specific heat").

Problems

4.1 A combustion experiment is performed by burning a mixture of fuel and oxygen in a constant-volume "bomb" surrounded by a water bath. During the experiment the temperature of the water is observed to rise. Regarding the mixture of fuel and oxygen as the system:

(a) Has heat when transferred?
(b) Has work been done?
(c) What is the sign of ΔU?

4.2 A liquid is irregularly stirred in a well-insulated container and undergoes a rise in temperature. Regarding the liquid as the system:

(a) Has heat been transferred?
(b) Has work been done?
(c) What is the sign of ΔU?

4.3 A vessel with rigid walls and covered with asbestos is divided into two parts by a partition. One part contains a gas, and the other is evacuated. If the partition is suddenly broken, show that the initial and final internal energies of the gas are equal.

4.4 A vessel with rigid walls and covered with asbestos is divided into two parts by an insulating partition. One part contains a gas at temperature T and pressure P. The other part contains a gas at temperature T' and pressure P'. The partition is removed. What conclusion may be drawn by applying the first law of thermodynamics?

4.5 A mixture of hydrogen and oxygen is enclosed in a rigid insulating container and exploded by a spark. The temperature and pressure both increase considerably. Neglecting the small amount of energy provided by the spark itself, what conclusion may be drawn by applying the first law of thermodynamics?

4.6 When a system is taken from state a to state b, in Fig. P4.6, along the path acb, 80 Btu of heat flow into the system, and the system does 30 Btu of work.

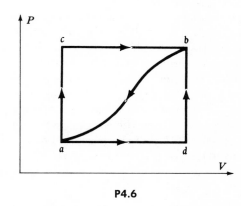

P4.6

(a) How much heat flows into the system along path adb if the work done is 10 Btu?

(b) When the system is returned from b to a along the curved path, the work done on the system is 20 Btu. Does the system absorb or liberate heat and how much?

(c) If $U_a = 0$ and $U_d = 40$ Btu, find the heat absorbed in the processes ad and db.

4.7 A cylindrical tube with rigid walls and covered with asbestos is divided into two parts by a rigid insulating wall with a small hole in it. A frictionless insulating piston is held against the perforated partition, thus preventing the gas that is on the other side from seeping through the hole. The gas is maintained at a pressure P_1 by another frictionless insulating piston. Imagine both pistons to move simultaneously in such a way that, as the gas streams through the hole, the pressure remains at the constant value P_1 on one side of the dividing wall and at a constant lower value P_2 on the other side, until all the gas is forced through the hole.   Prove that

$$U_1 + P_1V_1 = U_2 + P_2V_2.$$

4.8   An exhausted chamber with nonconducting walls is connected through a valve to the atmosphere, where the pressure is P_0.   The valve is opened, and air flows into the chamber until the pressure within the chamber is P_0.   Prove that $U_0 + P_0V_0 = U_f$, where U_0 and V_0 are the molar energy and molar volume of the air at the temperature and pressure of the atmosphere, and U_f is the molar energy of the air in the chamber.   (*Hint:* Connect to the chamber a cylinder equipped with a frictionless nonleaking piston.   Suppose the cylinder to contain exactly the amount of air that will enter the chamber when the valve is opened. As soon as the first small quantity of air enters the chamber, the pressure in the cylinder is reduced a small amount below atmospheric pressure, and the outside air forces the piston in.)

4.9   A bomb of volume V_B contains n moles of gas at high pressure. Connected to the bomb is a capillary tube through which the gas may slowly leak out into the atmosphere, where the pressure is P_0.   Surrounding the bomb and capillary is a water bath in which is immersed an electric resistor.   The gas is allowed to leak slowly through the capillary into the atmosphere while, at the same time, electric energy is dissipated in the resistor at such a rate that the temperature of the gas, the bomb, the capillary, and the water is kept equal to that of the outside air.   Show that, after as much gas as possible has leaked out during time τ, the change of internal energy is

$$\Delta U = vI\tau - P_0(nV_0 - V_B),$$

where V_0 = molar volume of the gas at atmospheric pressure,
   $v = pd$ across the resistor,
   I = current in the resistor.

4.10   A thick-walled insulated metal chamber contains n_1 moles of helium at high pressure P_1.   It is connected through a valve with a large, almost empty gasholder in which the pressure is maintained at a constant value P', very nearly atmospheric.   The valve is opened slightly, and the helium flows slowly and adiabatically into the gasholder until the pressures on the two sides of the valve are equalized. Prove that

$$\frac{n_2}{n_1} = \frac{U_1 - H'}{U_2 - H'},$$

where n_2 = number of moles of helium left in the chamber,
   U_1 = initial molar energy of helium in the chamber,
   U_2 = final molar energy of helium in the chamber,
   $H' = U' + P'V'$ (where U' = molar energy of helium in the gas-holder, V' = molar volume of helium in the gasholder).

4.11 Derive the equations listed in the accompanying table.

System	Heat capacity at constant extensive variable	Heat capacity at constant intensive variable
PVT system	$C_V = \left(\dfrac{\partial U}{\partial T}\right)_V$	$C_P = \left(\dfrac{\partial U}{\partial T}\right)_P + PV\beta$
Stressed bar	$C_\epsilon = \left(\dfrac{\partial U}{\partial T}\right)_\epsilon$	$C_\sigma = \left(\dfrac{\partial U}{\partial T}\right)_\sigma - \sigma\alpha$
Paramagnetic solid obeying Curie's equation	$C_m = \left(\dfrac{\partial U}{\partial T}\right)_m$	$C_{\mathscr{H}} = \left(\dfrac{\partial U}{\partial T}\right)_{\mathscr{H}} + \dfrac{\mu_0 \mathscr{M}^2}{C}$

4.12 It has been suggested that the kitchen in your house could be cooled in the summer by closing the kitchen from the rest of the house and opening the door to the electric refrigerator. Comment on this. State clearly and concisely the basis for your conclusions.

4.13 One mole of a gas obeys the equation of state

$$\left(P + \frac{a}{V^2}\right)(V - b) = RT,$$

and its internal energy is given by

$$U = cT - \frac{a}{V},$$

where a, b, c, and R are constants. Calculate the heat capacities C_V and C_P.

4.14 The equation of state of a monatomic solid is

$$PV + G = \Gamma U,$$

where V = molar volume,

G = a function of V only,

Γ = a constant.

Prove that

$$\Gamma = \frac{\beta V}{C_V k},$$

where k is the isothermal compressibility. This relation, first derived by Gruneisen, is of fundamental importance in the theory of the solid state.

4.15 Starting with the first law for a PVT system, derive the equations:

(a) $dQ = C_V \, dT + \left[\left(\dfrac{\partial U}{\partial V} \right)_T + P \right] dV.$

(b) $C_P = C_V + \left[\left(\dfrac{\partial U}{\partial V} \right)_T + P \right] V\beta.$

(c) $dQ = C_V \, dT + \dfrac{C_P - C_V}{V\beta} \, dV.$

4.16 (a) Energy is supplied electrically at a constant rate to a thermally insulated substance. The heating curve has the form shown in Fig. P4.16a. Draw a rough graph showing the dependence of heat capacity on temperature.

(b) Repeat for a heating curve of the form shown in Fig. P4.16b.

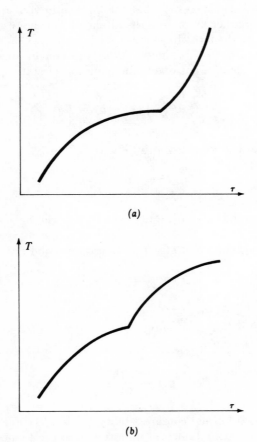

(a)

(b)

P4.16

4.17 The molar heat capacity at constant pressure of a gas varies with the temperature according to the equation

$$C_P = a + bT - \frac{c}{T^2},$$

where a, b, and c are constants. How much heat is transferred during an isobaric process in which n moles of gas undergo a temperature rise from T_1 to T_2?

4.18 The molar heat capacity at constant magnetic field of a paramagnetic solid at low temperatures varies with temperature and field according to the relation

$$C_{\mathscr{H}} = \frac{b + C\mathscr{H}^2}{T^2} + DT^3,$$

where b, C, and D are constants. How much heat is transferred during a process in which $\mathscr{H}$ remains constant at the value $\mathscr{H}_0$ and the temperature of n moles of material changes from T_1 to T_2?

4.19 A vapor expands quasi-statically in a piston and cylinder assembly. During the process the pressure and volume are related as follows:

P, lb$_f$/in.^{2}	V, ft^3
90	6.00
75	7.06
60	8.57
45	10.95
30	15.5
15	27.8

The energy change of the vapor is known to be $\Delta U = -75.2$ Btu. Calculate W in ft $\cdot$ lb$_f$ and Q in Btu for the process.

Chapter 5/
Thermal Properties of Gases

5.1/ Equation of State of a Gas

It was emphasized in Chap. 1 that a gas is the best-behaved thermometric substance because of the fact that the ratio of the pressure P of a gas at any temperature to the pressure P_t of the same gas at the triple point, as both P and P_t approach zero, approaches a value independent of the nature of the gas. The limiting value of this ratio, multiplied by 273.16°, was defined to be the ideal-gas temperature T of the system at whose temperature the gas exerts the pressure P. The reason for this regular behavior may be found by investigating the way in which the product PV of a gas depends on P.

Suppose that the pressure P and the molar volume V of a gas held at any constant temperature are measured over a wide range of values of the pressure, and the product PV is plotted as a function of P. Experiments of this sort were first performed by Amagat in France in 1870. Nowadays, such measurements are made at many bureaus of standards and universities. A typical set of isotherms of nitrogen is shown in Fig. 5.1. The relation between PV and P may be expressed by means of a power series of the form

$$PV = A(1 + B'P + C'P^2 + \cdots),$$

where A, B', C', etc., depend on the temperature and on the nature of the gas. It should be noticed in Fig. 5.1 that, in the pressure range

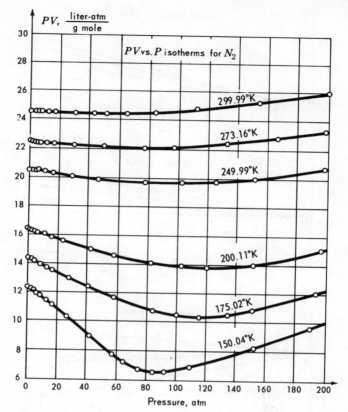

Fig. 5.1 Variation of PV of nitrogen with pressure at constant temperature. (A. S. Friedman, 1950.)

from 0 to about 40 atm, the relation between PV and P is practically linear, so that only the first two terms in the series are significant. In general, the greater the pressure range, the larger the number of terms required.

The remarkable property of gases that makes them so valuable in thermometry is displayed in Fig. 5.2, where the product PV is plotted against P for four different gases, all at the normal boiling temperature of sulfur in the top graph, all at the normal boiling temperature of water in the one beneath, all at the triple point of water in the next-lower graph, and all at the normal sublimation temperature of solid CO_2 in the lowest. In each case it is seen that, as the pressure approaches zero, the product PV approaches the same value for all gases at the same temperature. It follows from this that the coefficient A in the expansion for PV is *independent of the nature of the gas and depends only on temperature.* Thus

$$\lim_{P \to 0} (PV) = A = \text{function of temperature only.}$$

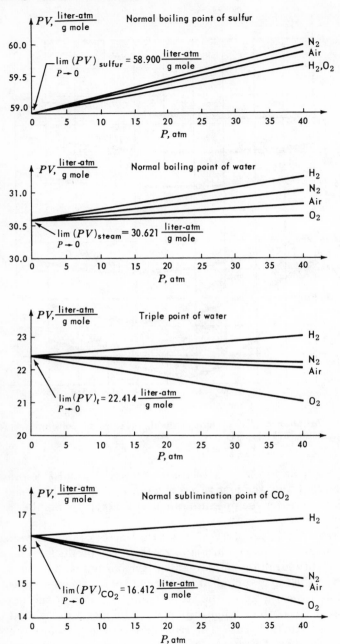

Fig. 5.2 The fundamental property of gases is that $\lim_{P \to 0} (PV)_T$ is independent of the nature of the gas and depends only on T.

Now consider the limiting values of the two ratios

$$\lim_{P \to 0} \frac{P}{P_t} \text{ (const } V) = \lim \frac{PV}{P_t V} = \frac{\lim (PV)}{\lim (PV)_t},$$

$$\lim_{P \to 0} \frac{V}{V_t} \text{ (const } P) = \lim \frac{PV}{PV_t} = \frac{\lim (PV)}{\lim (PV)_t}.$$

By definition (Chap. 1),

$$T = 273.16° \lim \frac{P}{P_t} \text{ (const } V) = 273.16° \lim \frac{V}{V_t} \text{ (const } P).$$

It follows that

$$T = 273.16° \frac{\lim (PV)}{\lim (PV)_t},$$

or

$$\lim (PV) = \left[\frac{\lim (PV)_t}{273.16°} \right] T.$$

The quantity in brackets is called the universal gas constant, and is denoted by R. Thus

$$\lim (PV) = A = RT,$$

and the equation of state for gases may be written

$$\frac{PV}{RT} = 1 + B'P + C'P^2 + \cdots.$$

A numerical value for R may be obtained from its defining equation

$$R = \frac{\lim (PV)_t}{273.16°}.$$

The best value obtained so far for $\lim (PV)_t$ is 22.4140 liter · atm/gm mole, or 2,271.16 joules/gm mole. Hence

$$R = \frac{22.4140 \text{ liter · atm/gm mole}}{273.16°K} = \frac{2,271.16 \text{ joules/gm mole}}{273.16°K}$$

$$R = \begin{cases} 0.08205 \text{ liter · atm/gm mole · °K,} \\ 8.314 \text{ joules/gm mole · °K,} \\ 1.987 \text{ cal/gm mole · °K} \quad \text{(thermochemical calorie),} \\ 1.986 \text{ Btu/lb mole · °R, or I.T. cal/gm mole · °K,} \\ 1,545 \text{ ft · lb}_f\text{/lb mole · °R,} \\ 10.73 \text{ psia · ft}^3\text{/lb mole · °R,} \\ 0.7302 \text{ atm · ft}^3\text{/lb mole · °R.} \end{cases}$$

The ratio PV/RT is called the *compressibility factor*, and is denoted by Z. Thus the equation of state for gases may be written

$$Z = 1 + B'P + C'P^2 + D'P^3 + \cdots.$$

An alternative expression for Z which is also in common use is

$$Z = 1 + \frac{B}{V} + \frac{C}{V^2} + \frac{D}{V^3} + \cdots$$

Both of these equations are known as *virial expansions*, and the coefficients B', C', D', ... and B, C, D, ... are called virial coefficients. B' and B are termed second virial coefficients; C' and C, third virial coefficients; etc. For a given material these coefficients are functions of temperature only.

Many other equations of state have been proposed for gases, but the virial equations are the only ones having a firm basis in theory. The methods of statistical mechanics allow the derivation of the virial equations and provide physical significance to the virial coefficients. Thus, for the expansion in $1/V$, the term B/V arises on account of interactions between pairs of molecules; the C/V^2 term, on account of three-body interactions; etc. Since two-body interactions are many times more common than three-body interactions, and three-body interactions are many times more common than four-body interactions, etc., the contributions to Z of successively higher-ordered terms fall off rapidly.

The coefficients of the expansion in pressure are related to the coefficients of the expansion in density $(1/V)$ as follows:

$$B' = \frac{B}{RT},$$

$$C' = \frac{C - B^2}{(RT)^2},$$

$$D' = \frac{D - 3BC + 2B^3}{(RT)^3},$$

etc.

These relations are obtained by elimination of P on the right-hand side of the expansion in pressure through use of the expansion in $1/V$. The resulting equation represents a power series in $1/V$ which may be compared term by term with the original virial expansion in $1/V$. This comparison provides equations which may be reduced to the above set.

Although it is the expansion in density, or $1/V$, which results directly as a consequence of statistical mechanics, nevertheless the expansion in pressure finds widespread use. As we have already seen, isotherms of PV, and hence of Z, are nearly linear at low pressure. Thus, for low pressures, a very satisfactory equation of state is

$$Z = \frac{PV}{RT} = 1 + B'P + \cdots = 1 + \frac{BP}{RT} + \cdots$$

At elevated temperatures this linear relationship is a good approximation even to high pressures. This is illustrated in Fig. 5.3, which shows the compressibility factor for hydrogen plotted against pressure at a number of temperatures.

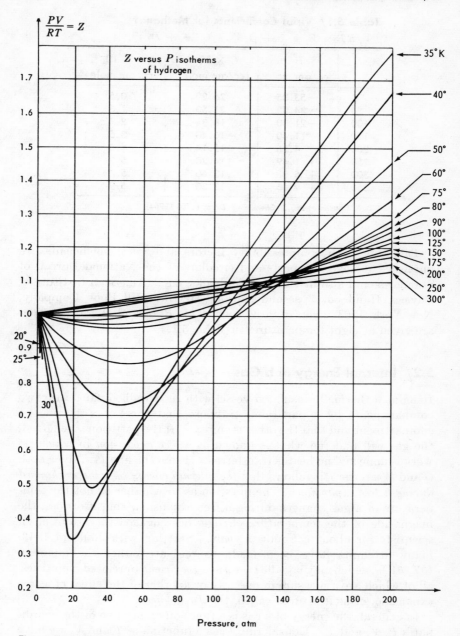

Fig. 5.3 Variation of Z of hydrogen with pressure at constant temperature. (A. S. Friedman, 1950.)

Table 5.1/ Virial Coefficients for Methane†

$$PV/RT = Z = 1 + B/V + C/V^2 + D/V^3$$

T, °C	B, cc/gm mole	$C \times 10^{-2}$, (cc/gm mole)^2	$D \times 10^{-4}$, (cc/gm mole)^3
0	−53.35	26.20	0.5
50	−34.23	21.50	1.3
100	−21.00	18.34	2.7
150	−11.40	16.40	3.5
200	− 4.16	15.14	4.3
250	+ 1.49	14.20	5.2
300	+ 5.98	13.60	5.7
350	+ 9.66	13.30	5.9

† D. R. Douslin et al., *J. Chem. Eng. Data,* 9:358 (1964).

Tables of both compressibility factors and virial coefficients are published in several reports and circulars of the National Bureau of Standards and also in various handbooks, e.g., "American Institute of Physics Handbook," second edition, McGraw-Hill Book Company, New York, 1963. Sets of virial coefficients B, C, and D, for methane, are given at eight temperatures in Table 5.1.

5.2/ Internal Energy of a Gas

Imagine a thermally insulated vessel with rigid walls divided into two compartments by a partition. Suppose that there is a gas in one compartment and that the other is empty. If the partition is removed, the gas will undergo what is known as a *free expansion* in which no work is done and no heat is transferred. From the first law, since both Q and W are zero, it follows that *the internal energy remains unchanged during a free expansion.* The question as to whether or not the temperature of a gas changes during a free expansion, and, if it does, the magnitude of the temperature change, has engaged the attention of scientists for about a hundred years. Starting with Joule in 1843, many attempts have been made to measure either the quantity $(\partial T/\partial V)_U$, which may be called the *Joule coefficient*, or related quantities, all of which are a measure in one way or another of the effect of a free expansion, or as it is often called, the *Joule effect*.

In general, the energy of a gas is a function of any two of the coordinates P, V, and T. Considering U as a function of T and V, we have

$$dU = \left(\frac{\partial U}{\partial T}\right)_V dT + \left(\frac{\partial U}{\partial V}\right)_T dV.$$

If no temperature change $(dT = 0)$ takes place in a free expansion

$(dU = 0)$, it follows that

$$\left(\frac{\partial U}{\partial V}\right)_T = 0,$$

or in other words, U does not depend on V. Considering U to be a function of T and P, we have

$$dU = \left(\frac{\partial U}{\partial T}\right)_P dT + \left(\frac{\partial U}{\partial P}\right)_T dP.$$

If no temperature change $(dT = 0)$ takes place in a free expansion $(dU = 0)$, it follows that

$$\left(\frac{\partial U}{\partial P}\right)_T = 0,$$

or in other words, U does not depend on P. It is apparent then that, if no temperature change takes place in a free expansion, U is independent of V and of P, and therefore U is a function of T only.

Two methods of studying the Joule effect have been employed. In the original method of Joule, two vessels connected by a short tube and stopcock were immersed in a water bath. One vessel contained air at high pressure, and the other was evacuated. The temperature of the water was measured before and after the expansion, the idea being to infer the temperature change of the gas from the temperature change of the water. Since the heat capacity of the vessels and water was approximately one thousand times as large as the heat capacity of the air, Joule was unable to detect any temperature change of the water, although, in the light of our present knowledge, the air must have suffered a temperature change of several degrees.

The second method of studying the Joule coefficient consists in an attempt to measure the temperature of the gas almost immediately after the free expansion, before the gas has had a chance to exchange heat with its surroundings, by using the gas itself as its own thermometer. In the experiments of Hirn in 1865, a vessel was divided into two equal compartments by a thin partition, which could be broken with the aid of a metal ball. Originally, both compartments contained air at atmospheric pressure. The air from one compartment was pumped into the other compartment, and the temperature of the compressed gas was allowed to come to its original value. The partition was then broken, and soon afterward the pressure was measured with the aid of a U-tube manometer containing a light liquid and found to be the value that existed when the gas originally occupied the whole vessel. It was therefore concluded that no temperature change took place. Cazin repeated this experiment in 1870 with similar apparatus.

The results of this method are doubtful because of the oscillations of the liquid in the manometer tube. If sufficient time elapses to allow the oscillations of the manometric liquid to subside, then, during this

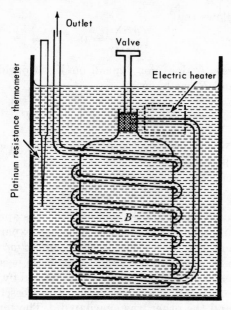

Fig. 5.4 Apparatus of Rossini and Frandsen for measuring $(\partial U/\partial P)_T$ of a gas.

time, there is a transfer of heat between the gas and the walls of the vessel which vitiates the results. Further complications arise from the conduction of heat through metal valve connections due to a temperature difference created by the rapidly streaming gas. In the experiments of Keyes and Sears in 1924, the gas was not used as its own thermometer, but instead, a platinum resistance thermometer was employed to measure the temperature immediately after expansion. Temperature changes of approximately the right order were measured, but only a few rough measurements were made.

A direct measurement of the temperature change associated with a free expansion is so difficult that it seems necessary to give up the idea of a precise measurement of the Joule coefficient. Modern methods of attacking the problem of the internal energy of a gas involve the measurement of the quantity $(\partial U/\partial P)_T$ by having the gas undergo an isothermal expansion in which heat is transferred and also work is done. The most extensive series of measurements of this kind was performed by Rossini and Frandsen in 1932 at the National Bureau of Standards by a method elaborated by Washburn. The apparatus is shown in Fig. 5.4. A bomb B contains n moles of gas at a pressure P and communicates with the atmosphere through a long coil wrapped around the bomb. The whole apparatus is immersed in a water bath the temperature of which may be maintained constant at exactly the same value as that of the surrounding atmosphere.

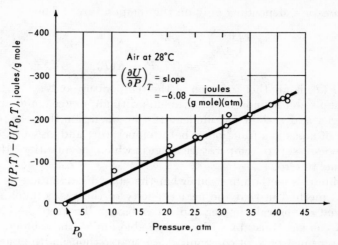

Fig. 5.5 **Dependence of the internal energy of a gas on the pressure.**

The experiment is performed as follows: When the valve is opened slightly, the gas flows slowly through the long coil and out into the air. At the same time, the temperature of the gas, the bomb, the coils, and the water is maintained constant by an electric heating coil immersed in the water. The electric energy supplied to the water is therefore the heat Q absorbed by the gas during the expansion. The work done by the gas during the entire process which reduces the pressure in the bomb to P_0 is

$$W = P_0(nV_0 - V_B),$$

where P_0 = atmospheric pressure,
V_0 = molar volume at atmospheric temperature and pressure,
V_B = volume of the bomb.

If $U(P,T)$ is the molar energy at pressure P and temperature T and $U(P_0,T)$ is the molar energy at atmospheric pressure and the same temperature, then, from the first law,

$$U(P,T) - U(P_0,T) = \frac{W - Q}{n},$$

provided that corrections have been made to take account of the energy changes due to the contraction of the walls of the bomb. In this way, the energy change was measured for various values of the initial pressure and was plotted against this pressure, as shown in Fig. 5.5. Since $U(P_0,T)$ is constant, it follows that the slope of the resulting curve at any value of P is equal to $(\partial U/\partial P)_T$. Within the pressure range of 1 to 40 atm, it is seen that $(\partial U/\partial P)_T$ *is independent of the pressure*, depending only on the temperature. Thus

$$\left(\frac{\partial U}{\partial P}\right)_T = f(T)$$

and

$$U = f(T)P + F(T),$$

where $F(T)$ is another function of the temperature only.

Rossini's and Frandsen's experiments with air, oxygen, and mixtures of oxygen and carbon dioxide lead to the conclusion that the internal energy of a gas is a function of both temperature and pressure. They found no pressure or temperature range in which the quantity $(\partial U/\partial P)_T$ was equal to zero.

Washburn's method has somewhat the same disadvantage as Joule's original method in that the heat capacity of the gas is much smaller than that of the calorimeter and water bath. To keep the temperature of the gas constant within reasonable limits, the temperature of the water must be kept constant to less than a thousandth of a degree. In Rossini's and Frandsen's measurements the final precision was estimated to be $2\frac{1}{2}$ percent.

5.3/ The Concept of an Ideal Gas

We have already pointed out that the terms B/V, C/V^2, etc., of the virial expansion arise on account of various kinds of molecular interactions. If no such interactions existed, the virial coefficients B, C, etc., would be zero and the virial expansion would reduce to

$$Z = 1, \qquad \text{or} \qquad PV = RT.$$

For a real gas, molecular interactions *do* exist, and exert an influence on the observed behavior of the gas. As the pressure of a real gas is reduced at constant temperature, V increases and the contributions of the terms B/V, C/V^2, etc., decrease. For a pressure approaching zero, Z approaches unity, not because of any change in the virial coefficients, but because V becomes infinite. Thus, in the limit as the pressure approaches zero, the equation of state assumes the simple form

$$Z = 1, \qquad \text{or} \qquad PV = RT.$$

We have also found that the internal energy of a real gas is a function of pressure as well as of temperature. This pressure dependency arises as a result of molecular interactions. If such interactions did not exist, no energy would be required to alter the average intermolecular distance. Since this is all that is accomplished when volume (and hence pressure) changes occur at constant temperature, we conclude that, in the absence of molecular interactions, the internal energy of a gas would depend on temperature only. These considerations of the behavior of a hypothetical gas in which no molecular interactions exist and of a real gas at the limiting pressure of zero lead us at this point to define an *ideal gas* whose properties, although not corresponding to those of any existing gas, are approximately those of a real gas at low pressures. By definition, an ideal gas satisfies the following equations at all temperatures and pressures:

$$\boxed{\begin{array}{c} PV = RT \\ \left(\dfrac{\partial U}{\partial V}\right)_T = 0 \end{array}} \qquad \text{ideal gas.}$$

The requirement that $(\partial U/\partial V)_T = 0$ may be written in other ways. Thus

$$\left(\frac{\partial U}{\partial P}\right)_T = \left(\frac{\partial U}{\partial V}\right)_T \left(\frac{\partial V}{\partial P}\right)_T,$$

and since $(\partial V/\partial P)_T = -RT/P^2 = -V/P$, and therefore is not zero, whereas $(\partial U/\partial V)_T$ is zero, it follows that, for an ideal gas,

$$\boxed{\left(\frac{\partial U}{\partial P}\right)_T = 0} \qquad \text{ideal gas.}$$

Finally, since both $(\partial U/\partial P)_T$ and $(\partial U/\partial V)_T$ are zero,

$$\boxed{U = f(T) \text{ only}} \qquad \text{ideal gas.}$$

Whether an actual gas may be treated as an ideal gas depends upon the error that may be tolerated in a given calculation. An actual gas at pressures below about two atmospheres may usually be treated as an ideal gas without introducing errors greater than a few percent. Even in the case of a saturated vapor in equilibrium with its liquid, the ideal-gas equation of state may be used with only a small error if the vapor pressure is low.

5.4/ Thermodynamic Equations

In Chap. 4 it was shown that, for an infinitesimal quasi-static process for any PVT system, the first law becomes

$$\text{đ}Q = dU + P\,dV.$$

Thus the molar heat capacity at constant volume is given by

$$C_V = \left(\frac{\text{đ}Q}{dT}\right)_V = \left(\frac{\partial U}{\partial T}\right)_V.$$

In the special case of an ideal gas, U is a function of T only, and therefore the partial derivative with respect to T is the same as the total derivative. Consequently, for an ideal gas we have, in general,

$$C_V = \frac{dU}{dT}$$

and

$$dQ = C_V\,dT + P\,dV. \tag{5.1}$$

Now, if all equilibrium states are represented by the ideal-gas equation

$$PV = RT,$$

then, for an infinitesimal quasi-static process,

$$P\,dV + V\,dP = R\,dT.$$

Substituting the above in Eq. (5.1), we get

$$dQ = (C_V + R)\,dT - V\,dP,$$

and dividing by dT,

$$\frac{dQ}{dT} = C_V + R - V\frac{dP}{dT}.$$

At constant pressure, the left-hand member becomes C_P; whence

$$C_P = C_V + R. \tag{5.2}$$

We have the result, therefore, that the molar heat capacity at constant pressure of an ideal gas is always larger than that at constant volume, the difference remaining constant and equal to R.

Since U is a function of T only, it follows that

$$C_V = \frac{dU}{dT} = \text{a function of } T \text{ only}$$

and

$$C_P = C_V + R = \text{a function of } T \text{ only}.$$

One more useful equation can be obtained. Since

$$dQ = (C_V + R)\,dT - V\,dP,$$

we get

$$dQ = C_P\,dT - V\,dP. \tag{5.3}$$

5.5/ Heat Capacities of Gases

The experimental determination of heat capacities of gases through use of the defining equations of the preceding chapter is a most difficult task. Such measurements are presently almost never made. Rather, such information is obtained by calculation through the methods of statistical mechanics from spectral data. This procedure yields heat capacities of gases at constant volume at the limiting pressure of zero.

Since the equations which define an ideal gas are also valid for the zero-pressure state and since the heat capacity of an ideal gas is independent of pressure, it is presumed that the zero-pressure heat capacity is identical with the ideal-gas heat capacity.   To put it another way, if a gas at zero pressure is imagined to obey the ideal-gas equations as it is compressed isothermally to finite pressures, this imaginary ideal gas would always have a heat capacity identical with the zero-pressure value.   Thus zero-pressure heat capacities are commonly referred to as ideal-gas heat capacities, or heat capacities for the ideal-gas state.   It is these heat capacities that are tabulated in compilations of thermodynamic data.   They are functions of temperature but not of pressure, and they depend on the gas.   The heat capacities of real gases are functions of pressure as well as of temperature, and are not often used. Other methods, to be considered later, are employed to take into account the effect of pressure on the thermodynamic properties of gases.

The general characteristics of molar-heat-capacity data for the *ideal-gas state* can be given quite simply as follows:

1. *All gases.*
   a. The molar heat at constant volume is independent of the volume.
   b. The molar heat at constant pressure is independent of the pressure.
   c. The molar heat at constant pressure is always larger than the molar heat at constant volume, the difference being equal to R.

2. *Monatomic gases*, such as He, A, and Ne, and most metallic vapors, such as the vapors of Na, Cd, and Hg.
   a. The molar heat at constant volume is constant over a wide temperature range, and is very nearly equal to $\frac{3}{2}R$, or 2.98 cal/gm mole · °C.
   b. The molar heat at constant pressure is constant over a wide temperature range, and is very nearly equal to $\frac{5}{2}R$, or 4.97 cal/gm mole · °C.
   c. The ratio C_P/C_V is constant over a wide temperature range, and is very nearly equal to 1.67.

3. *Diatomic gases*, namely, H_2, D_2, O_2, N_2, NO, and CO.
   a. The molar heat at constant volume is equal to about $\frac{5}{2}R$, or about 5 cal/gm mole · °C at room temperature, and increases slowly as the temperature is raised.
   b. The molar heat at constant pressure is equal to about $\frac{7}{2}R$, or about 7 cal/gm mole · °C at room temperature, and increases slowly as the temperature is raised.
   c. The ratio C_P/C_V is nearly constant at ordinary temperatures, being equal to about 1.40, and decreases as the temperature is raised.

4. *Polyatomic gases and gases that are chemically active*, such as CO_2, NH_3, CH_4, Cl_2, Br_2, etc.
   a. C_V, C_P, and C_P/C_V vary with the temperature, the variation being different for each different gas.

Table 5.2/ Molar Heat Capacities at Constant Pressure for the Ideal-gas State—300 to 1500°K†

Gas	Formula	a, cal/gm mole $\cdot °K$	$b \times 10^3$, cal/gm mole $\cdot °K^2$	$c \times 10^6$, cal/gm mole $\cdot °K^3$
Acetylene	C_2H_2	7.331	12.622	− 3.889
Ammonia	NH_3	6.086	8.812	− 1.506
Benzene	C_6H_6	−0.409	77.621	−26.429
Carbon dioxide	CO_2	6.214	10.396	− 3.545
Carbon monoxide	CO	6.420	1.665	− 0.196
Chlorine	Cl_2	7.576	2.424	− 0.965
Ethyl alcohol	C_2H_6O	6.990	39.741	−11.926
Hydrogen	H_2	6.947	−0.200	0.481
Hydrogen chloride	HCl	6.732	0.433	0.370
Methane	CH_4	3.381	18.044	− 4.300
Nitrogen	N_2	6.524	1.250	− 0.001
Oxygen	O_2	6.148	3.102	− 0.923
Sulfur dioxide	SO_2	7.116	9.512	3.511
Water	H_2O	7.256	2.298	0.283

† H. M. Spencer and coworkers, *J. Am. Chem. Soc.*, 56:2311 (1934), 64:2511 (1942), 67:1859 (1945); and *Ind. Eng. Chem.*, 40:2152 (1948).

Heat-capacity data for the ideal-gas state are often represented by empirical equations of the form

$$C_P = a + bT + cT^2,$$

where a, b, and c are constants. Values are given in Table 5.2 for these constants for a number of gases. These equations fit the data with an average deviation of better than 1 percent and a maximum deviation of about 2 percent.

5.6/ Quasi-static Adiabatic Process

When an ideal gas undergoes a quasi-static adiabatic process, the pressure, volume, and temperature change in a manner that is described by a relation between P and V, T and V, or P and T. In order to derive the relation between P and V, we start with Eqs. (5.1) and (5.3) of Sec. 5.4. Thus

$$\dot{Q} = C_V\,dT + P\,dV$$
$$= C_P\,dT - V\,dP.$$

Since, in an adiabatic process, $\dot{Q} = 0$,

$$V\,dP = C_P\,dT,$$
$$P\,dV = -C_V\,dT.$$

Dividing the first by the second,

$$\frac{dP}{P} = -\frac{C_P}{C_V}\frac{dV}{V},$$

and denoting the ratio of the molar heat capacities by the symbol γ, we have

$$\frac{dP}{P} = -\gamma\frac{dV}{V}.$$

This equation cannot be integrated until we know something about the behavior of γ. We have seen that, for monatomic gases, γ is constant, whereas for diatomic and polyatomic gases, it may vary with the temperature. It often requires, however, a large change of temperature to produce an appreciable change in γ. For example, in the case of carbon monoxide, a temperature rise from 0 to 2000°C produces a decrease in γ from 1.4 to 1.3. Most adiabatic processes that we deal with do not involve such a large temperature change. It is therefore often a good approximation in an adiabatic process that involves only a moderate temperature change to neglect the small accompanying change in γ. Regarding γ as constant and integrating, we obtain

$$\ln P = -\gamma \ln V + \ln \text{const},$$

or
$$\boxed{PV^\gamma = \text{const.}} \tag{5.4}$$

Equation (5.4) holds at all equilibrium states through which an ideal gas with constant heat capacities passes during a quasi-static adiabatic process. It is important to understand that a free expansion is an adiabatic process but not quasi-static. It is therefore entirely fallacious to attempt to apply Eq. (5.4) to the states traversed by an ideal gas during a free expansion.

A family of curves representing quasi-static adiabatic processes may be plotted on a PV diagram by assigning different values to the constant in Eq. (5.4). The slope of any adiabatic curve is

$$\left(\frac{\partial P}{\partial V}\right)_S = -(\gamma)(\text{const})V^{-\gamma-1}$$

$$= -\gamma\frac{P}{V},$$

where the subscript S is used to denote an adiabatic quasi-static process.

Quasi-static isothermal processes are represented by a family of equilateral hyperbolas obtained by assigning different values to T in the equation $PV = RT$. Since

$$\left(\frac{\partial P}{\partial V}\right)_T = -\frac{P}{V},$$

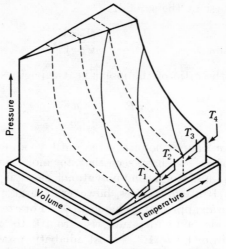

Fig. 5.6 PVT surface for an ideal gas. Isotherms are represented by dashed curves, and adiabatics by solid curves.

it follows that an adiabatic curve has a steeper negative slope than an isothermal curve at the same point.

The isothermal and adiabatic curves of an ideal gas may be shown in a revealing way on a PVT surface. If P, V, and T are plotted along rectangular axes, the resulting surface is shown in Fig. 5.6, where it may be seen that the adiabatic curves cut across the isotherms.

5.7 / Velocity of a Longitudinal Wave

Let c' be the velocity of propagation of a pressure increase in a fluid at rest. To show the relation of c' to the properties of the fluid, we consider the propagation of a pressure increase in a tube, as shown in Fig. 5.7.

The piston on the left is moved into the tube with constant velocity u by exertion of a force $A(P + \Delta P)$. The effect of this is to increase the pressure in front of the piston from P to $P + \Delta P$. This pressure increase propagates into the fluid with the constant velocity c'. The entire region affected by the pressure increase at time τ moves with velocity u, and the effect of the process is to increase the momentum of this region from zero to a finite value. The impulse-momentum principle may be applied to the entire tube.

At time τ the mass of fluid already set in motion is

$$m = \frac{c'\tau A}{V},$$

where V is the specific volume of undisturbed fluid. The impulse-

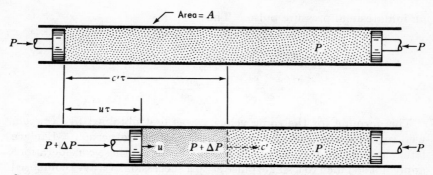

Fig. 5.7 **Propagation of a compression with constant velocity** c' **by motion of a piston with constant velocity** u. **Upper diagram at the start; lower diagram after time** τ.

momentum theorem gives

$$F\tau = \frac{\Delta(\Sigma m_i u_i)}{g_c},$$

where F, the resultant force acting on the entire fluid column, is given by $F = A \, \Delta P$. The quantity $\Delta(\Sigma m_i u_i)$ indicates the difference between the total momentum of the fluid at time τ and at zero time. The Σ indicates that we are considering all parts of the fluid. However, the only part of the fluid having momentum is that mass m which has been given the velocity u at time τ. Hence

$$\Delta(\Sigma m_i u_i) = mu,$$

where
$$m = \frac{c'\tau A}{V}.$$

Substitution of these elements into the impulse-momentum equation gives

$$A \, \Delta P\tau = \frac{c'\tau A u}{V g_c},$$

or
$$\Delta P = \frac{c'u}{V g_c}.$$

The change in total volume of the fluid column is $-u\tau A$, and the change in the specific volume of the fluid set in motion is

$$\Delta V = \frac{-u\tau A}{m} = \frac{-u\tau A}{c'\tau A/V} = -\frac{uV}{c'}.$$

Therefore

$$\frac{\Delta P}{\Delta V} = \frac{-c'u/V g_c}{uV/c'} = \frac{-(c')^2}{V^2 g_c}.$$

In the limit as ΔP approaches zero, the propagation velocity approaches the *sonic velocity* c, which is the velocity of propagation of an infinitesimal pressure pulse.   Thus

$$\lim_{\Delta P \to 0} \frac{\Delta P}{\Delta V} = \frac{dP}{dV} = -\frac{c^2}{V^2 g_c},$$

or

$$c^2 = -g_c V^2 \frac{dP}{dV}.$$

This formula for the sonic velocity was first obtained by Newton, who regarded the propagation process as being isothermal.   Laplace later showed that it is really adiabatic.   Actually, these considerations apply not so much to a single pulse as to a succession of waves composed of alternate compressions and rarefactions such as transmit sound. The temperature of a fluid rises with compression and falls with expansion unless heat is transferred.   The very existence of adjacent regions of compression and rarefaction with their associated differences in temperature provides the driving force for heat transfer between these regions.   However, at audible frequencies it is found that both the thermal conductivity and the temperature gradient are too small for any appreciable heat transfer to occur during the brief time that the temperature gradient exists at any one location.   At very high frequencies, of the order of 10^9 cycles per second, the temperature gradients become appreciable because of the very close spacing of the regions of compression and rarefaction, and the adiabatic condition is less closely approached.

Returning now to the expression for the sonic velocity, we identify the changes represented by dP/dV as being adiabatic by use of the subscript S:

$$c^2 = -g_c V^2 \left(\frac{dP}{dV}\right)_S.$$

For the special case of an ideal gas, we have shown that

$$\left(\frac{\partial P}{\partial V}\right)_S = -\frac{\gamma P}{V}.$$

Hence

$$c^2 = g_c \gamma P V,$$

where V is still the specific volume.   If V is to represent the molar volume, we must divide by the molecular weight M.   In this event,

$$c^2 = \frac{g_c \gamma P V}{M},$$

where V is now the molar rather than specific volume.   Replacing PV by RT, we have, finally,

$$c = \sqrt{\frac{g_c \gamma R T}{M}}.$$

The above formula enables us to calculate γ from experimental measurements of c and T. For example, the speed of sound in nitrogen at 62°F is about 1,140 ft/sec. We have, therefore, for nitrogen:

$$c = 1{,}140 \text{ ft/sec,}$$
$$T = 522°\text{R,}$$
$$R = 1{,}545 \text{ ft} \cdot \text{lb}_f/\text{lb mole} \cdot °\text{R,}$$
$$M = 28 \text{ lb}_m/\text{lb mole,}$$
$$g_c = 32.174 \; (\text{lb}_m/\text{lb}_f)(\text{ft/sec}^2);$$

whence

$$
\begin{aligned}
\gamma &= \frac{Mc^2}{g_c RT} \\
&= \frac{28 \text{ lb}_m/\text{lb mole} \times (1{,}140)^2 \text{ ft}^2/\text{sec}^2}{32.174 \text{ lb}_m \cdot \text{ft/lb}_f \cdot \text{sec}^2 \times 1{,}545 \text{ ft} \cdot \text{lb}_f/\text{lb mole} \cdot °\text{R} \times 522°\text{R}} \\
&= 1.402.
\end{aligned}
$$

The speed of a sound wave in a gas can be measured with fair accuracy by means of Kundt's tube. The gas is admitted to a cylindrical tube closed at one end and supplied at the other end with a movable piston capable of being set in vibration parallel to the axis of the tube. In the tube is a small amount of light powder. For a given frequency, a position of the piston can be found at which standing waves are set up. Under these conditions small heaps of powder pile up at the nodes. The distance between any two adjacent nodes is one-half a wavelength, and the speed of the waves is the product of the frequency and the wavelength. Values of γ obtained by this method are in good agreement with those obtained from both calorimetric measurements and statistical calculations.

Problems

5.1 For an ideal gas show that:

(a)
$$\beta = 1/T.$$
(b)
$$k = 1/P.$$

5.2 Using the virial expansion in the form

$$Z = 1 + B'P + C'P^2 + \cdots,$$

show that:

(a)
$$\beta = \frac{1}{T} + \frac{(dB'/dT)P + (dC'/dT)P^2 + \cdots}{1 + B'P + C'P^2 + \cdots}.$$

(b)
$$k = \frac{1}{P} - \frac{B' + 2C'P + \cdots}{1 + B'P + C'P^2 + \cdots}.$$

What are the limiting values of β and k as pressure approaches zero at constant temperature? Do these equations give the ideal-gas values for β and k when B', C', etc., are set equal to zero?

5.3 Using the virial expansion truncated to two terms,

$$Z = 1 + \frac{B}{V},$$

show that:

(a)
$$\beta = \frac{1 + B/V + (T/V)(dB/dT)}{T(1 + 2B/V)}.$$

(b)
$$k = \frac{1}{P + BRT/V^2}.$$

What are the limiting values of β and k as pressure approaches zero at constant temperature? Do these equations give the ideal-gas values for β and k when B is set equal to zero?

5.4 A cylindrical highball glass 6 in. high and 3 in. in diameter contains water up to the 4-in. level. A card is placed over the top and held there as the glass is inverted. When the support is removed, what mass of water must leave the glass in order that the rest of the water remain in the glass, neglecting the weight of the card? (*Caution:* Try this over a sink.)

5.5 The temperature of an ideal gas in a capillary of constant cross-sectional area varies exponentially from one end ($x = 0$) to the other ($x = L$) according to the equation

$$T = T_0 e^{-kx}.$$

If the volume of the capillary is V and the pressure P is uniform throughout, show that the number of moles of gas n is given by

$$PV = nR \frac{kLT_0}{e^{kL} - 1}.$$

Show that, as $k \rightarrow 0$, $PV \rightarrow nRT_0$, as it should.

5.6 Prove that the work done by an ideal gas with constant heat capacities during a quasi-static adiabatic expansion is equal to:

(a)
$$W = C_V(T_1 - T_2).$$

(b)
$$W = \frac{P_1 V_1 - P_2 V_2}{\gamma - 1}.$$

(c)
$$W = \frac{RT_1}{\gamma - 1}\left[1 - \left(\frac{P_2}{P_1}\right)^{(\gamma-1)/\gamma}\right].$$

5.7 (a) Show that the heat transferred during an infinitesimal quasi-static process of an ideal gas can be written

$$dQ = \frac{C_V}{R} V \, dP + \frac{C_P}{R} P \, dV.$$

Applying this equation to an adiabatic process, show that $PV^\gamma = \text{const.}$

(b) An ideal gas of volume 0.05 ft³ and pressure 120 lb$_f$/in.² undergoes a quasi-static adiabatic expansion until the pressure drops to 15 lb$_f$/in.². Assuming γ to remain constant at the value 1.4: (1) What is the final volume? (2) How much work is done?

5.8 (a) Derive the following formula for a quasi-static adiabatic process of an ideal gas, assuming γ to be constant:

$$TV^{\gamma-1} = \text{const.}$$

(b) At about 100 msec after detonation of a uranium fission bomb, the "ball of fire" consists of a sphere of gas with a radius of about 50 ft and a temperature of 300,000°K. Making very rough assumptions, estimate at what radius its temperature would be 3000°K.

5.9 (a) Derive the following formula for a quasi-static adiabatic process of an ideal gas, assuming γ to be constant:

$$\frac{T}{P^{(\gamma-1)/\gamma}} = \text{const.}$$

(b) Helium ($\gamma = \frac{5}{3}$) at 70°F and 1 atm pressure is compressed quasi-statically and adiabatically to a pressure of 5 atm. Assuming that the helium behaves as an ideal gas, what is the final temperature?

5.10 A horizontal insulated cylinder, closed at both ends, contains a frictionless nonconducting piston. On each side of the piston is 2 ft³ of an inert monatomic ideal gas at 1 atm and 80°F. Heat is slowly supplied to the gas on the left side until the piston has compressed the gas on the right side to 7.6 atm.

(a) How much work is done on the gas on the right side?

(b) What is the final temperature of the gas on the right side?

(c) What is the final temperature of the gas on the left side?

(d) How much heat is added to the gas on the left side?

5.11 (a) If y is the height above sea level, show that the decrease of atmospheric pressure due to a rise dy is given by

$$\frac{dP}{P} = -\frac{Mg}{g_c RT}\, dy,$$

where M = molecular weight of the air,

$\quad\;\; g$ = acceleration of gravity,

$\quad\;\; T$ = absolute temperature at height y.

(b) If the decrease in pressure in (a) is due to an adiabatic expansion, show that

$$\frac{dP}{P} = \frac{\gamma}{\gamma - 1}\frac{dT}{T}.$$

(c) From (a) and (b), taking $\gamma = 1.4$, calculate dT/dy in degrees Fahrenheit per mile.

5.12 An empirical equation, $PV^\delta = $ const, where δ is a constant, is often used to relate P and V for *any* quasi-static process. Assuming this equation to be valid for an ideal gas, show that

$$W = \frac{RT_1}{\delta - 1}\left[1 - \left(\frac{P_2}{P_1}\right)^{(\delta-1)/\delta}\right]$$

If the process is isothermal, $\delta = 1$. Show that the above equation reduces in this case to the isothermal work equation

$$W = RT \ln \frac{P_1}{P_2}.$$

5.13 For a gas at a pressure low enough so that the virial expansion may be truncated to

$$Z = 1 + B'P,$$

show that the equation for isothermal work in a quasi-static compression is

$$W = RT \ln \frac{P_1}{P_2},$$

the same as for an ideal gas.

5.14 For SO_2 at 157.5°C the virial coefficients are

$$B = -159 \text{ cc/gm mole,}$$
$$C = 9{,}000 \text{ (cc/gm mole)}^2.$$

Calculate the work of quasi-static isothermal compression of 1 lb mole of SO_2 from 1 atm to 75 atm at 157.5°C. Use the following forms of the virial equation:

(a) $$Z = 1 + \frac{B}{V} + \frac{C}{V^2}.$$

(b) $$Z = 1 + B'P + C'P^2,$$

where $$B' = \frac{B}{RT} \quad \text{and} \quad C' = \frac{C - B^2}{(RT)^2}.$$

Why do not both equations give exactly the same result?

5.15 Using the data of Table 5.1, prepare a plot of Z versus P for methane at 0°C from 0 to 400 atm. To what pressure does the virial expansion truncated to the second term represent a good approximation to the curve? To what pressure does the equation truncated to the third term represent a good approximation? If B', C', and D' are calculated from B, C, and D and are used in the virial expansion in pressure, what is the error in Z at 400 atm? Why should there be any error at all?

5.16 A rigid nonconducting tank with a volume of 80 ft³ is divided in half by a rigid membrane. An ideal monatomic gas ($C_V = 3$ Btu/

lb mole · °F) is contained in both halves of the tank.   In one half the temperature and pressure are 340°F and 4 psia, and in the other they are 120°F and 16 psia.   The membrane is broken, and complete mixing takes place.   What are the final temperature and pressure?

5.17   Consider the following series of quasi-static processes to be carried out with 1 lb mole of an ideal gas having a constant heat capacity, $C_V = 5$ Btu/lb mole · °F:

(a) The gas at 70°F and 1 atm is heated at constant volume to a temperature of 400°F.

(b) The gas is then expanded adiabatically to the initial temperature of 70°F.

(c) Finally, the gas is compressed isothermally to the initial pressure of 1 atm.

Calculate Q, W, and ΔU for each step and for the cycle.

5.18   Air is compressed quasi-statically from an initial state of 1 atm and 60°F to a final state of 5 atm and 60°F by three different processes:

(a) Heating at constant volume followed by cooling at constant pressure.

(b) Isothermal compression.

(c) Adiabatic compression followed by cooling at constant volume.

At these conditions air may be considered an ideal gas with a heat capacity $C_P = 7$ Btu/lb mole · °F.   Calculate Q, W, and ΔU for each process.   Sketch the paths followed in each process on a single PV diagram.

5.19   One pound mole of an ideal gas, initially at 70°F and 1 atm, undergoes the following changes: It is first compressed isothermally to a point such that, when it is heated at constant volume to 200°F, its final pressure is 10 atm.   Taking $C_V = 5$ Btu/lb mole · °F, calculate Q, W, and ΔU for the process.

5.20   From the data of Table 5.2, write equations for C_P for ammonia which give the molar heat capacity as a function of temperature in (a) °C, (b) °R, and (c) °F.

5.21   In the equation

$$\int_{T_1}^{T_2} C_P \, dT = C_{P_m}(T_2 - T_1),$$

where C_{P_m} is the mean heat capacity, show that, when C_P is linear with T, C_{P_m} is the heat capacity evaluated at the arithmetic average of T_1 and T_2.

5.22   The molar heat capacity of a gas is given by

$$C_P = 3.0 + 10.0 \times 10^{-3}T + 15.0 \times 10^{-6}T^2,$$

where T is in °K, and C_P has the usual units.   If the temperature of the gas is changed from 80 to 800°F, determine the value of $\int C_P \, dT$

in Btu/lb mole. Calculate the mean value of the heat capacity for this temperature interval. How does it compare with the heat capacity evaluated at the arithmetic average of T_1 and T_2?

5.23 Using data from Table 5.2, calculate the heat required (in Btu) to raise the temperature of 1 lb mole of carbon dioxide from 200 to 1500°F at a constant low pressure where CO_2 is essentially an ideal gas.

5.24 The heat capacity of a gas sample is to be calculated from the following data: The sample was put in a flask and came to the initial equilibrium conditions, 25°C and 910 mm Hg. A stopcock was then opened for a short time to allow the pressure inside the flask to drop to 760 mm Hg. With the stopcock again closed, the flask was warmed, and when it was again at 25°C, its pressure was found to be 780 mm Hg. Determine C_P in Btu/lb mole · °F. It may be assumed that the gas is ideal, that C_P is constant, and that expansion of the gas remaining in the flask was quasi-static and adiabatic.

5.25 One gram mole of solid NH_4Cl is contained in a cylinder at 350°C. At this temperature NH_4Cl decomposes slowly to give a gaseous mixture of NH_3 and HCl. If the cylinder is fitted with a frictionless piston which exerts a constant pressure of 1 atm, the entire charge of NH_4Cl can be decomposed by supplying the heat necessary to hold the temperature at 350°C. This heat requirement is 42,000 cal for the decomposition of 1 gm mole of NH_4Cl. Assuming the gases ideal and the volume of NH_4Cl negligible, calculate ΔU for the process.

5.26 The speed of a longitudinal wave in a mixture of helium and neon at 300°K was found to be 758 m/sec. What is the composition of the mixture?

5.27 The atomic weight of iodine is 127. A standing wave in iodine vapor at 400°K produces nodes that are 6.77 cm apart when the frequency is 1,000 vibrations/sec. Is iodine vapor monatomic or diatomic?

5.28 It has been proposed that a high-speed rapid transit system could be constructed to operate on the principle of a pneumatic tube. The vehicle would consist of a train of circular cross section running on rails in a closely fitting round tube. The tube in front of the train would be evacuated to a low pressure, and the train would be given a start by admitting atmospheric air behind it as it traveled a specified distance into the tube. The inlet port would then be closed and the train would be acted upon by the expanding air behind it and by the air being compressed in front of it. The train accelerates as long as the pressure behind it exceeds the pressure in front of it. Eventually, the reverse becomes true, and the train decelerates. When the pressure in front of the train builds up to atmospheric, the port at the far end of the tube opens to hold the front pressure at atmospheric, and the train continues to decelerate until it comes to a halt at the end of the tube solely as a result of the pressure forces. Thus the train is treated as a "floating"

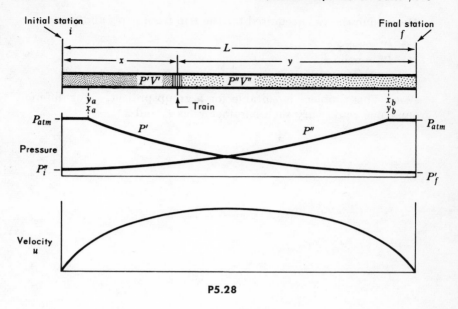

P5.28

piston in a tube.   Figure P5.28 gives a schematic picture of the process, showing roughly how the pressures and train velocity vary during a trip.

In working the problem, make the following assumptions:

(*a*) The train moves without friction.

(*b*) There is no leakage of air past the train.

(*c*) Air is an ideal gas.

(*d*) The train length is negligible compared with L.

(*e*) The compression and expansion of air in the tube are quasistatic, and P and V are related by the equation

$$PV^\delta = k,$$

where δ and k are constants.

(*f*) The train must stop at the final station without mechanical braking.

Consider now a transit tube of diameter D between two stations i and f traversed by a train of mass m.   The following parameters are specified:

$$L = 100 \text{ miles},$$
$$D = 10 \text{ ft},$$
$$m = 10^6 \text{ lb}_m,$$
$$x_a = 4 \text{ miles},$$
$$P_{\text{atm}} = 14.7 \text{ psia},$$
$$\delta = 1.1.$$

Determine the time required for the trip from i to f and plot:

(a) P' versus x.
(b) P'' versus x.
(c) u versus x.

Note: This problem is suitable for a group project. For different groups, one could vary such parameters as x_a and δ.

Chapter 6/
The Second Law of Thermodynamics

6.1/ Conversion of Work into Heat, and Vice Versa

When two stones are rubbed together under water, the work done against friction is transformed into internal energy, tending to produce a rise of temperature of the stones. As soon, however, as the temperature of the stones rises above that of the surrounding water, there is a flow of heat into the water. If the mass of water is large enough or if the water is continually flowing, there will be no appreciable rise of temperature, and the water can be regarded as a heat reservoir. Since the state of the stones is the same at the end of the process as at the beginning, the net result of the process is merely the conversion of mechanical work into heat. Similarly, when an electric current is maintained in a resistor immersed either in running water or in a very large mass of water, there is also a conversion of electrical work into heat, without any change in the thermodynamic coordinates of the wire. In general, work of any kind W may be done upon a system in contact with a reservoir, giving rise to a flow of heat Q without altering the state of the system. The system acts merely as an intermediary. It is apparent from the first law that the work W is equal to the heat Q, or in other words, the transformation of work into heat is accomplished with 100 percent efficiency. Moreover, this transformation can be continued indefinitely.

To study the converse process, namely, the conversion of heat into work, we must also have at hand a process or series of processes by means of which such a conversion may continue indefinitely without involving any resultant changes in the state of any system. At first thought, it might appear that the isothermal expansion of an ideal gas might be a suitable process to consider in discussing the conversion of heat into work. In this case there is no internal-energy change since the temperature remains constant, and therefore $W = Q$, or heat has been converted completely into work. This process, however, involves a change of state of the gas. The volume increases and the pressure decreases until atmospheric pressure is reached, at which the process stops. It therefore cannot be used indefinitely.

What is needed is a series of processes in which a system is brought back to its initial state, i.e., a *cycle*. Each of the processes that constitute a cycle may involve a flow of heat to or from the system and the performance of work by or on the system. For one complete cycle:

Let Q_H refer to amount of heat absorbed by the system,

      Q_C refer to amount of heat rejected by the system,

      ΣW refer to total amount of work done by the system.

The usual sign convention applies to all heat and work quantities. If $|Q_H|$ is larger than $|Q_C|$ and ΣW is positive (net work done by the system), the mechanical device by whose agency the system is caused to undergo the cycle is called a *heat engine*. It is convenient to speak of the system as the *working substance* and to say that the engine operates in a cycle. The purpose of a heat engine is to deliver work continuously to the surroundings by performing the same cycle over and over again. The net work of the cycle is the output, and the heat absorbed by the working substance is the input. The *thermal efficiency of the process* η is defined as

$$\text{Thermal efficiency} = \frac{\text{work output in any energy units}}{\text{heat input in the same energy units}},$$

or

$$\eta = \frac{\Sigma W}{Q_H}.$$

Applying the first law to one complete cycle, remembering that there is no net change of internal energy, we get

$$Q_H + Q_C = \Sigma W,$$

and therefore

$$\eta = \frac{Q_H + Q_C}{Q_H},$$

or

$$\boxed{\eta = 1 + \frac{Q_C}{Q_H}.}$$

Note that the numerical value of Q_C is always negative; of Q_H, positive.

Thus it is seen from this equation that η will be unity (efficiency 100 percent) when Q_C is zero. In other words, if an engine can be built to operate in a cycle in which there is no outflow of heat from the working substance, there will be 100 percent conversion of the heat absorbed into work. We shall see later under what conditions this is possible in principle and why it is not possible in practice.

The transformation of heat into work is usually accomplished in practice by two general types of engine, the *internal-combustion engine* and the *stationary power plant*. There are various types of internal-combustion engines, including the gasoline engine, the diesel engine, the jet engine, and the rocket motor. In all cases the products of combustion of the fuel itself directly supply the motive force and the work. Such engines are used primarily to produce motion of vehicles of various kinds.

The stationary power plant is used almost exclusively to produce electric power, and although small units may employ internal-combustion engines, generally the working substance of the plant is separate from the fuel. Heat is supplied to the working substance (usually H_2O) through conducting walls. Its source is either a combustion reaction of a fossil fuel or a nuclear reaction.

We are not in a position yet to describe the details of the cycle through which the working substance in a stationary power plant goes. It is not necessary, however, to know the exact nature of this cycle in order to understand that, during the cycle, water is heated to its boiling point and vaporized and that, for this purpose, there must be a flow of heat from an external source, which for purposes of analysis we may consider to be a heat reservoir. Furthermore, it is clear that after expansion the steam must be condensed at a lower temperature, thus involving a flow of heat into an external reservoir. Whether the absorption and rejection of heat are quasi-static or not is of no consequence. Usually, there are only two reservoirs, one at a higher temperature than the other, such as the boiler and condenser of a steam power plant. During both absorption and rejection of heat, there is in general a finite temperature difference between the working substance and the reservoir.

6.2/ Kelvin-Planck Statement of the Second Law

Reduced to simplest terms, the important characteristics of heat-engine cycles may be summed up as follows:

1. There is some process or series of processes during which there is an absorption of heat from an external reservoir at a high temperature (called, simply, the *hot reservoir*).

2. There is some process or series of processes during which heat is rejected to an external reservoir at a lower temperature (called, simply, the *cold reservoir*).

This is represented schematically in Fig. 6.1a.   No engine has ever been developed that converts the heat extracted from one reservoir into work without rejecting some heat to a reservoir at a lower temperature. This negative statement, which is the result of accumulated experience, constitutes the *second* law of thermodynamics, and has been formulated in several ways.   The original statement of Kelvin is, "It is impossible by means of inanimate material agency to derive mechanical effect from any portion of matter by cooling it below the temperature of the coldest of the surrounding objects."   In the words of Planck, "It is impossible to construct an engine which, working in a complete cycle, will produce no effect other than the raising of a weight and the cooling of a heat reservoir."   We may combine these statements into one equivalent statement, to which we shall refer hereafter as the *Kelvin-Planck statement of the second law*, thus:

It is impossible to construct an engine that, operating in a cycle, will produce no effect other than the extraction of heat from a reservoir and the performance of an equivalent amount of work.

If the second law were not true, it would be possible to drive a steamship across the ocean by extracting heat from the ocean or to run a

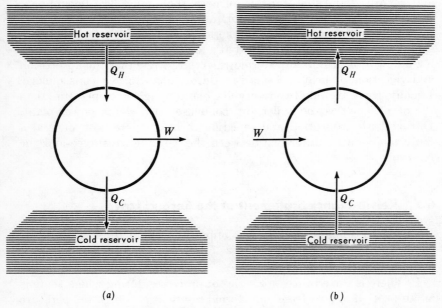

(a)   (b)

Fig. 6.1   Symbolic representations of (a) **a heat engine and** (b) **a refrigerator.**

power plant by extracting heat from the surrounding air. The student should notice that neither of these "impossibilities" violates the first law of thermodynamics. After all, both the ocean and the surrounding air contain an enormous store of internal energy, which, in principle, may be extracted in the form of a flow of heat. There is nothing in the first law to preclude the possibility of converting this heat completely into work. The second law, therefore, is nσt a deduction from the first, but stands by itself as a separate law of nature, referring to an aspect of nature different from that contemplated by the first law. The first law denies the possibility of creating or destroying energy; the second denies the possibility of utilizing energy in a particular way. The continual operation of a machine that creates its own energy and thus violates the first law is called *perpetual motion of the first kind.* The operation of a machine that utilizes the internal energy of only one heat reservoir, thus violating the second law, is called *perpetual motion of the second kind.*

6.3/ Refrigerator.   Clausius Statement of the Second Law

We have seen that a heat engine is a device by whose agency a working substance is taken through a cycle in such a direction that some heat is absorbed while the temperature is high, a smaller amount is rejected at a lower temperature, and a net amount of work is done on the outside. If we imagine a cycle performed in a direction opposite to that of an engine, the net result would be the absorption of some heat at a low temperature, the rejection of a *larger* amount at a higher temperature, and a net amount of work done *on* the working substance. A device that performs a cycle in this direction is called a *refrigerator*, and the working substance is called a *refrigerant.* Figure 6.1*b* represents a schematic diagram of a refrigerator.

For one complete cycle:

Let Q_H refer to amount of heat rejected by the refrigerant,

   Q_C refer to amount of heat absorbed by the refrigerant,

   ΣW refer to net work done on the refrigerant.

Here, again, the usual sign convention applies to all heat and work quantities. Since the refrigerant undergoes a cycle, there is no change in internal energy, and the first law becomes

$$Q_C + Q_H = \Sigma W,$$
or
$$Q_H = \Sigma W - Q_C.$$

That is, the absolute value of the heat rejected to the hot reservoir $|Q_H|$ is larger than the absolute value of the heat extracted from the cold reservoir $|Q_C|$ by the amount of work done on the system $|\Sigma W|$.

The purpose of a refrigerator is to extract as much heat as possible from the cold reservoir with the expenditure of as little work as possible. It is sufficient here merely to emphasize that work is always necessary to transfer heat from a cold to a hot reservoir. In household refrigerators, this work is usually done by an electric motor whose cost of operation appears regularly on the monthly bill. It would be a boon to mankind if no external supply of energy were needed, but it must certainly be admitted that experience indicates the contrary. This negative statement leads us to the *Clausius statement of the second law:*

It is impossible to construct a device that, operating in a cycle, will produce no effect other than the transfer of heat from a cooler to a hotter body.

At first sight, the Kelvin-Planck and the Clausius statements appear to be quite unconnected, but we shall see immediately that they are in all respects equivalent.

6.4/ The Equivalence of Kelvin-Planck and Clausius Statements

Let us adopt the following notation:

K = truth of Kelvin-Planck statement,
$-K$ = falsity of Kelvin-Planck statement,
C = truth of Clausius statement,
$-C$ = falsity of Clausius statement.

Two propositions or statements are said to be equivalent when the truth of one implies the truth of the second and the truth of the second implies the truth of the first. Using the symbol $\supset$ to mean "implies" and the symbol $\equiv$ to denote equivalence, we have, by definition,

$$K \equiv C$$

when $$K \supset C \quad \text{and} \quad C \supset K.$$

Now, it may easily be shown that

$$K \equiv C$$

also when $$-K \supset -C \quad \text{and} \quad -C \supset -K.$$

Thus, in order to demonstrate the equivalence of K and C, we have to show that a violation of one statement implies a violation of the second, and vice versa.

1. To prove that $-C \supset -K$, consider a refrigerator, shown in the left-hand side of Fig. 6.2, that requires *no work* to transfer $|Q_C|$ units of heat from a cold reservoir to a hot reservoir and that therefore violates

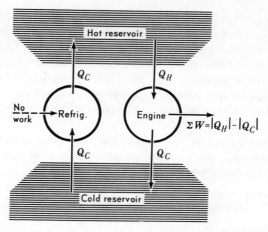

Fig. 6.2   Proof that $-C \supset -K$. **The refrigerator on the left is a violation of** C; **the refrigerator and engine acting together constitute a violation of** K.

the Clausius statement.   Suppose that a heat engine (on the right) also operates between the same two reservoirs in such a way that heat $|Q_C|$ is delivered to the cold reservoir.   The engine, of course, does not violate any law, but the refrigerator and engine *together* constitute a self-acting device that takes heat $|Q_H| - |Q_C|$ from the hot reservoir and converts *all* this heat into work without producing any change in the cold reservoir.   Therefore the refrigerator and engine together constitute a violation of the Kelvin-Planck statement.

2. To prove that $-K \supset -C$, consider an engine, shown on the left-hand side of Fig. 6.3, that rejects no heat to the cold reservoir and that

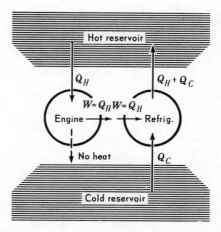

Fig. 6.3   Proof that $-K \supset -C$. **The engine on the left is a violation of** K; **the engine and refrigerator acting together constitute a violation of** C.

therefore violates the Kelvin-Planck statement. Suppose that a refrigerator (on the right) also operates between the same two reservoirs and uses up all the work liberated by the engine. The refrigerator violates no law, but the engine and refrigerator *together* constitute a self-acting device that transfers heat $|Q_C|$ from the cold to the hot reservoir without producing any changes elsewhere. Therefore the engine and refrigerator together constitute a violation of the Clausius statement.

We therefore arrive at the conclusion that both statements of the second law are equivalent. It is a matter of indifference which one is used in a particular argument.

Problems

6.1 Figure P6.1 represents an imaginary ideal-gas-engine cycle. Assuming constant heat capacities, show that the thermal efficiency is

$$\eta = 1 - \gamma \frac{(V_1/V_2) - 1}{(P_1/P_2) - 1}.$$

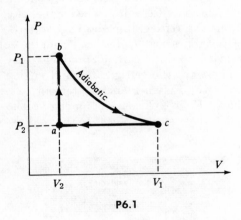

P6.1

6.2 Figure P6.2 represents an imaginary ideal-gas-engine cycle. Assuming constant heat capacities, show that the thermal efficiency is

$$\eta = \frac{1}{2C_V T_b} \frac{(P_1 - P_2)(V_1 - V_2)}{[1 - (P_2/P_1)] + \gamma[(V_1/V_2) - 1]}.$$

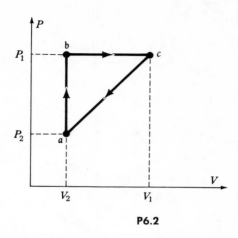

P6.2

6.3 A vessel contains 600 cm³ of helium gas at 2°K and $\frac{1}{36}$ atm. Take the zero of internal energy of helium to be at this point.

(a) The temperature is raised at constant volume to 288°K. Assuming helium to behave like an ideal monatomic gas, how much heat is absorbed, and what is the internal energy of the helium? Can this energy be regarded as stored heat or stored work?

(b) The helium is now expanded adiabatically to 2°K. How much work is done and what is the new internal energy? Has heat been converted into work without compensation, thus violating the second law?

(c) The helium is now compressed isothermally to its original volume. What are the quantities of heat and work in this process? What is the efficiency of the cycle? Plot on a PV diagram.

6.4 There are many paramagnetic solids whose internal energy is a function of temperature only, like an ideal gas. In an isothermal demagnetization, heat is absorbed from one reservoir and converted completely into work. Is this a violation of the second law? Why?

6.5 Would an atomic-energy power plant violate either the first law or the second law of thermodynamics? Explain.

6.6 Prove that it is impossible for two quasi-static adiabatics to intersect. (*Hint:* Assume that they do intersect, and complete the cycle with an isothermal. Show that the performance of this cycle violates the second law.)

Chapter 7/
Reversibility and Irreversibility

7.1/ Reversibility and Irreversibility

In thermodynamics, work is a macroscopic concept. The performance of work may always be described in terms of the raising or lowering of a weight or the winding or unwinding of a spring, i.e., by the operation of a device that serves to increase or decrease the potential energy of a mechanical system. Imagine, for the sake of simplicity, a suspended weight coupled by means of suitable pulleys to a system so that any work done by or on the system can be described in terms of the raising or lowering of the weight. Imagine, further, a series of reservoirs which may be put in contact with the system and in terms of which any flow of heat to or from the system may be described. We shall refer to the suspended weight and the series of reservoirs as the *local surroundings* of the system. The local surroundings are therefore those parts of the surroundings which interact *directly* with the system. Other mechanical devices and reservoirs that are accessible and that *might* interact with the system constitute the *auxiliary surroundings* of the system, or, for want of a better expression, the *rest of the universe*. The word "universe" is used here in a very restricted technical sense, with no cosmic or celestial implications. The universe merely means a finite portion of the world consisting of the system and those surroundings which may interact with the system.

Now suppose that a process occurs in which (1) the system proceeds from an initial state i to a final state f; (2) the suspended weight is lowered to an extent that W units of work are performed; and (3) a transfer of heat Q takes place from the system to the series of reservoirs. If, at the conclusion of this process, the system may be restored to its initial state i, the weight lifted to its former level, and the reservoirs caused to part with the same amount of heat Q, without producing any changes in any other mechanical device or reservoir in the universe, the original process is said to be *reversible*. In other words, *a reversible process is one that is performed in such a way that, at the conclusion of the process, both the system and the local surroundings may be restored to their initial states, without producing any changes in the rest of the universe.* A process that does not fulfill these stringent requirements is said to be *irreversible*.

The question immediately arises as to whether natural processes, i.e., the familiar processes of nature, are reversible or not. The purpose of this chapter is to show that it is a consequence of the second law of thermodynamics that all natural processes are irreversible. By considering representative types of natural processes and examining the features of these processes which are responsible for their irreversibility, we shall be able to state the conditions under which a process may be performed reversibly.

7.2/ External Mechanical Irreversibility

There is a large class of processes involving the isothermal transformation of work through a system (which remains unchanged) into internal energy of a reservoir. This type of process is depicted schematically in Fig. 7.1 and is illustrated by the following five examples:

1. Irregular stirring of a viscous liquid in contact with a reservoir.
2. Coming to rest of a rotating or vibrating liquid in contact with a reservoir.

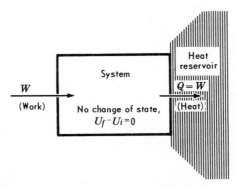

Fig. 7.1   Isothermal transformation of work through a system (which remains unchanged) into internal energy of a reservoir.

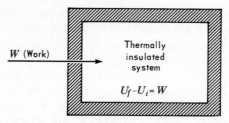

Fig. 7.2   Adiabatic transformation of work into internal energy of a system.

3. Inelastic deformation of a solid in contact with a reservoir.

4. Transfer of electricity through a resistor in contact with a reservoir.

5. Magnetic hysteresis of a material in contact with a reservoir.

In order to restore the system and its local surroundings to their initial states without producing changes elsewhere, Q units of heat would have to be extracted from the reservoir and converted completely into work. Since this would involve a violation of the second law, all processes of the above type are irreversible.

Another set of processes involves the adiabatic transformation of work into internal energy of a system. This is depicted schematically in Fig. 7.2, and is illustrated by the following examples, similar to the preceding list:

1. Irregular stirring of a viscous thermally insulated liquid.
2. Coming to rest of a rotating or vibrating thermally insulated liquid.
3. Inelastic deformation of a thermally insulated solid.
4. Transfer of electricity through a thermally insulated resistor.
5. Magnetic hysteresis of a thermally insulated material.

A process of this type is accompanied by a rise of temperature of the system from, say, T_i to T_f. In order to restore the system and its local surroundings to their initial states without producing changes elsewhere, the internal energy of the system would have to be decreased by extracting $U_f - U_i$ units of heat, thus lowering the temperature from T_f to T_i, and this heat would have to be completely converted into work. Since this violates the second law, all processes of the above type are irreversible.

The transformation of work into internal energy either of a system or of a reservoir is seen to take place through the agency of such phenomena as viscosity, friction, inelasticity, electric resistance, and magnetic hysteresis. These effects are known as *dissipative effects*, and the work is said to be dissipated. Processes involving the dissipation of work into internal energy are said to exhibit *external mechanical irreversibility.* It is a matter of everyday experience that dissipative effects, particularly friction, are always present in moving devices. Friction, of course, may be reduced considerably by suitable lubrication, but experience has shown that it can never be completely eliminated. If it could, a movable device could be kept in continual operation without violating either of the two laws of thermodynamics. Such a continual motion is known as *perpetual motion of the third kind.*

7.3/ Internal Mechanical Irreversibility

The following very important natural processes involve the transformation of internal energy of a system into mechanical energy and then back into internal energy again:

1. Ideal gas rushing into a vacuum (free expansion).
2. Gas seeping through a porous plug (throttling process).
3. Snapping of a stretched wire after it is cut.
4. Collapse of a soap film after it is pricked.

We shall prove the irreversibility of only the first.

During a free expansion, no interactions take place, and hence there are no local surroundings. The only effect produced is a change of state of an ideal gas from a volume V_i and temperature T to a larger volume V_f and the same temperature T. To restore the gas to its initial state, it would have to be compressed isothermally to the volume V_i. If the compression were performed quasi-statically and there were no friction between the piston and cylinder, an amount of work W would have to be done by some outside mechanical device, and an equal amount of heat would have to flow out of the gas into a reservoir at the temperature T. If the mechanical device and the reservoir are to be left unchanged, the heat would have to be extracted from the reservoir and converted completely into work. Since this last step is impossible, the process is irreversible.

In a free expansion, immediately after the stopcock is opened, there is a transformation of some of the internal energy into kinetic energy of "mass motion," or "streaming," and then this kinetic energy is dissipated through viscosity into internal energy again. Similarly, when a stretched wire is cut, there is first a transformation of internal energy into kinetic energy of irregular motion and of vibration and then the dissipation of this energy through inelasticity into internal energy again. In all the processes, the first energy transformation takes place as a result of mechanical instability, and the second by virtue of some dissipative effect. A process of this sort is said to exhibit *internal mechanical irreversibility.*

7.4/ External and Internal Thermal Irreversibility

Consider the following processes involving a transfer of heat between a system and a reservoir by virtue of a *finite* temperature difference:

1. Conduction or radiation of heat from a system to a cooler reservoir.
2. Conduction or radiation of heat through a system (which remains unchanged) from a hot reservoir to a cooler one.

To restore, at the conclusion of a process of this type, both the system and its local surroundings to their initial states, without producing changes elsewhere, heat would have to be transferred by means of a self-acting device from a cooler to a hotter body. Since this violates the second law (Clausius statement), all processes of this type are irreversible. Such processes are said to exhibit *external thermal irreversibility*.

A process involving a transfer of heat between parts of the same system because of nonuniformity of temperature is also obviously irreversible by virtue of the Clausius statement of the second law. Such a process is said to exhibit *internal thermal irreversibility*.

7.5/ Chemical Irreversibility

Some of the most interesting processes that go on in nature involve a spontaneous change of internal structure, chemical composition, density, crystal form, etc. Some important examples follow.

Formation of new chemical constituents:
1. All chemical reactions.

Mixing of two different substances:
2. Diffusion of two dissimilar inert ideal gases.
3. Mixing of alcohol and water.

Sudden change of phase:
4. Freezing of supercooled liquid.
5. Condensation of supersaturated vapor.

Transport of matter between phases in contact:
6. Solution of solid in water.
7. Osmosis.

Such processes are by far the most difficult to handle and must, as a rule, be treated by special methods. These methods constitute what is known as chemical thermodynamics. It can be shown that the diffusion of two dissimilar inert ideal gases is equivalent to two independent free expansions. Since a free expansion is irreversible, it follows that diffusion is irreversible. The student will have to accept at present the statement that the above processes are irreversible. Processes that involve a spontaneous change of chemical structure, density, phase, etc., are said to exhibit *chemical irreversibility*.

7.6/ Conditions for Reversibility

Most processes that occur in nature are included among the general types of process listed in the preceding articles. Consequently, we are entitled to conclude that it is a direct consequence of the second law of thermodynamics that *all natural processes are irreversible*.

A careful inspection of the various types of natural process shows that all of them involve one or both of the following features: (1) The conditions for mechanical, thermal, or chemical equilibrium, i.e., thermodynamic equilibrium, are not satisfied. (2) Dissipative effects, such as viscosity, friction, inelasticity, electric resistance, and magnetic hysteresis, are present. For a process to be reversible, it must not possess these features. If a process is performed quasi-statically, the system passes through states of thermodynamic equilibrium, which may be traversed just as well in one direction as in the opposite direction. If there are no dissipative effects, all the work done by the system during the performance of a process in one direction can be returned to the system during the reverse process. We are led, therefore, to the conclusion that a process will be reversible when (1) it is performed quasi-statically and (2) it is not accompanied by any dissipative effects.

Since it is impossible to satisfy these two conditions perfectly, it is obvious that a reversible process is purely an ideal abstraction, extremely useful for theoretical calculations (as we shall see) but quite devoid of reality. In this sense, the assumption of a reversible process in thermodynamics resembles the assumptions made so often in mechanics, such as those which refer to weightless strings, frictionless pulleys, and point masses.

A heat reservoir was defined as a body of very large mass capable of absorbing or rejecting an unlimited supply of heat without suffering appreciable changes in its thermodynamic coordinates. The changes that do take place are so very slow and so very minute that dissipative actions never develop. *Therefore, when heat enters or leaves a reservoir, the changes that take place in the reservoir are the same as those which would take place if the same quantity of heat were transferred reversibly.*

It is possible in the laboratory to approximate the conditions necessary for the performance of reversible processes. For example, if a gas is confined in a cylinder equipped with a well-lubricated piston and is allowed to expand very slowly against an opposing force provided either by a weight suspended from a frictionless pulley or by an elastic spring,

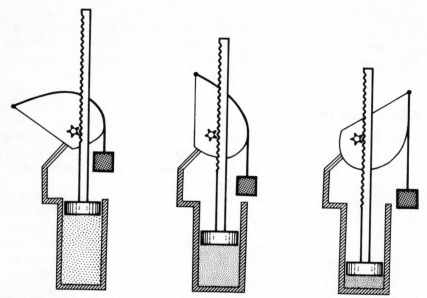

Fig. 7.3 Approximately reversible change of volume of a gas. (From Ernst Schmidt, "Thermodynamics," p. 91, Oxford University Press, Fair Lawn, N.J., 1949.)

the gas undergoes an approximately reversible process. A clever imaginary device for ensuring mechanical equilibrium at all times, due to Schmidt, is shown in Fig. 7.3. Similar considerations apply to a wire and to a surface film.

A reversible transfer of electricity through an electric cell may be imagined as follows: Suppose that a motor whose coils have a negligible resistance is caused to rotate until its back emf is only slightly different from the emf of the cell. Suppose, further, that the motor is coupled either to a weight suspended from a frictionless pulley or to an elastic spring. If neither the cell itself nor the connecting wires to the motor has appreciable resistance, a reversible transfer of electricity takes place.

Problem

7.1 Classify and discuss the following natural phenomena from the standpoint of irreversibility: a waterfall, the weathering of rocks, the rusting of iron, a forest fire, the tearing of a piece of cloth, lightning, a compressed spring dissolving in acid, spontaneous combustion of a coal pile, aging of a magnet, shelf aging of an electric cell.

Chapter 8/
The Carnot Cycle and
the Kelvin Temperature Scale

8.1/ Carnot Cycle

During a part of the cycle performed by the working substance in an
engine, some heat is absorbed from a hot reservoir; during another part
of the cycle, a smaller amount of heat is rejected to a cooler reservoir.
The engine is therefore said to operate between these two reservoirs.
Since it is a fact of experience that some heat is always rejected to the
cooler reservoir, the efficiency of an actual engine is never 100 percent.
If we assume that we have at our disposal two reservoirs at given temperatures, it is important to answer the following questions: (1) What
is the maximum efficiency that can be achieved by an engine operating
between these two reservoirs? (2) What are the characteristics of
such an engine? (3) Of what effect is the nature of the working
substance?

The importance of these questions was recognized by Nicolas Léonard
Sadi Carnot, a brilliant young French engineer who, in the year 1824,
before the first law of thermodynamics was firmly established, described
in a paper entitled "Sur la puissance motrice du feu" an ideal engine
operating in a particularly simple cycle known today as the *Carnot cycle*.

In describing and explaining the behavior of this ideal engine, Carnot
made use of three terms: *feu*, *chaleur*, and *calorique*. By *feu*, he meant
fire or flame, and when the word is so translated no misconceptions arise.
Carnot gave, however, no definitions for *chaleur* and *calorique*, but in a

footnote stated that they had the same meaning. If both of these words are translated as heat, then Carnot's reasoning is contrary to the first law of thermodynamics. There is, however, some evidence that, in spite of the unfortunate footnote, Carnot did not mean the same thing by *chaleur* and *calorique*. Carnot used *chaleur* when referring to heat in general, but when referring to the motive power of heat that is brought about when heat enters at high temperature and leaves at low temperature, he used the expression *chute de calorique*, never *chute de chaleur*. It is the opinion of a few scientists that Carnot had in the back of his mind the concept of entropy, for which he reserved the term *calorique*. This seems incredible, and yet it is a remarkable circumstance that, if the expression *chute de calorique* is translated "fall of entropy," many of the objections to Carnot's work raised by Kelvin, Clapeyron, Clausius, and others are no longer valid. In spite of possible mistranslations, Kelvin recognized the importance of Carnot's ideas, and put them in the form in which they appear today.

A Carnot cycle is a set of processes that can be performed by any thermodynamic system whatever, whether chemical, electrical, magnetic, or otherwise. The system or working substance is imagined first to be in thermal equilibrium with a cold reservoir at the temperature T_C. Four processes are then performed in the following order:

1. A reversible adiabatic process is performed in such a direction that the temperature rises to that of the hotter reservoir, T_H.

2. The working substance is maintained in contact with the reservoir at T_H, and a reversible isothermal process is performed in such a direction and to such an extent that heat Q_H is absorbed from the reservoir.

3. A reversible adiabatic process is performed in a direction opposite to process 1 until the temperature drops to that of the cooler reservoir, T_C.

4. The working substance is maintained in contact with the reservoir at T_C, and a reversible isothermal process is performed in a direction opposite to process 2 until the working substance is in its initial state. During this process, heat Q_C is rejected to the cold reservoir.

An engine operating in a Carnot cycle is called a *Carnot engine*. A Carnot engine operates between two reservoirs in a particularly simple way. All the heat that is absorbed is absorbed at a constant high temperature, namely, that of the hot reservoir. Also, all the heat that is rejected is rejected at a constant lower temperature, that of the cold reservoir. Since all four processes are reversible, the Carnot cycle is a reversible cycle.

8.2/ Examples of Carnot Cycles

The simplest example of a Carnot cycle is that of a gas (not necessarily an ideal gas), depicted on a PV diagram in Fig. 8.1. The dotted lines

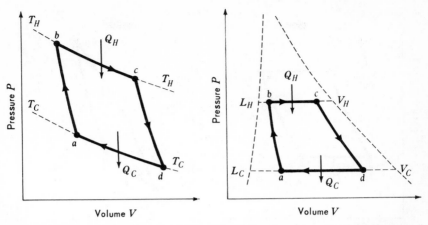

Fig. 8.1   Carnot cycle of a real gas.   **Fig. 8.2   Carnot cycle of a mixture of liquid and vapor.**

marked $T_H T_H$ and $T_C T_C$ are isothermals at the temperatures T_H and T_C, respectively, T_H being greater than T_C. The gas is originally in the state represented by the point a. The four processes are then:

1. $a \to b$, reversible adiabatic compression until the temperature rises to T_H.
2. $b \to c$, reversible isothermal expansion until any desired point such as c is reached.
3. $c \to d$, reversible adiabatic expansion until the temperature drops to T_C.
4. $d \to a$, reversible isothermal compression until the original state is reached.

During the isothermal expansion $b \to c$, heat Q_H is absorbed from the hot reservoir at T_H. During the isothermal compression $d \to a$, heat Q_C is rejected to the cooler reservoir at T_C.

A mixture of liquid and vapor may also be taken through a Carnot cycle. This is shown on a PV diagram in Fig. 8.2. The dotted line $L_H V_H$ denotes the isothermal isobaric vaporization of the liquid at the high temperature T_H; the line $L_C V_C$ that at the lower temperature T_C. Any point between L and V denotes a mixture of liquid and vapor. Starting at the point a, the four processes are as follows:

1. $a \to b$, reversible adiabatic compression until the temperature rises to T_H.
2. $b \to c$, reversible isothermal isobaric vaporization until any arbitrary point such as c is reached.
3. $c \to d$, reversible adiabatic expansion until the temperature drops to T_C.

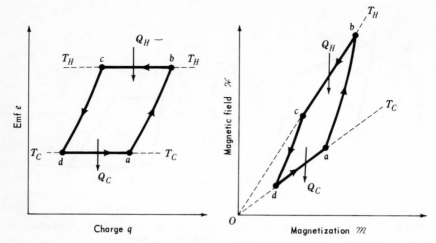

Fig. 8.3 Carnot cycle of a reversible electric cell.

Fig. 8.4 Carnot cycle of a paramagnetic substance.

4. $d \to a$, reversible isothermal isobaric condensation until the initial state is reached.

A Carnot cycle of a reversible electric cell is depicted on an eq diagram in Fig. 8.3. The lines $T_H T_H$ and $T_C T_C$ represent isothermals at the temperatures T_H and T_C, respectively. The point a indicates that the cell is well charged. The four processes are:

1. $a \to b$, reversible adiabatic transfer of electricity from $-$ to $+$ in the outside circuit until the temperature rises to T_H.
2. $b \to c$, reversible isothermal transfer of electricity from $+$ to $-$ in the outside circuit until an arbitrary point c is reached.
3. $c \to d$, reversible adiabatic transfer of electricity until the temperature drops to T_C.
4. $d \to a$, reversible isothermal transfer of electricity until the initial state is reached.

As a last example of a Carnot cycle, that of a paramagnetic substance is shown on an $\mathscr{H}\mathscr{M}$ diagram in Fig. 8.4. The lines OT_C and OT_H represent isothermals at the temperatures T_C and T_H, respectively. Starting at a, the four processes are:

1. $a \to b$, reversible adiabatic magnetization until the temperature rises to T_H.
2. $b \to c$, reversible isothermal demagnetization until an arbitrary point c is reached.
3. $c \to d$, reversible adiabatic demagnetization until the temperature drops to T_C.

4. $d \rightarrow a$, reversible isothermal magnetization until the initial state is reached.

The net work done in one cycle by a Carnot engine can be adjusted to any arbitrary amount by choosing the position of the point c, that is, by adjusting the extent of the isothermal process $b \rightarrow c$.   It is seen that the coordinates used to plot a Carnot cycle and the shape of the cycle depend on the nature of the working substance.   It will be shown, however, in the next chapter, that it is possible to find two coordinates in terms of which a graph of any Carnot cycle with *any* working substance is a rectangle.   Consequently, we shall represent a Carnot engine symbolically with the aid of a rectangle as shown in Fig. 8.5*a*. The letter R inside the rectangle indicates that the Carnot cycle is a reversible cycle.

If an engine is to operate between only two reservoirs and still operate in a reversible cycle, it must be a Carnot engine.   If any other cycle were performed between only two reservoirs, the necessary heat transfer would involve finite temperature differences and therefore could not be reversible.   Conversely, if any other cycle were performed reversibly, it would require a series of reservoirs, not merely two.   The expression "Carnot engine" therefore means "a reversible engine operating between only two reservoirs."

8.3/ Carnot Refrigerator

Since a Carnot cycle consists of reversible processes, it may be performed in either direction.   When it is performed in a direction opposite to that shown in the examples, it is a refrigeration cycle.   A Carnot refrigerator

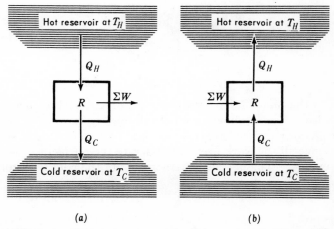

(a)   (b)

Fig. 8.5   Symbolic representations of (*a*) **Carnot engine and of** (*b*) **Carnot refrigerator.**

is represented symbolically in Fig. 8.5*b*. *The important feature of a Carnot refrigeration cycle which distinguishes it from any general reversed engine cycle is that the quantities Q_H, Q_C, and ΣW are numerically equal to those quantities when the cycle is performed in the opposite direction.* For example, exactly the same amount of heat that is absorbed by the Carnot engine from the hot reservoir is rejected to the hot reservoir when the cycle is reversed. This would not be the case if the cycle were not reversible.

8.4/ Carnot's Theorem and Corollary

We are now in a position to prove Carnot's theorem, which is stated as follows: *No engine operating between two given reservoirs can be more efficient than a Carnot engine operating between the same two reservoirs.*

Imagine a Carnot engine R and any other engine I working between the same two reservoirs and adjusted so that they both deliver the same amount of work, ΣW. It becomes convenient in the reasoning which follows to deal with the absolute values of the various Q and W terms. These will be indicated by $|Q|$ and $|W|$, so as to emphasize that we have not abandoned the usual sign conventions. Thus:

Carnot engine R	**Any other engine** I
1. Absorbs heat $|Q_H|$ from hot reservoir.	1. Absorbs heat $|Q'_H|$ from hot reservoir.
2. Performs work $|\Sigma W|$.	2. Performs work $|\Sigma W|$.
3. Rejects heat $|Q_H| - |\Sigma W|$ to cold reservoir.	3. Rejects heat $|Q'_H| - |\Sigma W|$ to cold reservoir.
4. Efficiency $\eta_R = |\Sigma W/Q_H|$.	4. Efficiency $\eta_I = |\Sigma W/Q'_H|$.

Let us assume that the efficiency of the engine I is greater than that of R. Thus

$$\eta_I > \eta_R,$$

$$\left| \frac{\Sigma W}{Q'_H} \right| > \left| \frac{\Sigma W}{Q_H} \right|,$$

and

$$|Q_H| > |Q'_H|.$$

Now let the engine I drive the Carnot engine R backward as a Carnot refrigerator. This is shown symbolically in Fig. 8.6. The engine and the refrigerator coupled together in this way constitute a self-acting device, since all the work needed to operate the refrigerator is supplied by the engine. The net heat extracted from the cold reservoir is

$$|Q_H| - |\Sigma W| - (|Q'_H| - |\Sigma W|) = |Q_H| - |Q'_H|,$$

which is positive. The net heat delivered to the hot reservoir is also $|Q_H| - |Q'_H|$. The effect, therefore, of this self-acting device is to

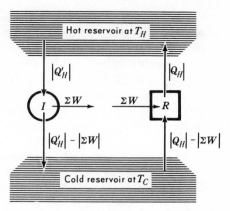

Fig. 8.6   Engine I operating a Carnot refrigerator.

transfer $|Q_H| - |Q'_H|$ units of heat from a cold reservoir to a hot reservoir. Since this is a violation of the second law of thermodynamics (Clausius' statement), our original assumption that $\eta_I > \eta_R$ is false and Carnot's theorem is proved. We may express this result in symbols, thus:

$$\eta_I \leq \eta_R.$$

The following corollary to Carnot's theorem may be easily proved: *All Carnot engines operating between the same two reservoirs have the same efficiency.*

Consider two Carnot engines R_1 and R_2, operating between the same two reservoirs. If we imagine R_1 driving R_2 backward, then Carnot's theorem states that

$$\eta_{R_1} \leq \eta_{R_2}.$$

If R_2 drives R_1 backward, then

$$\eta_{R_2} \leq \eta_{R_1}.$$

It therefore follows that

$$\eta_{R_1} = \eta_{R_2}.$$

It is clear from the above result that the nature of the working substance which is undergoing the Carnot cycle has no influence on the efficiency of the Carnot engine.

8.5/ The Kelvin Temperature Scale

In demonstrating that the efficiency of a Carnot engine is independent of the nature of the working substance and depends only on the temperatures of the two reservoirs it operates between, we have identified these temperatures with the ideal-gas temperature scale. However, the concept of the Carnot engine provides us with the opportunity to establish a truly *thermodynamic* temperature scale which is quite independent of the properties of any material substance.

Let us denote by θ temperatures measured by some arbitrarily chosen thermometer. Any of the various devices described in Chap. 1 would do. Thus θ represents temperatures on some empirical scale. Consider now two Carnot engines, one operating between a hot reservoir at temperature θ_H and a cold reservoir at temperature θ_C, and the second operating between θ_C and a still colder reservoir at temperature θ_0. Let the heat rejected by the first engine $|Q_C|$ be the heat absorbed by the second engine. The two engines working together thus constitute a third Carnot engine, which absorbs heat $|Q_H|$ from a reservoir at θ_H and rejects heat $|Q_0|$ to a reservoir at θ_0.

For the first engine the efficiency is given by

$$\eta_R = 1 - \frac{|Q_C|}{|Q_H|} = \phi(\theta_H, \theta_C),$$

where ϕ is an unknown function. Rearranging this equation, we get

$$\frac{|Q_H|}{|Q_C|} = \frac{1}{1 - \phi(\theta_H, \theta_C)} = f(\theta_H, \theta_C),$$

where f is also an unknown function.

For the second engine and for the two engines considered together as a third Carnot engine, the same equation must hold; thus

$$\frac{|Q_C|}{|Q_0|} = f(\theta_C, \theta_0),$$

and

$$\frac{|Q_H|}{|Q_0|} = f(\theta_H, \theta_0).$$

Since

$$\frac{|Q_H|}{|Q_C|} = \frac{|Q_H/Q_0|}{|Q_C/Q_0|},$$

we have the result that

$$f(\theta_H, \theta_C) = \frac{f(\theta_H, \theta_0)}{f(\theta_C, \theta_0)}.$$

Now the temperature θ_0 is arbitrarily chosen, and since it does not appear in the left-hand member of the above equation, it must therefore drop out of the ratio on the right. After it has been canceled, the numerator can be written $\psi(\theta_H)$ and the denominator $\psi(\theta_C)$, where ψ is another unknown function. Thus

$$\frac{|Q_H|}{|Q_C|} = \frac{\psi(\theta_H)}{\psi(\theta_C)}.$$

The ratio on the right is defined as the ratio of two *Kelvin* temperatures, and is denoted by T_H'/T_C'. We therefore, have, finally,

$$\frac{|Q_H|}{|Q_C|} = \frac{T_H'}{T_C'}.$$

Thus *two temperatures on the Kelvin scale are to each other as the absolute values of the heats absorbed and rejected, respectively, by a Carnot engine operating between reservoirs at these temperatures.* It is seen that the Kelvin temperature scale is independent of the peculiar characteristics of any particular substance. It therefore supplies precisely what is lacking in the ideal-gas scale.

At first thought it might seem that the ratio of two Kelvin temperatures would be impossible to measure, since a Carnot engine is an ideal engine, quite impossible to construct. The situation, however, is not so bad as it seems. The ratio of two Kelvin temperatures is the ratio of two heats that are transferred during two isothermal processes bounded by the same two adiabatics. The two adiabatic boundaries may be located experimentally, and the heats transferred during two isothermal "nearly reversible" processes can be measured with considerable precision. As a matter of fact, this is one of the methods used in measuring temperatures below 1°K.

To complete the definition of the Kelvin scale we proceed, as in Chap. 1, to assign the arbitrary value of 273.16°K to the temperature of the triple point of water T_t'. Thus

$$T_t' = 273.16°\text{K}.$$

For a Carnot engine operating between reservoirs at the temperatures T' and T_t', we have

$$\frac{|Q|}{|Q_t|} = \frac{T'}{T_t'},$$

or

$$T' = 273.16°\text{K}\,\frac{|Q|}{|Q_t|}.$$

Comparing this with the corresponding equation for the ideal-gas temperature T, namely,

$$T = 273.16°\text{K}\frac{\lim\,(PV)}{\lim\,(PV)_t},$$

it is seen that, in the Kelvin scale, $|Q|$ plays the role of a "thermometric property." This does not, however, have the objection attached to a coordinate of an arbitrarily chosen thermometer, inasmuch as the behavior of a Carnot engine is independent of the nature of the working substance.

8.6/ Absolute Zero

It follows from the equation

$$T' = 273.16°\text{K} \frac{|Q|}{|Q_t|}$$

that the heat transferred isothermally between two given adiabatics decreases as the temperature decreases. Conversely, the smaller the value of $|Q|$, the lower the corresponding T'. The smallest possible value of $|Q|$ is zero, and the corresponding T' is absolute zero. *Thus, if a system undergoes a reversible isothermal process without transfer of heat, the temperature at which this process takes place is called absolute zero.* In other words, at absolute zero, an isotherm and an adiabatic are identical.

It should be noticed that the definition of absolute zero holds for all substances and is therefore independent of the peculiar properties of any one arbitrarily chosen substance. Furthermore, the definition is in terms of purely macroscopic concepts. No reference is made to molecules or to molecular energy.

A Carnot engine absorbing heat $|Q_H|$ from a hot reservoir at T'_H and rejecting heat $|Q_C|$ to a cooler reservoir at T'_C has an efficiency

$$\eta_R = 1 - \frac{|Q_C|}{|Q_H|}.$$

Since

$$\frac{|Q_C|}{|Q_H|} = \frac{T'_C}{T'_H},$$

$$\eta_R = 1 - \frac{T'_C}{T'_H}.$$

For a Carnot engine to have an efficiency of 100 percent, it is clear that T'_C must be zero. Only when the lower reservoir is at absolute zero will all the heat be converted into work. Since nature does not provide us with a reservoir at absolute zero, a heat engine with 100 percent efficiency is a practical impossibility.

8.7/ Carnot Cycle of an Ideal Gas. Equality of Ideal-gas Temperature *T* and Kelvin Temperature *T'*

A Carnot cycle of an ideal gas is depicted on a PV diagram in Fig. 8.7. The two isothermal processes $b \rightarrow c$ and $d \rightarrow a$ are represented by equilateral hyperbolas whose equations are, respectively,

$$PV = R'T_H \quad \text{and} \quad PV = RT_C.$$

For any infinitesimal reversible process of an ideal gas, the first law may be written

$$đQ = C_V \, dT + P \, dV.$$

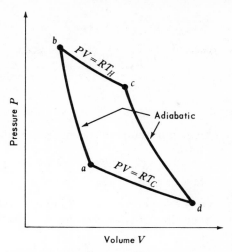

Fig. 8.7   Carnot cycle of an ideal gas.

Applying this equation to the isothermal process $b \rightarrow c$, the heat absorbed is found to be

$$|Q_H| = \int_{V_b}^{V_c} P \, dV$$

$$= RT_H \ln \frac{V_c}{V_b}.$$

Similarly, for the isothermal process $d \rightarrow a$, the absolute value of the heat rejected is

$$|Q_C| = RT_C \ln \frac{V_d}{V_a}.$$

Therefore

$$\frac{|Q_H|}{|Q_C|} = \frac{T_H \ln (V_c/V_b)}{T_C \ln (V_d/V_a)}.$$

Since the process $a \rightarrow b$ is adiabatic, we may write for any infinitesimal portion

$$-C_V \, dT = P \, dV,$$

or

$$-C_V \, dT = \frac{RT}{V} \, dV.$$

Integrating from a to b, we get

$$\frac{1}{R} \int_{T_C}^{T_H} C_V \frac{dT}{T} = \ln \frac{V_a}{V_b}.$$

Similarly, for the adiabatic process $c \rightarrow d$,

$$\frac{1}{R} \int_{T_C}^{T_H} C_V \frac{dT}{T} = \ln \frac{V_d}{V_c}.$$

Therefore
$$\ln \frac{V_a}{V_b} = \ln \frac{V_d}{V_c},$$

or
$$\ln \frac{V_c}{V_b} = \ln \frac{V_d}{V_a},$$

and we get, finally,

$$\frac{|Q_H|}{|Q_C|} = \frac{T_H}{T_C}.$$

Since, however, the Kelvin temperature scale is defined by the same sort of equation, we have

$$\frac{T_H}{T_C} = \frac{T'_H}{T'_C}.$$

If T' and T refer to any temperature and T'_t and T_t refer to the triple point of water, the preceding equation becomes

$$\frac{T}{T_t} = \frac{T'}{T'_t}.$$

Since $T'_t = T_t = 273.16°K$, it follows that

$$\boxed{T' = T.}$$

The Kelvin temperature is therefore numerically equal to the ideal-gas temperature and, in the proper range, may be measured with a gas thermometer.

Problems

8.1 An inventor claims to have developed an engine that takes in 100,000 Btu at a temperature of 400°K, rejects 40,000 Btu at a temperature of 200°K, and delivers 15 kwhr of mechanical work. Would you advise investing money to put this engine on the market?

8.2 A Carnot engine absorbs 1000 Btu of heat from a reservoir at the temperature of the normal boiling point of water and rejects heat to a reservoir at the temperature of the triple point of water. Find the heat rejected, the work done, and the efficiency.

8.3 Which is the more effective way to increase the efficiency of a Carnot engine: to increase T_H, keeping T_C constant, or to decrease T_C, keeping T_H constant?

8.4 Imagine any engine I and a Carnot engine R operating between the same two reservoirs. Suppose that they absorb from the hotter reservoir different amounts of heat, do different amounts of work, but reject to the cooler reservoir the *same* amounts of heat. Prove Carnot's theorem with the aid of the Kelvin-Planck statement of the second law.

8.5 In Sec. 8.4 suppose engine I to execute an *irreversible* cycle, and assume $\eta_I = \eta_R$. Show that this assumption leads to a result that is inconsistent with the assumed irreversibility of I, and therefore $\eta_I < \eta_R$.

8.6 Draw a symbolic diagram of a set of Carnot engines with the following characteristics: Each engine absorbs the heat rejected by the preceding one at the temperature at which it was rejected, and each engine delivers the same amount of work. Show that the temperature intervals between which these engines operate are all equal.

8.7 Take a gas whose equation of state is $P(V - b) = R\theta$ and whose C_V is a function of θ only through a Carnot cycle, and prove that $\theta = T$.

8.8 A body of total heat capacity A is cooled by a Carnot engine, and the heat rejected by the engine is absorbed by another body of total heat capacity B. Starting with the expression

$$dW = \frac{T_A - T_B}{T_A} dQ_A:$$

(a) Derive an expression relating T_A and T_B at any time.

(b) Derive an expression for the work obtained as a function of A, B, T_A and the initial temperatures T_{A_0} and T_{B_0}.

8.9 Robert Stirling, a Scottish minister, in 1816 devised a cycle known as the Stirling cycle. It is the basis for modern "regenerative" engines. The cycle consists of the following steps:

(a) An isothermal expansion from P_1, T_1, V_1 to P_2, T_1, V_2, during which heat Q_a flows to the engine and work W_a is done by the engine.

(b) A constant-volume process from P_2, T_1, V_2 to P_3, T_2, V_2, during which heat Q_b flows from the engine.

(c) An isothermal compression from P_3, T_2, V_2 to P_4, T_2, V_1, during which heat Q_c flows from the engine and work W_c is done on the engine.

(d) A constant-volume process from P_4, T_2, V_1 to P_1, T_1, V_1, during which heat Q_d flows to the engine.

Take the working substance to be an ideal gas, and sketch this cycle on a PV diagram. Show that the maximum efficiency for conversion of heat input into work is

$$\eta = \frac{W_a + W_b}{Q_a + Q_d} = \frac{(T_1 - T_2) \ln \dfrac{P_1}{P_2}}{T_1 \ln \dfrac{P_1}{P_2} + \dfrac{C_V}{R}(T_1 - T_2)}.$$

In a "regenerative" engine, Q_b is stored and used to supply the heat requirement Q_d. Thus the engine is its own source of the heat Q_d, and the only heat supplied to the engine is Q_a. If the regenerative process is reversible, show that the efficiency reduces to the Carnot efficiency.

8.10 Consider a metal rod, for which the linear expansivity α is known to be positive, to be the working substance of a Carnot engine. Show that adiabatic extension of the rod must cause its temperature to decrease and that adiabatic compression must cause its temperature to increase in order for the laws of thermodynamics to be satisfied.

Chapter 9/
Entropy

9.1 / Clausius' Theorem

Work diagrams in which a generalized force such as P, σ, γ, e, $\mathcal{E}$, or $\mathcal{H}$ is plotted against the corresponding generalized displacement V, ϵ, A, q, $\mathcal{P}$, and $\mathcal{M}$ have been used to indicate processes of various systems. An isothermal process or an adiabatic process is represented by a different curve on each diagram. In this chapter it is desired to formulate general principles that apply to all systems. If we let the symbol X denote any generalized force and the symbol x, its corresponding generalized displacement, a generalized work diagram in which X is plotted against x may be used to depict processes common to all systems, and will thus be suitable for general discussions.

Consider a reversible process represented by the smooth curve $i \rightarrow f$ on the generalized work diagram shown in Fig. 9.1. The nature of the system is immaterial. The dotted curves through i and f, respectively, represent portions of adiabatic processes. Let us draw a curve $a \rightarrow b$ representing an isothermal process in such a way that the area under the smooth curve if is equal to the area under the zigzag path $iabf$. Then the work done in traversing both paths is the same, or

$$W_{if} = W_{iabf}.$$

Now
$$Q_{if} = U_f - U_i + W_{if}$$

and
$$Q_{iabf} = U_f - U_i + W_{iabf}.$$

Therefore
$$Q_{if} = Q_{iabf}.$$

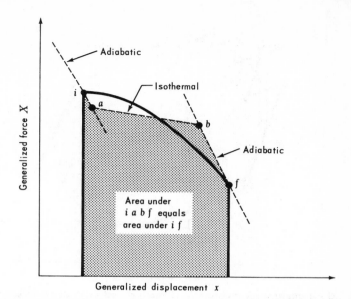

Fig. 9.1 Generalized work diagram. ($i \rightarrow f$, any reversible process; $i \rightarrow a$, reversible adiabatic process; $a \rightarrow b$, reversible isothermal process; $b \rightarrow f$, reversible adiabatic process.)

But since no heat is transferred in the two adiabatic processes ia and bf, we have

$$Q_{if} = Q_{ab}.$$

If we are given, therefore, a reversible process in which the temperature may change in any manner, it is always possible to find a reversible zigzag path between the same two states, consisting of an adiabatic followed by an isothermal followed by an adiabatic, such that the heat transferred during the isothermal portion is the same as that transferred during the original process.

Now consider the smooth closed curve representing a reversible cycle on the work diagram shown in Fig. 9.2. Since no two adiabatic lines can intersect (see Prob. 6.6), a number of adiabatic lines may be drawn, dividing the cycle into a number of adjacent strips. A zigzag closed path may now be drawn, consisting of alternate adiabatic and isothermal portions, such that the heat transferred during all the isothermal portions is equal to the heat transferred in the original cycle. Consider the two isothermal processes ab at the temperature T_1, during which heat $|Q_1|$ is absorbed, and cd at the temperature T_2, during which heat $|Q_2|$ is rejected. Since ab and cd are bounded by the same adiabatics, $abcd$ is a Carnot cycle, and we may write

$$\frac{|Q_1|}{T_1} = \frac{|Q_2|}{T_2}.$$

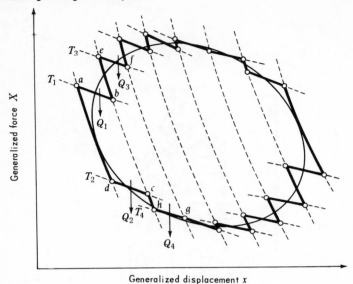

Fig. 9.2   Generalized work diagram.   (Smooth closed curve = reversible cycle; zigzag closed path = alternate reversible isothermal and adiabatic processes.)

For the sake of convenience and simplicity, we have been using the absolute values of Q_1 and Q_2.   Let us now adhere to the sign convention and regard any Q as an algebraic symbol, positive for heat absorbed and negative for heat rejected.   We may then write

$$\frac{Q_1}{T_1} + \frac{Q_2}{T_2} = 0,$$

where Q_1 stands for a positive number, and Q_2 for a negative number. Since the isothermals ef and gh are bounded by the same two adiabatics, $efgh$ is also a Carnot cycle, and

$$\frac{Q_3}{T_3} + \frac{Q_4}{T_4} = 0.$$

If a similar equation is written for each pair of isothermals bounded by the same two adiabatics and if all the equations are added, the result is obtained that

$$\frac{Q_1}{T_1} + \frac{Q_2}{T_2} + \frac{Q_3}{T_3} + \frac{Q_4}{T_4} + \cdots = 0.$$

Since no heat is transferred during the adiabatic portions of the zigzag cycle, we may write

$$\sum \frac{Q}{T} = 0,$$

where the summation is taken over the complete zigzag cycle.

Now imagine the cycle divided into a very large number of strips by drawing a large number of adiabatics close together. If we connect these adiabatics with small isothermals in the manner already described, a zigzag path may be traced that may be made to approximate the original cycle as closely as we please.   When these isothermal processes become infinitesimal, the ratio $đQ/T$ for an infinitesimal isothermal between two adjacent adiabatics is equal to the ratio $đQ/T$ for the infinitesimal piece of the original cycle bounded by the same two adiabatics.   In the limit, therefore, we may write, for any reversible cycle,

$$_R\oint \frac{đQ}{T} = 0.$$

The circle through the integral sign signifies that the integration takes place over the complete cycle, and the latter R emphasizes the fact that the equation is true only for a reversible cycle.   This result is known as *Clausius' theorem*.

9.2/ Entropy and the Second Law

Let an initial equilibrium state of any thermodynamic system be represented by the point i on any convenient diagram such as the generalized work diagram of Fig. 9.3.   Denote a final equilibrium state by the point f.   It is possible to take the system from i to f along any number of different reversible paths since i and f are equilibrium states. Suppose the system is taken from i to f along the reversible path R_1 and then back to i again along another reversible path R_2.   The two paths obviously constitute a reversible cycle, and from Clausius'

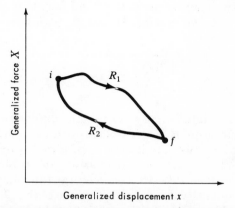

Fig. 9.3   Two reversible paths joining two equilibrium states of a system.

theorem, we may write

$$\oint_{R_1 R_2} \frac{dQ}{T} = 0.$$

The above integral may be expressed as the sum of two integrals, one for the path R_1 and the other for the path R_2. We have, then,

$$_{R_1}\int_i^f \frac{dQ}{T} + {_{R_2}}\int_f^i \frac{dQ}{T} = 0,$$

or

$$_{R_1}\int_i^f \frac{dQ}{T} = - {_{R_2}}\int_f^i \frac{dQ}{T}.$$

Since R_2 is a reversible path,

$$_{R_1}\int_i^f \frac{dQ}{T} = {_{R_2}}\int_i^f \frac{dQ}{T}.$$

Since R_1 and R_2 were chosen at random and represent *any* two reversible paths, the above equation expresses the important fact that $_R\int_i^f dQ/T$ *is independent of the reversible path connecting i and f.* It therefore follows that *there exists a function of the thermodynamic coordinates of a system whose value at the final state minus its value at the initial state equals the integral* $_R\int_i^f dQ/T$. This function is called the *entropy,* and is denoted by S. If S_i is the entropy at the initial state and S_f that at the final state, we have the result that

$$\boxed{_R\int_i^f \frac{dQ}{T} = S_f - S_i,}$$

where the difference $S_f - S_i$ is the *entropy change.*

Finally, if the two equilibrium states i and f are infinitesimally near, the integral sign may be eliminated and $S_f - S_i$ becomes dS. The equation then becomes

$$\boxed{\frac{dQ_R}{T} = dS,}$$

where dS is an exact differential, since it is the differential of an actual function. The subscript R written along with dQ indicates that the preceding equation is true only if dQ is transferred reversibly.

It should be noticed that the existence of an entropy function is deduced in the same manner as that of an energy function, i.e., by showing that a certain quantity is independent of the path. In neither case, however, are we able to calculate one value of the function.

9.3/ Principle of Carathéodory

We have arrived at the mathematical formulation of the second law by the conventional historical method initiated by the engineer Carnot and elaborated by the physicists Kelvin and Clausius. These men thought in terms of practical engines, ideal engines, and physical models. Starting with a statement expressing the impossibility of converting heat completely into work, or the impossibility of spontaneous heat flow from a colder to a hotter body, an ideal engine of maximum efficiency was described. With the aid of this ideal engine, an absolute temperature scale was defined and the Clausius theorem proved. On the basis of the Clausius theorem, the existence of an entropy function was inferred. From a mathematical point of view, this procedure is somewhat unsatisfactory. The mathematician prefers what is known as an "axiomatic treatment," i.e., a statement of the minimum number of fundamental axioms and then a purely formal mathematical deduction from these axioms.

In 1909, the mathematician Carathéodory set himself the problem of finding a statement of the second law which, without the aid of Carnot engines and refrigerators, but only by mathematical deduction, would lead to the existence of an entropy function satisfying the equation $dQ_R = T \, dS$. He was led to his formulation of the second law by a mathematical theorem which he proved and which may be stated in its simplest form as follows:

Imagine a space of three dimensions with rectangular coordinates x, y, z. *In the neighborhood of any arbitrary point P_0 there are points which are not accessible from P_0 along solution curves of the equation*

$$A(x,y,z) \, dx + B(x,y,z) \, dy + C(x,y,z) \, dz = 0,$$

if and only if the equation is integrable. The equation is said to be integrable if there exist functions $\lambda(x,y,z)$ and $F(x,y,z)$ such that

$$A \, dx + B \, dy + C \, dz = \lambda \, dF.$$

The proof of this purely mathematical theorem is somewhat involved, and it will not be given here. It holds for any number of variables.

Let us now consider how this theorem has a bearing on thermodynamics. Consider a system whose states are determined, for the sake of argument, by three thermodynamic coordinates x, y, and z. Then the first law in differential form may be written

$$dQ = A \, dx + B \, dy + C \, dz,$$

where A, B, and C are functions of x, y, and z. The adiabatic, reversible transitions of this system are subject to the condition

$$dQ = A \, dx + B \, dy + C \, dz = 0.$$

Let us now take as our mathematical statement of the second law the following:

In the neighborhood of any arbitrary initial state P_0 of a physical system there exist neighboring states which are not accessible from P_0 along quasistatic adiabatic paths.

It follows from Carathéodory's theorem that this is possible if and only if there exist functions T and S such that

$$đQ = A\, dx + B\, dy + C\, dz = T\, dS.$$

Thus, by stating the second law in terms of the inaccessibility of certain states by adiabatic paths and by using a mathematical theorem, Carathéodory inferred the existence of an entropy function and an integrating factor connected with Kelvin temperature. This is the barest outline of the axiomatic treatment, and is given only to inspire those of a mathematical turn of mind to read and learn more about it.†

9.4/ Entropy of an Ideal Gas

If a system absorbs an infinitesimal amount of heat $đQ_R$ during a reversible process, the entropy change of the system is equal to

$$dS = \frac{đQ_R}{T}.$$

It is interesting to notice that, although $đQ_R$ is an inexact differential, the ratio $đQ_R/T$ is exact. The reciprocal of the Kelvin temperature is therefore the integrating factor of $đQ_R$. If $đQ_R$ is expressed as a sum of differentials involving thermodynamic coordinates, then, upon dividing by T, the expression may be integrated and the entropy of the system obtained. As an example of this procedure, consider one of the expressions for $đQ_R$ of an ideal gas, namely,

$$đQ_R = C_P\, dT - V\, dP.$$

Dividing by T, we get

$$\frac{đQ_R}{T} = C_P \frac{dT}{T} - \frac{V}{T}\, dP,$$

or

$$dS = C_P \frac{dT}{T} - R \frac{dP}{P}.$$

Let us now calculate the entropy change ΔS of the gas between an arbitrarily chosen *reference state* with coordinates T_r, P_r and any other

---

† S. Chandrasekhar, "Stellar Structure," chap. 1, University of Chicago Press, Chicago, 1939, and Dover Publications, New York, 1957.

H. A. Buchdahl, *Z. Physik* (in English), **152**:425 (1958).

L. A. Turner, *Am. J. Phys.*, **28**:781 (1960).

F. W. Sears, *Am. J. Phys.*, **31**:747 (1963).

P. T. Landsberg, *Nature*, **201**:485 (1964).

state with coordinates T, P. Integrating between these two states, we get

$$\Delta S = \int_{T_r}^{T} C_P \frac{dT}{T} - R \ln \frac{P}{P_r}.$$

Suppose we ascribe to the reference state an entropy S_r and choose *any arbitrary numerical value* for this quantity. Then an entropy S may be associated with the other state where $S - S_r = \Delta S$. To make the discussion simpler, let C_P be constant. Then

$$S - S_r = C_P \ln \frac{T}{T_r} - R \ln \frac{P}{P_r},$$

and this may be rewritten

$$S = C_P \ln T - R \ln P + (S_r - C_P \ln T_r + R \ln P_r).$$

Denoting the quantity in parentheses by the *constant* S_0, we get finally

$$S = C_P \ln T - R \ln P + S_0.$$

Substituting for T and P thousands of different values, we may calculate thousands of corresponding values of S which, after tabulation, constitute an *entropy table*. Any one value from this table, taken alone, will have no meaning. The difference between two values, however, will be an actual entropy change.

Let us now return to the original differential equation

$$dS = C_P \frac{dT}{T} - R \frac{dP}{P}.$$

Again, for simplicity, assuming C_P to be constant, we may take the indefinite integral and obtain

$$S = C_P \ln T - R \ln P + S_0,$$

where S_0 is the constant of integration. Since this is precisely the equation obtained previously, we see that, in taking the indefinite integral of dS, we do not obtain an "absolute entropy," but merely an entropy referred to a nonspecified reference state whose coordinates are contained within the constant of integration. Thus, for an ideal gas,

$$\boxed{S = \int C_P \frac{dT}{T} - R \ln P + S_0.}$$

To calculate the entropy of an ideal gas as a function of T and V, we use the other expression for dQ_R of an ideal gas. Thus

$$\frac{dQ_R}{T} = C_V \frac{dT}{T} + \frac{P}{T} dV,$$

$$dS = C_V \frac{dT}{T} + R \frac{dV}{V}.$$

Proceeding in the same way as before, we get for the entropy, referred to an unspecified reference state, the expression

$$S = \int C_V \frac{dT}{T} + R \ln V + S_0,$$

which becomes, if C_V is constant,

$$S = C_V \ln T + R \ln V + S_0.$$

9.5/ TS Diagram

For each infinitesimal amount of heat that enters a system during an infinitesimal portion of a reversible process, there is an equation

$$dQ_R = T\, dS.$$

It follows, therefore, that the total amount of heat transferred in a reversible process is given by

$$Q_R = \int_i^f T\, dS.$$

This integral can be interpreted graphically as the area under a curve on a diagram in which T is plotted along the Y axis and S along the X axis. The nature of the curve on the TS diagram is determined by the kind of reversible process that the system undergoes. Obviously, an isothermal process is a horizontal line.

In the case of a reversible adiabatic process, we have

$$dS = \frac{dQ_R}{T} \qquad \text{and} \qquad dQ_R = 0;$$

whence, if T is not zero,

$$dS = 0$$

and S is constant. Therefore, during a reversible adiabatic process, the entropy of a system remains constant, or in other words, the system undergoes an *isentropic process*. An isentropic process on a TS diagram is obviously a vertical line. It is therefore clear that the two isothermal and the two adiabatic processes which go to make up a Carnot cycle form a rectangle on a TS diagram, no matter what the working substance is. Only reversible processes may be plotted on a TS diagram since entropy has been defined only for equilibrium states.

The TS diagram is particularly convenient for representing reversible cycles. The closed curve shown in Fig. 9.4 consisting of an upper portion R_1 and a lower portion R_2 represents a reversible engine cycle. The area under R_1 (positive area) is equal to the heat absorbed Q_1, and the area under R_2 (negative area), to the heat rejected Q_2. The area

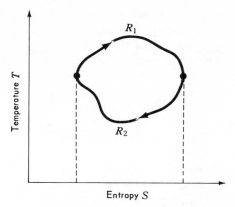

Fig. 9.4   Reversible cycle on a TS diagram.

inside the closed curve is therefore $Q_1 + Q_2$, or W.   Since the efficiency of the engine is $1 + Q_2/Q_1$, it may be measured directly from the diagram.

9.6/ Entropy and Reversibility

In order to understand the physical meaning of entropy and its significance, it is necessary to study all the entropy changes that take place when a system undergoes a process.   If we calculate the entropy change of the system and add to this the entropy change of the local surroundings, we obtain a quantity that is the sum of all the entropy changes brought about by this particular process.   We may call this the *entropy change of the universe* due to the process in question.

When a finite amount of heat is absorbed or rejected by a reservoir, extremely small changes in the coordinates take place in every unit of mass.   The entropy change of a unit of mass is therefore very small. Since, however, the total mass of a reservoir is large, the total entropy change is finite.   Suppose that a reservoir is in contact with a system and that heat Q is absorbed by the reservoir at the temperature T. The reservoir undergoes nondissipative changes determined entirely by the quantity of heat absorbed.   Exactly the same changes *in the reservoir* would take place if the same amount of heat Q were transferred reversibly.   Hence the entropy change of the reservoir is Q/T.   Therefore, *whenever a reservoir absorbs heat Q at the temperature T from any system during any kind of process, the entropy change of the reservoir is Q/T.*

Consider now the entropy change of the universe that is brought about by the performance of any reversible process.   The process will, in general, be accompanied by a flow of heat between a system and a set of reservoirs ranging in temperature from T_i to T_f. During *any* infinitesimal portion of the process, an amount of heat $đQ_R$ is transferred between the system and one of the reservoirs at the temperature T. Let $đQ_R$ be a positive number. If $đQ_R$ is absorbed by the system, then

$$dS \text{ of the system} = + \frac{đQ_R}{T},$$

$$dS \text{ of the reservoir} = - \frac{đQ_R}{T},$$

and the entropy change of the universe is zero. If $đQ_R$ is rejected by the system, the same equations apply, but $đQ_R$ is a negative number. If $đQ_R$ is zero, neither the system nor the reservoir will have an entropy change and the entropy change of the universe is still zero. Since this is true for any infinitesimal portion of the reversible process, it is true for all such portions, and therefore we may conclude that, *when a reversible process is performed, the entropy of the universe remains unchanged.*

9.7/ Entropy and Irreversibility

When a system undergoes an irreversible process between an initial equilibrium state and a final equilibrium state, the entropy change of the system is equal to

$$S_f - S_i = {}_R\!\int_i^f \frac{đQ}{T},$$

where R indicates *any reversible process arbitrarily chosen* by which the system may be brought from the given initial state to the given final state. No integration is performed over the original irreversible path. The irreversible process is replaced by a reversible one. This can easily be done when the initial and the final states of the system are equilibrium states. When either the initial or the final state is a nonequilibrium state, special methods must be used. At first, we shall limit ourselves to irreversible processes all of which involve initial and final states of equilibrium.

Processes Exhibiting External Mechanical Irreversibility

A. Those involving the isothermal dissipation of work through a system (which remains unchanged) into internal energy of a reservoir, such as:

1. Irregular stirring of a viscous liquid in contact with a reservoir.
2. Coming to rest of a rotating or vibrating liquid in contact with a reservoir.
3. Inelastic deformation of a solid in contact with a reservoir.

4. Transfer of electricity through a resistor in contact with a reservoir.

5. Magnetic hysteresis of a material in contact with a reservoir.

In the case of any process involving the isothermal transformation of work W through a system into internal energy of a reservoir, there is no entropy change of the system because the thermodynamic coordinates do not change. There is a flow of heat Q into the reservoir where $Q = W$. Since the reservoir absorbs Q units of heat at the temperature T, its entropy change is Q/T, or W/T. The entropy change of the universe is therefore W/T, which is a positive quantity.

B. Those involving the adiabatic dissipation of work into internal energy of a system, such as:

1. Irregular stirring of a viscous thermally insulated liquid.

2. Coming to rest of a rotating or vibrating thermally insulated liquid.

3. Inelastic deformation of a thermally insulated solid.

4. Transfer of electricity through a thermally insulated resistor.

5. Magnetic hysteresis of a thermally insulated material.

In the case of any process involving the adiabatic transformation of work W into internal energy of a system whose temperature rises from T_i to T_f at constant pressure, there is no flow of heat to or from the surroundings, and therefore the entropy change of the local surroundings is zero. To calculate the entropy change of the system, the original irreversible process must be replaced by a reversible one that will take the system from the given initial state (temperature T_i, pressure P) to the final state (temperature T_f, pressure P). Let us replace the irreversible performance of work by a reversible isobaric flow of heat from a series of reservoirs ranging in temperature from T_i to T_f. The entropy change of the system will then be

$$S_f - S_i \text{ (system)} = {}_R\!\int_{T_i}^{T_f} \frac{dQ}{T}.$$

For an isobaric process,

$$dQ_R = C_P \, dT,$$

and

$$S_f - S_i \text{ (system)} = \int_{T_i}^{T_f} C_P \frac{dT}{T}.$$

Finally, if C_P is assumed constant,

$$S_f - S_i \text{ (system)} = C_P \ln \frac{T_f}{T_i},$$

and the entropy change of the universe is $C_P \ln (T_f/T_i)$, which is a positive quantity.

Processes Exhibiting Internal Mechanical Irreversibility

Those involving the transformation of internal energy of a system into mechanical energy and then back into internal energy again, such as:

1. Ideal gas rushing into a vacuum (free expansion).
2. Gas seeping through a porous plug (throttling process).
3. Snapping of a stretched wire after it is cut.
4. Collapse of a soap film after it is pricked.

In the case of a free expansion of an ideal gas, the entropy change of the local surroundings is zero. To calculate the entropy change of the system, the free expansion must be replaced by a reversible process that will take the gas from its original state (volume V_i, temperature T) to the final state (volume V_f, temperature T). Evidently, the most convenient reversible process is a reversible isothermal expansion at the temperature T from a volume V_i to the volume V_f. The entropy change of the system is then

$$S_f - S_i \text{ (system)} = {}_R\!\int_{V_i}^{V_f} \frac{dQ}{T}.$$

For an isothermal process of an ideal gas,

$$dQ_R = P \, dV,$$

and

$$\frac{dQ_R}{T} = R \frac{dV}{V},$$

whence

$$S_f - S_i \text{ (system)} = R \ln \frac{V_f}{V_i},$$

and the entropy change of the universe is $R \ln (V_f/V_i)$, which is a positive number.

Processes Exhibiting External Thermal Irreversibility

Those involving a transfer of heat by virtue of a finite temperature difference, such as:

1. Conduction or radiation of heat from a system to its cooler surroundings.
2. Conduction or radiation of heat through a system (which remains unchanged) from a hot reservoir to a cooler one.

In the case of the conduction of Q units of heat through a system (which remains unchanged) from a hot reservoir at T_H to a cooler reservoir at T_C, the following steps are obvious:

$$S_f - S_i \text{ (system)} = 0,$$

$$S_f - S_i \text{ (hot reservoir)} = -\frac{|Q|}{T_H},$$

$$S_f - S_i \text{ (cold reservoir)} = +\frac{|Q|}{T_C},$$

$$S_f - S_i \text{ (universe)} = \frac{|Q|}{T_C} - \frac{|Q|}{T_H}.$$

Processes Exhibiting Chemical Irreversibility

Those involving a spontaneous change of internal structure, chemical composition, density, etc., such as:

1. A chemical reaction.
2. Diffusion of two dissimilar inert ideal gases.
3. Mixing of alcohol and water.
4. Freezing of supercooled liquid.
5. Condensation of a supersaturated vapor.
6. Solution of a solid in water.
7. Osmosis.

Assuming the diffusion of two dissimilar inert ideal gases to be equivalent to two separate free expansions, for one of which

$$S_f - S_i \text{ (universe)} = R \ln \frac{V_f}{V_i},$$

and taking a mole of each gas so that $V_f = 2V_i$, we obtain

$$S_f - S_i \text{ (universe)} = 2R \ln 2,$$

which is a positive number. All the results of this article are summarized in Table 9.1.

9.8/ Entropy and Nonequilibrium States

The calculation of the entropy changes associated with the irreversible processes discussed in Sec. 9.7 presented no special difficulties because, in all cases, the system either did not change at all (in which case only the entropy changes of reservoirs had to be calculated) or the terminal states of a system were equilibrium states that could be connected by a suitable reversible process. Consider, however, the following process involving internal thermal irreversibility. A thermally conducting

Table 9.1/ Entropy Change of the Universe Due to Natural Processes

Type of irreversibility	Irreversible process	Entropy change of the system	Entropy change of the local surroundings	Entropy change of the universe
External mechanical irreversibility	Isothermal dissipation of work through a system into internal energy of a reservoir	0	$\dfrac{W}{T}$	$\dfrac{W}{T}$
External mechanical irreversibility	Adiabatic dissipation of work into internal energy of a system	$C_P \ln \dfrac{T_f}{T_i}$	0	$C_P \ln \dfrac{T_f}{T_i}$
Internal mechanical irreversibility	Free expansion of an ideal gas	$R \ln \dfrac{V_f}{V_i}$	0	$R \ln \dfrac{V_f}{V_i}$
External thermal irreversibility	Transfer of heat through a medium from a hot to a cooler reservoir	0	$\dfrac{|Q|}{T_C} - \dfrac{|Q|}{T_H}$	$\dfrac{|Q|}{T_C} - \dfrac{|Q|}{T_H}$
Chemical irreversibility	Diffusion of two dissimilar inert ideal gases	$2R \ln 2$	0	$2R \ln 2$

bar, brought to a nonuniform temperature distribution by contact at one end with a hot reservoir and at the other end with a cold reservoir, is removed from the reservoirs and then thermally insulated and kept at constant pressure. An internal flow of heat will finally bring the bar to a uniform temperature, but the transition will be from an initial nonequilibrium state to a final equilibrium state. It is obviously impossible to find one reversible process by which the system may be brought from the same initial to the same final state. What meaning, therefore, may be attached to the entropy change associated with this process?

Let us consider the bar to be composed of an infinite number of infinitesimally thin sections, each of which has a different initial temperature but all of which have the same final temperature. Suppose we imagine all the sections to be insulated from one another and all kept at the same pressure and then each section to be put in contact successively with a series of reservoirs ranging in temperature from the initial temperature of the particular section to the common final temperature. This defines an infinite number of reversible isobaric processes, which may be used to take the system from its initial nonequilibrium state to its final equilibrium state. We shall now define the entropy change as the result of integrating dQ/T over all these reversible processes. In other words, in the absence of one reversible process to take the system from i to f, we conceive of an infinite number of reversible processes, one for each volume element.

As an example, consider the uniform bar of length L depicted in Fig. 9.5. A typical volume element at x has a mass

$$dm = \rho A\ dx,$$

where ρ is the density, and A the cross-sectional area. The heat capacity of the section is

$$C_P\ dm = C_P \rho A\ dx.$$

Let us suppose that the initial temperature distribution is linear, so that the section at x has an initial temperature

$$T_i = T_0 - \frac{T_0 - T_L}{L}\ x.$$

If no heat is lost and if we assume for the sake of simplicity that the thermal conductivity, density and heat capacity of all sections remain constant, the final temperature will be

$$T_f = \frac{T_0 + T_L}{2}.$$

Integrating dQ/T over a reversible isobaric transfer of heat between the volume element and a series of reservoirs ranging in temperature

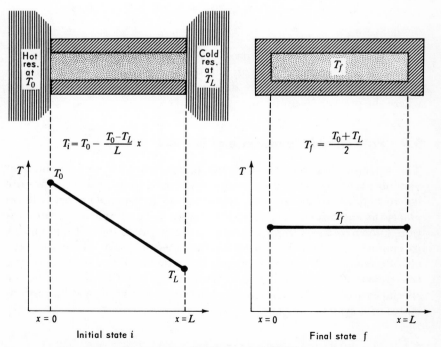

Fig. 9.5 Process exhibiting internal thermal irreversibility.

from T_i to T_f, we get, for the entropy change of *this one volume element*,

$$C_{P}\rho A \, dx \int_{T_i}^{T_f} \frac{dT}{T} = C_{P}\rho A \, dx \ln \frac{T_f}{T_i}$$

$$= C_{P}\rho A \, dx \ln \frac{T_f}{T_0 - \dfrac{T_0 - T_L}{L} x}$$

$$= -C_{P}\rho A \, dx \ln \left(\frac{T_0}{T_f} - \frac{T_0 - T_L}{LT_f} x \right).$$

Upon integrating over the whole bar, the total entropy change is

$$S_f - S_i = -C_{P}\rho A \int_0^L \ln \left(\frac{T_0}{T_f} - \frac{T_0 - T_L}{LT_f} x \right) dx,$$

which, after integration† and simplification, becomes

$$S_f - S_i = mC_P \left(1 + \ln T_f + \frac{T_L}{T_0 - T_L} \ln T_L - \frac{T_0}{T_0 - T_L} \ln T_0 \right).$$

To show that the entropy change is positive, let us take a convenient numerical case such as $T_0 = 400°\text{K}$, $T_L = 200°\text{K}$; whence $T_f = 300°\text{K}$. Then

$$S_f - S_i = mC_P(1 + 5.704 + 5.298 - 2 \times 5.992)$$
$$= 0.019mC_P.$$

The same method may be used to compute the entropy change of a system during a process from an initial nonequilibrium state characterized by a nonuniform pressure distribution to a final equilibrium state where the pressure is uniform.

9.9/ Principle of the Increase of Entropy

The entropy change of the universe associated with each of the irreversible processes treated up to now was found to be positive. We are led to believe, therefore, that whenever an irreversible process takes place, the entropy of the universe increases. To establish this proposition, known as the *entropy principle*, in a general manner, it is sufficient to confine our attention to adiabatic processes only, since we have already seen that the entropy principle is true for all processes involving the irreversible transfer of heat. We start the proof by considering the special case of an adiabatic irreversible process between two equilibrium states of a system.

$$\dagger \int \ln (a + bx) \, dx = \frac{1}{b} (a + bx)[\ln (a + bx) - 1].$$

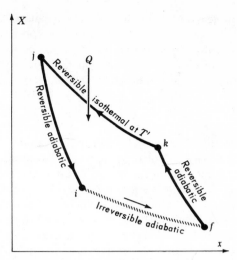

Fig. 9.6   Cycle which contradicts the second law unless $S_f > S_i$.

1. Let the initial state of the system be represented by the point i on the generalized work diagram of Fig. 9.6, and suppose that the system undergoes an *irreversible adiabatic process* to the state f. Then the entropy change is

$$\Delta S = S_f - S_i.$$

A temperature change may or may not have taken place. Whether or not, let us cause the system to undergo a *reversible adiabatic process* $f \rightarrow k$ in such a direction as to bring its temperature to that of any arbitrarily chosen reservoir, say, at T'. Then, since $S_f = S_k$,

$$\Delta S = S_k - S_i.$$

Now suppose that the system is brought into contact with the reservoir and caused to undergo a *reversible isothermal process* $k \rightarrow j$ until its entropy is the same as at the beginning. A final *reversible adiabatic process* $j \rightarrow i$ will now bring the system back to its initial state; and since $S_j = S_i$,

$$\Delta S = S_k - S_j.$$

The only heat transfer Q that has taken place in the cycle is during the isothermal process $k \rightarrow j$, where

$$Q = T'(S_j - S_k).$$

A net amount of work W has been done in the cycle, where

$$W = Q.$$

It is clear from the second law of thermodynamics that the heat Q cannot have entered the system, that is, Q cannot be positive, for then we should have a cyclic process in which no effect has been produced other than the extraction of heat from a reservoir and the performance of an equivalent amount of work. Therefore $Q \leq 0$, and

$$T'(S_j - S_k) \leq 0,$$

and finally

$$\Delta S \geq 0.$$

2. If we assume that the original irreversible adiabatic process took place without any change in entropy, it would be possible to bring the system back to i by means of one reversible adiabatic process. Moreover, since the net heat transferred in this cycle is zero, the net work would also be zero. Therefore, under these circumstances, the system and its surroundings would have been restored to their initial states without producing changes elsewhere, which implies that the original process was reversible. Since this is contrary to our original assertion, the entropy of the system cannot remain unchanged. Therefore

$$\Delta S > 0.$$

3. Let us now suppose that the system is not homogeneous and not of uniform temperature and pressure and that it undergoes an irreversible adiabatic process in which mixing and chemical reaction may take place. If we assume that the system may be subdivided into parts (each one infinitesimal, if necessary) and that it is possible to ascribe a definite temperature, pressure, composition, etc., to each part, so that each part will have a definite entropy depending on its coordinates, then we may define the entropy of the whole system as the sum of the entropies of its parts. If we now assume that it is possible to take *each part* back to its initial state by means of the reversible processes described in step 1, using the same reservoir for each part, it follows that ΔS of the whole system is positive.

It should be emphasized that we have had to make two assumptions, namely, (1) that the entropy of a system may be defined by subdividing the system into parts and summing the entropies of these parts, and (2) that reversible processes may be found or imagined by which mixtures may be unmixed and reactions may be caused to proceed in the opposite direction. The main justification for these assumptions, and therefore for the entropy principle, lies in the fact that they lead to results in complete agreement with experiment.

The behavior of the entropy of the universe as a result of *any* kind of process may now be represented in the following succinct manner:

$$\Delta S \text{ (universe)} \geq 0,$$

where the equality sign refers to reversible processes and the inequality sign to irreversible processes. *This equation is the mathematical formulation of the second law.*

Thus the second law provides an answer to the question that is not contained within the scope of the first law, namely: In what direction does a process take place? The answer is that a process always takes place in such a direction as to cause an increase in the entropy of the universe, i.e., in the system plus its surroundings.

9.10/ Application of the Entropy Principle

We have seen that, whenever irreversible processes take place, the entropy of the universe increases. In the actual operation of a device, such as an engine or a refrigerator, it is often possible to calculate the sum of all the entropy changes. The fact that this sum is positive enables us to draw useful conclusions concerning the behavior of the device. An important example from the field of refrigeration will illustrate the power and simplicity of the entropy principle. Suppose it is desired to freeze water or to liquefy air, i.e., to lower the temperature of a body of finite mass from the temperature T_1 of its surroundings to any desired temperature T_2. A refrigerator operating in a cycle between a reservoir at T_1 and the body itself is utilized. After a finite number of complete cycles has been traversed, as shown in Fig. 9.7, a quantity of heat $|Q|$ has been removed from the body, a quantity of work $|W|$ has been supplied to the refrigerator, and a quantity of

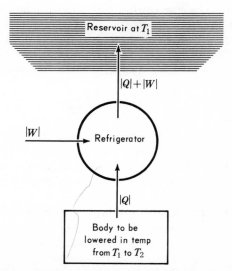

Fig. 9.7 Operation of a refrigerator in lowering the temperature of a body from that of its surroundings T_1 to any desired value T_2.

heat $|Q| + |W|$ has been rejected to the reservoir. Listing the entropy changes, we have

$$\Delta S \text{ of body} = S_2 - S_1,$$
$$\Delta S \text{ of refrigerant} = 0,$$
$$\Delta S \text{ of reservoir} = \frac{|Q| + |W|}{T_1}.$$

Applying the entropy principle,

$$S_2 - S_1 + \frac{|Q| + |W|}{T_1} \geq 0.$$

Multiplying by T_1 and transposing, we get

$$|W| \geq T_1(S_1 - S_2) - |Q|.$$

It follows that the smallest possible value for $|W|$ is

$$|W|(\min) = T_1(S_1 - S_2) - |Q|.$$

If tables of the thermodynamic properties of the material are available, a knowledge of the initial and final states is all that is needed to read from the tables the values of $S_1 - S_2$ and, if the body undergoes an isobaric process, of $|Q|$. The calculated value of $|W|(\min)$ is used to provide an estimate of the minimum cost of operation of the refrigeration plant.

9.11 / Entropy and Unavailable Energy

Consider a system consisting of a heat reservoir at temperature T to exist in surroundings having the uniform and constant temperature T_0, which is lower than T. The surroundings are equivalent to a second heat reservoir. If a Carnot engine is operated between the system and its surroundings, a quantity of heat Q supplied to the engine will be partially converted into work according to the equation

$$W = Q\left(1 - \frac{T_0}{T}\right).$$

This represents the maximum amount of work which may be produced from the heat Q supplied to the engine by the system. One may therefore adopt the view that only a part of the heat energy Q is *available* for conversion into work with respect to a surroundings temperature T_0.

Suppose now that the quantity of heat Q is transferred directly from a heat reservoir at temperature T_1 to another heat reservoir at a lower temperature T_2, both existing in surroundings at the still lower temperature T_0. We wish to show that, because of the irreversible transfer of heat from T_1 to T_2, the fraction of the quantity of heat Q available for conversion into work for a given T_0 has decreased. The maximum work which could have been obtained from the heat Q before its irreversible transfer to the temperature level T_2 is given by

$$\text{Maximum work before transfer} = Q\left(1 - \frac{T_0}{T_1}\right).$$

After its irreversible transfer to the reservoir at T_2, the maximum work available is

$$\text{Maximum work after transfer} = Q\left(1 - \frac{T_0}{T_2}\right).$$

The difference between these quantities represents an amount of energy E that could have been converted to work prior to the irreversible heat-transfer process but which cannot be so converted after the process. Thus E represents an amount of energy which has become unavailable for conversion into work as the result of the irreversible heat transfer, and is given by

$$E = Q\left(1 - \frac{T_0}{T_1}\right) - Q\left(1 - \frac{T_0}{T_2}\right)$$
$$= T_0\left(\frac{Q}{T_2} - \frac{Q}{T_1}\right).$$

But the quantity $(Q/T_2 - Q/T_1)$ is the total entropy change of the two heat reservoirs as a result of the irreversible heat-transfer process. Thus

$$E = T_0\,\Delta S_{\text{total}}.$$

The energy which became unavailable is seen to be directly proportional to the total entropy change resulting from the irreversible process. That the proportionality factor is the absolute temperature of the surroundings T_0 may seem remarkable, because the surroundings were not involved in the irreversible process. But this fact shows clearly that the energy made unavailable for conversion into work depends on, or is determined with respect to, a particular T_0. In practice, this temperature is taken as that naturally available to us, i.e., the temperature of the atmosphere or of cooling water.

The foregoing derivation was specific for the special case of irreversible heat transfer between two heat reservoirs. We shall now present a more abstract derivation to establish the generality of the relation between E and the total entropy change associated with an irreversible process.

Consider a system which undergoes a change of state by an irreversible process. We assume that the system exists in surroundings which in effect constitute a heat reservoir at temperature T_0. The first law requires that

$$\Delta U = Q - W,$$

where Q is heat exchanged between the system and its surroundings. The entropy change of the surroundings caused by this transfer of heat is

$$\Delta S_0 = \frac{-Q}{T_0}.$$

The minus sign on Q arises because the sign convention for Q is taken with reference to the system, whereas here we are determining the entropy change of the surroundings.

Now, after the irreversible process has occurred, let us consider the restoration of the *system* to its initial state *by a completely reversible process*. For this process the first law may be written

$$\Delta U_{rev} = Q_{rev} - W_{rev},$$

where the designation "rev" indicates the reversible restoration process. The entropy change of the surroundings during this process is

$$\Delta S_{0rev} = \frac{-Q_{rev}}{T_0}.$$

For the complete cycle—original irreversible process plus reversible restoration—we have

$$\Delta U + \Delta U_{rev} = Q - W + (Q_{rev} - W_{rev}).$$

But for the cycle there can be no net change of the internal energy of the system; therefore

$$0 = Q - W + (Q_{rev} - W_{rev}),$$
or
$$Q + Q_{rev} = W + W_{rev}.$$

Furthermore, there can be no net change of the entropy of the *system* for the complete cycle. Thus the total entropy change which occurs as a result of the two processes is the sum of the entropy changes of the surroundings:

$$\Delta S_{total} = \frac{-(Q + Q_{rev})}{T_0}.$$

Since this is the total entropy change of the cycle, it must also be the total entropy change brought about by the original irreversible process, for the restoration process was reversible and hence caused no change in the total entropy.

Therefore the total entropy change resulting from the original irreversible process is

$$\Delta S_{total} = \frac{-(Q + Q_{rev})}{T_0} = \frac{-(W + W_{rev})}{T_0},$$
or
$$-(W + W_{rev}) = T_0\,\Delta S_{total}.$$

The quantity $W + W_{rev}$ is the net work of the cycle and as such represents the *extra* work required to restore the system to its initial state, for had the original process been reversible, no *extra* work would have been necessary for restoration of the system by a reversible process. This extra work is therefore the negative of work which would have been obtained had the original process been reversible but which became unavailable because of the irreversibility of the actual process. Thus $-(W + W_{rev})$ is the quantity we have designated E. Hence we have as a general equation

$$E = T_0 \, \Delta S_{total}.$$

This equation states that *the energy that becomes unavailable for work during an irreversible process is T_0 times the total entropy change in the system and surroundings resulting from an irreversible process.* It must be understood that energy which becomes unavailable for work is not energy which is lost, for the first law is always valid.

The engineering significance of this result is clear. The greater the irreversibility of a process, the greater the increase in total entropy accompanying it, and the greater amount of energy which becomes unavailable for work. Since work is a form of energy of high monetary value, every irreversibility in a process carries with it a price.

Problems

9.1 (*a*) Derive the expression for the efficiency of a Carnot engine directly from a TS diagram.

(*b*) Compare the efficiencies of cycles a and b of Fig. P9.1.

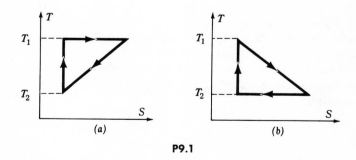

P9.1

9.2 Prove that the slope on a TS diagram (*a*) of an isochoric curve is T/C_V; (*b*) of an isobaric curve is T/C_P.

9.3 Show that the entropy of an ideal gas with constant heat capacities may be written

$$S = C_V \ln P + C_P \ln V + \text{const.}$$

9.4 An electric current of 10 amp is maintained for 1 sec in a resistor of 25 ohms while the temperature of the resistor is kept constant at 27°C.

(*a*) What is the entropy change in the resistor?

(*b*) What is the entropy change of the universe?

The same current is maintained for the same time in the same resistor, but now thermally insulated, whose initial temperature is 27°C. If the resistor has a mass of 10 gm and $C_P = 0.20$ cal/gm · °C:

(*c*) What is the entropy change of the resistor?

(*d*) What is the entropy change of the universe?

9.5 (*a*) One pound mass of water at 500°R is brought into contact with a heat reservoir at 600°R. When the water has reached 600°R, what is the entropy change of the water? Of the heat reservoir? Of the universe?

(*b*) If the water had been heated from 500 to 600°R by first bringing it into contact with a reservoir at 550°R and then with a reservoir at 600°R, what would have been the entropy change of the universe?

(*c*) Explain how the water might be heated from 500 to 600°R with almost no change of entropy of the universe.

9.6 A thermally insulated cylinder closed at both ends is fitted with a frictionless heat-conducting piston which divides the cylinder into two parts. Initially, the piston is clamped in the center, with 1 ft³ of air at 500°R and 2 atm pressure on one side and 1 ft³ of air at 500°R and 1 atm pressure on the other side. The piston is released and reaches equilibrium in pressure and temperature at a new position. Compute the final pressure and temperature and the total increase of entropy. What irreversible process has taken place?

9.7 A piece of hot metal (mass m, specific heat at constant pressure C_P, temperature T_1) is immersed in a cooler liquid (m',C'_P,T'_1) adiabatically and isobarically. Prove that the condition of equilibrium, namely, $T_2 = T'_2$, may be obtained by rendering the entropy change of the universe a maximum subject to the condition that the heat lost by the metal equals the heat gained by the liquid.

9.8 A mass m of water at T_1 is isobarically and adiabatically mixed with an equal mass of water at T_2. Show that the entropy change of the universe is

$$2mC_P \ln \frac{(T_1 + T_2)/2}{\sqrt{T_1 T_2}},$$

and prove that this is positive by drawing a semicircle of diameter $T_1 + T_2$.

9.9 Solve the problem of Sec. 9.8 when only the hot reservoir is removed, and show that the entropy change of the universe is

$$mC_P \left(1 + \frac{T_0 - T_L}{2T_L} - \frac{T_0}{T_0 - T_L} \ln \frac{T_0}{T_L}\right).$$

9.10 A body of finite mass is originally at a temperature T_1, which is higher than that of a reservoir at the temperature T_2. Suppose an engine operates in a cycle between the body and the reservoir until it lowers the temperature of the body from T_1 to T_2, thus extracting heat Q from the body. The engine does work W and rejects heat to the reservoir at T_2. Show that the maximum work obtainable from the engine is

$$W(\text{max}) = T_2(S_2 - S_1) - Q,$$

where Q, S_1, and S_2 refer to the body.

9.11 One pound mole of an ideal gas is compressed isothermally but irreversibly at 127°C from 1 to 10 atm by a piston in a cylinder. The heat removed from the gas during compression flows to a heat reservoir at 27°C. The actual work required is 20 percent greater than the reversible work for the same compression. Calculate the entropy change of the gas, the entropy change of the heat reservoir, and the total entropy change in Btu/°R.

9.12 A rigid nonconducting tank with a volume of 120 ft³ is divided into two equal parts by a thin membrane. Hydrogen gas is contained on one side of the membrane at 50 psia and 100°F. The other side is a perfect vacuum. The membrane is suddenly ruptured, and the H_2 gas fills the tank. What is the entropy change of the hydrogen? Consider hydrogen to be an ideal gas for which $C_P = 7$ Btu/lb mole · °F.

9.13 The molar heat capacity of an ideal gas is given as a function of temperature by the equation

$$C_P = 3.0 + 10.0 \times 10^{-3}T + 15.0 \times 10^{-6}T^2,$$

where T is in °K, and C_P has the usual units. If the temperature of the gas is raised from 80 to 800°F at constant pressure, calculate the entropy change of the gas in Btu/lb mole · °R.

Chapter 10/
Thermodynamic Functions
for Pure Substances

10.1/ Enthalpy

The primary thermodynamic functions have already been introduced in the development of the zeroth, first, and second laws. They are temperature T, pressure P, volume V, internal energy U, and entropy S. Several additional thermodynamic functions are defined in this chapter which are composites of those already discussed. Their use is simply a matter of convenience.

The enthalpy of a system is defined as

$$H = U + PV.$$

In order to study the properties of this function, consider the change in enthalpy that takes place when a system undergoes an infinitesimal reversible process from an initial equilibrium state to a final equilibrium state. We have

$$dH = dU + P\,dV + V\,dP.$$

But

$$\text{d}Q = dU + P\,dV;$$

therefore

$$dH = \text{d}Q + V\,dP.$$

Dividing both sides by dT,

$$\frac{dH}{dT} = \frac{\text{d}Q}{dT} + V\frac{dP}{dT},$$

and at constant P,

$$\left(\frac{\partial H}{\partial T}\right)_P = \left(\frac{dQ}{dT}\right)_P = C_p \qquad \text{(property 1)}.$$

Since

$$dH = dQ + V\,dP,$$

the change in enthalpy during an isobaric process is equal to the heat that is transferred. That is,

$$\left.\begin{array}{l} H_2 - H_1 = Q, \\[2mm] \text{or} \qquad H_2 - H_1 = \displaystyle\int_1^2 C_P\,dT \end{array}\right\} \qquad \text{(isobaric) (property 2)}.$$

The change in enthalpy of a system undergoing an adiabatic process has an interesting graphical interpretation. Since

$$dH = dQ + V\,dP,$$

then, for an adiabatic process,

$$H_2 - H_1 = \int_1^2 V\,dP \qquad \text{(adiabatic) (property 3)}.$$

The above integral represents the area to the left of an adiabatic curve on a PV diagram. This area does *not* represent work.

One of the most interesting properties of the enthalpy function is in connection with a *throttling process*. Imagine a cylinder thermally insulated and equipped with two nonconducting pistons on opposite sides of a porous wall, as shown in Fig. 10.1a. The wall, shaded in horizontal lines, is a porous plug, a narrow constriction, or a series of small holes. Between the left-hand piston and the wall there is a gas at a pressure P_1 and a volume V_1; and since the right-hand piston is against

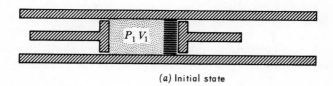

(a) Initial state

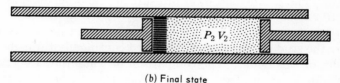

(b) Final state

Fig. 10.1   Throttling process.

the wall, any gas being thus prevented from seeping through, the initial state of the gas is an equilibrium state. Now imagine moving both pistons simultaneously in such a way that a *constant pressure* P_1 is maintained on the left-hand side of the wall and a constant lower pressure P_2 is maintained on the right-hand side. After all the gas has seeped through the porous wall, the final equilibrium state of the system will be as shown in Fig. 10.1*b*. Such a process is a throttling process.

A throttling process is obviously an irreversible one since the gas passes through nonequilibrium states on its way from the initial equilibrium state to its final equilibrium state. These nonequilibrium states cannot be described by thermodynamic coordinates, but an interesting conclusion can be drawn about the initial and final equilibrium states. Applying the first law to the throttling process,

$$Q = U_2 - U_1 + W,$$

we have

$$Q = 0$$

and

$$W = \int_0^{V_2} P_2 \, dV + \int_{V_1}^0 P_1 \, dV.$$

Since both pressures remain constant,

$$W = P_2 V_2 - P_1 V_1.$$

The above expression is sometimes called *flow work*, since it represents the work necessary to keep the gas flowing. Therefore

$$0 = U_2 - U_1 + P_2 V_2 - P_1 V_1,$$

or

$$U_2 + P_1 V_1 = U_2 + P_2 V_2,$$

and finally,

$$H_1 = H_2 \qquad \text{(throttling process) (property 4)}.$$

In a throttling process, therefore, the initial and final enthalpies are equal. One is not entitled to say that the enthalpy remains constant, since one cannot speak of the enthalpy of a system that is passing through such nonequilibrium states. In plotting a throttling process on any diagram, the initial and final equilibrium states may be represented by points. The intermediate states, however, cannot be plotted.

A continuous throttling process may be achieved by a pump that maintains a constant high pressure on one side of a constriction or porous wall and a constant lower pressure on the other side, as shown in Fig. 10.2.

The four properties of the enthalpy function must be clearly understood by the student, for they will be used continually throughout the remainder of this book. The comparison of the internal energy and the enthalpy given in Table 10.1 will help the student to remember these properties.

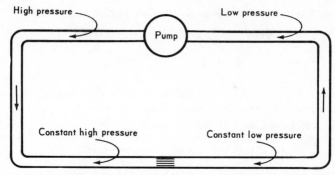

Fig. 10.2   Apparatus for performing a continuous throttling process.

Table 10.1/ Comparison of U and H

Internal energy U	Enthalpy H
In general: $dU = \text{d}Q - P\,dV$ $\left(\dfrac{\partial U}{\partial T}\right)_V = C_V$	In general: $dH = \text{d}Q + V\,dP$ $\left(\dfrac{\partial H}{\partial T}\right)_P = C_P$
Isochoric process: $U_2 - U_1 = Q$ $U_2 - U_1 = \displaystyle\int_1^2 C_V\,dT$	Isobaric process: $H_2 - H_1 = Q$ $H_2 - H_1 = \displaystyle\int_1^2 C_P\,dT$
Adiabatic process: $U_2 - U_1 = -\displaystyle\int_1^2 P\,dV$	Adiabatic process: $H_2 - H_1 = \displaystyle\int_1^2 V\,dP$
Free expansion: $U_1 = U_2$	Throttling process: $H_1 = H_2$
For an ideal gas: $U = \int C_V\,dT + \text{const}$	For an ideal gas: $H = \int C_P\,dT + \text{const}$

10.2/ Helmholtz Function

The Helmholtz function is defined as

$$\boxed{A = U - TS.}$$

For an infinitesimal reversible process,

$$dA = dU - T\,dS - S\,dT$$

and

$$dU = \text{d}Q - P\,dV = T\,dS - P\,dV.$$

Hence

$$\boxed{dA = -P\,dV - S\,dT.}$$

From this if follows: (1) For a *reversible isothermal process,*

$$dA = -P \, dV,$$

or
$$A_2 - A_1 = - \int_1^2 P \, dV.$$

Hence the change of the Helmholtz function during a reversible isothermal process equals the work done *on* the system.   (2) For a *reversible, isothermal, and isochoric process,*

$$dA = 0 \qquad \text{and} \qquad A = \text{const.}$$

These properties are of interest in chemistry and are useful in considering chemical reactions that take place isothermally and isochorically. The main importance, however, of the Helmholtz function is its use in statistical mechanics, where it plays a fundamental role.   It is possible by statistical methods to calculate the Helmholtz function of some substances as a function of T and V.   The equation of state of a substance is then obtained from the relationship

$$P = - \left(\frac{\partial A}{\partial V} \right)_T$$

and the entropy from

$$S = - \left(\frac{\partial A}{\partial T} \right)_V.$$

10.3/ Gibbs Function

The Gibbs function is defined as

$$\boxed{G = H - TS.}$$

For an infinitesimal reversible process,

$$dG = dH - T \, dS - S \, dT$$

and
$$dH = đQ + V \, dP = T \, dS + V \, dP;$$

whence
$$\boxed{dG = V \, dP - S \, dT.}$$

In the case of a *reversible, isothermal, isobaric process,*

$$dG = 0 \qquad \text{and} \qquad G = \text{const.}$$

This is a particularly important result in connection with processes involving a change of phase.   Sublimation, fusion, and vaporization take place isothermally and isobarically, and can be conceived of as occurring reversibly. Hence, during such processes, the Gibbs function of the system remains constant. If we denote by the symbols G', G'', and G''' the molar Gibbs functions of a saturated solid, saturated liquid, and saturated vapor, respectively, the equation of the fusion curve is

$$G' = G'',$$

the equation of the vaporization curve is

$$G'' = G''',$$

and the equation of the sublimation curve is

$$G' = G'''.$$

At the triple point two equations hold simultaneously, namely,

$$G' = G'' = G'''.$$

All the G's can be regarded as functions of P and T only, and hence the two equations above serve to determine the P and the T of the triple point uniquely.

The Gibbs function is of the utmost importance in chemical thermodynamics since chemical reactions can be conceived of as taking place at constant P and T.

10.4/ Names and Symbols for the Thermodynamic Functions

No science has developed in neat, logical steps. The history of any science shows periods of tremendous growth in which many research workers throughout the world try, discard, and try again new ideas, new definitions, and new symbols. In thermodynamics this situation has been aggravated by the fact that many workers have borne in mind only the particular needs of a special branch of thermodynamics, such as engineering or chemical thermodynamics, without attempting to adopt a point of view suitable for all branches. It is not surprising, therefore, that there are many different names and symbols for the thermodynamic functions.

Practically all authors of modern textbooks are agreed upon the name entropy and the symbol S. For the internal-energy function both E and U are used, but U has become more common. The symbol for enthalpy is almost invariably H, but there are three other names that are widely used: heat content, total heat, and heat function. It is the opinion of the authors that to designate this function by any expression involving the word "heat" is objectionable, for two reasons: (1) The beginner is apt to receive the erroneous impression that heat, in general, is a function or that a body has a certain amount of heat in it. (2) The change in enthalpy is the heat transferred *only for an isobaric process.*

If, for this reason, the enthalpy is called the "heat function at constant pressure," then, to be consistent, we should have to call U the "heat function for constant volume." Since, however, the change in internal energy is equal to the work done in an adiabatic process, we should then have as an alternative name for internal energy the "adiabatic work function." Although the idea of assigning to a function a name that suggests a property of the function is an appealing one, the fact remains that the thermodynamic functions have *many* properties, and it is not satisfactory to choose one property for the purpose of nomenclature.

The situation with regard to the Helmholtz and Gibbs functions is really serious and has led to great confusion and error in calculations, as is shown in the accompanying table.

	Helmholtz function	Gibbs function
Most American chemists	Work function A	Free energy F
Many physicists	Free energy F	Thermodynamic potential G
Compromise suggested by several symbols committees	Helmholtz function A	Gibbs function G

Space is lacking to discuss the arguments for and against these names and symbols. The deplorable fact remains that many scientists and engineers use the same name and the same symbol for two entirely different functions. The only feasible solution, in the opinion of the authors, is to compromise by selecting unambiguous, noncommittal names and symbols, giving up entirely the expression "free energy" and the symbol F.

10.5/ Two Mathematical Theorems

Theorem 1

If a relation exists among x, y, and z, we may imagine z expressed as a function of x and y; whence

$$dz = \left(\frac{\partial z}{\partial x}\right)_y dx + \left(\frac{\partial z}{\partial y}\right)_x dy.$$

If we let

$$M = \left(\frac{\partial z}{\partial x}\right)_y \quad \text{and} \quad N = \left(\frac{\partial z}{\partial y}\right)_x,$$

then

$$dz = M\,dx + N\,dy,$$

where z, M, and N are all functions of x and y. Differentiating M

partially with respect to y and N with respect to x, we get

$$\left(\frac{\partial M}{\partial y}\right)_x = \frac{\partial^2 z}{\partial x \, \partial y},$$

$$\left(\frac{\partial N}{\partial x}\right)_y = \frac{\partial^2 z}{\partial y \, \partial x}.$$

Since the two second derivatives on the right are equal, it follows that

$$\boxed{\left(\frac{\partial M}{\partial y}\right)_x = \left(\frac{\partial N}{\partial x}\right)_y.}$$

This is known as the *condition for an exact differential*.

Theorem 2

If a quantity f is a function of x, y, and z and a relation exists among x, y, and z, then f may be regarded as a function of *any two* of x, y, and z. Similarly, any one of x, y, and z may be considered to be a function of f and one other of x, y, and z. Thus, regarding x to be a function of f and y,

$$dx = \left(\frac{\partial x}{\partial f}\right)_y df + \left(\frac{\partial x}{\partial y}\right)_f dy.$$

Considering y to be a function of f and z,

$$dy = \left(\frac{\partial y}{\partial f}\right)_z df + \left(\frac{\partial y}{\partial z}\right)_f dz.$$

Substituting this expression for dy in the preceding equation, we get

$$dx = \left[\left(\frac{\partial x}{\partial f}\right)_y + \left(\frac{\partial x}{\partial y}\right)_f \left(\frac{\partial y}{\partial f}\right)_z\right] df + \left[\left(\frac{\partial x}{\partial y}\right)_f \left(\frac{\partial y}{\partial z}\right)_f\right] dz.$$

But

$$dx = \left(\frac{\partial x}{\partial f}\right)_z df + \left(\frac{\partial x}{\partial z}\right)_f dz.$$

Equating the dz terms of the last two equations, we get

$$\boxed{\begin{aligned} \left(\frac{\partial x}{\partial y}\right)_f \left(\frac{\partial y}{\partial z}\right)_f &= \left(\frac{\partial x}{\partial z}\right)_f, \\ \left(\frac{\partial x}{\partial y}\right)_f \left(\frac{\partial y}{\partial z}\right)_f \left(\frac{\partial z}{\partial x}\right)_f &= 1. \end{aligned}}$$

10.6/ Maxwell's Equations

A PVT system has been defined as any system of constant mass whose equilibrium states are describable by the three thermodynamic coordinates P, V, and T. In describing the behavior of such a system it is convenient to make use of the four functions:

1. The internal energy U.
2. The enthalpy $H = U + PV$.
3. The Helmholtz function $A = U - TS$.
4. The Gibbs function $G = H - TS$.

Any one of these may be regarded as a function of *any two* of P, V, and T. Suppose, for example, that both U and S are expressed as functions of V and T, thus:

$$U = \text{function of } (V,T)$$
and
$$S = \text{function of } (V,T).$$

The second equation may be imagined to be solved for T in terms of S and V; substituting this value of T in the first equation, we should then have

$$U = \text{function of } (S,V).$$

Consequently, we may go further and say that any one of the eight quantities P, V, T, S, U, H, A, and G may be expressed as a function of *any two others*.

Now imagine a PVT system undergoing an infinitesimal reversible process from one equilibrium state to another.

1. The internal energy changes by an amount

$$dU = \text{d}Q - P\,dV$$
$$= T\,dS - P\,dV,$$

where U, T, and P are all imagined to be functions of S and V.

2. The enthalpy changes by an amount

$$dH = dU + P\,dV + V\,dP$$
$$= T\,dS + V\,dP,$$

where H, T, and V are all imagined to be functions of S and P.

3. The Helmholtz function changes by an amount

$$dA = dU - T\,dS - S\,dT$$
$$= -P\,dV - S\,dT,$$

where A, P, and S are all imagined to be functions of V and T.

4. The Gibbs function changes by an amount

$$dG = dH - T\,dS - S\,dT$$
$$= V\,dP - S\,dT,$$

where G, V, and S are all imagined to be functions of P and T.

Since U, H, A, and G are actual functions, their differentials are exact differentials of the type

$$dz = M\,dx + N\,dy,$$

where z, M, and N are all functions of x and y. Therefore

$$\left(\frac{\partial \bar{M}}{\partial y}\right)_x = \left(\frac{\partial N}{\partial x}\right)_y.$$

Applying this result to the four exact differentials dU, dH, dA, and dG,

1. $dU = T\,dS - P\,dV;$ hence $\left(\dfrac{\partial T}{\partial V}\right)_S = -\left(\dfrac{\partial P}{\partial S}\right)_V;$

2. $dH = T\,dS + V\,dP;$ hence $\left(\dfrac{\partial T}{\partial P}\right)_S = \left(\dfrac{\partial V}{\partial S}\right)_P;$

3. $dA = -P\,dV - S\,dT;$ hence $\left(\dfrac{\partial P}{\partial T}\right)_V = \left(\dfrac{\partial S}{\partial V}\right)_T;$

4. $dG = V\,dP - S\,dT;$ hence $\left(\dfrac{\partial V}{\partial T}\right)_P = -\left(\dfrac{\partial S}{\partial P}\right)_T.$

The four equations on the right are known as *Maxwell's equations.* It is not necessary for the student to memorize them since they are so easily derived. Maxwell's equations do not refer to a process, but merely express relations that hold at any equilibrium state of a PVT system.

10.7/ First $T\,dS$ Equation

The entropy of a PVT system can be imagined as a function of T and V; whence

$$dS = \left(\frac{\partial S}{\partial T}\right)_V dT + \left(\frac{\partial S}{\partial V}\right)_T dV$$

and

$$T\,dS = T\left(\frac{\partial S}{\partial T}\right)_V dT + T\left(\frac{\partial S}{\partial V}\right)_T dV.$$

For a reversible process,

$$\dbar Q = T\,dS \qquad \text{and} \qquad \frac{\dbar Q}{dT} = T\frac{dS}{dT}.$$

At constant volume,

$$\left(\frac{\dbar Q}{dT}\right)_V = C_V = T\left(\frac{\partial S}{\partial T}\right)_V,$$

or

$$T\left(\frac{\partial S}{\partial T}\right)_V = C_V,$$

and from Maxwell's third equation,

$$\left(\frac{\partial S}{\partial V}\right)_T = \left(\frac{\partial P}{\partial T}\right)_V;$$

whence

$$T\, dS = C_V\, dT + T\left(\frac{\partial P}{\partial T}\right)_V dV.$$

We shall call the above equation the *first T dS equation*.   It is useful in a variety of ways.

Consider, for example, the reversible isothermal compression of 1 mole of a gas from an initial volume V_1 to a final volume V_2.   Since the temperature is constant, the entropy change at constant T is given by

$$\Delta S_T = \int_{V_1}^{V_2} \left(\frac{\partial P}{\partial T}\right)_V dV.$$

If the pressures encountered in the process are not too high, we may use the virial equation truncated to the first two terms as our equation of state.   Thus

$$\frac{PV}{RT} = 1 + \frac{B}{V},$$

or

$$P = \frac{RT}{V} + \frac{BRT}{V^2}.$$

By differentiation, recalling that B is a function of T,

$$\left(\frac{\partial P}{\partial T}\right)_V = \frac{R}{V} + \frac{R}{V^2}\left(B + T\frac{dB}{dT}\right).$$

Therefore

$$\Delta S_T = R\int_{V_1}^{V_2}\frac{dV}{V} + R\left(B + T\frac{dB}{dT}\right)\int_{V_1}^{V_2}\frac{dV}{V^2},$$

or

$$\Delta S_T = R\ln\frac{V_2}{V_1} + R\left(B + T\frac{dB}{dT}\right)\left(\frac{1}{V_1} - \frac{1}{V_2}\right).$$

10.8/ Second T dS Equation

If the entropy of a PVT system is regarded as a function of T and P, then

$$dS = \left(\frac{\partial S}{\partial T}\right)_P dT + \left(\frac{\partial S}{\partial P}\right)_T dP$$

and

$$T\, dS = T\left(\frac{\partial S}{\partial T}\right)_P dT + T\left(\frac{\partial S}{\partial P}\right)_T dP.$$

Since, as before,

$$\frac{dQ}{dT} = T\frac{dS}{dT},$$

then at constant pressure

$$\left(\frac{dQ}{dT}\right)_P = C_P = T\left(\frac{\partial S}{\partial T}\right)_P.$$

Therefore

$$T\left(\frac{\partial S}{\partial T}\right)_P = C_P,$$

and from Maxwell's fourth equation,

$$\left(\frac{\partial S}{\partial P}\right)_T = -\left(\frac{\partial V}{\partial T}\right)_P;$$

whence

$$T\,dS = C_P\,dT - T\left(\frac{\partial V}{\partial T}\right)_P dP.$$

We shall call the above equation the *second T dS equation*. Two important applications follow.

1. Reversible Isothermal Change of Pressure

When T is constant,

$$T\,dS = -T\left(\frac{\partial V}{\partial T}\right)_P dP$$

and

$$Q = -T\int\left(\frac{\partial V}{\partial T}\right)_P dP.$$

Remembering that the coefficient of volume expansion is

$$\beta = \frac{1}{V}\left(\frac{\partial V}{\partial T}\right)_P,$$

we obtain

$$Q = -T\int V\beta\,dP,$$

which can be integrated when the dependence of V and β on the pressure is known.   In the case of a solid or liquid, neither V nor β is very sensitive to a change in pressure.   For example, in the case of mercury, Bridgman found that as the pressure was increased by 1,000 atm at 0°C, the volume of 1 gm mole of mercury changed from 14.72 to 14.67 cm^3, a change of only 0.34 percent; and the volume expansivity changed from 181×10^{-6} °C^{-1} to 174×10^{-6} °C^{-1}, a 4 percent change.   The volume and the expansivity of most solids and liquids behave similarly, and therefore V and β may be taken out from under the integral sign and replaced by average values $\langle V\rangle$ and $\langle\beta\rangle$.   (The signs $\langle\ \rangle$ around a quantity indicate an average value.)   We have, then,

$$Q = -T\langle V\rangle\langle\beta\rangle\int_{P_1}^{P_2} dP,$$

or

$$Q = -T\langle V\rangle\langle\beta\rangle(P_2 - P_1).$$

It is seen from this result that, as the pressure is increased isothermally, heat will flow *out* if $\langle\beta\rangle$ is positive, but, for a substance with a negative expansivity (such as water between 0 and 4°C), an isothermal increase of pressure causes an absorption of heat.

If the pressure of 1 gm mole of mercury at 0°C and 1 atm is increased reversibly and isothermally by 1,000 atm, the following values may be used in the calculation of the heat transferred:

$$T = 273°K,$$
$$\langle V \rangle = 14.7 \text{ cm}^3/\text{gm mole},$$
$$\langle \beta \rangle = 178 \times 10^{-6} °K^{-1},$$
$$P_2 - P_1 = 1{,}000 \text{ atm} = 1.013 \times 10^9 \text{ dynes/cm}^2.$$

Hence

$$Q = - \frac{273°K \times 14.7 \text{ cm}^3/\text{gm mole} \times 178 \times 10^{-6} °K^{-1} \times 1{,}000 \text{ atm}}{41.292 \text{ cm}^3 \cdot \text{atm/cal}}$$
$$= -17.3 \text{ cal/gm mole}.$$

It is interesting to compare the heat liberated with the work done during the compression

$$W = \int P \, dV;$$

but at constant temperature

$$dV = \left(\frac{\partial V}{\partial P} \right)_T dP$$

and

$$W = \int \left(\frac{\partial V}{\partial P} \right)_T P \, dP.$$

Remembering that the isothermal compressibility is

$$k = - \frac{1}{V} \left(\frac{\partial V}{\partial P} \right)_T,$$

then

$$W = - \int_{P_1}^{P_2} VkP \, dP.$$

The isothermal compressibility is also fairly insensitive to a change of pressure. Bridgman showed that the compressibility of mercury at 0°C changed from 3.88×10^{-12} to 3.79×10^{-12} cm^2/dyne (a 2 percent change) as the pressure was increased by 1,000 atm. We may therefore again replace V and k by average values and obtain

$$W = - \frac{\langle V \rangle \langle k \rangle}{2} (P_2{}^2 - P_1{}^2).$$

Taking for mercury

$$\langle k \rangle = 3.84 \times 10^{-12} \text{ cm}^2/\text{dyne}$$

and noting that

$$P_2{}^2 - P_1{}^2 \cong P_2{}^2 = (1{,}000 \text{ atm})^2 (1.013 \times 10^6 \text{ dynes/cm}^2 \cdot \text{atm})^2$$
$$= 1.03 \times 10^{18} \text{ (dynes/cm}^2)^2,$$

we get

$$W = - \frac{(14.7 \text{ cm}^3/\text{gm mole})(3.84 \times 10^{-12} \text{ cm}^2/\text{dyne})(1.03 \times 10^{18} \text{ dynes}^2/\text{cm}^4)}{(2)(4.184 \times 10^7) \text{ergs/cal}}$$
$$= - \frac{5.76 \times 10^7 \text{ dyne} \cdot \text{cm/gm mole}}{8.368 \times 10^7 \text{ ergs/cal}}$$
$$= -0.687 \text{ cal/gm mole}.$$

It is seen, therefore, that when the pressure on a gram mole of mercury at 0°C is increased by 1,000 atm, 17.3 cal of heat is liberated but only 0.687 cal of work is done! The extra amount of heat comes, of course, from the store of internal energy, which has changed by an amount

$$U_2 - U_1 = Q - W$$
$$= -17.3 \text{ cal/gm mole} + 0.687 \text{ cal/gm mole}$$
$$= -16.6 \text{ cal/gm mole.}$$

A similar result is obtained in the case of any substance with a positive expansivity. For a substance with a negative expansivity, heat is absorbed and the internal energy is increased.

2. Reversible Adiabatic Change of Pressure

Since the entropy remains constant,

$$T \, dS = 0 = C_P \, dT - T \left(\frac{\partial V}{\partial T} \right)_P dP,$$

or

$$dT = \frac{T}{C_P} \left(\frac{\partial V}{\partial T} \right)_P dP$$
$$= \frac{TV\beta}{C_P} \, dP.$$

In the case of a solid or liquid, an increase of pressure of as much as 1,000 atm produces only a small temperature change. Also, experiment shows that C_P hardly changes even for an increase of 10,000 atm. The above equation, therefore, when applied to a solid or a liquid, may be written

$$\Delta T = \frac{T \langle V \rangle \langle \beta \rangle}{\langle C_P \rangle} (P_2 - P_1).$$

It is clear from the above that an adiabatic increase of pressure will produce an increase of temperature in any substance with a positive expansivity and a decrease in temperature in a substance with a negative expansivity.

If the pressure on a mole of mercury at 0°C is increased isentropically by 1,000 atm, the mean heat capacity $\langle C_P \rangle$ is 6.69 cal/gm mole · °K and the temperature change will be

$$\Delta T = \frac{273°\text{K} \times 14.7 \text{ cm}^3/\text{gm mole} \times 178 \times 10^{-6} \text{ °K}^{-1} \times 1,000 \text{ atm}}{6.69 \text{ cal/gm mole} \cdot °\text{C} \times 41.292 \text{ cm}^3 \cdot \text{atm/cal}}$$
$$= 2.58°\text{C.}$$

10.9/ Energy Equation

If a PVT system undergoes an infinitesimal reversible process between two equilibrium states, the change of internal energy is

$$dU = T \, dS - P \, dV,$$

and by the first $T\,dS$ equation

$$T\,dS = C_V\,dT + T\left(\frac{\partial P}{\partial T}\right)_V dV.$$

Combining both equations, we get

$$dU = C_V\,dT + \left[T\left(\frac{\partial P}{\partial T}\right)_V - P\right]dV,$$

where U is imagined as a function of T and V. But

$$dU = \left(\frac{\partial U}{\partial T}\right)_V dT + \left(\frac{\partial U}{\partial V}\right)_T dV,$$

and consequently

$$\boxed{\left(\frac{\partial U}{\partial V}\right)_T = T\left(\frac{\partial P}{\partial T}\right)_V - P.} \quad \text{and } C_V = \left(\frac{\partial U}{\partial T}\right)_V$$

The above equation, known as the *energy equation*, enables us to draw conclusions about the internal energy of any PVT system whose equation of state is known. For example:

1. Ideal Gas

$$P = \frac{RT}{V},$$

$$\left(\frac{\partial P}{\partial T}\right)_V = \frac{R}{V},$$

and
$$\left(\frac{\partial U}{\partial V}\right)_T = T\frac{R}{V} - P = 0.$$

Therefore U does not depend on V but is a function of T only.

2. Real Gas at Low to Moderate Pressure: Two-term Virial Equation

$$P = \frac{RT}{V} + \frac{BRT}{V^2},$$

$$\left(\frac{\partial P}{\partial T}\right)_V = \frac{R}{V} + \frac{R}{V^2}\left(B + T\frac{dB}{dT}\right),$$

and

$$\left(\frac{\partial U}{\partial V}\right)_T = \frac{RT}{V} + \frac{RT}{V^2}\left(B + T\frac{dB}{dT}\right) - \frac{RT}{V} - \frac{BRT}{V^2}$$

$$= \frac{RT^2}{V^2}\frac{dB}{dT}.$$

Since dB/dT is known from experiment to be positive for most gases at normal temperatures, it is clear that the internal energy of a real gas usually increases as the volume increases. It is interesting to note that, as the pressure approaches zero, the volume approaches infinity. Thus, for a real gas,

$$\lim_{P \to 0} \left(\frac{\partial U}{\partial V} \right)_T = 0.$$

It does *not* follow that the limiting value of $(\partial U / \partial P)_T$ is zero. This derivative is given by

$$\left(\frac{\partial U}{\partial P} \right)_T = \frac{(\partial U / \partial V)_T}{(\partial P / \partial V)_T}.$$

Differentiation of the virial equation gives

$$\left(\frac{\partial P}{\partial V} \right)_T = -\frac{RT}{V^2} - \frac{2BRT}{V^3}.$$

From this we have

$$\left(\frac{\partial U}{\partial P} \right)_T = \frac{-T(dB/dT)}{1 + 2B/V}.$$

Thus

$$\lim_{P \to 0} \left(\frac{\partial U}{\partial P} \right)_T = -T \frac{dB}{dT},$$

which is finite. This result is in accord with the experimental results of Rossini and Frandsen as described in Sec. 5.2.

10.10/ Difference in Heat Capacities

Equating the first and second $T\,dS$ equations,

$$C_P\,dT - T \left(\frac{\partial V}{\partial T} \right)_P dP = C_V\,dT + T \left(\frac{\partial P}{\partial T} \right)_V dV.$$

Solving for dT,

$$dT = \frac{T \left(\frac{\partial P}{\partial T} \right)_V}{C_P - C_V}\,dV + \frac{T \left(\frac{\partial V}{\partial T} \right)_P}{C_P - C_V}\,dP.$$

But

$$dT = \left(\frac{\partial T}{\partial V} \right)_P dV + \left(\frac{\partial T}{\partial P} \right)_V dP.$$

Therefore

$$\left(\frac{\partial T}{\partial V} \right)_P = \frac{T \left(\frac{\partial P}{\partial T} \right)_V}{C_P - C_V}$$

and

$$\left(\frac{\partial T}{\partial P} \right)_V = \frac{T \left(\frac{\partial V}{\partial T} \right)_P}{C_P - C_V}.$$

Both the above equations yield the result that

$$C_P - C_V = T \left(\frac{\partial V}{\partial T}\right)_P \left(\frac{\partial P}{\partial T}\right)_V.$$

It was shown in Art. 2.4 that

$$\left(\frac{\partial P}{\partial T}\right)_V = - \left(\frac{\partial V}{\partial T}\right)_P \left(\frac{\partial P}{\partial V}\right)_T.$$

Substituting the above value of $(\partial P/\partial T)_V$ in the equation just derived for the difference in the heat capacities, we obtain, finally,

$$C_P - C_V = -T \left(\frac{\partial V}{\partial T}\right)_P^2 \left(\frac{\partial P}{\partial V}\right)_T.$$

This is one of the important equations of thermodynamics and shows that:

1. Since $(\partial P/\partial V)_T$ is always negative for all known substances and $(\partial V/\partial T)_P{}^2$ must be positive, then $C_P - C_V$ can never be negative, or C_P can never be less than C_V.
2. As $T \rightarrow 0$, $C_P \rightarrow C_V$, or *at the absolute zero the two heat capacities are equal.*
3. $C_P = C_V$ when $(\partial V/\partial T)_P = 0$. For example, at 4°C, at which the density of water is a maximum, $C_P = C_V$.

Laboratory measurements of the heat capacity of solids and liquids usually take place at constant pressure and therefore yield values of C_P. It would be extremely difficult to measure with any degree of accuracy the C_V of a solid or liquid. Values of C_V, however, must be known for purposes of comparison with theory. The equation for the difference in the heat capacities is very useful in calculating C_V in terms of C_P and other measurable quantities. Remembering that

$$\beta = \frac{1}{V} \left(\frac{\partial V}{\partial T}\right)_P \qquad \text{and} \qquad k = - \frac{1}{V} \left(\frac{\partial V}{\partial P}\right)_T,$$

we may write the equation in the form

$$C_P - C_V = \frac{TV \left[\frac{1}{V}\left(\frac{\partial V}{\partial T}\right)_P\right]^2}{-\frac{1}{V}\left(\frac{\partial V}{\partial P}\right)_T},$$

$$C_P - C_V = \frac{TV\beta^2}{k}.$$

As an example of the use of the above equation, let us calculate the molar heat capacity at constant volume of mercury at 0°C and 1 atm pressure.   From experiment we have:

$$C_P = 6.69 \text{ cal/gm mole} \cdot {}^\circ\text{K},$$
$$T = 273^\circ\text{K},$$
$$V = 14.72 \text{ cm}^3/\text{gm mole},$$
$$\beta = 181 \times 10^{-6} \, {}^\circ\text{K}^{-1},$$
$$k = 3.88 \times 10^{-12} \text{ cm}^2/\text{dyne};$$

whence

$$C_P - C_V = \frac{273^\circ\text{K} \times 14.72 \text{ cm}^3/\text{gm mole} \times (181)^2 \times 10^{-12} \, {}^\circ\text{K}^{-2}}{3.88 \times 10^{-12} \text{ cm}^2/\text{dyne}}$$
$$= 3.39 \times 10^7 \text{ ergs/gm mole} \cdot {}^\circ\text{K}$$

or

$$C_P - C_V = \frac{3.39 \times 10^7 \text{ ergs/gm mole} \cdot {}^\circ\text{K}}{4.19 \times 10^7 \text{ ergs/cal}}$$
$$= 0.809 \text{ cal/gm mole} \cdot {}^\circ\text{K}$$

and

$$C_V = (6.69 - 0.809) \text{ cal/gm mole} \cdot {}^\circ\text{K}$$
$$= 5.88 \text{ cal/gm mole} \cdot {}^\circ\text{K}.$$

Finally, $\gamma = \dfrac{C_P}{C_V} = \dfrac{6.69}{5.88} = 1.14.$

10.11/ Ratio of Heat Capacities

The two $T\,dS$ equations are

$$T\,dS = C_P\,dT - T\left(\frac{\partial V}{\partial T}\right)_P dP,$$
$$T\,dS = C_V\,dT + T\left(\frac{\partial P}{\partial T}\right)_V dV.$$

At constant S,

$$C_P\,dT_S = T\left(\frac{\partial V}{\partial T}\right)_P dP_S,$$
$$C_V\,dT_S = -T\left(\frac{\partial P}{\partial T}\right)_V dV_S.$$

Dividing, $\dfrac{C_P}{C_V} = -\left[\dfrac{\left(\dfrac{\partial V}{\partial T}\right)_P}{\left(\dfrac{\partial P}{\partial T}\right)_V}\right]\left(\dfrac{\partial P}{\partial V}\right)_S.$

But the quantity in brackets is equal to

$$-\left(\frac{\partial V}{\partial P}\right)_T.$$

Therefore $\boxed{\dfrac{C_P}{C_V} = \dfrac{(\partial P/\partial V)_S}{(\partial P/\partial V)_T}.}$

The *adiabatic compressibility* is defined as

$$k_S = -\frac{1}{V}\left(\frac{\partial V}{\partial P}\right)_S;$$

and, as usual,

$$k = -\frac{1}{V}\left(\frac{\partial V}{\partial P}\right)_T.$$

We have, therefore,

$$\frac{C_P}{C_V} = \gamma = \frac{k}{k_S},$$

from which k_S may be calculated. In the case of mercury at 0°C and 1 atm pressure,

$$\gamma = 1.14,$$
$$k = 3.88 \times 10^{-12} \text{ cm}^2/\text{dyne};$$

whence

$$k_S = \frac{3.88 \times 10^{-12} \text{ cm}^2/\text{dyne}}{1.14}$$
$$= 3.41 \times 10^{-12} \text{ cm}^2/\text{dyne}$$
$$= 3.46 \times 10^{-6} \text{ atm}^{-1}.$$

Problems

10.1 Nitrogen gas at 25°C and 2 atm pressure passes through a partly opened valve (Joule-Kelvin expansion) in an insulated pipe. The pressure on the downstream side of the valve is 1 atm. If nitrogen under these conditions behaves as an ideal gas:

(*a*) What is the temperature on the downstream side?

(*b*) What is the change in entropy accompanying the passage of 1 gm mole of gas through the valve?

(*c*) Is the process reversible?

10.2 (*a*) Derive the equations

$$\left(\frac{\partial H}{\partial P}\right)_T = V - T\left(\frac{\partial V}{\partial T}\right)_P$$
$$= V(1 - \beta T)$$
$$= \frac{-RT^2}{P}\left(\frac{\partial Z}{\partial T}\right)_P.$$

(*b*) For an ideal gas, show H to be a function of temperature only by proving that

$$\left(\frac{\partial H}{\partial P}\right)_T = 0.$$

(*c*) For a gas which obeys the equation of state

$$Z = \frac{PV}{RT} = 1 + B'P,$$

show that

$$\left(\frac{\partial H}{\partial P}\right)_T = -RT^2\frac{dB'}{dT}.$$

(d) For a gas which obeys the equation of state

$$Z = \frac{PV}{RT} = 1 + \frac{B}{V},$$

show that
$$\left(\frac{\partial H}{\partial P}\right)_T = \frac{B - T(dB/dT)}{1 + 2B/V}.$$

10.3 For a gas which obeys the equation of state

$$Z = \frac{PV}{RT} = 1 + B'P,$$

show that
$$\left(\frac{\partial S}{\partial P}\right)_T = -\frac{R}{P} - R\left(B' + T\frac{dB'}{dT}\right).$$

Compare this result with that for an ideal gas.

10.4 Let us define an enthalpy deviation and an entropy deviation for a real gas by

$$\Delta H' = H^{id} - H \qquad \text{and} \qquad \Delta S' = S^{id} - S,$$

where H^{id} and S^{id} are values of the enthalpy and entropy that the gas would have if it were an ideal gas at the temperature and pressure of the system.

(a) Using the results of Probs. 10.2c and 10.3 for a gas which obeys the equation of state

$$Z = \frac{PV}{RT} = 1 + B'P,$$

show that
$$\Delta H' = RPT^2 \frac{dB'}{dT}$$

and
$$\Delta S' = RP\left(B' + T\frac{dB'}{dT}\right).$$

(b) Values of B' as a function of T and values of the vapor pressure as a function of T for n-hexane (C_6H_{14}) are given in the following table:

T, °K	B', atm^{-1}	Vapor pressure, atm
313	−0.0661	0.383
323	−0.0589	0.548
333	−0.0529	0.767
343	−0.0477	1.054
353	−0.0428	1.424
363	−0.0388	1.89
373	−0.0350	2.47

Prepare plots of $\Delta H'$ and $\Delta S'$ for n-hexane at its vapor pressure versus temperature.

(c) If $B' = B/RT$, show that

$$Z = 1 + \frac{BP}{RT},$$

$$\Delta H' = PT\left(\frac{dB}{dT} - \frac{B}{T}\right),$$

$$\Delta S' = P\frac{dB}{dT}.$$

10.5 When 1 gm of solid naphthalene ($C_{10}H_8$) is burned in oxygen saturated with water vapor at constant volume in a bomb calorimeter, 9620 cal are evolved at 25°C. Note that the water formed during the combustion condenses but the CO_2 formed is a gas. If this combustion process occurred at constant pressure instead of at constant volume at 25°C, what would be the heat evolved? Oxygen and carbon dioxide may be assumed to be ideal gases.

10.6 The latent heat of vaporization of water at 212°F and 1 atm is 970.3 Btu/lb$_m$. What is ΔH for the vaporization of 1 lb$_m$ of water at these conditions? If the volume change of vaporization is 26.81 ft^3/lb$_m$, what is ΔU for the vaporization process?

10.7 A gas at high pressure flows through a duct; a thermometer in the duct reads 200°K. A small amount of gas is bled out of this duct through an insulated throttle valve open to the atmosphere. The temperature of the gas leaving the throttle is measured as 180°K. What is the pressure of the gas in the high-pressure duct?

The gas obeys the equation of state

$$\frac{PV}{RT} = 1 + \left(b - \frac{a}{T}\right)\frac{P}{RT},$$

where $b = 20$ cm^3/gm mole,
$a = 40,000$ (°K)(cm^3/gm mole).

The molar heat capacity of the gas at low pressure is

$$C_P = 10 + 0.02T,$$

where T is in degrees Kelvin.

10.8 Very pure liquid water can be subcooled at atmospheric pressure to temperatures considerably below 32°F. Assume that 1 lb$_m$ has been cooled as a liquid to 22°F. A small ice crystal (whose mass may be considered negligible) is now added to "seed" the subcooled liquid. If the subsequent change of state occurs adiabatically and at 1 atm:

(a) What is the final state of the system?
(b) What fraction of the system freezes?

(c) What is the entropy change of the system during this adiabatic process?

(d) Is the process reversible?

Data: Latent heat of fusion of water at 32°F = 143.35 Btu/lb$_m$; specific heat of subcooled liquid water = 1.01 Btu/lb$_m$ · °F.

10.9   One pound-mole of an ideal gas originally confined in a vessel at 500°R and 200 psia is allowed to expand through a valve into an evacuated vessel whose volume is nine times that of the first.   The system is thermally and mechanically insulated from the surroundings. What are the numerical values of W, Q, ΔU, ΔH, ΔS, ΔA, and ΔG (units of Btu, lb moles, and °R) for this process after sufficient time has elapsed so that the temperatures of the two tanks have equalized?

10.10   (a) Derive the equation

$$\left(\frac{\partial C_V}{\partial V}\right)_T = T\left(\frac{\partial^2 P}{\partial T^2}\right)_V.$$

(b) Prove that C_V of an ideal gas is a function of T only.

(c) In the case of a gas obeying the equation of state

$$\frac{PV}{RT} = 1 + \frac{B}{V},$$

where B is a function of T only, show that

$$C_V - C_V^\circ = -\frac{RT}{V}\frac{d^2}{dT^2}BT,$$

where C_V° is the heat capacity for the ideal-gas state, i.e., the heat capacity as $P \rightarrow 0$ and $V \rightarrow \infty$.

10.11   (a) Derive the equation

$$\left(\frac{\partial C_P}{\partial P}\right)_T = -T\left(\frac{\partial^2 V}{\partial T^2}\right)_P.$$

(b) Prove that C_P of an ideal gas is a function of T only.

(c) In the case of a gas obeying the equation of state

$$\frac{PV}{RT} = 1 + B'P,$$

where B' is a function of T only, show that

$$C_P - C_P^\circ = -RTP\frac{d^2}{dT^2}B'T,$$

where C_P° is the heat capacity for the ideal-gas state, i.e., the heat-capacity as $P \rightarrow 0$.

10.12 Starting with the first Maxwell equation, derive the remaining three by using only the relations

$$\left(\frac{\partial x}{\partial y}\right)_z \left(\frac{\partial y}{\partial z}\right)_x \left(\frac{\partial z}{\partial x}\right)_y = -1,$$

$$\left(\frac{\partial x}{\partial y}\right)_f \left(\frac{\partial y}{\partial z}\right)_f \left(\frac{\partial z}{\partial x}\right)_f = +1.$$

10.13 Derive the following equations:

(a) $U = A - T\left(\frac{\partial A}{\partial T}\right)_V = -T^2\left(\frac{\partial A/T}{\partial T}\right)_V.$

(b) $C_V = -T\left(\frac{\partial^2 A}{\partial T^2}\right)_V.$

(c) $H = G - T\left(\frac{\partial G}{\partial T}\right)_P = -T^2\left(\frac{\partial G/T}{\partial T}\right)_P$ Gibbs-Helmholtz equation.

(d) $C_P = -T\left(\frac{\partial^2 G}{\partial T^2}\right)_P.$

10.14 From the fact that dV/V is an exact differential, derive the relation

$$\left(\frac{\partial \beta}{\partial P}\right)_T = -\left(\frac{\partial k}{\partial T}\right)_P.$$

10.15 Derive the third $T\,dS$ equation,

$$T\,dS = C_V\left(\frac{\partial T}{\partial P}\right)_V dP + C_P\left(\frac{\partial T}{\partial V}\right)_P dV,$$

and show that the three $T\,dS$ equations may be written:

(1) $$T\,dS = C_V\,dT + \frac{\beta T}{k}\,dV,$$

(2) $$T\,dS = C_P\,dT - V\beta T\,dP,$$

(3) $$T\,dS = \frac{C_V k}{\beta}\,dP + \frac{C_P}{\beta V}\,dV.$$

10.16 The pressure on 1 gm of water is increased by 1,000 atm reversibly and adiabatically. Calculate the temperature change when the initial temperature has the three different values given below:

Temp., °C	Specific volume V, cm³/gm	β, °C^{-1}	C_P, cal/gm · °C
0	1.000	$-\ 67 \times 10^{-6}$	1.0087
5	1.000	$+\ 15 \times 10^{-6}$	1.0048
50	1.012	$+465 \times 10^{-6}$	0.9983

10.17 Measurements of thermal expansion and compressibility of a gas yield the equations

$$\left(\frac{\partial V}{\partial T}\right)_P = \frac{R}{P} + \frac{a}{T^2} \quad \text{and} \quad \left(\frac{\partial V}{\partial P}\right)_T = -Tf(P),$$

where a is a constant and $f(P)$ is a function of the pressure only. At low pressures, the heat capacity at constant pressure has the value for a monatomic ideal gas. Show that:

(a) $f(P) = \dfrac{R}{P^2}.$

(b) The equation of state is

$$PV = RT - \frac{aP}{T}.$$

(c) $C_P = \dfrac{2aP}{T^2} + \frac{5}{2}R.$

10.18 Derive the equations:

(a) $C_V = -T\left(\dfrac{\partial P}{\partial T}\right)_V \left(\dfrac{\partial V}{\partial T}\right)_S.$

(b) $\left(\dfrac{\partial V}{\partial T}\right)_S = -\dfrac{C_V k}{\beta T}.$

(c) $\dfrac{(\partial V/\partial T)_S}{(\partial V/\partial T)_P} = \dfrac{1}{1 - \gamma}.$

10.19 Derive the equations:

(a) $C_P = T\left(\dfrac{\partial V}{\partial T}\right)_P \left(\dfrac{\partial P}{\partial T}\right)_S.$

(b) $\left(\dfrac{\partial P}{\partial T}\right)_S = \dfrac{C_P}{V\beta T}.$

(c) $\dfrac{(\partial P/\partial T)_S}{(\partial P/\partial T)_V} = \dfrac{\gamma}{\gamma - 1}.$

10.20 The pressure on 1 ft³ of water at 75°F (62.2 lb$_m$) is increased reversibly and isothermally from 1 to 3,000 atm.

(a) How much heat is transferred?

(b) How much work is done?

(c) What is the change in internal energy?

(d) What is the change in enthalpy?

Take $\beta = 140 \times 10^{-6}$ °F^{-1} and $k = 45 \times 10^{-6}$ atm^{-1}.

Chapter 11/
Properties of Pure Substances

11.1/ *PV* Diagram for a Pure Substance

If 1 lb$_m$ of water at about 200°F is introduced into a vessel about 50 ft^3 in volume from which all the air has been exhausted, the water will evaporate completely and the system will be in the condition known as *unsaturated vapor*, the pressure of the vapor being less than 1 atm. On the *PV* diagram shown in Fig. 11.1 this state is represented by the point *A*. If the vapor is then compressed slowly and isothermally, the pressure will rise until there is *saturated vapor* at the point *B*. If the compression is continued, condensation takes place, the pressure remaining constant so long as the temperature remains constant. The straight line *BC* represents the isothermal isobaric condensation of water vapor, the constant pressure being called the *vapor pressure*. At any point between *B* and *C*, water and steam are in equilibrium; at the point *C*, there is only liquid water, or *saturated liquid*. Since a very large increase of pressure is needed to compress liquid water, the line *CD* is almost vertical. At any point on the line *CD* the water is said to be in the *liquid phase*, at any point on *AB* in the *vapor phase*, and at any point on *BC* there is equilibrium between the liquid and the vapor phases. *ABCD* is a typical isotherm of a pure substance on a *PV* diagram.

At other temperatures the isotherms are of similar character, as shown in Fig. 11.1. It is seen that the lines representing equilibrium between liquid and vapor phases, or *vaporization lines*, get shorter as the

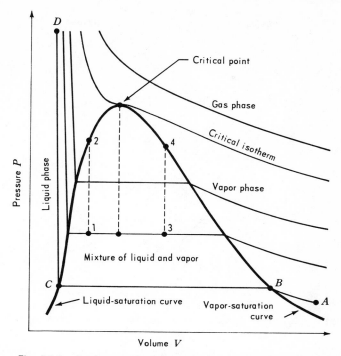

Fig. 11.1   Isotherms of a pure substance on a PV diagram.

temperature rises until a certain temperature is reached, the *critical temperature*, above which there is no longer any distinction between a liquid and a vapor.   The isotherm at the critical temperature is called the *critical isotherm*, and the point that represents the limit of the vaporization lines is called the *critical point*.   It is seen that the critical isotherm exhibits a horizontal inflection at the critical point.   The pressure and volume at the critical point are known as the *critical pressure* and the *critical volume*, respectively.   All points at which the liquid is saturated lie on the *liquid-saturation curve*, and all points representing saturated vapor lie on the *vapor-saturation curve*.   The two saturation curves denoted by heavy lines meet at the critical point. Above the critical point the isotherms are continuous curves that at large volumes and low pressures approach equilateral hyperbolas, i.e., the isotherms of an ideal gas.

In Fig. 11.2 the point V refers to saturated vapor at the temperature T_1.   If this vapor is heated at constant pressure until its temperature rises to T_2, a point such as S will be reached and the vapor is said to be *superheated*, the difference $T_2 - T_1$ being the *number of degrees superheat*.   Superheated vapor is unsaturated vapor.   If the line $V'S'$ represents the same number of degrees superheat as the line VS, then

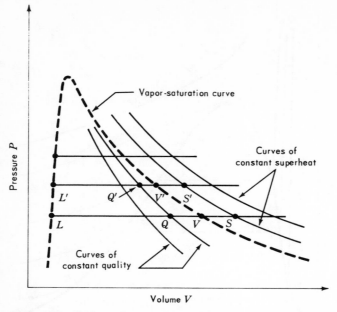

Fig. 11.2   Curves of constant quality and curves of constant superheat.

all points such as S and S' determine a curve known as a *curve of constant superheat*.

The point V denotes saturated vapor, or 100 percent vapor and 0 percent liquid. The point L, however, denotes 0 percent vapor and 100 percent liquid at the same temperature. At intermediate points such as Q the percentage vapor, or *quality*, varies. If the point Q' represents the same quality with respect to V' that the point Q represents with respect to V, then Q and Q' lie on a curve known as a *curve of constant quality*.

In the two PV diagrams shown in Figs. 11.1 and 11.2 the low-temperature region representing the solid phase has not been shown. The solid region and the region of equilibrium between solid and vapor are indicated by isotherms of the same general character as those in Fig. 11.1. The horizontal portion of one of these isotherms represents the transition from saturated solid to saturated vapor, or *sublimation*. There is obviously one such line that is the boundary between the liquid-vapor region and the solid-vapor region. This *line* is associated with the *triple point*. In the case of ordinary water, the triple point is at a pressure of 0.00602 atm and a temperature of 0.01°C.

11.2/ Critical Point

From the description of the critical point given above it is clear that it represents the state at which vapor and liquid phases in equilibrium become indistinguishable from one another, because their properties, e.g., densities, refractive indices, etc., are identical. For a pure substance the critical point is also the highest temperature and pressure at which liquid and vapor phases can exist in equilibrium. The horizontal inflection point exhibited by the critical isotherm at the critical point implies the following mathematical conditions:

$$\left(\frac{\partial P}{\partial V}\right)_T = \left(\frac{\partial^2 P}{\partial V^2}\right)_T = 0.$$

The experimental observation of the properties exhibited by fluids in the neighborhood of the critical point is extraordinarily difficult, and the literature abounds with observations which are apparently incorrect. Several of the reasons for this are:

At the critical point the isothermal compressibility becomes infinite. As a result the gravitational field of the earth causes large density gradients from top to bottom in the fluid under observation. What one wants is data taken in the absence of a gravitational field. Such data are not yet available.

Thermal equilibrium is most difficult to obtain in systems near the critical point. This results from the fact that the heat capacity of such systems is very large. Thus the system must be held at constant temperature for long periods before experimental observations become meaningful.

Visual observation of systems near the critical point is hampered by strong scattering of light caused by a phenomenon known as *the critical opalescence*.

If a pure substance is heated slowly and uniformly in a sealed vertical tube of constant volume, observation shows that one of three results will be obtained. Consider the tube filled with a mixture of liquid and vapor in equilibrium, with the meniscus separating the phases initially near the bottom of the tube. Heating produces vaporization of the liquid, and the meniscus falls to the bottom of the tube as the last of the liquid vaporizes. If the meniscus is near the top of the tube, heating causes sufficient expansion of the liquid so that the meniscus rises to the top of the tube as the last of the vapor condenses. These processes may be readily followed on the PV diagram of Fig. 11.1 along the vertical lines $1 \rightarrow 2$ and $3 \rightarrow 4$.

The third possibility is represented by the vertical line on Fig. 11.1 passing through the critical point. If one starts with the appropriate amounts of liquid and vapor in the tube, heating produces little change in the level of the meniscus. As the critical point is approached, the meniscus becomes less distinct, then becomes hazy, and finally disappears. The temperature at which the meniscus vanishes is the critical temperature. Most measurements of critical temperatures have

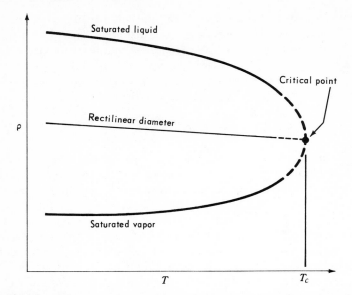

Fig. 11.3   Extrapolation of the rectilinear diameter to the critical temperature.

been made by this technique.   Because of the difficulties already mentioned, such experiments must be made with the greatest care.

The critical pressure may be measured at the same time as the critical temperature by noting the pressure at which the meniscus disappears.   The critical volume, however, is much more difficult to determine.   This measurement is most commonly carried out by measuring the densities of both saturated liquid and saturated vapor as a function of temperature to as close to the critical temperature as possible.   The vapor and liquid densities are then plotted versus temperature, and a line representing the arithmetic average of these densities is constructed as shown in Fig. 11.3.   This last line is usually called the rectilinear diameter, and experiment shows it to be virtually linear. Extrapolation to the critical temperature yields the critical density.

The density-temperature relationship for the saturated phases as shown in Fig. 11.3 was for a time believed to show irregularities near the critical point.   However, the curve is now believed to be smooth, as shown.

Critical data for a few substances are given in Table 11.1.

11.3/ Vapor Pressure of Liquids and Solids

When a liquid is in equilibrium with its vapor at a given temperature, the vapor exerts a pressure that depends only on the temperature. In general, the higher the temperature, the greater the vapor pressure. The temperature at which the vapor pressure equals 760 mm is known as the *normal boiling point.*

Table 11.1/ Critical Data

Substance	Critical temp., °K	Critical pressure, atm	Critical volume, cm³/gm mole	Critical density, gm/cm³
Helium (4)	5.3	2.26	57.8	0.0693
Helium (3)	3.34	1.15	72.6	0.0413
Hydrogen (normal)	33.3	12.80	65.0	0.0310
Deuterium (normal)	38.4	16.4	30.0	0.0668
Nitrogen	126.2	33.5	90.1	0.311
Oxygen	154.8	50.1	78	0.41
Ammonia	405.5	111.3	72.5	0.235
Freon 12	384.7	39.6	218	0.555
Carbon dioxide	304.2	72.9	94.0	0.468
Sulfur dioxide	430.7	77.8	122	0.524
Water	647.4	218.3	56	0.32
Carbon disulfide	552	78	170	0.44

As the temperature is reduced, a temperature is reached at which some of the liquid starts to solidify. This temperature and the corresponding vapor pressure constitute the triple point at which solid, liquid, and vapor exist in equilibrium.

A number of empirical equations, of varying degrees of complexity, have been proposed to represent the vapor pressure of a liquid as a function of temperature. The simplest of these, and one that is entirely satisfactory for many purposes, reflects the observation that a plot of the logarithm of vapor pressure versus the reciprocal of absolute temperature is very nearly linear:

$$\ln P = A - \frac{B}{T},$$

where A and B are constants for a given substance.

A three-constant equation, known as the Antoine equation, is widely used and is more accurate:

$$\ln P = A - \frac{B}{T + C}.$$

At temperatures below the triple-point temperature only solid and vapor are present. The solid is in equilibrium with the vapor, which exerts a pressure that is again a function of temperature only.

11.4/ PT Diagram for a Pure Substance

If the vapor pressure of a solid is measured at various temperatures until the triple point is reached and then that of the liquid is measured until the critical point is reached, the results when plotted on a PT diagram appear as in Fig. 11.4. If the substance at the triple point is compressed until there is no vapor left and the pressure on the resulting

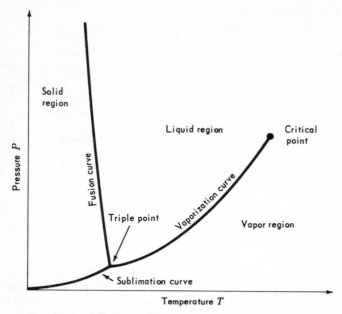

Fig. 11.4 *PT* **diagram for a substance such as water.**

mixture of liquid and solid is increased, the temperature will have to be changed for equilibrium to exist between the solid and the liquid. Measurements of these pressures and temperatures give rise to a third curve on the *PT* diagram, starting at the triple point and continuing indefinitely. The points representing the coexistence of (1) solid and vapor lie on the *sublimation curve*, (2) liquid and vapor lie on the *vaporization curve*, (3) liquid and solid lie on the *fusion curve*. In the particular case of water, the sublimation curve is called the *frost line*, the vaporization curve is called the *steam line*, and the fusion curve is called the *ice line*.

The slopes of the sublimation and the vaporization curves for all substances are positive. The slope of the fusion curve, however, may be positive or negative. The fusion curve of most substances has a positive slope. Water is one of the important exceptions. When an equation known as the Clapeyron equation is derived later in this chapter, it will be seen that any substance, such as water, which expands upon freezing has a fusion curve with a negative slope, whereas the opposite is true for a substance which contracts upon freezing.

11.5/ Triple Point

The pressure and temperature at which all three phases of a pure substance coexist may be measured with the apparatus that is used to

Table 11.2/ Triple-point Data

Substance	Temp., °K	Pressure, mm Hg
Helium (4) (λ point)	2.172	37.8
Hydrogen (normal)	13.96	54.1
Deuterium (normal)	18.63	128
Neon	24.57	324
Nitrogen	63.18	94
Oxygen	54.36	1.14
Ammonia	195.40	45.57
Carbon dioxide	216.55	3,880
Sulfur dioxide	197.68	1.256
Water	273.16	4.58

Table 11.3/ Triple Points of Water

Phases in equilibrium	Pressure	Temp., °C
Ice I, liquid, vapor	4.579 mm Hg	+ 0.01
Ice I, liquid, ice III	2,115 kg/cm²	−22.0
Ice I, ice II, ice III	2,170 kg/cm²	−34.7
Ice II, ice III, ice V	3,510 kg/cm²	−24.3
Ice III, liquid, ice V	3,530 kg/cm²	−17.0
Ice V, liquid, ice VI	6,380 kg/cm²	+ 0.16
Ice VI, liquid, ice VII	22,400 kg/cm²	+81.6

measure vapor pressure. The triple point is merely the point of intersection of the sublimation and vaporization curves. It must be understood that only on a PT diagram is the triple point represented by a
point. On a PV diagram it is a line, and on a UV diagram it is a tri-
angle. Triple-point data for some interesting substances are given in
Table 11.2.

Investigating the ice line of water at very high pressures, Bridgman
and Tammann discovered five new modifications of ice, designated as
ice II, III, V, VI, and VII, ordinary ice being denoted by ice I. Two
other modifications of ice, IV and VIII, were found to be unstable.
Equilibrium conditions among these forms of ice and liquid give rise to
six other triple points, which, along with the low-pressure triple point,
are listed in Table 11.3.

11.6/ *PVT* Surface

All the information that is represented on both the PV and the PT
diagrams can be shown on one diagram if the three coordinates P, V,

and T are plotted along rectangular axes.   The result is called the PVT surface.   Two such surfaces are shown in Figs. 11.5 and 11.6, the first for a substance like water that expands upon freezing and the second for a substance like CO_2 that contracts upon freezing.   These diagrams are not drawn to scale, the volume axis being considerably foreshortened. If the student imagines a PVT surface projected on the PV plane, he

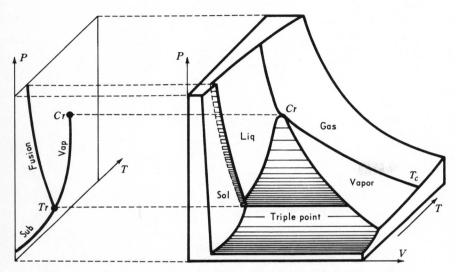

Fig. 11.5 PVT surface for a substance which expands upon freezing.

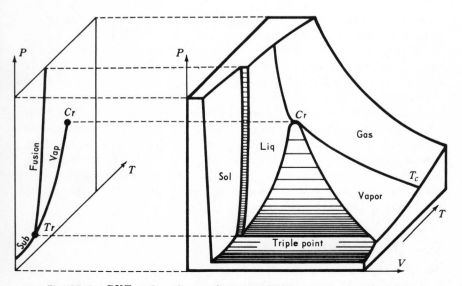

Fig. 11.6 PVT surface for a substance which contracts upon freezing.

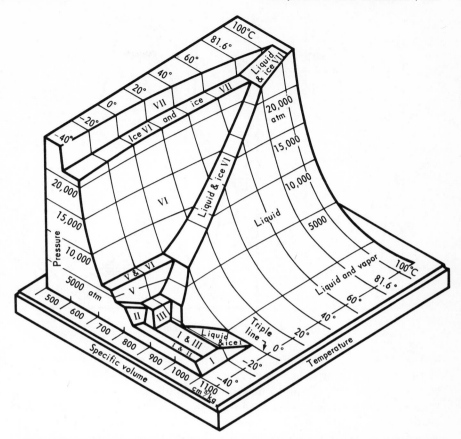

Fig. 11.7 PVT **surface for water, showing all the triple points.   Constructed by Verwiebe on the basis of measurements by Bridgman.**

will see the usual PV diagram.   Upon projecting the surface on the PT plane, the whole solid-vapor region projects into the sublimation curve, the whole liquid-vapor region projects into the vaporization curve, the whole solid-liquid region projects into the fusion curve, and finally the "triple-point line" projects into the triple point.   The critical point is denoted by the letters Cr, and the triple point by Tr.   The critical isotherm is marked T_c.   A substance with no free surface and with a volume determined by that of the container is called a gas when its temperature is above the critical temperature, otherwise it is called a vapor.

All the triple points of water are shown on the PVT surface in Fig. 11.7, which was constructed by Verwiebe on the basis of measurements by Bridgman.

The PVT surface and accompanying PT projection for helium given

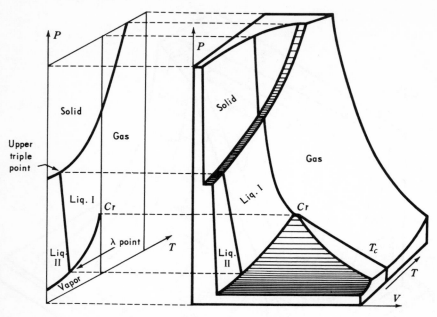

Fig. 11.8 PVT **surface for helium.**

in Fig. 11.8 show that helium has a number of remarkable properties. If we start at the critical point ($T_c = 5.3°$K, $P_c = 2.3$ atm) and lower the temperature, the liquid remaining in equilibrium with its vapor, a triple point is reached (known as the λ point) at which three different phases are in equilibrium but there is no solid. Instead of solid helium, another modification of liquid helium, known as helium II, is formed. The coordinates of the λ point are $T = 2.172°$K, $P = 0.0497$ atm (37.8 mm). Further reduction of the temperature (by rapid evaporation) is still not attended by the formation of the solid. In order to produce solid helium from either liquid I or liquid II, the pressure must be increased to over 25 atm, in which case a triple point (the upper triple point) is reached at which both the liquids and the solid are in equilibrium. *There is no triple point for solid, liquid, and vapor.*

The transition from liquid I to liquid II takes place with no "latent" heat and with no change of volume. Such a transition is known as a phase change of the second order; its treatment is beyond the scope of this book. When the two liquids are in equilibrium, they both have the same density. Other properties, however, are remarkably different. For example, the thermal conductivity of liquid helium II is very much larger than that of liquid I, so much so, in fact, that a temperature gradient, which gives rise to bubbling in liquid I, does not exist in liquid II, and thus one can tell when liquid II is formed by noting that the liquid suddenly becomes quiescent. Perhaps the most interesting property of liquid II is its remarkably low viscosity. It flows very rapidly through capillary tubes and goes through tightly packed porous materials as if through a sieve. Other interesting properties of liquid helium II are that it has a large heat capacity at constant pressure and a negative volume expansivity.

11.7/ Expansivity

The volume expansivity of a gas may be calculated from the equation of state or more simply from any empirical equation representing the relation between volume and temperature at constant pressure. The volume expansivity of liquids and solids is usually calculated from an empirical equation representing the relation between density and temperature at constant pressure. Since the specific volume V is the reciprocal of the density ρ, it follows that

$$\beta = -\frac{1}{\rho}\frac{\partial \rho}{\partial T}.$$

In cases where it is inconvenient or inadvisable to measure the density of a solid over a wide temperature range, the volume expansivity may be calculated from the linear expansivity. Suppose that the three rectangular dimensions of a unit mass of solid are L_1, L_2, and L_3. Then

$$V = L_1 L_2 L_3,$$
$$\frac{\partial V}{\partial T} = L_2 L_3 \frac{\partial L_1}{\partial T} + L_1 L_3 \frac{\partial L_2}{\partial T} + L_1 L_2 \frac{\partial L_3}{\partial T},$$
$$\frac{1}{V}\frac{\partial V}{\partial T} = \frac{1}{L_1}\frac{\partial L_1}{\partial T} + \frac{1}{L_2}\frac{\partial L_2}{\partial T} + \frac{1}{L_3}\frac{\partial L_3}{\partial T},$$

and
$$\beta = \alpha_1 + \alpha_2 + \alpha_3,$$

where α_1, α_2, and α_3 are the linear expansivities along the three directions. If the solid is isotropic, then

$$\alpha_1 = \alpha_2 = \alpha_3 = \alpha$$
and
$$\beta = 3\alpha.$$

In general, the volume expansivity of all materials depends on both the temperature and the pressure. As an example of the way β depends on pressure, consider the values for mercury listed in Table 11.7. It requires an enormous change of pressure to give rise to an appreciable change in β. At ordinary pressures of 1 to 10 atm, β can be regarded as practically constant for most materials.

The temperature variation of β is much more significant. This is shown for copper at atmospheric pressure in Table 11.8 and is plotted for four different metals in Fig. 11.9. It is seen that the volume expansivity decreases as the temperature is lowered, approaching zero as the temperature approaches absolute zero. Most pure solids behave in a manner similar to that shown in Fig. 11.9, but there are several interesting exceptions. A type of iron known as α iron, for example, behaves normally from 0 to about 1000°K; then its volume expansivity takes a sudden drop, becoming negative at about 1100°K.

The curves drawn in Fig. 11.9 show an interesting regularity, namely, the higher the melting point, the lower the volume expansivity. As a result, in the temperature interval from absolute zero to the melting point, all metals expand approximately the same fraction of their original volumes. It seems as though a metal like tin, realizing it is going to melt soon, expands rapidly with the temperature, whereas platinum, with a high melting point, slows down its rate.

One of the most interesting substances is water. The temperature variation of β of both ice and water is given in Table 11.4 and is plotted in Fig. 11.10. It is a remarkable fact that the volume expansivity is negative at very low temperatures and also in the well-known region from 0 to 4°C.

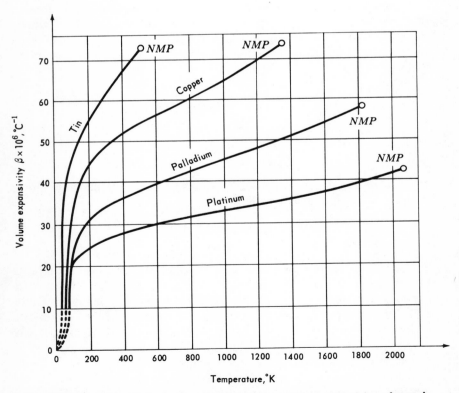

Fig. 11.9 Normal temperature variation of the volume expansivity of metals. (NMP stands for the normal melting point.)

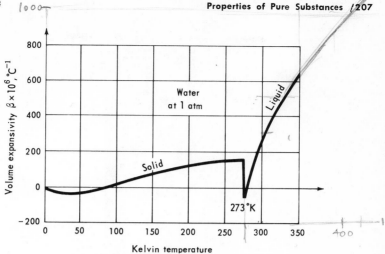

Fig. 11.10   Temperature variation of β of water.

Table 11.4/ Temperature Variation of β of Ice and of Water

Temp., °K	$\beta \times 10^6$, °C^{-1}	Temp., °K	$\beta \times 10^6$, °C^{-1}
0	0	279	+ 32
23	− 18.3	281	+ 61
73	+ 2.4	283	+ 89
123	+ 50.4	293	+208
173	+102	303	+304
223	+137	313	+390
273 (solid)	+158	323	+465
273 (liquid)	− 67	333	+522
275	− 31	343	+586
277	+ 1	353	+643

$\sim 60°F$ (handwritten annotation near 293 K row)

11.8/ Compressibility

The isothermal compressibility of a gas may be calculated from an empirical equation expressing the dependence of V upon P at constant temperature.   In the case of solids and liquids the change in volume (or the change in one dimension) produced by a known change in pressure is measured at constant temperature and the average compressibility is calculated from the expression

$$\langle k \rangle = -\frac{1}{V_0}\frac{V - V_0}{P - P_0}.$$

If the change in pressure is not too large, $\langle k \rangle$ is approximately the true isothermal compressibility.

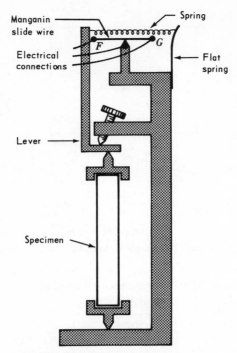

Fig. 11.11 Bridgman piezometer.

In the apparatus known as a *piezometer* used by Bridgman for solids, a bar of the solid is contained in a strong iron container filled with oil. The pressure of the oil is varied by a hydrostatic press, and the change in length of the solid relative to that of the iron container is measured by the motion it produces in a high-resistance manganin wire, which moves past a fixed contact G, as shown in Fig. 11.11. The resistance of the part of the wire between the end F and the fixed contact G is measured with the aid of a potentiometer. The quantity that is measured is the linear compressibility; i.e.,

$$\delta = -\frac{1}{L}\frac{\partial L}{\partial P}.$$

If the three rectangular dimensions of the solid are L_1, L_2, and L_3, then

$$V = L_1 L_2 L_3,$$

$$\frac{\partial V}{\partial P} = L_2 L_3 \frac{\partial L_1}{\partial P} + L_1 L_3 \frac{\partial L_2}{\partial P} + L_1 L_2 \frac{\partial L_3}{\partial P},$$

$$\frac{1}{V}\frac{\partial V}{\partial P} = \frac{1}{L_1}\frac{\partial L_1}{\partial P} + \frac{1}{L_2}\frac{\partial L_2}{\partial P} + \frac{1}{L_3}\frac{\partial L_3}{\partial P},$$

and

$$k = -\frac{1}{V}\frac{\partial V}{\partial P} = \delta_1 + \delta_2 + \delta_3.$$

If the solid is isotropic, all the δ's are equal and

$$k = 3\delta.$$

In general, the isothermal compressibility of all substances is a func tion of both pressure and temperature. The pressure dependence is exemplified by the values given in Table 11.7 for mercury at 0°C. It is seen that the change is only about 20 percent for an increase of pressure of 7,000 atm.

The effect of temperature on the isothermal compressibility is somewhat greater, as shown in Table 11.8 for copper at atmospheric pressure. The isothermal compressibility of copper is plotted against the Kelvin temperature in Fig. 11.12. Above about 100°K the rise of k is approximately linear.

$$\frac{cm^2}{dyne} = \frac{10^5 cm^2}{N} = \frac{10^6 cm^2}{kp} = \frac{10^6}{ata} = \frac{10^6}{14.6 \, psi} \, \frac{1}{}$$

Table 11.5/ Velocity of Sound and Compressibility of Water

Temp., °C	c, km/sec	$\beta \times 10^6$, °C^{-1}	C_P, joule/ gm · °C	ρ, gm/cm^3	$k \times 10^{12}$, cm^2/dyne	$k_s \times 10^{12}$, cm^2/dyne
0	1.404	−67	4.2177	0.99986	50.8	50.8
10	1.448	89	4.1922	0.99973	48.1	48.0
20	1.483	208	4.1819	0.99823	45.8	45.5
30	1.510	304	4.1785	0.99568	44.6	43.9
40	1.530	390	4.1786	0.99225	43.8	42.7
50	1.544	465	4.1807	0.98807	43.7	42.0
60	1.552	522	4.1844	0.98324	43.7	41.5
70	1.555	586	4.1896	0.97781	44.1	41.3
80	1.555	643	4.1964	0.97183	44.8	41.3

$$\frac{44 \times 10^{-6}}{14} = 3.1 \times 10^{-6}$$

$$\frac{1}{psia}$$

Table 11.6/ Temperature Variation of C_P of H_2O

Temp., °K	C_P, cal/ gm mole · °C	Temp., °K	C_P, cal/ gm mole · °C
0	0	233	7.63
10	0.66	253	8.14
20	0.423	273 (solid)	8.64
40	1.57	273 (liquid)	18.09
60	2.39	280	18.03
80	3.09	300	18.00
100	3.75	340	18.03
150	5.16	373	18.09
200	6.57		

Table 11.7/ Pressure Variation of Properties of Mercury at 0°C

P, atm	V, cm³/ gm mole	$\beta \times 10^6$, °C⁻¹	$k \times 10^{12}$, cm²/dyne	C_P, cal/ gm mole · °C	$C_P - C_V$, cal/ gm mole · °C	C_V, cal/ gm mole · °C	γ
1	14.72	181	3.88	6.69	0.810	5.88	1.14
1,000	14.67	174	3.79	6.69	0.768	5.92	1.13
2,000	14.62	168	3.69	6.69	0.731	5.96	1.12
3,000	14.57	164	3.60	6.68	0.709	5.97	1.12
4,000	14.51	160	3.48	6.68	0.695	5.98	1.12
5,000	14.45	158	3.38	6.68	0.695	5.98	1.12
6,000	14.42	155	3.25	6.68	0.694	5.99	1.11
7,000	14.38	152	3.12	6.68	0.692	5.99	1.11

The adiabatic compressibility is obtained most readily by measuring the velocity of sound c and using the equation derived in Chap. 5, namely, $c = \sqrt{g_c/\rho k_S}$. Eliminating C_V from the equations derived in Art. 10.10 and 10.11,

$$\frac{C_P}{C_V} = \frac{k}{k_S} \qquad \text{and} \qquad C_P - C_V = \frac{TV\beta^2}{k},$$

we get the useful relation

$$k - k_S = \frac{TV\beta^2}{C_P}.$$

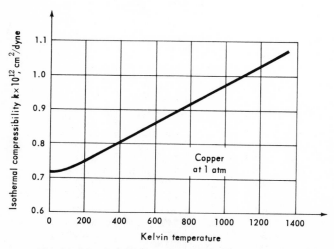

Fig. 11.12   Temperature variation of k of copper.

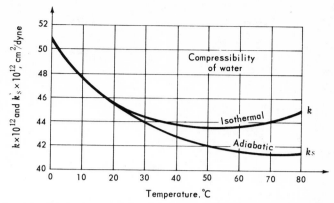

Fig. 11.13 **Temperature variation of isothermal and adiabatic compressibilities** of water.

It follows, therefore, that

$$k_S = \frac{g_c}{\rho c^2} \quad \text{and} \quad k = \frac{1}{\rho}\left(\frac{g_c}{c^2} + \frac{\beta^2 T}{C_P}\right).$$

The data needed to calculate k_S and k of water between 0 and 80°C are listed in Table 11.5, and both k_S and k are plotted in Fig. 11.13.

11.9/ Heat Capacity at Constant Pressure

The experimental measurement of C_P has already been discussed in Chap. 4. One important result of such measurements is the discovery that the C_P of solids and liquids is extremely insensitive to changes in the pressure. For example, for a change of pressure from 1 to 7,000 atm, the C_P of mercury changes from 6.69 to 6.68 cal/gm mole · °C.

The temperature dependence of C_P, however, is of considerable importance. In Table 11.8 the values of C_P of copper are given over a very wide temperature range. These values are plotted in Fig. 11.14. It is seen that C_P approaches zero as the temperature approaches zero and that, as the temperature rises, C_P continuously increases without approaching a constant value. This is the normal behavior of C_P and applies for most pure metals and many compounds. There are, of course, exceptions, among which α iron is interesting. In the temperature range from 1000 to 1100°K, where the volume expansivity of α iron takes a sudden drop, the C_P takes a sudden rise and then drops just as rapidly. Also of interest is the behavior of certain paramagnetic salts in the neighborhood of absolute zero. Below 2°K, C_P rises and then, as the temperature approaches zero, approaches zero again. This behavior is of great importance in connection with the production of very low temperatures by adiabatic demagnetization.

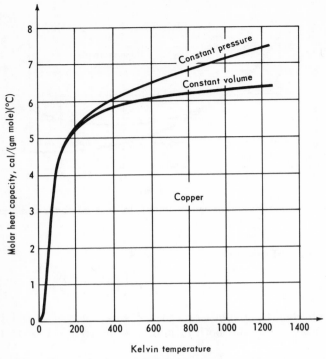

Fig. 11.14   Temperature variation of C_P and C_V of copper.

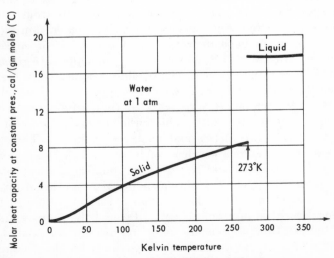

Fig. 11.15   Temperature variation of C_P of water.

The behavior of ice is quite normal until the melting point is reached, at which C_P rises to a value more than twice as large, as shown in Table 11.6 and Fig. 11.15.

11.10/ Heat Capacity at Constant Volume

It has been mentioned that the C_V of solids and liquids is almost impossible to measure and must therefore be calculated from known values of C_P with the aid of the equation

$$C_P - C_V = \frac{TV\beta^2}{k}.$$

In Table 11.7 this calculation is shown for mercury at 0°C at a number of different pressures. It is seen that the C_V of mercury varies less than 2 percent for a pressure change of 7,000 atm. The C_V of other substances is also quite insensitive to a change of pressure.

The temperature variation of C_V, however, is very pronounced and is also of great theoretical significance. In Table 11.8 all the quantities that are used to calculate C_V of copper are listed, along with the final values of C_V. These are plotted along with C_P in Fig. 11.14. It is to be noted that C_V and C_P are practically identical at low temperatures but become quite different at high temperatures, where C_V, unlike C_P, approaches a constant value in the neighborhood of 6 cal/gm mole · °C. This is the normal behavior of most pure metals and compounds.

A tremendous amount of data is required to set up a table such as Table 11.8. The complete temperature dependence of molar volume, volume expansivity, isothermal compressibility, and molar heat capacity at constant pressure is not known for all the substances whose temperature variation of C_V must be known. It is therefore fortunate that an approximate relation exists which is sufficiently accurate to allow the calculation of $C_P - C_V$ in a much simpler manner. If we rewrite the equation

$$C_P - C_V = \frac{V\beta^2 T}{k}$$

in the form

$$C_P - C_V = \frac{V\beta^2}{kC_P{}^2} C_P{}^2 T$$

and denote by the symbol A

$$A = \frac{V\beta^2}{kC_P{}^2},$$

experiment shows that A remains approximately constant as the temperature changes. The approximate constancy of A is shown in the case of copper in Table 11.9, where it is seen that A does not depart appreciably from the average value of 1.55×10^{-5} gm mole/cal.

With this simplification, the equation for the difference in the heat capacities takes the form

$$C_P - C_V = A C_P^2 T,$$

where A is a constant which can be calculated from one value of each of V, k, β, and C_P at *one* convenient temperature. The equation in this form, known as the Nernst-Lindemann equation, is the one that has actually been used to calculate the temperature variation of C_V of most solids.

The results of such calculations for a few representative substances are shown in Fig. 11.16. In all cases, C_V approaches zero as the temperature approaches zero and approaches a constant value of about

Table 11.8/ Temperature Variation of Properties of Copper
Values in parentheses are extrapolated

T, °K	V, cm³/ gm mole	$\beta \times 10^6$, °C⁻¹	$k \times 10^{12}$, cm²/dyne	C_P, cal/ gm mole · °C	$C_P - C_V$, cal/ gm mole · °C	C_V, cal/ gm mole · °C	γ
0	(7.0)	(0)	(0.710)	(0)	0	0	1.00
50	(7.002)	(11.5)	(0.712)	1.38	0.00154	1.38	1.00
100	(7.008)	31.5	0.721	3.88	0.0230	3.86	1.00
150	(7.018)	41.0	0.733	5.01	0.0577	4.95	1.01
200	(7.029)	45.6	0.748	5.41	0.0931	5.32	1.02
250	7.043	48.0	0.762	5.65	0.127	5.52	1.02
300	7.062	49.2	0.776	5.87	0.157	5.71	1.03
500	7.115	54.2	0.837	6.25	0.298	5.95	1.05
800	7.256	60.7	0.922	6.70	0.555	6.14	1.09
1200	7.452	69.7	1.030	7.34	1.00	6.34	1.16

Table 11.9/ Values of A for Copper

Temp., °K	$A \times 10^5$, gm mole/cal
50	1.61
100	1.54
150	1.53
200	1.60
250	1.59
300	1.52
500	1.57
800	1.55
1200	1.55

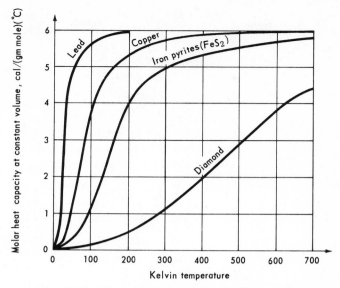

Fig. 11.16   Temperature variation of C_V of solids.

6 cal/gm mole · °C as the temperature is raised.   The actual temperature region, however, where C_V becomes 6 cal/gm mole · °C, is different
for each substance, being around 100°K for Pb and about 2000°K for
diamond.   In many cases this asymptotic value is reached in the
neighborhood of room temperature, about 300°K.   Since at this temperature C_V and C_P are not very different, the C_P of many substances
has a value in the neighborhood of 6 cal/gm mole · °C at room temperature.   This fact was first noticed by Dulong and Petit, in recognition of whom the value of 6 cal/gm mole · °C approached by the C_V
of all solids at high temperatures is called the *Dulong and Petit value*.
The C_V's of some substances, notably Na, Cu, Fe, and FeS_2, exceed the
Dulong and Petit value at very high temperatures.

11.11/ Change of Phase.   Clapeyron's Equation

In the familiar phase transitions—melting, vaporization, and sublimation—as well as in some less familiar transitions such as from one crystal
modification to another, the temperature and pressure remain constant
whereas the internal energy, enthalpy, entropy, and volume change.
Consider 1 mole of material in phase (') with molar internal energy U',
molar enthalpy H', molar entropy S', and molar volume V'.   All these
properties are functions of T and P and hence remain constant during
the phase transitions which end with some material in phase (''),
where the molar properties are represented by U'', H'', S'', and V''.

Let x be the fraction of the initial phase which has been transformed into the final phase. Then the properties of the two-phase mixture are given by

$$U = (1 - x)U' + xU'',$$
$$H = (1 - x)H' + xH'',$$
$$S = (1 - x)S' + xS'',$$
$$V = (1 - x)V' + xV'',$$

and the molar properties are seen to be linear functions of x.

Since the phase transition occurs at constant pressure, the heat (commonly known as the latent heat) transferred per mole is equal to the enthalpy change:

$$Q = \Delta H = H'' - H',$$

and if the process is reversible, the entropy change is given by

$$\Delta S = S'' - S' = \frac{Q}{T} = \frac{\Delta H}{T} = \frac{H'' - H'}{T},$$

or
$$\Delta H = T(S'' - S') = T \, \Delta S.$$

The existence of a latent heat ΔH implies that there is a change in entropy. Since $G = H - TS$, then at constant temperature

$$\Delta G = \Delta H - T \, \Delta S.$$

We have just shown that $\Delta H = T \, \Delta S$; hence ΔG is zero for a phase transition of a pure substance.

The total differential of G is given by

$$dG = -S \, dT + V \, dP.$$

Therefore

$$S = - \left(\frac{\partial G}{\partial T} \right)_P \qquad \text{and} \qquad V = \left(\frac{\partial G}{\partial P} \right)_T.$$

Since S and V change during a phase transition occurring at a given T and P, it is clear that the derivatives of G are different on opposite sides of the point of transition. We may therefore characterize the familiar phase transitions by either of the following equivalent statements:

1. There are changes of internal energy, enthalpy, entropy, and volume.

2. The first-order derivatives of the Gibbs function change discontinuously, although there is no change in the Gibbs function itself.

Changes which occur in the Gibbs function, the entropy, and the volume during a phase transition are crudely represented by the three graphs of Fig. 11.17.

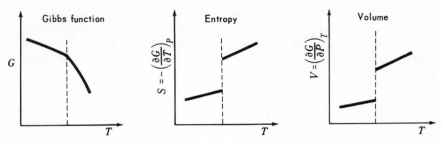

Fig. 11.17   Property changes auring a phase transition.

Since the Gibbs function remains constant during a change of phase, we may write for such a change at T and P:

$$G' = G'';$$

and for the same change of phase at $T + dT$ and $P + dP$:

$$G' + dG' = G'' + dG''.$$

Subtraction gives

$$dG' = dG'',$$

or

$$-S' \, dT + V' \, dP = -S'' \, dT + V'' \, dP.$$

Therefore

$$\frac{dP}{dT} = \frac{S'' - S'}{V'' - V'} = \frac{\Delta S}{\Delta V},$$

and finally,

$$\boxed{\frac{dP}{dT} = \frac{\Delta H}{T \, \Delta V}.}$$

This equation, known as Clapeyron's equation, applies to any change of phase that takes place at constant T and P.

Throughout the remainder of this chapter we shall make use of the following notation: The subscript s will designate saturated solid; the subscript f (for fluid) will designate saturated liquid; and the subscript g (for gas) will designate saturated vapor.   The use of a double subscript will denote a change of phase: sf for fusion (solid to fluid), fg for vaporization (fluid to gas), and sg for sublimation (solid to gas). The reason for adopting this notation is that it is consistent with that of the steam tables used so extensively by engineers.

11.12/ Vaporization

With the notation just described, Clapeyron's equation for vaporization becomes

$$\frac{dP}{dT} = \frac{H_{fg}}{TV_{fg}},$$

where dP/dT is the slope of the vapor-pressure curve, and H_{fg} and V_{fg} are the latent heat and the volume change of vaporization, respectively, all at the conditions of vaporization T and P. The latent heat of vaporization may be calculated by means of this equation if the vapor pressure is known as a function of temperature. Thus

$$H_{fg} = T \frac{dP}{dT} V_{fg} = T \frac{dP}{dT} (V_g - V_f).$$

For temperatures well below the critical, an approximate form of this equation may be employed to estimate latent heats of vaporization. At these conditions, $V_g \gg V_f$; whence V_f can be dropped out. If the vapor is assumed to behave as an ideal gas,

$$V_g = \frac{RT}{P},$$

and the Clapeyron equation becomes

$$H_{fg} = \frac{RT^2}{P} \frac{dP}{dT}.$$

As an example of the use of this equation, consider H_2O at $100°C$ and 760 mm Hg. Experiment shows that, as the temperature increases from 99 to $101°C$, the vapor pressure increases from 733.7 to 788.0 mm Hg. Therefore, taking

$$\frac{dP}{dT} = \frac{\Delta P}{\Delta T} = \frac{788.0 - 733.7}{101 - 99} = 27.15 \text{ mm/°C},$$

we have

$$H_{fg} = \frac{1.987 \text{ cal/gm mole} \cdot °K \times (373)^2 (°K)^2 \times 27.15 \text{ mm/°K}}{760 \text{ mm}}$$
$$= 9864 \text{ cal/gm mole}$$
$$= \tfrac{9864}{18} = 548 \text{ cal/gm}$$
$$= 548 \times 1.8 = 986 \text{ Btu/lb}_m.$$

This value is about 2 percent larger than the correct value because of the approximations involved.

The latent heat of vaporization may be measured calorimetrically by means of an apparatus like that depicted in Fig. 11.18. A liquid L_2 whose latent heat is to be measured is contained in a small vessel and has immersed in it a small heating coil R_2 as shown in Fig. 11.18. Completely surrounding this vessel is a temperature bath consisting of a mixture of air and the vapor of another liquid, L_1. By choosing a suitable liquid L_1 and keeping it at its boiling point by means of the

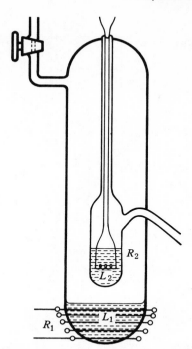

Fig. 11.18   Apparatus for measuring heat of vaporization.

heating coil R_1 in the presence of air at the proper pressure, the temperature bath may be maintained at any desired temperature. At this chosen temperature, the liquid L_2 is in equilibrium with its vapor. The small vessel containing L_2 communicates with another vessel on the outside (not shown in the figure), which may be maintained at any desired temperature by a separately controlled heating or cooling device.

If the temperature of the outside container is maintained at less than that of L_2, a pressure gradient is produced, and some of L_2 will distill over. By maintaining a small current in the heating coil R_2, the temperature of L_2 is kept equal to that of its surroundings, and the energy necessary to vaporize it is thus supplied. There is, therefore, a steady distillation of L_2 into the outside container, the heat of vaporization being supplied by the heating coil R_2 and the heat of condensation being withdrawn by the surroundings of the outside container. Moreover, all the energy supplied by the heater R_2 is used to vaporize L_2 since there is no heat loss between the inner tube and its surroundings. Consequently, if n moles is vaporized by electric energy supplied at the rate vI in a time τ, the heat of vaporization per mole is

$$H_{fg} = \frac{(vI)\tau}{n}.$$

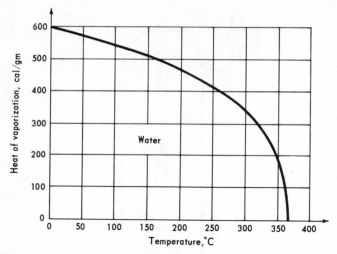

Fig. 11.19   Temperature variation of heat of vaporization of water.

With apparatus similar to that just described, Henning, Aubrey, and Griffiths, and others have measured the heat of vaporization of water at various temperatures. The experimental results are plotted in Fig. 11.19.

11.13/ Fusion

Clapeyron's equation for fusion is

$$\frac{dP}{dT} = \frac{H_{sf}}{TV_{sf}}.$$

Since H_{sf} and T are positive, the slope of the fusion curve is determined by the sign of $V_{sf} = V_f - V_s$. If the substance expands on melting, $V_f > V_s$, and the slope is positive. This is the usual case. Water, however, contracts on melting and has, therefore, a fusion curve with a negative slope.

The simplest method of measuring the heat of fusion of a solid is to supply electric energy at a constant rate and to measure the temperature at convenient time intervals. A plot of temperature versus time represents a heating curve in which the phase transition appears as a straight line, as shown in Fig. 11.20. If n moles of solid melts in time $\Delta\tau$, with electric energy supplied at the rate vI, then

$$H_{sf} = \frac{(vI)\,\Delta\tau}{n}.$$

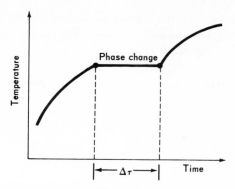

Fig. 11.20   Determination of the heat of fusion from a heating curve.

11.14/ Sublimation

Heats of sublimation are usually measured indirectly by measuring the vapor pressure as a function of temperature and using Clapeyron's equation. The same assumptions may be made as in the case of vaporization, namely,

$$V_g \gg V_s \qquad \text{and} \qquad V_g = \frac{RT}{P}.$$

Clapeyron's equation can then be written

$$H_{sg} = R \frac{dP/P}{dT/T^2}$$
$$= -R \frac{d \ln P}{d(1/T)},$$

from which it can be seen that H_{sg} is equal to $-R$ times the slope of the curve obtained when $\ln P$ is plotted against $1/T$. Vapor pressures of solids are usually measured over only a small range of temperature. Within this range the graph of $\ln P$ versus $1/T$ is practically linear, or

$$\ln P = -\frac{A}{T} + B,$$

where A and B are constants for a given substance.

For example, within the temperature interval from 700 to 739°K, the vapor pressure of magnesium satisfies with reasonable accuracy the equation

$$\ln P = -\frac{17,330}{T} + 19.78.$$

Therefore, from 700 to 739°K, the heat of sublimation of magnesium is approximately $R \times 17,330 = 34,400$ cal/gm mole. Actually, the heat of sublimation does vary with temperature, and if reliable vapor-pressure data exist over a reasonable temperature range, the temperature variation of H_{sg} can be obtained.

Problems

11.1 If P and T are the actual pressure and temperature of a gas and P_C and T_C are the critical pressure and critical temperature of the gas, then the *reduced* pressure P_R and *reduced* temperature T_R are defined by

$$P_R = \frac{P}{P_C} \quad \text{and} \quad T_R = \frac{T}{T_C}.$$

These quantities are useful for establishing generalized correlations of the properties of gases. Such correlations are based on the principle of corresponding states: All gases, when compared at the same reduced pressure and reduced temperature, have nearly the same compressibility factor, and all deviate from ideal-gas behavior to about the same degree.

This principle, although only approximate in nature, allows reasonable estimates to be made of the properties of gases for which no data are available. One equation of state based on this principle which is satisfactory for nonpolar gases at low to moderate pressures gives the compressibility factor as

$$Z = \frac{PV}{RT} = 1 + \frac{BP}{RT} = 1 + \frac{B^*P_R}{T_R},$$

where B^* is a reduced virial coefficient and is a function of reduced temperature only:

$$B^* = \frac{BP_C}{RT_C} = 0.070 - \frac{0.422}{T_R{}^2}.$$

In addition, the reduced vapor pressure is given as a function of reduced temperature by

$$\ln P_R = 6.44 \left(1 - \frac{1}{T_R}\right).$$

(a) Prepare a graph of Z plotted as a function of P_R showing isotherms at values of T_R equal to 0.7, 0.8, 0.9, 0.95, 1.00, 1.05, 1.20, 1.50, and 2.00 for a pressure range of P_R from 0 to 0.7. Note that isotherms for T_R less than unity terminate at the vapor pressure. Draw in the curve of Z versus P_R for saturated vapor.

(b) The enthalpy and entropy deviations were defined in Prob. 10.4;

$$\Delta H' = H^{id} - H \qquad \Delta S' = S^{id} - S.$$

It was also shown in Prob. 10.4c that

$$\Delta H' = PT \left(\frac{dB}{dT} - \frac{B}{T} \right) \quad \text{and} \quad \Delta S' = P \frac{dB}{dT}.$$

Using the definitions of P_R, T_R, and B^*, show that these equations become

$$\frac{\Delta H'}{RT_C} = P_R \left(T_R \frac{dB^*}{dT_R} - B^* \right),$$

$$\frac{\Delta S'}{R} = P_R \frac{dB^*}{dT_R}.$$

Prepare plots of $\Delta H'/RT_C$ and $\Delta S'/R$ versus P_R similar to those constructed for Z in (a).

(c) For n-hexane,

$$T_C = 508°\text{K} \quad \text{and} \quad P_C = 29.9 \text{ atm.}$$

Using the plots prepared in part b, determine $\Delta H'$ and $\Delta S'$ for n-hexane at its vapor pressure at 323, 343, and 363°K, and compare the results with those obtained in Prob. 10.4b.

11.2 The following table gives vapor pressures and specific volumes of saturated liquid and vapor phases for benzene.

Temp., °F	P, psia	V_f, ft³/lb$_m$	V_g, ft³/lb$_m$
430	286.3	0.0258	0.3102
440	310.5	0.0262	0.2818
450	336.7	0.0268	0.2565
460	364.2	0.0273	0.2328
470	393.4	0.0279	0.2112

(a) Determine the constants A and B to give the best fit to the vapor-pressure data by the equation

$$\ln P = A - \frac{B}{T}.$$

Using this equation, determine dP/dT at 450°F, and then calculate the latent heat of vaporization of benzene at 450°F by Clapeyron's equation.

(b) Repeat part a for a vapor-pressure equation of the form

$$\ln P = A - \frac{B}{T + C}.$$

(c) Determine dP/dT at 450°F from a plot of the vapor-pressure data, and calculate the latent heat of vaporization from it.

(d) Calculate the latent heat of vaporization of benzene at 450°F by means of the approximate equation

$$H_{fg} = \frac{RT^2}{P}\frac{dP}{dT}.$$

(e) Compare the results of the preceding calculations, and discuss them from the standpoint of accuracy. Can you devise a means of getting a more accurate value? The reported value for the latent heat is 103.1 Btu/lb$_m$.

11.3 The pressure on 1 lb$_m$ of copper is increased reversibly and isothermally from 1 to 5,000 atm at 300°K.

(a) How much heat in Btu is transferred during the compression?

(b) How much work is done during the compression?

(c) Determine the change of internal energy.

(d) What would have been the rise of temperature if the copper had been subjected to a reversible adiabatic compression?

(Assume the density, volume expansivity, isothermal compressibility, and heat capacity to remain practically constant. The values are given in Table 11.8.)

11.4 At 0°C, aluminum has the following properties: atomic weight = 27.0 gm/mole, density = 2.70 gm/cm³, C_P = 0.220 cal/gm · °C, $\beta = 71.4 \times 10^{-6}$ °C⁻¹, $k = 1.34 \times 10^{-6}$ atm⁻¹. Calculate, at 0°C;

(a) The molar heat capacity at constant volume.

(b) The ratio γ.

(c) The adiabatic compressibility.

(d) The constant A in the Nernst-Lindemann equation.

11.5 Prove that the slope of the sublimation curve (P versus T) of a substance at the triple point is greater than that of the vaporization curve at the same point.

Chapter 12/
Thermodynamic Diagrams and Tables

12.1/ Types of Thermodynamic Diagram

The PV diagram, which we have had occasion to refer to a number of times, is an example of the common thermodynamic diagrams widely used in engineering calculations for PVT systems. Actually, a thermodynamic diagram in two dimensions can be constructed by choosing any pair of thermodynamic properties as rectangular coordinates. The phase boundaries on such a plot appear as curves. Superimposed are various other curves which represent the functional relationships connecting the coordinate variables at constant values of another thermodynamic property. For example, on a PV diagram it is common to display curves relating P to V at constant T, or isotherms. One could also include curves of constant enthalpy, or isenthalps, curves of constant entropy, or isentrops, etc. As a matter of fact, such an extensive PV diagram is never used in practice, simply because other choices for the properties representing the rectangular coordinates have proved to be much more convenient. The diagrams in general use are those which plot temperature versus entropy (TS diagram), enthalpy versus entropy (HS, or Mollier diagram), and the logarithm of pressure versus enthalpy ($\ln P\ H$ diagram).

The preparation of an accurate thermodynamic diagram or, alternatively, of a set of thermodynamic tables is an exacting task. One must start with experimental data, such as heat capacities and PVT

data and, through the equations of thermodynamics, calculate the required properties, such as enthalpy and entropy. The raw data must themselves be accurate, and the calculations must be carried out with great precision.

12.2/ TS Diagram for a Pure Substance

The entropy of a single-phase PVT system may be taken to be a function of T and P, as shown by the second $T\,dS$ equation:

$$dS = C_P \frac{dT}{T} - \left(\frac{\partial V}{\partial T}\right)_P dP.$$

If we consider an isobaric process, this equation may be integrated for a change of the system from one equilibrium state to another to give

$$S_2 - S_1 = \int_{T_1}^{T_2} \frac{C_P}{T} dT \qquad \text{const } P. \tag{12.1}$$

Equation (12.1) yields *changes* in entropy, and if we wish to have numerical values for S itself, we must arbitrarily assign a value to S for some particular state, known as the *reference state*. For example, the entropy of saturated liquid water at 32°F and under its vapor pressure of 0.0886 psia is usually taken as zero. All other entropies for H_2O are then referred to this state.

The phase boundaries for a substance such as CO_2 are shown in Fig. 12.1. A single isobar is represented by the series of lines $ABCDEF$, which corresponds to the isobaric reversible processes by which solid CO_2 is transformed finally into vapor. Thus:

AB = isobaric heating of solid to its melting point,
BC = isobaric isothermal melting,
CD = isobaric heating of liquid to its boiling point,
DE = isobaric isothermal vaporization,
EF = isobaric heating of vapor.

Entropy changes along curves AB, CD, and EF may be calculated by Eq. (12.1). Steps BC and BE are both isobaric and isothermal. Equation (12.1) is obviously not applicable. The entropy changes for these phase transitions must be calculated either from measured values of the latent heats or by means of Clapeyron's equation. It is clear that to establish each isobar such as $ABCDEF$ in Fig. 12.1 it is necessary to have the required latent heats and heat capacities at the particular pressure of the isobar. Even if such data were available (and they usually are not), it would still be necessary to relate one isobar to

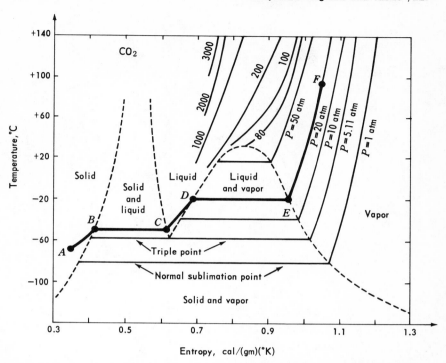

Fig. 12.1 *TS* **diagram for CO₂. The two dashed lines bounding the solid-liquid region are not intended to be correctly located.**

another so that all values of S could be referred back to the reference state. We must therefore have, at least for one temperature, sufficient data to allow the calculation of the change of entropy with pressure at constant temperature. For a single-phase region such a relation is obtained by integration of the second $T\,dS$ equation at constant T:

$$S_2 - S_1 = - \int_{P_1}^{P_2} \left(\frac{\partial V}{\partial T}\right)_P dP \qquad \text{const } T. \qquad (12.2)$$

For the evaluation of the integral on the right of Eq. (12.2) one must have volumetric data for the substance as a function of both T and P. Through the use of Eqs. (12.1) and (12.2) one can establish as many isobars on the TS diagram as wanted, within the range of the variables for which data are available.

In addition to isobars, it is common to find isochors and isenthalps included on a TS diagram. We have already shown that the total differential dH is given by

$$dH = T\,dS + V\,dP.$$

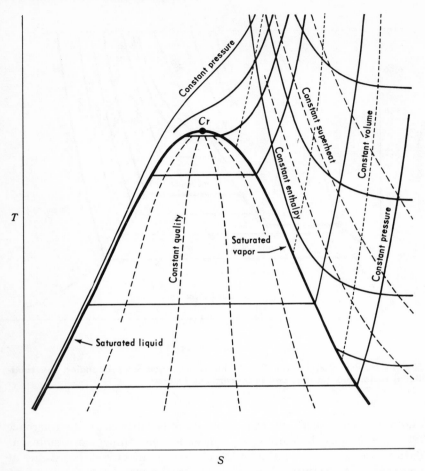

Fig. 12.2 Sketch of TS diagram for water, showing liquid, liquid-vapor, and vapor regions.

This is a general equation for PVT systems, valid for two-phase as well as for single-phase regions. It shows H to be functionally related to S and P. Hence

$$dH = \left(\frac{\partial H}{\partial S}\right)_P dS + \left(\frac{\partial H}{\partial P}\right)_S dP.$$

Comparing this equation with the preceding one, we get

$$\left(\frac{\partial H}{\partial S}\right)_P = T \quad \text{and} \quad \left(\frac{\partial H}{\partial P}\right)_S = V.$$

The integral forms of these two equations may be written

$$\Delta H = \int_{S_1}^{S_2} T \, dS \qquad \text{const } P,$$

and

$$\Delta H = \int_{P_1}^{P_2} V \, dP \qquad \text{const } S.$$

Once isobars have been established on the TS diagram, enthalpy changes along an isobar are readily calculated from the first of these two integral equations. The second is required to relate enthalpies on different isobars so as to refer all values to an arbitrarily assigned value for some reference state. For H_2O, the enthalpy, like the entropy, is usually assigned the value zero for saturated liquid at 32°F. Calculations of this nature allow one to construct isenthalps on the TS diagram. Isochors may be plotted directly from PVT data where available. In other regions values of V are given by the relation $V = (\partial H/\partial P)_S$. A sketch of the TS diagram for the liquid, liquid-vapor, and vapor regions of water is shown by Fig. 12.2. Isobars are shown for all three regions, whereas isochors and isenthalps are not indicated in the liquid-vapor region. In this region lines of constant quality are often shown, and in the vapor region, lines of constant superheat are frequently added. Superheat is a term which refers to the temperature difference by which the actual temperature exceeds the saturation temperature for the same pressure. Thus steam at atmospheric pressure and 300°F is said to show $300 - 212 = 88$°F of superheat.

12.3/ Mollier Diagram

Once the thermodynamic properties have been calculated for the purpose of preparing one type of diagram, for example, the TS diagram just discussed, the values are available for replotting on any coordinate scale one wishes. The type of diagram perhaps most commonly employed by engineers is the HS, or Mollier, diagram. The general outlines of such a diagram are shown on Fig. 12.3. The curve $ABCDEF$ represents a typical reversible isobaric transition from solid at A to vapor at F. Thus:

AB = isobaric heating of solid to melting point (slope increasing),
BC = isobaric isothermal melting of solid (slope constant),
CD = isobaric heating of liquid to boiling point (slope increasing),
DE = isobaric isothermal vaporization of liquid (slope constant),
EF = isobaric superheating of vapor (slope increasing).

Since the slope is given by $(\partial H/\partial S)_P = T$, all sublimation, fusion, and vaporization lines are straight, and the higher the temperature, the

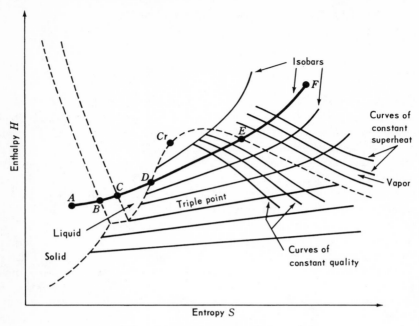

Fig. 12.3   Mollier diagram for water.

steeper the slope.   Where the heating process is manifested by a temperature rise, the slope increases throughout the process.

A detailed Mollier diagram for steam is included in Appendix B.

12.4/ LnP H Diagram

Another very useful diagram for engineering calculations is obtained by plotting pressure on a logarithm scale versus enthalpy.   The general outline of such a diagram is shown in Fig. 12.4.   The series of steps leading at constant pressure from solid at A to vapor at F is again shown by the isobar $ABCDEF$.

Since the latent heat of vaporization is the difference between the enthalpy of saturated vapor and the enthalpy of saturated liquid, this quantity is represented by horizontal line segments such as DE. It is obvious from Fig. 12.4 that the heat of vaporization decreases with increasing temperature and becomes zero at the critical point. The heats of sublimation are represented by horizontal lines traversing the solid-vapor region.   At the triple point the heat of sublimation is evidently equal to the sum of the heat of fusion and the heat of vaporization.

The shapes of the isotherms on the ln P versus H diagram is of interest.   For an ideal gas the isotherms would be vertical lines.   For

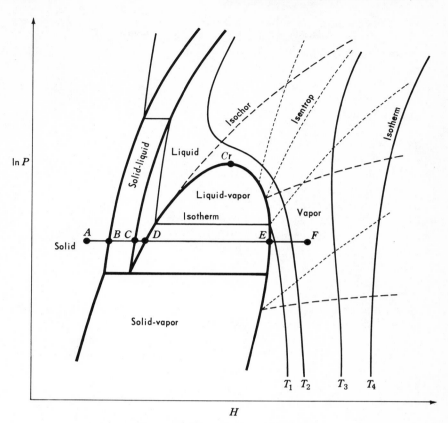

Fig. 12.4   Sketch of a ln$P$ H diagram.

a real substance the general character of the isotherms is indicated in Fig. 12.4 by the lines labeled T_1, T_2, T_3, and T_4, where $T_4 > T_3 > T_2 > T_1$. It is seen that an increase in pressure at constant temperature causes an increase in enthalpy in some regions of the diagram and a decrease in others.

12.5/ Tables of Thermodynamic Properties

Thermodynamic diagrams can surely be drawn to a scale large enough so that numerical values for the properties can be read from them. Even so, it is convenient to have the same data available in tabular form.   This provides greater accuracy than is possible from readings of graphs.   Values are given at close enough intervals so that linear interpolation is sufficiently accurate for all practical purposes.   Both tables and diagrams are to be found in the engineering literature and in handbooks of data for the most common substances.

Because of their great industrial importance, data for water and steam have been extensively compiled. The resulting tables, known simply as steam tables, are in widespread use. We have therefore included in Appendix B two complete tables for saturated and superheated steam. The first table gives the properties of saturated liquid and saturated vapor at even values of temperature. For each temperature the following data will be found:

Vapor pressure P, psia and in. Hg,
Specific volume of saturated liquid V_f, ft^3/lb$_m$,
Specific volume change of vaporization V_{fg}, ft^3/lb$_m$,
Specific volume of saturated vapor V_g, ft^3/lb$_m$,
Enthalpy of saturated liquid H_f, Btu/lb$_m$,
Enthalpy change of vaporization (latent heat) H_{fg}, Btu/lb$_m$,
Enthalpy of saturated vapor H_g, Btu/lb$_m$,
Entropy of saturated liquid S_f, Btu/lb$_m \cdot$ °R,
Entropy change of vaporization S_{fg}, Btu/lb$_m \cdot$ °R,
Entropy of saturated vapor S_g, Btu/lb$_m \cdot$ °R.

The second table gives specific volumes, enthalpies, and entropies of superheated steam as functions of both pressure and temperature. In addition, for each even value of pressure, the saturation temperature is listed along with the specific volumes, enthalpies, and entropies of saturated liquid and saturated vapor.

The evaluation of property changes through use of the steam tables is illustrated by the following example: Superheated steam at 70 psia and 400°F is expanded reversibly and adiabatically (i.e., at constant entropy) to a final pressure of 15 psia. What is the enthalpy change of the steam during this process? From the superheat tables we find the initial enthalpy and entropy to be

$$H_1 = 1232.8 \text{ Btu/lb}_m,$$
$$S_1 = 1.6960 \text{ Btu/lb}_m \cdot \text{°R}.$$

Since $S_2 = S_1$, the final entropy of the steam at 15 psia is

$$S_2 = 1.6960 \text{ Btu/lb}_m \cdot \text{°R}.$$

At 15 psia the entropy of *saturated* vapor is 1.7548 Btu/lb$_m \cdot$ °R. Evidently the final state of the steam is a mixture of saturated vapor and saturated liquid (wet steam), because the entropy is less than that of saturated steam. S_2 is therefore given by

$$S_2 = (1 - x)S_{f_2} + xS_{g_2},$$

where x is the quality. Thus

$$1.6960 = (1 - x)0.3135 + (x)1.7548,$$
and
$$x = 0.9592.$$

The final enthalpy is

$$H_2 = (1 - x)H_{f_2} + xH_{g_2}$$
$$= (0.0408)(181.1) + (0.9592)(1150.7)$$
$$= 1111.1,$$

and the enthalpy change is

$$\Delta H = H_2 - H_1 = 1111.1 - 1232.8$$
$$= -121.7 \text{ Btu/lb}_m.$$

Problems

12.1 (a) Prove that the slope of a curve on a Mollier diagram representing a reversible isothermal process is equal to

$$T - \frac{1}{\beta}.$$

(b) Prove that the slope of a curve on a Mollier diagram representing a reversible isochoric process is equal to

$$T + \frac{\gamma - 1}{\beta}.$$

12.2 (a) With the aid of a Mollier diagram, show that, when a saturated liquid undergoes a throttling process, cooling and partial vaporization result.

(b) The pressure of CO_2 at the triple point is about 5 atm. Show with the aid of a $\ln P\ H$ diagram that, if saturated liquid CO_2 at room temperature undergoes a throttling process to atmospheric pressure, "dry ice" will be formed.

12.3 Show from the steam tables that, at any temperature, the value of the Gibbs function is the same for both saturated liquid and saturated vapor.

12.4 One pound mass of steam undergoes the following quasi-static processes. Determine Q and W in each case:

(a) Cooling at constant volume from an initial state of 50 psia and 500°F to a final temperature of 300°F.

(b) The same as (a), but at constant pressure.

12.5 Determine the differences between the enthalpy, internal energy, and entropy of steam at 900°F and 500 psia and at 300°F and 40 psia. Base your results on 1 lb mole. Compare answers obtained from the steam tables with those calculated, assuming steam to be an ideal gas. See Table 5.2 for C_P of steam.

12.6 Steam at 80 psia and 400°F is expanded at constant enthalpy (as through a valve) to 14.7 psia.

(a) What is the temperature of the steam in the final state? If steam under these conditions were an ideal gas, what would be the final temperature?

(b) What is its specific volume in the final state?

(c) What is the entropy change of the steam?

12.7 (a) One pound mass of steam is confined in a cylinder by a piston at 100 psia and 500°F. Calculate the work done by the steam if it is allowed to expand isothermally and quasi-statically to 35 psia. What is the heat absorbed by the steam from the surroundings during the process?

(b) Steam at 100 psia and 500°F is allowed to expand adiabatically and quasi-statically until its pressure is 35 psia. Determine the final temperature of the steam. What is the work done by the steam?

(c) Explain the difference between the work values obtained in (a) and (b).

12.8 At 450°F a mixture of saturated steam and liquid water exists in equilibrium. If the specific volume of the mixture is 0.6673 ft³/lb$_m$, calculate from data in the steam tables:

(a) Percent moisture.

(b) Enthalpy of the mixture, Btu/lb$_m$.

(c) Entropy of the mixture, Btu/lb$_m$ · °R.

12.9 Steam at 50 psia is known to have an enthalpy of 1038.0 Btu/lb$_m$. What is its temperature? What is its entropy? What is its internal energy?

12.10 A piston-and-cylinder engine operating in cycles and using steam as the working fluid executes the following steps:

(a) Steam at 75 psia and 350°F is heated at constant volume to a pressure of 110 psia.

(b) The steam is then expanded quasi-statically and adiabatically back to the initial temperature of 350°F.

(c) The steam is finally compressed isothermally and quasi-statically to the initial pressure of 75 psia.

Determine the efficiency of the conversion of heat into work for this engine.

12.11 A tank having a volume of 100 ft³ contains 1 ft³ of liquid water and 99 ft³ of water vapor at standard atmospheric pressure. Heat is transferred to the contents of the tank until the liquid water has just evaporated. How much heat must be added?

12.12 A closed vessel of 10 ft³ capacity is filled with saturated steam at 250 psia. If, subsequently, 25 percent of the steam is condensed, how much heat must be removed and what is the final pressure?

12.13 Describe the characteristics and sketch the paths of the following processes on PV, $\ln P\ H$, TS, and HS diagrams:

(a) Continuous throttling of saturated liquid.

(b) Condensing superheated vapor to subcooled liquid.

(c) Adiabatic reversible expansion of saturated vapor.

(d) Constant-volume heating of saturated liquid.

(e) Isothermal expansion, starting at the critical point.

Chapter 13/
Applications of Thermodynamics
to Engineering Systems

13.1/ Flow Processes

The development in Chap. 4 of the mathematical expression of the first law in the form

$$\Delta U = U_2 - U_1 = Q - W$$

was based on three related ideas: the existence of an internal-energy function, the principle of conservation of energy, and the thermo-dynamic definition of heat. Our applications of this equation have been to systems of constant mass which experience no changes in kinetic or gravitational potential energy. Moreover, we have dealt primarily with systems whose properties are uniform throughout at the initial and final conditions of the system.

The engineer must usually deal with much more complex situations. The vast majority of engineering processes involve the flow of fluids, and it is the purpose of this chapter to extend the applications of thermodynamics to such processes.

The general problem of fluid flow is extremely complicated. There may be present any or all of the following conditions:

1. Pressure, temperature, velocity, density, and other property variations in all directions in the fluid.
2. Changes in gravitational potential energy and in kinetic energy of the fluid as it flows from one point to another.

3. Turbulence and other dissipative effects, all encompassed under the general term fluid friction and arising because of the viscous nature of fluids. In this chapter we limit ourselves to systems in which flow is unidirectional and in which surface, electrical, and magnetic effects are negligible.

We idealize our systems to the extent of imagining that, if we proceed from any given point in a fluid stream in a direction *perpendicular to the flow direction*, there will be no change of pressure, temperature, velocity, density, or other property. Thus the properties assigned at any cross section of a flowing stream are considered uniform over the stream at values representing the average values one would obtain by integration over the actual stream. We also make the basic assumption that the thermodynamic properties of a flowing stream are the same as for the fluid at rest at the same temperature, pressure, and density. These idealizations are necessary to make engineering problems tractable, and experience shows that the errors introduced are negligible for all practical purposes.

13.2/ Energy Equations for Closed Systems

A closed system is one which may exchange energy as heat and work with its surroundings but which cannot exchange mass. Since matter does not flow across the boundaries of the system, the mass of the system is necessarily constant. The simple first-law equation

$$\Delta U = Q - W$$

applies to such a system. We wish now to generalize this equation so that it may be applied to systems consisting of several parts between which matter may flow. However, we still impose the restriction of a closed system, so that the total mass in all parts of the system taken together is constant. As we shall see, this restriction does not limit the kinds of processes that may be considered. Rather, it prescribes the proper choice of a system in any given application.

Systems of several parts may interact with the surroundings in such a way that more than one heat term and more than one work term must be included in the energy equation. We therefore replace Q and W by ΣQ and ΣW, where the summation signs merely indicate that all terms of the type considered must be included. These quantities then represent the *total* heat transfer to the system and the *total* work produced by the system.

Since the system consists of several parts, we must sum the internal energy over all parts of the system in its original and final states. We then can determine the change in *total* internal energy of the system as the result of carrying out a process.

This internal-energy summation may be done in two ways:

1. Energy may be summed over the identifiable *regions of space* included in the system. The resulting equation is

$$\Delta \sum_R (mU) = \Sigma Q - \Sigma W, \tag{13.1}$$

or equivalently, $$\sum_R \Delta(mU) = \Sigma Q - \Sigma W. \tag{13.2}$$

It clearly does not matter whether we take the difference of sums or the sum of the differences. The sign $\sum_R$ indicates a sum over *regions of space*. The quantity (mU) gives the total internal energy of a region, and this may change both in the mass m and in the internal energy per unit mass U from beginning to end of the process.

2. Energy may be summed over the identifiable *mass elements* making up the system. In this case

$$\sum_m (m\,\Delta U) = \Sigma Q - \Sigma W. \tag{13.3}$$

The sign $\sum_m$ indicates a sum over the mass elements which make up the system.

It is very often useful to replace the internal energy U in these equations by the enthalpy H. There are two reasons for this. First, the resulting equations are usually simpler, and second, tables of properties (e.g., steam tables) rarely list values of U but always give complete data for H. By definition,

$$H = U + PV.$$

Therefore

$$\Delta \sum_R (mH) = \Delta \sum_R (mU) + \Delta \sum_R (mPV),$$

or

$$\sum_R \Delta(mH) = \sum_R \Delta(mU) + \sum_R \Delta(mPV),$$

and

$$\sum_m (m\,\Delta H) = \sum_m (m\,\Delta U) + \sum_m (m\,\Delta PV).$$

Combination of each of these expressions with the appropriate form of the energy equation, Eqs. (13.1), (13.2), or (13.3), leads immediately to

$$\Delta \sum_R (mH) = \Sigma Q - \Sigma W + \Delta \sum_R (mPV), \tag{13.4}$$

$$\sum_R \Delta(mH) = \Sigma Q - \Sigma W + \sum_R \Delta(mPV), \tag{13.5}$$

and

$$\sum_m (m\,\Delta H) = \Sigma Q - \Sigma W + \sum_m (m\,\Delta PV). \tag{13.6}$$

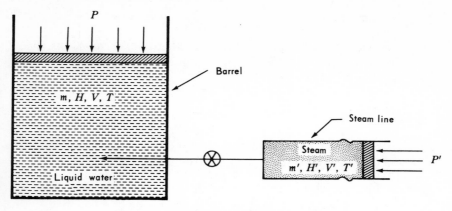

Fig. 13.1   Injection of steam into water.

The use of Eqs. (13.4), (13.5), and (13.6) is best illustrated by example. A crude method for determining the enthalpy of steam in a steam line is to bleed steam from the line through a hose into a barrel of water. The mass of the barrel with its contents and the temperature of the water are recorded at the beginning and end of the process. The condensation of steam by the water raises the temperature of the water.

Our energy equations are written for a system of constant mass. It is therefore essential to choose the system so that it includes not only the water originally in the barrel, but also the steam in the line that will be condensed by the water during the process. We may imagine a piston in the steam line that separates the steam in the line into two parts: that which will enter the barrel and that which will remain in the line. This view is represented schematically in Fig. 13.1. In addition to the piston in the steam line, another piston is shown which separates the water in the barrel from the atmosphere. Both the atmosphere and the steam in the line exert forces (shown as pressures, i.e., forces distributed over an area) which act on the system. These forces move during the process and therefore do work, which must be included in the ΣW term.

The pressure P exerted by the atmosphere on the water in the barrel is taken as constant, but the other properties of the water change during the process. Thus the mass changes from m_1 to m_2; the specific enthalpy, from H_1 to H_2; the specific volume, from V_1 to V_2; and the temperature, from T_1 to T_2. In the steam line, however, the intensive properties T', P', H', and V' remain constant. The mass of steam considered as part of the system goes from an initial value of m' to zero. From a mass balance,

$$m_2 - m_1 = m'.$$

The work terms are as follows (note that $P = P_1 = P_2$):

$$W_{\text{barrel}} = \int_{m_1 V_1}^{m_2 V_2} P\, d(mV) = P \int_{m_1 V_1}^{m_2 V_2} d(mV) = P(m_2 V_2 - m_1 V_1)$$
$$= m_2 P_2 V_2 - m_1 P_1 V_1,$$

and

$$W_{\text{line}} = \int_{m'V'}^{0} P'\, d(m'V') = P' \int_{m'V'}^{0} d(m'V') = -P'm'V' = -m'P'V'.$$

Therefore $\qquad \Sigma W = m_2 P_2 V_2 - m_1 P_1 V_1 - m'P'V'.$

If we assume that the steam line and the barrel are well insulated, we may neglect heat transfer and set $\Sigma Q = 0$.

Application of Eq. (13.4) requires the selection of regions of space over which to make the summations $\sum_R$. These are quite obviously the barrel and the steam line. Thus Eq. (13.4) becomes

$$\underbrace{\underbrace{m_2 H_2}_{\substack{\sum_R \text{final}}} - \underbrace{(m_1 H_1 + m'H')}_{\substack{\sum_R \text{initial}}}}_{\Delta \sum_R (mH)} = \underbrace{-m_2 P_2 V_2 + m_1 P_1 V_1 + m'P'V'}_{-\Sigma W}$$

$$+ \underbrace{\underbrace{m_2 P_2 V_2}_{\substack{\sum_R \text{final}}} - \underbrace{(m_1 P_1 V_1 + m'P'V')}_{\substack{\sum_R \text{initial}}}}_{\Delta \sum_R (mPV)}.$$

Since the mPV terms all cancel, the final equation is

$$m_2 H_2 = m_1 H_1 + m'H'.$$

This equation shows that for this process the total enthalpy of the system at the end is the same as the total enthalpy of the system at the start.

Were we to choose to work with Eq. (13.5), we should have

$$\underbrace{\underbrace{(m_2 H_2 - m_1 H_1)}_{\Delta(mH)_{\text{barrel}}} + \underbrace{(0 - m'H')}_{\Delta(mH)_{\text{line}}}}_{\sum_R \Delta(mH)} = \underbrace{-m_2 P_2 V_2 + m_1 P_1 V_1 + m'P'V'}_{-\Sigma W}$$

$$+ \underbrace{\underbrace{(m_2 P_2 V_2 - m_1 P_1 V_1)}_{\Delta(mPV)_{\text{barrel}}} + \underbrace{(0 - m'P'V')}_{\Delta(mPV)_{\text{line}}}}_{\sum_R \Delta(mPV)}.$$

Again the final equation is

$$m_2 H_2 = m_1 H_1 + m'H'.$$

Equations (13.4) and (13.5) are two equivalent versions of the same summation process, and there is nothing outside of personal preference to recommend the use of one over the other. Equation (13.6), however, makes use of a different idea, i.e., the summation over mass elements. The obviously identifiable mass elements here are the initial mass of water in the tank m_1 and the initial mass of steam in the line m'. We must now follow these mass elements through the process to see how their properties are altered. At the end of the process the mass m_1 is still liquid water in the barrel and it now has the properties H_2 and V_2. The mass m' has been transferred from the line to the barrel, where it also has the properties H_2 and V_2. With this analysis in mind we may write Eq. (13.6):

$$\underbrace{m_1(H_2 - H_1) + m'(H_2 - H')}_{\sum_m (m\,\Delta H)} = \underbrace{-m_2 P_2 V_2 + m_1 P_1 V_1 + m' P' V'}_{-\Sigma W}$$

$$+ \underbrace{m_1(P_2 V_2 - P_1 V_1) + m'(P_2 V_2 - P' V')}_{\sum_m (m\,\Delta PV)}.$$

Upon rearrangement this becomes

$$(m_1 + m')H_2 - m_1 H_1 - m'H' = -m_2 P_2 V_2 + m_1 P_1 V_1 + m' P' V'$$
$$+ (m_1 + m')P_2 V_2 - m_1 P_1 V_1 - m' P' V'.$$

Substitution of m_2 for $(m_1 + m')$ reduces this equation to the one obtained before:

$$m_2 H_2 = m_1 H_1 + m'H'.$$

The student who notes the similarity between the process considered here and the throttling process described in Sec. 10.1 will not be surprised by this result. For both processes the total final enthalpy of the system is unchanged from the total initial enthalpy.

Consider the following experimental results: Steam from a line at 100 psia is bled into a barrel of water for which $m_1 = 300$ lb$_m$ and $T_1 = 50°F$. At the end of the process the measured values are $m_2 = 320$ lb$_m$ and $T_2 = 120°F$. Clearly, $m' = 20$ lb$_m$. From the steam tables,

$$H_1 = 18.07 \text{ Btu/lb}_m,$$
$$H_2 = 87.91 \text{ Btu/lb}_m,$$

where the enthalpy of liquid water at atmospheric pressure is taken to be the same as *saturated* liquid water at the temperature considered. The error introduced is negligible, because the effect of pressure on liquid properties is slight except near the critical point. Solution for H' gives

$$H' = \frac{m_2 H_2 - m_1 H_1}{m'} = \frac{(320)(87.91) - (300)(18.07)}{20} = 1135.5 \text{ Btu/lb}_m.$$

Since saturated steam at 100 psia has an enthalpy of 1187.3 Btu/lb$_m$, the steam in the line is wet. Its quality is easily calculated to be 0.9423, or 94.23 percent vapor.

One observation to be made about this problem is that, in the derivation of the energy equation which applies to it, the mPV terms arising from the substitution of $H - PV$ for U and the mPV terms representing work quantities all canceled. It is readily shown that this is true for any process of this type for which the pressure is constant *in each part* of the system. It is *not* necessary that the pressure be the *same* in all parts of the system. Where P is constant in each part of the system, i.e., in each region of space, the work terms will be of the form

$$W = P\,\Delta(mV)$$

and

$$\Sigma W = \sum_R [P\,\Delta(mV)].$$

Equation (13.5) then becomes, since $\Delta(mPV) = P\,\Delta(mV)$,

$$\sum_R \Delta(mH) = \Sigma Q - \sum_R [P\,\Delta(mV)] + \sum_R [P\,\Delta(mV)],$$

or

$$\sum_R \Delta(mH) = \Sigma Q.$$

This equation may also be written

$$\Delta \sum_R (mH) = \Sigma Q,$$

because taking the difference of the sums is identical with summing the differences. In either case the equation states that the total enthalpy change for the entire system is equal to the total heat transferred. One can equally well sum over the mass elements of the system and write

$$\sum_m (m\,\Delta H) = \Sigma Q.$$

This result is a generalization of one of the fundamental properties of the enthalpy function as presented in Sec. 10.1. It was shown there (property 2) that the change in enthalpy during an isobaric process is equal to the heat that is transferred. It was implicit in that derivation that the pressure be not only constant during the process, but also uniform throughout the system. We now see that uniformity of pressure is not a necessary condition, provided that each part of the system is maintained at *constant* pressure.

For problems of the type considered in this section one may sum over regions of space or over the mass elements of the system. The same answer must always be obtained. The choice may be considered a matter of personal preference. However, in some problems the proper choice may greatly simplify the solution procedure. Consider the following problem.

A tank of 50-ft³ capacity contains 1,000 lb$_m$ of liquid water in equilibrium with pure water vapor, which fills the rest of the tank, at a temperature of 212°F and 1 atm absolute pressure. From a water line at slightly above atmospheric pressure 1,500 lb$_m$ of water at 160°F is to be bled into the tank. How much heat must be transferred to the contents of the tank during this process if the temperature and pressure in the tank are not to change?

The system must be chosen to include the initial contents of the tank and the water to be added during the process. A schematic diagram of the system is shown in Fig. 13.2. Since the tank at all times contains liquid and vapor in equilibrium at 212°F and 1 atm abs, the properties H_f and V_f for the liquid and H_g and V_g for the vapor in the tank are the same at the end as at the start of the process. The properties H' and V' of the liquid water in the line are also constant. As liquid is added to the tank, it displaces some of the vapor that is present initially, and this vapor must condense. Thus the tank at the end of the process contains as liquid all the 1,000 lb$_m$ of liquid initially present in the tank. This 1,000 lb$_m$ of liquid is present as saturated liquid at 212°F both at the beginning and end of the process, and hence does not change in properties. In addition, the 1,500 lb$_m$ of liquid added to the tank remains liquid, but it changes from liquid at 160°F to saturated liquid at 212°F. Also, the vapor which condenses adds to the liquid in the tank at the end of the process. Let the amount of vapor which condenses be y lb$_m$. This mass of material changes from saturated vapor at 212°F to saturated liquid at 212°F during the process. The part of the vapor which does *not* condense remains as saturated vapor at 212°F and therefore does not change in properties.

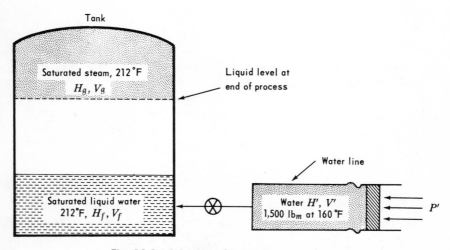

Fig. 13.2   Injection of water into a tank.

In this analysis of the problem we have identified four mass elements which constitute the system and have described their changes during the process. This suggests that we make our summation over changes which occur in these mass elements. Two of the mass elements— the initial 1,000 lb$_m$ of liquid in the tank and the mass of vapor which does not condense—undergo no change in properties, and may be omitted from the summation. The two remaining mass elements to be considered are the 1,500 lb$_m$ of water added to the tank from the line and the y lb$_m$ of vapor which condenses. Since pressure is constant in both the tank and the line, the appropriate energy equation is

$$\sum_m (m\ \Delta H) = \Sigma Q.$$

Carrying out the summation, we have

$$\Sigma Q = 1{,}500(H_f - H') + y(H_f - H_g).$$

From the steam tables,

$$H_f = 180.07 \text{ Btu/lb}_m,$$
$$H' = 127.87 \text{ Btu/lb}_m,$$
$$H_g = 1150.4 \text{ Btu/lb}_m.$$

Thus

$$\Sigma Q = 1500(180.07 - 127.87) + y(180.07 - 1150.4)$$
$$= 78{,}300 - 970.3y.$$

We must now determine y. This is most easily done by noting that the sum of the volume changes of the mass elements of the system that we have already identified must be equal to the total volume change of the system. The total volume change of the system is just the volume of the 1,500 lb$_m$ of water at 160°F that is added to the tank. Since the total volume change is negative,

$$\Sigma(m\ \Delta V) = -1{,}500V'.$$

The same mass elements that change in enthalpy also change in volume. Thus

$$1{,}500(V_f - V') + y(V_f - V_g) = -1{,}500V',$$

or

$$1{,}500V_f + y(V_f - V_g) = 0.$$

From the steam tables,

$$V_f = 0.01672 \text{ ft}^3/\text{lb}_m,$$
$$V_g = 26.83 \text{ ft}^3/\text{lb}_m.$$

Therefore

$$(1{,}500)(0.01672) + y(0.01672 - 26.83) = 0.$$

Solution for y gives

$$y = 0.9355 \text{ lb}_m.$$

For the total heat transferred we have

$$\Sigma Q = 78,300 - (970.3)(0.9355)$$
$$= 77,390 \text{ Btu.}$$

Analysis of this problem through identification of mass elements has led to a very simple solution. If we had summed over regions, we should eventually have reached the same result, but the calculations would have been much more tedious.

Processes of the type considered so far are commonly called "unsteady-state-flow processes," because of one's natural tendency to focus attention on the barrel or tank. By careful choice of the system for purposes of writing an energy equation, we have been able to treat these processes as though they were "nonflow." Indeed, no flow does occur at the start or end of the process, and therefore we need no kinetic-energy terms in our equations. Moreover, we have ignored the possibility of changes in gravitational potential energy when material is transferred from one location to another. Terms to account for this are easily included, but are rarely needed.

13.3/ Energy Equations for Steady-state-flow Processes

We wish now to consider the kind of process that is referred to as "steady-state flow." Such processes are of primary importance in engineering because the mass production of materials and energy demands continuous operation of processes. The term steady-state-flow process implies the continuous flow of material through an apparatus. The inflow of mass is at all times exactly matched by the outflow of mass, so that there is no accumulation of material within the apparatus. Moreover, conditions at all points within the apparatus are steady or constant with time. Thus, at any point in the apparatus, the thermodynamic properties are constant; although they may vary from point to point, they do not change with time at a given point.

Consider the schematic diagram of Fig. 13.3, which shows a region of space bounded by the heavy curves and by the line segments 1-1, 2-2, and 3-3. This region is called the *control volume*. The material contained in the control volume is shown by the light shading. In addition, we recognize three other regions of space which communicate with the control volume: one to the left of 1-1, another to the right of 2-2, and a third to the right of 3-3. These we shall call regions 1, 2, and 3, respectively. For the process considered, regions 1 and 2 contain fluid which flows into the control volume, and region 3 collects fluid which flows from the control volume. There is no limitation on the number of inlets to and outlets from the control volume. We consider here a total of three by way of example.

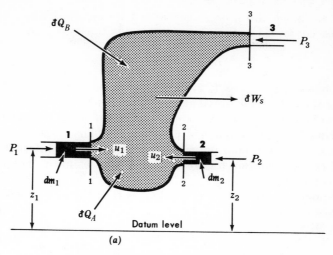

Fig. 13.3a   Flow system at time τ.

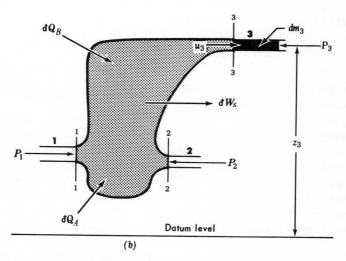

Fig. 13.3b   Flow system at time $\tau + d\tau$.

Our *system* is chosen to include not only the fluid contained initially in the control volume, but in addition all fluid which will enter the control volume during some arbitrarily selected time interval.   Thus the initial configuration of the system as shown in Fig. 13.3a includes the masses dm_1 and dm_2 which are to flow into the control volume during a differential time interval.   The final configuration of the system after time $d\tau$ is shown in Fig. 13.3b.   Here regions 1 and 2 no longer contain the masses dm_1 and dm_2; however, the mass dm_3 has collected in region 3. Since the process considered is one of steady-state flow, the mass contained in the control volume is constant, and

$$dm_3 = dm_1 + dm_2.$$

The masses in regions 1, 2, and 3 are considered to have the properties of the fluid as measured at 1-1, 2-2, and 3-3, respectively. These properties include a velocity u and an elevation above a datum plane z, as well as the thermodynamic properties. Thus these masses have kinetic and gravitational potential energy as well as internal energy, and an energy equation for steady-flow processes must contain terms for all these forms of energy.

We know from the study of mechanics that the kinetic energy of a mass m is equal to

$$E_k = \frac{mu^2}{2g_c},$$

where u is velocity, and g_c is the dimensional constant discussed in Sec. 2.5 and included to allow the use of any self-consistent set of units. The gravitational potential energy of a mass m is

$$E_p = \frac{mzg}{g_c},$$

where z is the height above some arbitrarily chosen datum level, and g is the local acceleration of gravity.

We are now able to write an energy equation for steady-state-flow processes. Note that we have chosen our system to be one of constant mass, i.e., the mass contained in the control volume plus the mass which is to enter during the time interval considered. Thus we may apply the first law in the form already developed, provided that we add terms to account for changes in kinetic and potential energy. Since we have identified the regions of space which make up the system, we sum over these regions. For a differential time interval, we have

$$\Delta \sum_R (U\, dm) + \Delta \sum_R \left(\frac{u^2\, dm}{2g_c}\right) + \Delta \sum_R \left(\frac{zg\, dm}{g_c}\right) = \Sigma\, dQ - \Sigma\, dW.$$

Since the mass of the control volume and the properties of the fluid in the control volume remain unchanged with time, the summations in the above equation over regions of space may omit this region. The summations need include only the regions from which and to which fluid flows during the process considered. These are regions 1, 2, and 3 of Fig. 13.3. At the end of the time interval, only the exit regions will contain part of the mass of the system, whereas at the start only the inlet regions contain mass constituting part of the system. With respect to Fig. 13.3, the internal-energy term is therefore

$$\Delta \sum_{R} (U \, dm) = U_3 \, dm_3 - U_1 \, dm_1 - U_2 \, dm_2.$$

This result can be expressed more simply by writing

$$\Delta \sum_{R} (U \, dm) = \Sigma(U \, dm)_{\text{out}} - \Sigma(U \, dm)_{\text{in}} = \Delta(U \, dm)_{\substack{\text{flowing} \\ \text{streams}}}.$$

The kinetic- and potential-energy terms may be expressed similarly. Thus the energy equation may be written

$$\Delta(U \, dm)_{\substack{\text{flowing} \\ \text{streams}}} + \Delta \left(\frac{u^2 \, dm}{2g_c} \right)_{\substack{\text{flowing} \\ \text{streams}}} + \Delta \left(\frac{zg \, dm}{g_c} \right)_{\substack{\text{flowing} \\ \text{streams}}} = \Sigma \, dQ - \Sigma \, dW,$$

where Δ denotes the difference between streams flowing out and streams flowing in.

The $\Sigma \, dQ$ term includes all heat transferred to the system. For the example of Fig. 13.3 it would consist of $dQ_A + dQ_B$. The $\Sigma \, dW$ term includes work quantities of two types. The one shown in Fig. 13.3 and designated dW_s represents *shaft work*, i.e., work transmitted across the boundaries of the system by a rotating or reciprocating shaft. The other work quantities are of the kind already considered, which result from the action of external pressures in regions 1, 2, and 3 on the moving boundaries of the system. Thus, for the process of Fig. 13.3,

$$\Sigma \, dW = P_3 V_3 \, dm_3 - P_1 V_1 \, dm_1 - P_2 V_2 \, dm_2 + dW_s.$$

This can also be written

$$\Sigma \, dW = \Delta(PV \, dm)_{\substack{\text{flowing} \\ \text{streams}}} + dW_s.$$

Substitution in the energy equation and rearrangement gives

$$\Delta(U \, dm)_{\substack{\text{flowing} \\ \text{streams}}} + \Delta(PV \, dm)_{\substack{\text{flowing} \\ \text{streams}}}$$
$$+ \Delta \left(\frac{u^2 \, dm}{2g_c} \right)_{\substack{\text{flowing} \\ \text{streams}}} + \Delta \left(\frac{zg \, dm}{g_c} \right)_{\substack{\text{flowing} \\ \text{streams}}} = \Sigma \, dQ - dW_s.$$

If dm is factored, this equation may be written more simply as

$$\Delta \left[\left(U + PV + \frac{u^2}{2g_c} + \frac{zg}{g_c} \right) dm \right]_{\substack{\text{flowing} \\ \text{streams}}} = \Sigma \, dQ - dW_s.$$

By definition, $H = U + PV$, and we have, finally,

$$\boxed{\Delta \left[\left(H + \frac{u^2}{2g_c} + \frac{zg}{g_c} \right) dm \right]_{\substack{\text{flowing} \\ \text{stremas}}} = \Sigma \, dQ - dW_s.} \qquad (13.7)$$

Equation (13.7) is the energy equation for a steady-flow process as written for an infinitesimal time interval $d\tau$. If we divide through by $d\tau$ and denote the various rates by

$$\dot{m} = \frac{dm}{d\tau},$$

$$\dot{Q} = \frac{dQ}{d\tau},$$

and

$$\dot{W}_s = \frac{dW_s}{d\tau},$$

we have

$$\Delta \left[\left(H + \frac{u^2}{2g_c} + \frac{zg}{g_c} \right) \dot{m} \right]_{\substack{\text{flowing} \\ \text{streams}}} = \Sigma \dot{Q} - \dot{W}_s, \tag{13.8}$$

which expresses the energy equation in terms of rates, all of which are constant in a steady-state-flow process.

One special case of Eq. (13.8) is very often encountered. If only a single stream enters and a single stream leaves the control volume, then $\dot{m}$ must be the same for both, and Eq. (13.8) becomes

$$\Delta \left(H + \frac{u^2}{2g_c} + \frac{zg}{g_c} \right) \dot{m} = \Sigma \dot{Q} - \dot{W}_s. \tag{13.9}$$

Division by $\dot{m}$ gives

$$\Delta \left(H + \frac{u^2}{2g_c} + \frac{zg}{g_c} \right) = \frac{\Sigma \dot{Q}}{\dot{m}} - \frac{\dot{W}_s}{\dot{m}} = \Sigma Q - W_s,$$

or

$$\Delta H + \frac{\Delta u^2}{2g_c} + \Delta z \left(\frac{g}{g_c} \right) = \Sigma Q - W_s, \tag{13.10}$$

where each term now refers to a unit mass of fluid passing through the control volume. All terms in this equation, as in all the energy equations of this chapter, must be expressed in the same energy units. Careful attention must be paid to this, for H and Q are usually given in thermal units (e.g., Btu), whereas kinetic energy, potential energy, and work are usually expressed in mechanical units (e.g., ft · lb$_f$). The correct use of conversion factors must be mastered.

Consider now the application of Eq. (13.8) to a specific example. Saturated steam at 50 psia is to be mixed continuously with a stream of water at 60°F to produce hot water at 180°F at the rate of 500 lb$_m$/min. The inlet and exit lines leading to the mixing device all have an internal diameter of 2 in. At what rate must steam be supplied?

Evidently, $\dot{W}_s = 0$. We shall assume that the apparatus is insulated so that, to a good approximation, $\Sigma \dot{Q} = 0$. Presumably, also, the device is small enough so that the inlet and outlet elevations are almost the same and the potential-energy terms may be neglected. The velocity of the outlet hot-water stream is given by $u = \dot{m}V/A$, where $\dot{m}$ is 500 lb_m/min, V is the specific volume of water at 180°F, and $A = (\pi/4)D^2$. From the steam tables $V = 0.01651$ ft³/lb_m. Thus

$$u = \frac{(500 \text{ lb}_m/\text{min})(0.01651 \text{ ft}^3/\text{lb}_m)}{(\pi/4)(\tfrac{2}{12} \text{ ft})^2(60 \text{ sec/min})} = 6.3 \text{ ft/sec.}$$

From this we can calculate the kinetic energy of the outlet water stream:

$$\frac{\dot{m}u^2}{2g_c} = \frac{(500 \text{ lb}_m/\text{min})(6.3 \text{ ft/sec})^2}{(2)(32.174 \text{ lb}_m \cdot \text{ft/lb}_f \cdot \text{sec}^2)} = 308 \text{ ft} \cdot \text{lb}_f/\text{min,}$$

or
$$\frac{308 \text{ ft} \cdot \text{lb}_f/\text{min}}{778 \text{ ft} \cdot \text{lb}_f/\text{Btu}} = 0.396 \text{ Btu/min.}$$

This is an entirely negligible energy quantity compared with the energy changes being considered. (Note that the process raises the temperature of nearly 500 lb_m of water per minute from 60 to 180°F. This requires about 60,000 Btu.) We may therefore neglect the kinetic-energy terms for both water streams. Since we do not yet know the flow rate of the steam, we shall for the present neglect this kinetic-energy term also. We can later see if this is justified. Equation (13.8) therefore reduces to

$$H_3\dot{m}_3 - H_2\dot{m}_2 - H_1\dot{m}_1 = 0,$$

where the subscript 3 refers to the outlet stream; 2, to the inlet water; and 1, to the inlet steam.

From the steam tables:

$$H_1 = 1174.0 \text{ Btu/lb}_m,$$
$$H_2 = 28.07 \text{ Btu/lb}_m,$$
$$H_3 = 147.92 \text{ Btu/lb}_m.$$

Also
$$\dot{m}_3 = 500 \text{ lb}_m/\text{min,}$$
$$\dot{m}_2 = \dot{m}_3 - \dot{m}_1 = 500 - \dot{m}_1.$$

Substitution in the energy equation gives

$$(147.91)(500) - (28.07)(500 - \dot{m}_1) - 1{,}174.0\dot{m}_1 = 0,$$
$$\dot{m}_1 = 52.29 \text{ lb}_m/\text{min.}$$

The velocity of this stream is

$$u_1 = \frac{\dot{m}_1 V_1}{(\pi/4)D^2} = \frac{(52.29 \text{ lb}_m/\text{min})(8.522 \text{ ft}^3/\text{lb}_m)}{(\pi/4)(\tfrac{2}{12} \text{ ft})^2(60 \text{ sec/min})},$$
$$= 354 \text{ ft/sec.}$$

Its kinetic energy is

$$\frac{\dot{m}_1 u_1^2}{2g_c} = \frac{(52.29 \text{ lb}_m/\text{min})(354 \text{ ft/sec})^2}{(2)(32.174 \text{ lb}_m \cdot \text{ft/lb}_f \cdot \text{sec}^2)} = 101{,}800 \text{ ft} \cdot \text{lb}_f/\text{min},$$

or

$$\frac{101{,}800}{778} = 131 \text{ Btu/min}.$$

We may now rewrite our energy balance to include the kinetic-energy term for the steam flow:

$$(147.91)(500) - (28.07)(500 - \dot{m}_1) - 1{,}174.0\dot{m}_1 - 131 = 0,$$
$$\dot{m}_1 = 52.18 \text{ lb}_m/\text{min}.$$

The inclusion of the kinetic-energy term has resulted in only a 0.2 percent change in our answer. In this example, as in many others, the kinetic-energy term is not significant even though a stream of rather high velocity is considered. Of course, in cases where kinetic-energy changes are a primary object or result of a process, the kinetic-energy terms are important. For example, the acceleration of an air stream to a high velocity in a wind tunnel requires a considerable work expenditure to produce the kinetic-energy change. For the calculation of this work, one could hardly omit the kinetic-energy terms from the energy equation. The same general comments apply to gravitational potential-energy effects. They are often quite negligible. However, the work generated in a hydroelectric power plant depends directly on the change in elevation of the water flowing through the plant, and the potential-energy terms are of major importance in the energy equation.

13.4/ General Energy Equations

In deriving the energy equation for steady-state-flow processes, we found it useful to introduce the concept of a control volume. The resulting energy equation is seen to connect the properties of the streams flowing into and out of the control volume with the heat and work quantities crossing the boundaries of the control volume. We can extend the use of this concept to include unsteady-state-flow processes. The control volume is still a bounded region of space; however, the boundaries may be flexible to allow for expansion or contraction of the control volume. Furthermore, the mass contained in the control volume need no longer be constant. We deal now with transient conditions, where rates and properties vary with time. During an infinitesimal time interval $d\tau$, the mass entering the control volume may be different from the mass leaving the control volume. The difference must clearly be accounted for by the accumulation or depletion of mass within the control volume. Similarly, the difference between the transport of energy out of the control volume and into it by flowing streams need no longer be accounted for solely by the heat and work terms. Energy may be accumulated or depleted within the control volume. To state the situation precisely, the energy crossing the boundaries of the control volume as heat and work, $\Sigma \, dQ - \Sigma \, dW$, must equal the change in energy of the material contained within the control volume itself *plus* the net energy transport of the flowing streams. The energy change of the material in the control volume is $d(mU)_{\text{control volume}}$, and the net energy transport of the flowing streams as shown by Eq. (13.7) is

$$\Delta \left[\left(H + \frac{u^2}{2g_c} + \frac{zg}{g_c} \right) dm \right]_{\substack{\text{flowing} \\ \text{streams}}}$$

The energy equation therefore becomes

$$d(mU)_{\substack{\text{control} \\ \text{volume}}} + \Delta \left[\left(H + \frac{u^2}{2g_c} + \frac{zg}{g_c} \right) dm \right]_{\substack{\text{flowing} \\ \text{streams}}} = \Sigma \, dQ - \Sigma \, dW.$$

(13.11)

The work term $\Sigma \, dW$ may include shaft work, but may also include a term for work resulting from the expansion or contraction of the control volume itself.

Equation (13.11) is the most general expression for an energy equation that we shall attempt. It has inherent limitations. For example, it assumes no changes in the kinetic and potential energies of the control volume. For the vast majority of applications the control volume may be assumed to change just in internal energy. It is completely impractical to try to write a single energy equation that can be used for all applications. The only suitable guide where complexities arise is strict adherence to the law of conservation of energy, which is the basis for all energy equations. It might be remarked that Eq. (13.11) reduces to Eq. (13.7) for steady-state-flow processes. [The first term of Eq. (13.11) is zero, and $\Sigma \, dW$ becomes dW_s.] For a nonflow process, where the control volume contains the entire system, $dm = 0$, and Eq. (13.11) reduces to

$$d(mU) = dQ - dW.$$

If the system contains several parts, we need to sum the internal-energy term over the parts:

$$\Sigma \, d(mU) = \Sigma \, dQ - \Sigma \, dW,$$

which is the differential form of Eq. (13.2).

As an example of the use of Eq. (13.11), let us see how we should arrive at the energy equation for the process illustrated by Fig. 13.2. We take the tank as our control volume. There is no shaft work, and no expansion work. Therefore, $\Sigma \ dW = 0$. Equation (13.11) becomes

$$\Sigma \ dQ = d(mU)_{\text{tank}} - H' \ dm'.$$

The minus sign on $H' \ dm'$ arises because it is an inflowing stream. Since it is the only stream, we may arbitrarily set $z' = 0$, thus eliminating the potential-energy term. The kinetic-energy term has been dropped on the assumption that the process is carried out slowly enough so that flow is at low velocity. We must now integrate over the duration of the process. Since H' is constant, the result is

$$\Sigma Q = \Delta(mU)_{\text{tank}} - m'H'.$$

By the definition of enthalpy,

$$\Delta(mU)_{\text{tank}} = \Delta(mH)_{\text{tank}} - \Delta(PmV)_{\text{tank}}.$$

However, both the volume of the tank $(mV)_{\text{tank}}$ and the pressure in the tank are constant. Therefore $\Delta(PmV)_{\text{tank}} = 0$. As a result,

$$\Sigma Q = \Delta(mH)_{\text{tank}} - m'H'.$$

This equation expresses the fact that for this process the heat transferred is equal to the total enthalpy change caused by the process. This is the same idea upon which we based our earlier solution to this problem.

Clearly, energy equations may be developed from more than one point of view. Different applications yield most readily to different approaches. No formula can substitute for a thorough understanding of the meaning of the law of conservation of energy.

Equation (13.11) may be written in terms of rates by dividing through by $d\tau$:

$$\frac{d(mU)_{\substack{\text{control} \\ \text{volume}}}}{d\tau} + \Delta \left[\left(H + \frac{u^2}{2g_c} + \frac{zg}{g_c} \right) \dot{m} \right]_{\substack{\text{flowing} \\ \text{streams}}} = \Sigma \dot{Q} - \Sigma \dot{W}.$$

This equation applies at any instant during processes where conditions and flow rates change continuously. Other forms are, of course, also possible. For example, multiplication by $d\tau$ and integration over the time interval from zero to τ gives

$$\Delta(mU)_{\substack{\text{control} \\ \text{volume}}} + \int_0^\tau \Delta \left[\left(H + \frac{u^2}{2g_c} + \frac{zg}{g_c} \right) \dot{m} \right] d\tau = \Sigma Q - \Sigma W.$$

The integral can be evaluated only if the various quantities of the integrand are known as functions of time. This requires detailed information describing the process as a function of time.

13.5/ The Throttling Process (Joule-Kelvin Effect)

The throttling process was discussed briefly in Sec. 10.1, and in Sec. 13.2 we noted an example of such a process. We shall now review the basic features of a throttling process and then develop the thermodynamic equations which apply to it.

A throttling process is said to occur when fluid flowing steadily in a pipe passes an obstruction, such as a porous plug or a partly closed valve, which causes a discrete pressure drop in the flowing fluid in the absence of heat transfer and without appreciable kinetic-energy change of the fluid. Clearly, no shaft work is accomplished. For such a steady-flow process Eq. (13.10) reduces to

$$\Delta H = H_2 - H_1 = 0.$$

Thus, in a throttling process, the downstream enthalpy is the same as the upstream enthalpy. It should be noted that the downstream station must be far enough removed from the obstruction so as to be located beyond any local high-velocity jet immediately adjacent to the obstruction.

In addition to its engineering applications, the throttling process may be used to provide experimental information on the properties of fluids. This was in fact the object of Joule and Kelvin in their original experiments on throttling processes. In their work a cotton plug was used to provide an obstruction to flow, and gas passed through it parallel to the axis of the pipe. In modern measurements a cup of a strong porous material capable of withstanding a large force allows the gas to seep through in a radial direction. Rigid precautions are taken to provide adequate thermal insulation for the plug and the portion of the pipe near the plug. Suitable manometers and thermometers are used to measure the pressure and temperature of the gas on both sides of the plug.

The experiment is performed in the following way: The pressure and temperature on the high-pressure side of the plug P_i and T_i are chosen arbitrarily. The pressure on the other side of the plug P_f is then set at any value less than P_i, and the temperature of the gas T_f is measured. P_i and T_i are kept the same, and P_f is changed to another value, and the corresponding T_f is measured. This is done for a number of different values of P_f, the corresponding T_f being measured in each case. P_f is the independent variable of the experiment, and T_f, the dependent variable. The results provide a set of discrete points on a TP diagram, one point being P_iT_i and the others being the various P_f's and T_f's indicated in Fig. 13.4 by numbers 1 to 7. Although the points shown in the figure do not refer to any particular gas, they are typical of most gases. It can be seen that, if a throttling process takes

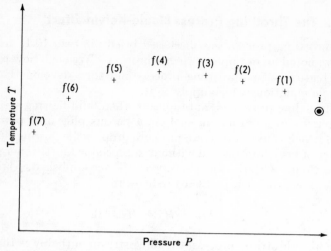

Fig. 13.4 Isenthalpic states of a gas.

place between the states P_iT_i and P_fT_f (3), there is a rise of temperature. Between P_iT_i and P_fT_f (7) however, there is a drop of temperature. In general, the temperature change of a gas upon seeping through a porous plug depends on the three quantities P_i, T_i, and P_f, and may be an increase or a decrease, or there may be no change whatever.

The eight points plotted in Fig. 13.4 represent equilibrium states of some constant mass of the gas, say, 1 lb_m, at which the gas has the same enthalpy. All equilibrium states of the gas corresponding to this enthalpy must lie on some curve, and it is reasonable to assume that this curve can be obtained by drawing a smooth curve through the discrete points. Such a curve is called an *isenthalpic curve*. The student must understand that *an isenthalpic curve is not the graph of a throttling process*. No such graph can be drawn because in any throttling process the intermediate states traversed by a gas cannot be described by means of thermodynamic coordinates. An isenthalpic curve is the locus of all points representing equilibrium states of the same enthalpy. The porous-plug experiment is performed to provide a few of these points, the rest being obtained by interpolation.

The temperature on the high-pressure side T_i is now changed to another value, P_i being kept the same. P_f is again varied, and the corresponding T_f's measured. Upon plotting the new P_iT_i and the new P_f's and T_f's, another discrete set of points is obtained, which determines another isenthalpic curve corresponding to a different enthalpy. In this way, a series of isenthalpic curves is obtained. Such a series is shown in Fig. 13.5 for nitrogen.

The numerical value of the slope of an isenthalpic curve on a TP

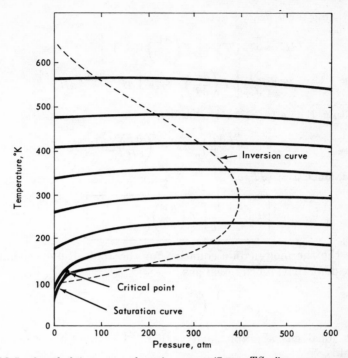

Fig. 13.5   Isenthalpic curves for nitrogen. (From TS diagram prepared by F. Din; published by Butterworth Scientific Publications, London, 1958.)

diagram at any point is called the *Joule-Kelvin coefficient*, and will be denoted by μ.   Thus

$$\mu = \left(\frac{\partial T}{\partial P}\right)_H$$

The locus of all points at which the Joule-Kelvin coefficient is zero, i.e., the locus of the maxima of the isenthalpic curves, is known as the *inversion curve* and is shown in Fig. 13.5 as a dotted closed curve.   The region inside the inversion curve where μ is positive is called the region of cooling, whereas outside, where μ is negative, is the region of heating.

In general, the difference in enthalpy between two neighboring equilibrium states is

$$dH = T\, dS + V\, dP,$$

and according to the second $T\, dS$ equation,

$$T\, dS = C_P\, dT - T\left(\frac{\partial V}{\partial T}\right)_P dP.$$

Substituting for $T\,dS$, we get

$$dH = C_P\,dT - \left[T\left(\frac{\partial V}{\partial T}\right)_P - V\right]dP,$$

or

$$dT = \frac{1}{C_P}\left[T\left(\frac{\partial V}{\partial T}\right)_P - V\right]dP + \frac{1}{C_P}\,dH.$$

Regarding T as a function of P and H,

$$dT = \left(\frac{\partial T}{\partial P}\right)_H dP + \left(\frac{\partial T}{\partial H}\right)_P dH;$$

whence, since $\mu = (\partial T/\partial P)_H$,

$$\boxed{\mu = \frac{1}{C_P}\left[T\left(\frac{\partial V}{\partial T}\right)_P - V\right].}$$

This is the thermodynamic equation for the Joule-Kelvin coefficient. It is evident that, for an ideal gas,

$$\mu = \frac{1}{C_P}\left(T\frac{R}{P} - V\right) = 0.$$

For an ideal gas a graph such as Fig. 13.5 would show horizontal isenthalps.

The most important application of the Joule-Kelvin effect is in the liquefaction of gases.

13.6/ Liquefaction of Gases by the Joule-Kelvin Effect

An inspection of the isenthalpic curves and the inversion curve of Fig. 13.5 shows that, for the Joule-Kelvin effect to give rise to cooling, the initial temperature of the gas must be below the point where the inversion curve cuts the temperature axis, i.e., below the maximum inversion temperature. For many gases, room temperature is already below the maximum inversion temperature, so that no precooling is necessary. Thus, if air is compressed to a pressure of 200 atm and a temperature of 52°C, then, after throttling to a pressure of 1 atm, it will be cooled to 23°C. On the other hand, if helium, originally at 200 atm and 52°C, is throttled to 1 atm, its temperature will rise to 64°C.

Figure 13.6 shows that, for the Joule-Kelvin effect to produce cooling in hydrogen, the hydrogen must be cooled below 200°K. Liquid nitrogen is used in most laboratories for this purpose. To produce Joule-Kelvin cooling in helium, the helium is first cooled with the aid of liquid hydrogen. Table 13.1 gives the maximum inversion temperatures of a few gases commonly used in low-temperature work.

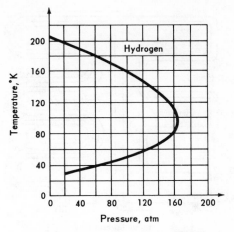

Fig. 13.6   Inversion curve for hydrogen.

It is clear from Fig. 13.5 that, once a gas has been precooled to a temperature lower than the maximum inversion temperature, the optimum pressure from which to start throttling corresponds to a point on the inversion curve. Starting at this pressure and ending at atmospheric pressure, the largest temperature drop is produced. This, however, is not large enough to produce liquefaction. Consequently, the gas that has been cooled by throttling is used to cool the incoming gas, which, after throttling, becomes still cooler. After many repetitions of these successive coolings, the gas is lowered to such a temperature that, after throttling, it becomes partly liquefied. The device used for this purpose is a *countercurrent heat exchanger*, and is shown in Fig. 13.7.

The gas, after precooling, is sent through the middle tube of a long coil of double-walled pipe. After throttling, it flows back through the outer annular space surrounding the middle pipe. For the heat exchanger to be efficient, the temperature of the gas as it leaves must

Table 13.1/ Maximum Inversion Temperatures

Gas	Maximum inversion temperature, °K
Carbon dioxide	~1500
Argon	723
Nitrogen	621
Air	603
Hydrogen	202
Helium	~ 40

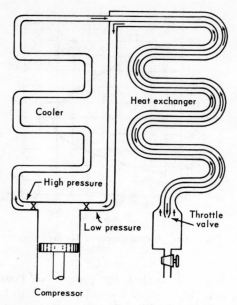

Fig. 13.7   Liquefaction of a gas by means of the Joule-Kelvin effect.

differ only slightly from the temperature at which it entered. To accomplish this, the heat exchanger must be quite long and well insulated.

When steady-state operation is finally reached, liquid is formed at a constant rate: For every pound of gas supplied, a certain fraction y is liquefied, the remaining fraction $1 - y$ is returned to the compressor. Considering the heat exchanger and throttling valve as completely insulated, as shown in Fig. 13.8, we have a flow process in which no shaft work is done and no heat is transferred, the kinetic- and potential-energy terms being negligible.   It therefore follows that the enthalpy of the entering gas is equal to the enthalpy of y lb$_m$ of emerging liquid plus the enthalpy of $(1 - y)$ lb$_m$ of emerging gas.   If

$$H_1 = \text{enthalpy of entering gas at } T_1, P_1,$$
$$H_L = \text{enthalpy of emerging liquid at } T_L, P_L,$$
$$H_2 = \text{enthalpy of emerging gas at } T_2, P_2,$$

then
$$H_1 = yH_L + (1 - y)H_2,$$

or

$$\boxed{y = \frac{H_2 - H_1}{H_2 - H_L}.}$$

Now, for steady-state operation, H_L is determined by the pressure on the liquid, which fixes the temperature, and hence is constant. H_2

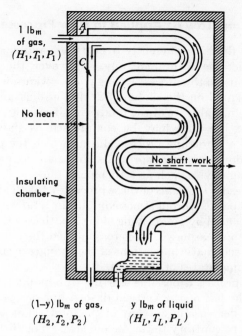

1 lb$_m$ of gas, (H_1, T_1, P_1)

No heat

Insulating chamber

No shaft work

$(1-y)$ lb$_m$ of gas, (H_2, T_2, P_2) y lb$_m$ of liquid (H_L, T_L, P_L)

Fig. 13.8   Throttling valve and heat exchanger in steady-state operation.

is determined by the pressure drop in the return tube and the temperature at C, which is only a little below that at A.   Hence it remains constant. H_1 refers to a temperature T_1 that is fixed, but at a pressure that may be chosen at will.   Therefore the fraction liquefied y may be varied only by varying H_1, which depends on P_1.   Since

$$y = \frac{H_2 - H_1}{H_2 - H_L},$$

y will be a maximum when H_1 is a minimum; and since H_1 may be varied only by varying the pressure, the condition that it be a minimum is that

$$\left(\frac{\partial H_1}{\partial P}\right)_{T=T_1} = 0.$$

But

$$\left(\frac{\partial H}{\partial P}\right)_T = -\left(\frac{\partial H}{\partial T}\right)_P \left(\frac{\partial T}{\partial P}\right)_H = -C_P \mu.$$

Hence, for y to be a maximum,

$$\mu = 0 \qquad \text{at} \qquad T = T_1,$$

or the point (T_1, P_1) must lie on the inversion curve.

13.7/ The Second Law as Applied to Flow Processes

The flow of real fluids is inherently irreversible, and is always accompanied by an increase in total entropy. However, the degree of irreversibility depends on the process taking place. Consider the *adiabatic* processes represented on the sketch of a Mollier diagram in Fig. 13.9. Assume that the initial state of the fluid is in all cases given by point 1. From this point the fluid may be compressed as shown by line *a*. Line *b* indicates a throttling process, during which the pressure drops but no work is done. Line *c* represents an expansion process through a work-producing device such as a turbine. Lines *a*, *b*, and *c* are not intended to represent the *paths* of these processes, for all are irreversible. Since the fluid passes through nonequilibrium states, its properties cannot be represented by points lying along a path on a thermodynamic diagram. For this reason we have crosshatched the lines to show that they are merely schematic indications of the changes occurring between the initial and final states of the fluid.

No adiabatic process is possible starting from point 1 which leads to final states to the left of the vertical dashed line of Fig. 13.9, for this would require a decrease in entropy of the fluid. For adiabatic processes this would be contrary to the second law. The throttling process represented by process *b* is seen to be inevitably irreversible, for if H_2 is to be the same as H_1, it is clear that S_2 must be greater than S_1.

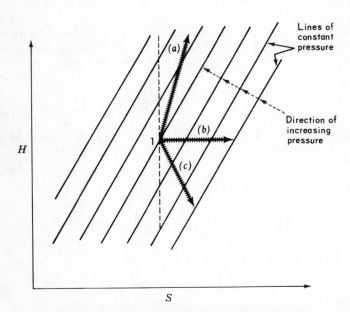

Fig. 13.9   Adiabatic flow process on Mollier diagram.

Processes a and c, however, which involve work, can in the limit be imagined to occur at constant entropy, i.e., reversibly. These limiting processes proceed along the vertical dashed line of Fig. 13.9, in the direction of increasing pressure for reversible, adiabatic compression and in the direction of decreasing pressure for reversible, adiabatic expansion. They represent reversible flow processes, and are idealizations, not attainable with real fluids. However, the work for such processes is readily calculated.

If the potential- and kinetic-energy terms of Eq. (13.10) are negligible, it reduces for either compression or expansion to

$$(\Delta H)_S = -W_s,$$

where the subscript S indicates that the enthalpy change occurs at constant entropy. Through this equation we may calculate the *minimum* adiabatic work required for compression of a fluid in a flow process operating between two given pressures and the *maximum* adiabatic work attainable from expansion in a flow process between two given pressures. For example, if superheated steam at 860°F and 180 psia is expanded through a turbine to atmospheric pressure, the maximum adiabatic work is calculated as follows: From the Mollier diagram for steam given in Appendix B, we have

$$H_1 = 1455 \text{ Btu/lb}_m.$$

From this initial point on the Mollier diagram we follow a constant-entropy (vertical) line to where it intersects the atmospheric-pressure line. At this point we find

$$H_2 = 1181 \text{ Btu/lb}_m.$$

Hence
$$W_s = -(\Delta H)_S = (H_1 - H_2)_S = 1455 - 1181$$
$$= 274 \text{ Btu/lb}_m.$$

This is the maximum work attainable from each pound of steam expanded. In any actual process the work would be less, perhaps 70 or 80 percent of this figure. However, thermodynamics provides us with the limiting value only.

The second law is of little use in numerical calculations without the assumption of reversibility. Only in this case does it provide an equality. For irreversible processes we have an inequality. It is often of value to calculate the results one could obtain in a flow process were it carried out reversibly. For such calculations we use an appropriate energy equation and the second law in the form $\Delta S_{total} = 0$. It is not necessary to know any details as to how the process is carried out. One needs merely end conditions and the assumption of reversibility. We illustrate with the following example: A complicated process has been devised to make heat continuously available at a temperature

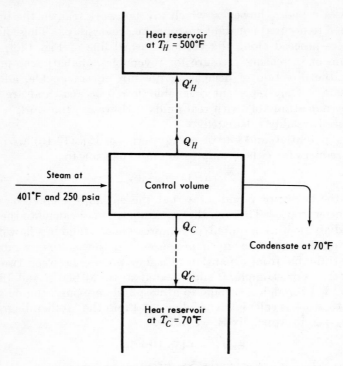

Fig. 13.10   Reversible flow process.

level of 500°F. The only source of energy is steam, saturated at 250 psia. Cooling water is available in large supply at 70°F. How much heat can be transferred from the process to a heat reservoir at 500°F for every pound of steam condensed in the process?

Let us assume that steam flows continuously and that it is condensed and subcooled to the cooling-water temperature by the time it emerges. The properties of the inlet steam and outlet condensate are given by the steam tables as:

$T_1 = 401°F,$ $T_2 = 70°R,$
$H_1 = 1201.4 \text{ Btu/lb}_m,$ $H_2 = 38.0 \text{ Btu/lb}_m,$
$S_1 = 1.5267 \text{ Btu/lb}_m \cdot °R,$ $S_2 = 0.0745 \text{ Btu/lb}_m \cdot °R.$

The second law denies the possibility that the *only* effect of this process could be the transfer of heat from the steam at temperatures between 70 and 401°F to a heat reservoir at 500°F. However, in this process we have cooling water available at 70°F. Thus we may consider that the *two* results of the process are transfer of heat from the steam to a heat reservoir at 500°F *and* the transfer of heat to another heat reservoir at 70°F. A representation of the process is shown in Fig. 13.10.

If we neglect potential- and kinetic-energy terms, Eq. (13.10) as written for the control volume becomes

$$\Delta H = \Sigma Q = Q_H + Q_C,$$

or $\qquad 38.0 - 1201.4 = Q_H + Q_C \qquad$ Btu/lb$_m$.

We now apply the second law, $\Delta S_{\text{total}} = 0$. The entropy change of the steam is simply

$$\Delta S = S_2 - S_1 = 0.0745 - 1.5267 = -1.4522 \text{ Btu/lb}_m \cdot {}^\circ\text{R}.$$

The entropy change of the heat reservoir at 500°R is

$$\frac{Q'_H}{(500 + 460)} \frac{\text{Btu}}{\text{lb}_m \cdot {}^\circ\text{R}},$$

and the entropy change of the heat reservoir at 70°F is

$$\frac{Q'_C}{(70 + 460)} \frac{\text{Btu}}{\text{lb}_m \cdot {}^\circ\text{R}}.$$

The sum of these three entropy changes is zero. However, Q_H and Q_C, taken with reference to the control volume in the energy equation, are opposite in sign to Q'_H and Q'_C, taken with reference to the heat reservoirs in the entropy expressions. Thus, in terms of Q_H and Q_C, the total entropy change is

$$\Delta S_{\text{total}} = -1.4522 - \frac{Q_H}{960} - \frac{Q_C}{530} = 0.$$

The energy equation and this entropy equation constitute two equations in two unknowns, and may be solved for Q_H and Q_C. The results are

$$Q_H = -1036.0 \text{ Btu/lb}_m \text{ of steam,}$$
$$Q_C = -127.4 \text{ Btu/lb}_m \text{ of steam.}$$

The minus signs merely indicate that heat is transferred away from the control volume.

In any actual process more heat would be transferred to the cold reservoir and less to the hot. In order to solve the problem for any case except that of complete reversibility, one would have to know the details of how the process is actually carried out.

13.8 / The Mechanical-energy Balance

Consider the steady-state flow of fluid through a control volume to which there is but one entrance and one exit. The energy equation which applies is Eq. (13.10):

$$\Delta H + \frac{\Delta u^2}{2g_c} + \Delta z \left(\frac{g}{g_c}\right) = \Sigma Q - W_s.$$

We have seen in Sec. 10.1 that, for infinitesimal changes between equilibrium states, the enthalpy change is given by

$$dH = đQ + V\,dP.$$

Integration of this equation for finite changes of state is possible only if the system traverses a succession of equilibrium states. If we assume for the moment that the steady-flow process being considered here does indeed carry fluid through such a succession of equilibrium states, we can determine the enthalpy change for the process by

$$\Delta H = H_2 - H_1 = \int đQ + \int_1^2 V\,dP = \Sigma Q + \int_1^2 V\,dP.$$

Substitution in the energy equation yields

$$-W_s = \int_1^2 V\,dP + \frac{\Delta u^2}{2g_c} + \Delta z\left(\frac{g}{g_c}\right).$$

The assumption made in deriving this equation that the fluid passes through a succession of equilibrium states is equivalent for real fluids to the assumption that the process is reversible. The viscous nature of real fluids leads to frictional effects that make flow processes inherently irreversible. As it stands, this equation is valid only for an imaginary nonviscous fluid. For real fluids it is at best approximate. An additional term may be incorporated in the equation to account for mechanical energy dissipated through fluid friction. The resulting equation is known as the *mechanical-energy balance:*

$$\boxed{-W_s = \int_1^2 V\,dP + \frac{\Delta u^2}{2g_c} + \Delta z\left(\frac{g}{g_c}\right) + \Sigma F,}$$

where ΣF is the friction term. The determination of numerical values for ΣF is a problem in fluid mechanics, not thermodynamics, and will not be considered here.

Evaluation of the integral $\int V\,dP$ presents the problem of knowing the path, that is, the VP relation, along which to integrate. For an irreversible process, no path can be fixed exactly. One must therefore assume a VP relation for the flow process which approximates the real process, insofar as this is possible.

Bernoulli's famous equation is a special case of the mechanical-energy balance applying to nonviscous, incompressible fluids which do not exchange shaft work with the surroundings. For nonviscous fluids, ΣF is zero. For incompressible fluids,

$$\int_1^2 V\,dP = V\,\Delta P = \frac{\Delta P}{\rho}.$$

Thus Bernoulli's equation becomes

$$\frac{\Delta P}{\rho} + \frac{\Delta u^2}{2g_c} + \Delta z \left(\frac{g}{g_c}\right) = 0,$$

or

$$\Delta \left[\frac{P}{\rho} + \frac{u^2}{2g_c} + z \left(\frac{g}{g_c}\right)\right] = 0.$$

This may also be written

$$\boxed{\frac{P}{\rho} + \frac{u^2}{2g_c} + z \left(\frac{g}{g_c}\right) = \text{const.}}$$

The severe limitations on this equation should be carefully noted.

Problems

13.1 A tank of 100-ft³ capacity contains 3,000 lb_m of liquid water in equilibrium with its vapor, which fills the remainder of the tank. The temperature and pressure are 450°F and 422.6 psia, respectively. A quantity of 2,000 lb_m of water at 150°F is to be pumped into the tank without removing any steam. How much heat must be added during this process if the pressure and temperature in the tank are to remain at their initial values?

13.2 A tank contains 1 lb_m of steam at a pressure of 300 psia and a temperature of 700°F. It is connected through a valve to a vertical cylinder which contains a frictionless piston. The piston is loaded with a weight such that a pressure of 100 psia is necessary to support it. Initially, the piston is at the bottom of the cylinder. The valve is opened slightly, so that steam flows into the cylinder until the pressure is uniform throughout the system. The final temperature of the steam in the tank is found to be 440°F. Calculate the temperature of the steam in the cylinder if no heat is transferred from the steam to the surroundings.

13.3 Consider a steady (constant T and P) supply of gas or vapor connected through a valve to a closed tank containing the same gas or vapor at a lower pressure. The valve is opened so that gas or vapor flows into the tank and is then shut again.

(a) Develop a general equation relating n_1 and n_2, the moles (or mass) of gas or vapor in the tank at the beginning and end of the process, to the properties U_1 and U_2, the internal energy of the gas or vapor in the tank at the beginning and end of the process, and H', the enthalpy of the gas or vapor in the steady supply, and to Q, the heat transferred to the material in the tank during the process.

(b) Reduce the general equation to its simplest form for the special case of an ideal gas with constant heat capacities.

(c) Further reduce the equation obtained in (b) for the case of $n_1 = 0$.

(d) Further reduce the equation obtained in (c) for the case where, in addition, $Q = 0$.

(e) Apply the appropriate equation to the case where a steady supply of hydrogen at 80°F and 2 atm flows into an evacuated tank of 150-ft^3 volume, and calculate how many pound moles of hydrogen will flow into the tank when the pressures are equalized if:

(1) It is assumed that no heat flows from the gas to the tank or through the tank walls.

(2) The tank weighs 900 lb$_m$, is perfectly insulated, has a specific heat of 0.11 Btu/lb$_m$ · °F, has an initial temperature of 80°F, and is heated by the gas so as always to be at the temperature of the gas in the tank. Assume hydrogen to be an ideal gas with a molal heat capacity at constant pressure of 7 Btu/lb mole · °F.

13.4 Develop equations which may be solved to give the final temperature of the gas remaining in a tank after the tank has been bled from an initial pressure p_1 to a final pressure p_2. Known quantities are the initial temperature, the tank volume, the heat capacity of the gas, the total heat capacity of the containing tank, p_1, and p_2. Assume the tank to be always at the temperature of the gas remaining in the tank, the gas to be ideal with constant heat capacities, and the tank to be perfectly insulated.

13.5 An inventor has developed a complicated process for making heat continuously available at an elevated temperature. Saturated steam at 220°F is used as the only source of energy. Assuming that there is plenty of cooling water available at 75°F, what is the maximum amount of heat which could be made available at a temperature level of 400°F per Btu of heat given up by the steam?

13.6 A chemical plant has saturated steam available at 400 psia but, requires steam at 150 psia. In addition, the plant also has exhaust steam available, saturated at 40 psia. It has been suggested that the 40 psia steam be compressed to 150 psia, obtaining the required work by expanding the 400-psia steam to 150 psia. The two streams at 150 psia could then be mixed. Calculate the amounts of each kind of steam required to give enough steam at 150 psia to supply 1,000,000 Btu/hr by condensation only (i.e., no subcooling). Perform these calculations for an ideal system. Rework the problem for a practical process, and suggest a method or methods for carrying out the process.

13.7 When nitrogen at 100 atm and 80°F expands adiabatically through a throttle to 1 atm, the temperature drops to 45°F. A process for liquefying nitrogen is to consist of an exchanger system with no moving parts. The nitrogen will enter at 100 atm and 80°F. Unliquefied gas will leave the system at 70°F and 1 atm, and liquid nitrogen will be withdrawn saturated at 1 atm. It is estimated that the system can be well enough insulated so that the heat leak from the surroundings will be 25 Btu/lb mole of entering nitrogen. It is claimed that at least 5 percent of the entering nitrogen can be liquefied in one pass through the apparatus. Do you think this is correct? Show the basis for your answer.

Data: The latent heat of nitrogen at its normal boiling point of 77.4°K is 1335 cal/gm mole. The specific heat of nitrogen gas may be taken as constant at 0.240 Btu/lb$_m$ · °F.

13.8 A lightweight portable power-supply system consists of a 1-ft^3 bottle of compressed helium, connected to a small adiabatic turbine. The bottle is initially charged to 2,000 psia at 80°F, and operates the turbine continuously until the pressure declines to 100 psia. The turbine exhausts at 5 psia. Neglecting all heat transfer to the gas, calculate the maximum possible useful work which can be obtained during the process. Assume helium to be an ideal gas with constant heat capacities $C_P = 5$, $C_V = 3$.

13.9 A frictionless piston slides in a cylinder as shown in Fig. P13.9. The piston works to compress a spring, which exerts a force on the piston directly proportional to the distance x. Steam from a line having constant properties (P_1, T_1, U_1, H_1, V_1, etc.) is admitted to the cylinder through the valve and is allowed to flow until the properties of the steam in the cylinder reach the values P_2, T_2, U_2, H_2, V_2, etc. Derive an expression giving $H_2 - H_1 = f(P_2, V_2)$. Neglect heat transfer.

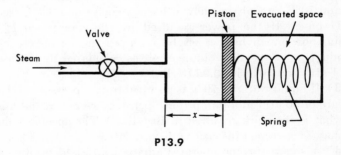

P13.9

13.10 The vessel shown in Fig. P13.10 is initially evacuated. It is closed at the top by a frictionless piston having a mass of 100 lb$_m$. Initially, it rests on the shoulders of the vessel as shown. The vessel is connected to a steady supply of air at 200 psig and 70°F. Air is allowed to flow into the vessel until its volume doubles. If no heat is transferred to the air, what is the air temperature in the vessel at the

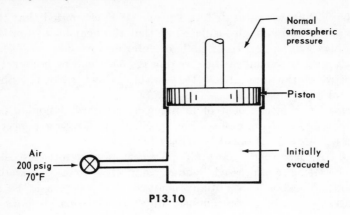

P13.10

end of the process? Consider air an ideal gas for which $C_P = 7$ and $C_V = 5$.

13.11 A tank with a volume of 10 ft³ is initially evacuated. Atmospheric air seeps into the tank through small holes slowly enough so that heat transfer through the walls maintains the gas at the ambient temperature of 27°C. Calculate the amount of heat added to or removed from the tank up to the time the pressures equalize at 1 atm.

13.12 A stream of air is accelerated to a very high velocity in the following steady-state-flow process: Air is taken from the atmosphere at 1 atm and 70°F and is passed into an adiabatic compressor, where its pressure is raised. It emerges at a fairly high temperature, and is then run through a heat exchanger, where some heat is removed. From there it enters a nozzle, in which it expands to its original conditions of 1 atm and 70°F, except that now it has a velocity of 1,000 ft/sec in an 8-in.-ID pipe. If the power required by the compressor is 40,300 Btu/min, how much heat must be removed in the heat exchanger (Btu/min)? The specific volume of air as calculated by the ideal-gas law at 1 atm and 70°F is 13.35 ft³/lb$_m$.

13.13 If liquid water at 70°F is pumped from a pressure of 1 atm to a pressure of 50 atm in a pump that operates reversibly and adiabatically, what is the work required in Btu/lb$_m$? The specific volume of water may be assumed insensitive to pressure.

13.14 A steam turbine operates adiabatically and produces 4,000 hp. Steam enters the turbine at 300 psia and 900°F. Exhaust steam from the turbine is saturated vapor at 5 psia. What is the steam rate in lb$_m$/hr through the turbine? What is the efficiency of the turbine compared with isentropic operation? Efficiency $= W/W_{\text{isentropic}}$.

13.15 (a) An insulated evacuated tank having a volume of 50 ft³ is attached to a constant-pressure line containing steam at 50 psia, superheated 10°F. Steam is allowed to flow into the tank until the pressure has risen to 50 psia. Assuming the tank to be well insulated and to have a negligible heat capacity, how many pounds *mass* of steam will enter the tank?

(b) Prepare graphs showing the mass of steam in the tank and the temperature of the steam in the tank as a function of pressure.

13.16 A 100 ft³/min positive-displacement (piston and cylinder) constant-speed vacuum pump is to be used to evacuate air from a 1,000-ft³ tank initially at 1 atm abs pressure. If air is essentially an ideal gas and if the entire process is isothermal, what is the absolute minimum time that will be required to reduce the tank pressure to 10 mm Hg abs? (*Note:* No specification of the intake volume per stroke has been given, for this is part of the problem of determining the absolute minimum time requirement. All that is necessary is that the volume per stroke times the strokes per minute equal 100 ft³/min. Hence the speed and intake volume of the pump are interdependent.)

13.17 Saturated steam at 25 psia is to be compressed adiabatically in a centrifugal compressor to 95 psia at the rate of 200 lb_m/min. The efficiency of the compressor (compared with isentropic operation) is 70 percent; that is, efficiency = $W_{isentropic}/W$. What is the horsepower requirement of the compressor and what is the final state of the steam, i.e., what are its properties H, S, T, and V?

13.18 The basic cycle for a steam power plant is shown in Fig. P13.18. Assume that steam is generated in the boiler at 500 psia and superheated to 1000°F. It is fed to an adiabatic turbine which has an efficiency of 75 percent, where efficiency = $W/W_{isentropic}$. The turbine exhausts to a condenser maintained at 5 psia. Condensate is then pumped as liquid back to the boiler. Assume that no subcooling of the condensate occurs in the condenser and that the work of pumping

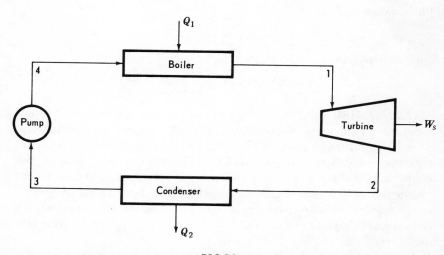

P13.18

the condensate to the boiler is negligible. Calculate W_s, the work of the turbine in Btu/lb$_m$ of steam. For power generation of 200,000 kw, what is the rate of steam circulation in lb$_m$/hr? How much heat must be supplied to the steam by the boiler, and how much heat must be given up in the condenser, in Btu/hr? What is the thermal efficiency of the cycle? How does it compare with the thermal efficiency of a Carnot cycle operating between the temperature levels 1000 and 162.25°F?

13.19 Refrigeration at a temperature level of 150°R is required for a certain process. A cycle using helium gas has been proposed to operate as follows: Helium at 1 atm is compressed adiabatically to 5 atm, water-cooled to 60°F, and sent to a heat exchanger, where it is cooled by returning helium. From there it goes to an adiabatic expander, which delivers work to be used to help drive the compressor. The helium then enters the refrigerator, where it absorbs enough heat to raise its temperature to 140°R. It returns to the compressor by way of the heat exchanger.

Helium may be considered an ideal gas with a constant molar heat capacity at constant pressure of 5. If the efficiencies of the compressor and expander are 80 percent and if the minimum temperature difference in the exchanger is 10°F, at what rate must the helium be circulated to provide refrigeration at a rate of 100 Btu/min? What is the net power requirement of the process? Sketch the cycle, and show the temperatures at the various points. What is the coefficient of performance of the cycle? How does it compare with the Carnot COP?

$$\text{COP} = \text{coefficient of performance} = \frac{\text{refrigeration rate}}{\text{power supplied}}.$$

For compression,

$$\text{Efficiency} = \frac{W_{\text{isentropic}}}{W},$$

and for expansion,

$$\text{Efficiency} = \frac{W}{W_{\text{isentropic}}}.$$

13.20 A Hilsch vortex tube is a device with no moving parts which separates a high-pressure gas stream into two low-pressure streams, one at a temperature above and one at a temperature below that of the entering gas stream. It consists of a tube with an inlet port at the center which directs the high-pressure gas stream into the tube perpendicular to the tube axis and tangent to the tube wall. Adjacent to the inlet there is an orifice in the tube. The cooler stream exits from the tube end beyond the orifice, and the warmer stream exits from the other end.

A particular test of a Hilsch tube gave the following results: Air entered at 75 psia and 19.3°C. The exit streams left at atmospheric pressure, with temperatures of −21.8 and 26.5°C, respectively. The ratio of warm air to cool air was 5.39. Are these results consistent with the requirements of the laws of thermodynamics? Take air to be an ideal gas for which $C_P = 7$ Btu/lb mole · °F.

13.21 (a) Show that

$$\mu C_P = T^2 \left(\frac{\partial V/T}{\partial T} \right)_P .$$

In the region of moderate pressures, the equation of state of 1 mole of a gas may be written

$$\frac{PV}{RT} = 1 + B'P + C'P^2,$$

where the second and third virial coefficients B' and C' are functions of the temperature only.

(b) Show that, as the pressure approaches zero,

$$\mu C_P \rightarrow RT^2 \frac{dB'}{dT} .$$

(c) Show that the equation of the inversion curve is

$$P = - \frac{dB'/dT}{dC'/dT} .$$

13.22 The Joule-Kelvin coefficient μ is a measure of the temperature change during a throttling process. A similar measure of the temperature change produced by an isentropic change of pressure is provided by the coefficient μ_S, where

$$\mu_S = \left(\frac{\partial T}{\partial P} \right)_S .$$

Prove that

$$\mu_S - \mu = \frac{V}{C_P} .$$

13.23 Indicate on a rough freehand TS diagram the states of a substance at various places in a Joule-Kelvin liquefier when it is liquefying gas at a constant rate.

13.24 Hot water could in theory be used as a heat source for the generation of work. If hot water is available at 210°F and if an infinite heat sink is available at 70°F, what is the minimum amount of water that would be required for the production of 1 Btu of work?

13.25 A refrigerator is to be built to cool a brine solution from 70 to 20°F continuously. Heat is to be discarded to the atmosphere at a temperature of 80°F.

What is the absolute minimum power requirement of the refrigerator if 100 gal of brine is to be cooled per minute?

How much heat must be discarded to the atmosphere?

Data for the brine: $C_P = 0.83$ Btu/lb$_m$ · °F, $\rho = 71.8$ lb$_m$/ft³.

13.26 Compute the absolute minimum quantity of steam in pounds per hour that is required to manufacture ice at the rate of 1 ton/hr under the following conditions:

Water for making ice is supplied at 60°F.

Steam is at 200 psia and 500°F. (No other energy source is available.)

The ice is not subcooled.

The temperature of the surroundings is 70°F.

The latent heat of fusion of ice is 143.3 Btu/lb$_m$ at 32°F.

13.27 An ideal gas with constant heat capacities is caused to flow adiabatically through a nozzle from a region where the pressure and temperature are P_i and T_i, respectively, to a constricted region where the values are P and T. Assuming the initial velocity to be negligible:

(a) Show that the final velocity u is

$$u = \sqrt{2g_c C_P T_i \left(1 - \frac{T}{T_i}\right)}.$$

(b) Assuming the expansion in the nozzle to be isentropic, show that

$$u = \sqrt{2g_c C_P T_i \left[1 - \left(\frac{P}{P_i}\right)^{(\gamma-1)/\gamma}\right]}$$

$$= \sqrt{2g_c \frac{\gamma}{\gamma - 1} R T_i \left[1 - \left(\frac{P}{P_i}\right)^{(\gamma-1)/\gamma}\right]}.$$

13.28 Steam approaches a horizontal nozzle at a pressure of 100 psia and a temperature of 500°F at negligible velocity. It reaches the discharge end of the nozzle at a pressure of 70 psia. Assuming the flow to be isentropic:

(a) Find the velocity in the nozzle discharge.

(b) Find the area of the nozzle-discharge cross section required to pass a flow of 1 lb/sec.

Chapter 14/
Applications of Thermodynamics
to Special Systems

14.1/ Simple Systems

In Chaps. 2 to 4 we considered a number of thermodynamic systems which are describable in terms of just three coordinates. Such *simple systems* include as one class the PVT system, which we have discussed in considerable detail. So commonly encountered is the PVT system that it is often thought of as *the* type of system to which thermodynamics applies. Hence other types of simple systems, such as a stressed bar, a surface, an electric cell, etc., are thought of as being something special. It is our purpose in this chapter to consider further such "special systems."

Table 4.1 on page 72 displays the forms the first law assumes for the various simple systems that we have considered. Since these equations are written for infinitesimal quasi-static processes, we may substitute $T\,dS$ for $đQ$ in each equation:

PVT system:	$dU = T\,dS - P\,dV.$

Stressed bar:	$dU = T\,dS + \sigma\,d\epsilon$
Surface:	$dU = T\,dS + \gamma\,dA$
Reversible cell:	$dU = T\,dS + e\,dq$
Dielectric:	$dU = T\,dS + \mathcal{E}\,d\mathcal{P}$
Magnetic material:	$dU = T\,dS + \mu_0 \mathcal{H}\,d\mathcal{M}$

It is clear from the similarities among these equations that derivations starting from the equation for a PVT system have their counterparts or analogies for the other simple systems. For stressed bars, σ replaces $-P$ and ϵ replaces V; for surfaces, γ replaces $-P$ and A replaces V; and similarly for the other systems.

14.2/ Stressed Bars

Replacing $-P$ and V by σ and ϵ in the second $T\,dS$ equation, we have immediately

$$T\,dS = C_\sigma\,dT + T\left(\frac{\partial\epsilon}{\partial T}\right)_\sigma d\sigma$$

$$= C_\sigma\,dT + T\alpha\,d\sigma,$$

where α is the linear expansivity. It is interesting to consider whether the temperature of a bar stressed reversibly and adiabatically will rise or fall. For such a process $dS = 0$, and the above equation may be written

$$\left(\frac{\partial T}{\partial\sigma}\right)_S = -\frac{T\alpha}{C_\sigma}.$$

Thus $(\partial T/\partial\sigma)_S$, the change of temperature with stress in a reversible, adiabatic process is positive when α is negative and negative for positive α. We have four cases to consider:

	Tension		Compression	
	Positive α	Negative α	Positive α	Negative α
$(\partial T/\partial\sigma)_S$ is	−	+	−	+
Change in σ is	+	+	−	−
$\therefore$ Change in T is	−	+	+	−

From these results we see that a bar of steel at room temperature, for which α is positive, decreases in temperature when stressed in tension but increases in temperature under compression. Rubber, on the other hand, shows a negative value of α, and its temperature changes are opposite those of steel.

For consistent units in the second $T\,dS$ equation,

$$T\,dS = C_\sigma\,dT + T\alpha\,d\sigma,$$

the terms must represent energy *per unit volume*. This results from the dimensions of the term $T\alpha\,d\sigma$. For example, for T in °R, α in in./in. $\cdot$ °R, and σ in $lb_f/in.^2$, the units of $T\alpha\,d\sigma$ are in. $\cdot$ $lb_f/in.^3$ The units of C_σ are therefore in. $\cdot$ $lb_f/in.^3$ $\cdot$ °R.

We can get an idea of the size of the temperature changes caused by stress from a specific example. Consider steel at 300°K.

$$\alpha = 12 \times 10^{-6} \text{ in./in.} \cdot °K = 1 \times 10^{-6} \text{ ft/in.} \cdot °K.$$

To a good approximation we may calculate C_σ from C_P. If $C_P = 0.12$ cal/gm $\cdot$ °K, and if the density of steel is taken as 7.8 gm/cm³,

$$C_\sigma = (0.12 \text{ cal/gm} \cdot °K)(7.8 \text{ gm/cm}^3)(16.4 \text{ cm}^3/\text{in.}^3)(778/252 \text{ ft} \cdot \text{lb}_f/\text{cal})$$
$$= 47 \text{ ft} \cdot \text{lb}_f/\text{in.}^3 \cdot °K.$$

Hence

$$\left(\frac{\partial T}{\partial \sigma}\right)_S = -\frac{T\alpha}{C_\sigma} = \frac{-(300°K)(1 \times 10^{-6} \text{ ft/in.} \cdot °K)}{(47 \text{ ft} \cdot \text{lb}_f/\text{in.}^3 \cdot °K)}$$
$$\cong -6 \times 10^{-6} \text{ (°K)}/(\text{lb}_f/\text{in.}^2)$$
$$\cong -1 \times 10^{-5} \text{ (°R)}/(\text{lb}_f/\text{in.}^2).$$

If T, α, and C_σ are rather insensitive to stress, then $T\alpha/C_\sigma$ may be considered constant, and we may write

$$\Delta T = -\frac{T\alpha}{C_\sigma} (\Delta\sigma) \qquad \text{const } S.$$

Hence a steel bar stressed reversibly and adiabatically to 100,000 lb$_f$/in.² in tension would show a temperature decrease of about 1°F. The requirement of reversibility here implies that the proportional limit of the steel is not exceeded.

14.3/ Surfaces

Substitution of γ and A for $-P$ and V in the first $T \, dS$ equation yields

$$T \, dS = C_A \, dT - T\left(\frac{\partial\gamma}{\partial T}\right)_A dA.$$

Imagine a spherical drop of liquid having a surface area A_0, which is the minimum area possible for the volume considered. Suppose that the drop is drawn out into a thin film with the aid of a wire framework until the surface area reaches a value A, very much larger than the original value. If this is done reversibly and isothermally and *if the surface tension is a function of temperature only*, then $T \, dS = đQ$, and from the above equation

$$Q = -T \frac{d\gamma}{dT} (A - A_0).$$

Moreover, the work of the process is

$$W = -\int_{A_0}^{A} \gamma \, dA = -\gamma(A - A_0).$$

From the first law, we then have

$$U - U_0 = \left(\gamma - T\frac{d\gamma}{dT}\right)(A - A_0).$$

Since A is very much larger than A_0, we may equally well write

$$U - U_0 = \left(\gamma - T\frac{d\gamma}{dT}\right)A,$$

where U_0 is the energy of the liquid with practically no surface, and U is the energy of the liquid with the large surface area A. Hence

$$\boxed{\frac{U - U_0}{A} = \gamma - T\frac{d\gamma}{dT}.}$$

In the process of expanding the area of the original drop, it is assumed that the *bulk* properties of the liquid enclosed within the surface do not change. Thus $U - U_0$ is interpreted as the energy associated with the surface only, and $(U - U_0)/A$ is the *surface energy per unit area*. This quantity is seen to have the same dimensions as γ. If γ is expressed in dynes/cm, the energy is given in dyne $\cdot$ cm/cm^2, or ergs/cm^2. With the aid of the above equation, values of surface energy per unit area may be calculated once the surface tension has been measured as a function of temperature.

In the neighborhood of the critical temperature the surface tension of all liquids is zero. The surface tension of a pure liquid in equilibrium with its vapor can usually be represented by a formula of the type

$$\gamma = \gamma_0\left(1 - \frac{t}{t'}\right)^n,$$

where γ_0 = surface tension at 0°C,

$\quad\quad t'$ = a temperature a few degrees below the critical temperature,

$\quad\quad n$ = a constant between 1 and 2.

For example, in the case of water, $\gamma_0 = 75.5$ dynes/cm, $t' = 368$°C, and $n = 1.2$. Since $d\gamma/dT$ is the same as $d\gamma/dt$, all the quantities necessary to calculate $(U - U_0)/A$ are at hand. The steps in the calculation are given in Table 14.1, and both γ and $(U - U_0)/A$ are plotted in Fig. 14.1.

The surface energy per unit area is an important quantity in the kinetic theory of liquids. According to this theory, evaporation takes place when a molecule of liquid possesses sufficient energy to escape through the film at the surface of the liquid. A relation exists, therefore, between the heat of vaporization and the surface energy. If the student compares the surface-energy curve of Fig. 14.1 with the heat-of-vaporization curve of Fig. 11.19 (page 220), he will notice that both

Table 14.1/ Calculation of Surface Energy of a Water Film

Temp., °C	Temp., °K	γ, dynes/cm	$\dfrac{d\gamma}{dT}$	$T\,\dfrac{d\gamma}{dT}$	$\dfrac{U-U_0}{A} = \gamma - T\,\dfrac{d\gamma}{dT}$, ergs/cm²
0	273	75.5	−0.248	− 67.6	143
50	323	63.1	−0.241	− 77.8	141
100	373	51.5	−0.233	− 86.8	138
150	423	40.0	−0.223	− 94.3	134
200	473	29.0	−0.212	−100	129
250	523	18.9	−0.197	−103	122
300	573	9.6	−0.176	−101	111
350	623	1.6	−0.126	− 78.5	80.1
368	641	0	0	0	0

quantities vary with the temperature in a similar manner, both becoming zero in the neighborhood of the critical temperature.

Surface energy per unit area is usually very small, and the total surface energy associated with a system becomes important only when the area becomes very large with respect to the volume or mass of the system. This situation is encountered when one deals with mists, foams, aerosols, etc. Consider, for example, $1\ lb_m$ of liquid water in equilibrium with its vapor at 100°C. Let this mass of water consist of n spherical

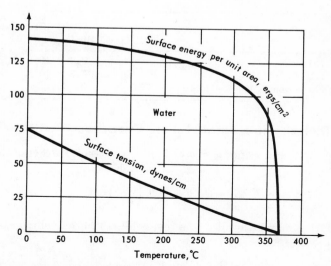

Fig. 14.1   Temperature variation of surface tension and surface energy per unit area of water.

droplets of radius r. The volume of liquid per drop is $\frac{4}{3}\pi r^3$. The volume of 1 lb_m of water at 100°C is 0.01672 ft^3/lb_m. Thus the number of drops is

$$n = \frac{0.01672 \ ft^3/lb_m}{\frac{4}{3}\pi r^3},$$

where r is drop radius in feet. The area per drop is $4\pi r^2$. Thus the total area of n drops is

$$A = 4\pi r^2 \frac{0.01672 \ ft^3/lb_m}{\frac{4}{3}\pi r^3}$$
$$= \frac{0.05016 \ ft^3/lb_m}{r}.$$

From Table 14.1, at 100°C we find the surface energy per unit area to be 138 ergs/cm², or

$$\frac{(138 \ ergs/cm^2)(929 \ cm^2/ft^2)}{1055 \times 10^7 \ ergs/Btu} = 122 \times 10^{-7} \ Btu/ft^2.$$

Thus

$$\text{Surface energy}/lb_m = \frac{(122 \times 10^{-7} \ Btu/ft^2)(0.0502 \ ft^3/lb_m)}{r}$$
$$= \frac{6.1 \times 10^{-7} \ Btu \cdot ft/lb_m}{r},$$

where r is the drop radius. We may now calculate values of surface energy/lb_m for various values of r:

r	Surface energy, Btu/lb_m
1 in.	7.3×10^{-6}
0.001 in.	7.3×10^{-3}
1 micron = 10^{-4} cm	0.186

14.4/ Dielectric in a Parallel-plate Capacitor

Substituting $\mathcal{E}$ and $\mathcal{P}$ for $-P$ and V in the second $T \, dS$ equation, we have

$$T \, dS = C_{\mathcal{E}} \, dT + T \left(\frac{\partial \mathcal{P}}{\partial T}\right)_{\mathcal{E}} d\mathcal{E}.$$

This equation may be applied to a reversible isothermal change of field, in which case it reduces to

$$dQ = T \left(\frac{\partial \mathcal{P}}{\partial T}\right)_{\mathcal{E}} d\mathcal{E},$$

or to a reversible adiabatic change of field, for which it becomes

$$\left(\frac{\partial T}{\partial \mathscr{E}}\right)_S = -\frac{T}{C_\mathscr{E}}\left(\frac{\partial \mathscr{P}}{\partial T}\right)_\mathscr{E}.$$

The second of these is known as the *electrocaloric effect*.

14.5 / Magnetic Material in a Magnetic Field

The second $T\,dS$ equation for a material in a magnetic field is obtained by substituting $\mu_0 \mathscr{H}$ for $-P$ and $\mathscr{M}$ for V in the corresponding equation for a PVT system:

$$T\,dS = C_\mathscr{H}\,dT + \mu_0 T\left(\frac{\partial \mathscr{M}}{\partial T}\right)_\mathscr{H} d\mathscr{H}.$$

For a reversible, isothermal change of field, this becomes

$$đQ = \mu_0 T\left(\frac{\partial \mathscr{M}}{\partial T}\right)_\mathscr{H} d\mathscr{H}.$$

In the case of a paramagnetic material, such as a crystal containing magnetic ions separated by a large number of nonmagnetic particles, the degree of orientation of the magnetic ions, which determines the magnitude of the magnetization $\mathscr{M}$, is controlled by two factors: the magnetic field $\mathscr{H}$ and the temperature T. If $\mathscr{H}$ is kept constant, an increase in temperature is associated with an increase in the energy of vibration, with a consequent reduction in the degree of orientation of the ions. Experiment therefore shows that, for paramagnetic materials, $(\partial \mathscr{M}/\partial T)_\mathscr{H}$ is *always* negative. Thus the preceding equation shows that such materials reject heat when the field is increased and absorb heat when the field is decreased isothermally.

For a reversible, adiabatic change of field the second $T\,dS$ equation becomes

$$\left(\frac{\partial T}{\partial \mathscr{H}}\right)_S = -\frac{\mu_0 T}{C_\mathscr{H}}\left(\frac{\partial \mathscr{M}}{\partial T}\right)_\mathscr{H}.$$

Thus a paramagnetic material experiences a temperature rise when the field is increased adiabatically, and a temperature drop upon adiabatic demagnetization. This phenomenon is called the *magnetocaloric effect*, and is used today to produce extremely low temperatures, below 1°K. Experiments of this sort were first performed in 1933 by Giauque in America and were then taken up by Kurti and Simon in England and by De Haas and Wiersma in Holland. In these experiments a paramagnetic salt is cooled to as low a temperature as possible with the aid of liquid helium. A strong magnetic field is then applied, producing a rise of temperature in the substance and a consequent flow of heat to the surrounding helium, some of which is thereby evaporated. After a while, the substance is both strongly magnetized and as cold as possible. At this moment, the space surrounding the substance is evacuated. The magnetic field is now reduced to zero, and the temperature of the paramagnetic salt drops to a very low value.

In the experiments of Kurti and Simon the adiabatic demagnetization was accomplished by switching the magnet off and wheeling it away. In the experiments at Leiden, the whole calorimeter was swung out of the magnetic field.

The next step is to measure the temperature. For this purpose, separate coils of wire surrounding the paramagnetic salt are used. The paramagnetic susceptibility $\mathcal{M}/\mathcal{H}$, which is a function of the temperature, is measured by means of a special a-c bridge. A new temperature scale is now defined with the aid of Curie's equation. The new temperature T^*, called the *magnetic temperature*, is defined as

$$T^* = \frac{\text{Curie's constant}}{\text{susceptibility}} = \frac{C\mathcal{H}}{\mathcal{M}}.$$

It is seen that, in the region where Curie's law holds, T^* is the real Kelvin temperature, whereas, in the region around absolute zero, T^* is expected to differ somewhat from the Kelvin temperature. A series of results obtained by de Klerk is shown in Fig. 14.2, where the final magnetic temperature of chromium–potassium alum is plotted against the initial magnetic field, the initial temperature being 1.17°K.

The properties of cerium–magnesium nitrate are particularly noteworthy. Parallel to the axis of a crystal of this compound the magnetic susceptibility is practically zero, whereas perpendicular to this

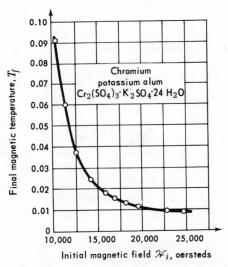

Fig. 14.2 De Klerk's results in the adiabatic demagnetization of chromium–potassium alum. (Initial temperature = 1.17°K.)

axis the susceptibility is quite reasonable in magnitude and *obeys Curie's equation all the way down to 0.006°K:* Starting at $T_i = 1°K$, $\mathcal{H}_i = 7,130$ oersteds (570,000 amp/m), the salt needs merely to be rotated from the perpendicular to the parallel position and its temperature will drop to 6 millidegrees.

14.6 / Mixtures of Ideal Gases

We have not previously considered the effect of composition on the properties of PVT systems. To present a general and comprehensive treatment of the thermodynamics of solutions would carry us far beyond the intended scope of this text. However, it is desirable to introduce the subject and to develop the methods useful for mixtures of ideal gases.

Imagine several vessels, each having a total volume V_t and all held at the same temperature T. Let the first such vessel contain n_1 moles of a pure gas at pressure p_1; the second, n_2 moles of a different pure gas at pressure p_2; etc. In general, each vessel contains n_i moles of pure gas i at a pressure p_i. We impose the restriction that in each case the conditions of temperature and pressure are such that the equation of state for an ideal gas is essentially valid. We now combine the contents of all vessels into a single vessel of the same volume V_t and at the same temperature T. Experiment shows that the pressure of the combined gases P is the sum of the initial pressures. That is,

$$P = \sum_i p_i.$$

This observation is known as *Dalton's law*. It expresses the fact that the total pressure of a mixture of ideal gases is equal to the sum of the pressures exerted by the individual gases as each occupies the total volume alone at the temperature of the mixture.

For each of the pure ideal gases occupying the volume V_t, we have

$$p_i = \frac{n_i RT}{V_t}.$$

By Dalton's law

$$P = \Sigma p_i = (\Sigma n_i)\frac{RT}{V_t}.$$

Thus

$$\frac{p_i}{P} = \frac{n_i}{\Sigma n_i} = y_i,$$

or

$$p_i = y_i P,$$

where y_i is the mole fraction of component i in the mixture. The p_i's are known as *partial pressures*, and the above equation shows that the partial pressure of a constituent in a mixture of ideal gases is proportional to the total pressure. The mole fractions are, of course, subject to the restriction that

$$\Sigma y_i = 1.$$

The observation that the partial pressure of a gas in a mixture of ideal gases is the same as the pressure which that gas alone exerts in the total mixture volume leads one to the idea that, in a mixture of ideal gases, each gas exists independent of the others and has therefore a complete set of properties in the mixture identical with those it has when it occupies the total volume alone at the same temperature. This proposition is the essential element of *Gibbs's theorem*, which may be stated as follows: *The total thermodynamic property* $(nU, nC_V, nH, nC_P, nS, nA,$ and $nG)$ *of a mixture of ideal gases is the sum of the properties that the individual gases would have if each occupied the total mixture volume alone at the same temperature.*

Suppose we have a mixture of ideal gases occupying a total volume V_t. Let the numbers of moles of the individual gases be represented by n_1, n_2, n_3, etc. The total number of moles n is given by

$$n = \Sigma n_i.$$

According to Gibbs's theorem the total internal energy of the gas mixture is

$$nU = \Sigma(n_i U_{0_i}),$$

where U_{0_i} is the molar internal energy of pure i were the n_i moles of it to occupy the total volume V_t alone at the pressure p_i.

For an ideal gas, the internal energy is a function of temperature only. Hence U_i is not changed by increasing the pressure from p_i to P at constant temperature. The above equation may therefore equally well be written

$$nU = \Sigma(n_i U_i),$$

where U_i is the molar internal energy of pure i at the mixture T and P. Division by n yields

$$\boxed{U = \Sigma(y_i U_i).}$$

Heat capacities and the enthalpy for ideal gases are also independent of pressure. Therefore completely analogous derivations for these properties show that

$$\boxed{\begin{aligned} C_V &= \Sigma(y_i C_{V_i}), \\ H &= \Sigma(y_i H_i), \\ C_P &= \Sigma(y_i C_{P_i}). \end{aligned}}$$

The entropy of an ideal gas *is* a function of pressure. It was shown in Sec. 9.4 that, for an infinitesimal change of state for an ideal gas,

$$dS = C_P \frac{dT}{T} - R \frac{dP}{P}.$$

At constant T, this becomes

$$dS = -R\frac{dP}{P}.$$

For a pressure change from p_i to P, the entropy changes from S_{0_i} to S_i, and integration gives

$$S_i - S_{0_i} = -R\ln\frac{P}{p_i}.$$

If p_i represents the partial pressure of component i in a mixture of ideal gases at a total pressure P, then $p_i = y_iP$, and

$$S_i - S_{0_i} = R\ln y_i,$$

or
$$S_{0_i} = S_i - R\ln y_i.$$

Clearly, S_i is the entropy of pure i at pressure P, whereas S_{0_i} is the entropy of pure i at pressure p_i, both at the same temperature.

By Gibbs's theorem, the total entropy of a mixture of ideal gases is

$$nS = \Sigma(n_iS_{0_i}).$$

Substitution for S_{0_i} yields

$$nS = \Sigma(n_iS_i) - R\Sigma(n_i\ln y_i).$$

We may divide this equation by n to get

$$\boxed{S = \Sigma(y_iS_i) - R\Sigma(y_i\ln y_i),}$$

or
$$S - \Sigma(y_iS_i) = R\Sigma\left(y_i\ln\frac{1}{y_i}\right).$$

In this equation S is the entropy of 1 mole of a mixture of ideal gases at temperature T and pressure P, in which the compositions of the constituents are given by the mole fractions y_i. The S_i's are the molar entropies of the pure constituents *at T and P*. Thus the difference $S - \Sigma(y_iS_i)$ represents the entropy change upon mixing ideal gases at constant T and P.

As an example, consider the mixing of $\frac{1}{2}$ mole of helium and $\frac{1}{2}$ mole of neon to form 1 mole of an equimolar mixture at constant T and P. Then

$$S - \Sigma(y_iS_i) = R(\tfrac{1}{2}\ln 2 + \tfrac{1}{2}\ln 2)$$
$$= R\ln 2.$$

On the right-hand side of this expression there are no quantities such as heat capacities that distinguish one gas from another. The result is the same for the mixing of any two inert ideal gases, no matter how similar or dissimilar they are. If, however, the two gases are identical, the concept of mixing has no meaning, and there is no entropy change. From the microscopic point of view, this means that the mixing of any two dissimilar gases brings about the same degree of disorder, whereas the mixing of two identical gases introduces no element of disorder.

The application of mathematics to the macroscopic processes of nature usually gives rise to continuous results. Our experience suggests that, as the two gases become more and more alike, the entropy change due to mixing should get smaller and smaller, approaching zero as the gases become identical. The fact that this is not the case is known as *Gibbs's paradox*. The paradox has been resolved by Bridgman in the following way: To recognize that two gases are dissimilar requires a set of experimental operations. These operations become more and more difficult as the gases become more and more alike, but, at least in principle, the operations are possible. In the limit, when the gases become identical, there is a discontinuity in the instrumental operations inasmuch as no instrumental operation exists by which the gases may be distinguished. Hence a discontinuity in a function such as that of an entropy change is to be expected.

The Gibbs function is defined by the equation

$$G = H - TS.$$

If G, H, and S in this equation represent the molar properties of a mixture of ideal gases, we may substitute for H and S by the equations just developed:

$$\begin{aligned}
G &= \Sigma(y_i H_i) - T\Sigma(y_i S_i) + RT\Sigma(y_i \ln y_i) \\
&= \Sigma[y_i(H_i - TS_i)] + RT\Sigma(y_i \ln y_i) \\
&= \Sigma(y_i G_i) + RT\Sigma(y_i \ln y_i),
\end{aligned}$$

or

$$\boxed{G = \Sigma[y_i(G_i + RT \ln y_i)].}$$

14.7/ Chemical Equilibrium

Consider a homogeneous mixture of 1 mole of hydrogen and 1 mole of oxygen at room temperature and at atmospheric pressure. It is a well-known fact that this mixture will remain indefinitely at the same temperature, pressure, and composition. The most careful measurements over a long period of time will disclose no appreciable spontaneous change of state. One might be inclined to deduce from this that such a mixture represents a system in a state of thermodynamic equilibrium. This, however, is not the case. If a small piece of platinized asbestos is introduced, or if an electric spark is created across two electrodes, an explosion takes place involving a sudden change in the temperature, the pressure, and the composition. If at the end of the explosion the system is brought back to the same temperature and pressure, it will be found that the composition is now $\frac{1}{2}$ mole of oxygen, no measurable amount of hydrogen, and 1 mole of water vapor.

The piece of material such as platinized asbestos by whose agency a chemical reaction is started is known as a *catalyst*. If chemical combination is started in a mixture of 1 mole of hydrogen and 1 mole of oxygen with different amounts and different kinds of catalysts, and the final composition of the mixture is measured in each case, it is found that (1) the final composition does not depend upon the amount of catalyst used; (2) the final composition does not depend on the kind of catalyst used; (3) the catalyst itself is the same at the end of the reaction as at the beginning. These results lead us to the following conclusions:

1. The initial state of the mixture is a state of mechanical and thermal equilibrium but not of chemical equilibrium.
2. The final state is a state of thermodynamic equilibrium.
3. The transition from the initial nonequilibrium state to the final equilibrium state is accompanied by a chemical reaction that is too slow to be measured when it takes place spontaneously. Through the agency of the catalyst the reaction is caused to take place more rapidly.

Imagine a vessel divided into two compartments by a removable partition as shown in Fig. 14.3(a). Suppose that one compartment contains a dilute solution of sodium chloride and water which is maintained at a pressure of 1 atm and at a temperature of 20°C, the mole fraction of the salt being, say, 0.01. Under these conditions the solution is in thermodynamic equilibrium. Suppose that the other com-

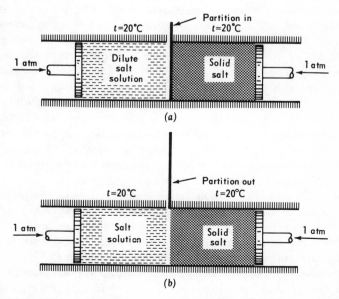

Fig. 14.3 Transport of matter across the boundary between two phases.

partment contains solid salt in equilibrium also at a pressure of 1 atm and a temperature of 20°C. Now imagine that the partition is removed (Fig. 14.3b) and that the pressure and temperature of the whole system are kept constant at the original values. Experiment shows that some solid salt dissolves; i.e., the mole fraction of the salt in the solution increases spontaneously at constant pressure and temperature. After a while, the change ceases and the mole fraction is found to be about 0.1.

Focusing our attention on the solution from the moment it was put in contact with the solid salt, we are led to the following conclusions:

1. The initial state of the solution (at the moment it was put in contact with the solid salt) is one of mechanical and thermal equilibrium but not of chemical equilibrium.

2. The final state of the solution is a state of thermodynamic equilibrium.

3. The transition from the initial nonequilibrium state to the final equilibrium state is accompanied by a transport of a chemical constituent into the solution.

14.8/ Thermodynamic Description of Nonequilibrium States

A *phase* is defined as a system or a portion of a system composed of any number of chemical constituents satisfying the requirements that (1) it is homogeneous and (2) it has a definite boundary. The hydrogen-oxygen mixture described in Sec. 14.7 is a gaseous phase of two chemical constituents and of constant mass. The salt solution is a liquid phase of two chemical constituents whose mass, when it is in contact with the solid-salt phase, is variable. Although the initial states of both these phases are nonequilibrium states, it is possible to describe them in terms of thermodynamic coordinates. Since each phase is in mechanical and thermal equilibrium, a definite P and T may be ascribed to each; since each has a definite boundary, each has a definite volume; and since each is homogeneous, the composition of each phase may be described by specifying the number of moles of each constituent. In general, a phase consisting of c chemical constituents in mechanical and thermal equilibrium may be described with the aid of the coordinates P, V, T, n_1, n_2, . . . , n_c.

Under a given set of conditions a phase may undergo a change of state in which some or all of these coordinates change. While this is going on, the phase passes through states, not of thermodynamic equilibrium, but of mechanical and thermal equilibrium only. These states are connected by an equation of state that is a relation among P, V, T, and the n's. Whether a phase is in chemical equilibrium or not, it has a definite internal energy and enthalpy. Both U and H may be regarded as functions of P, V, T, and the n's, and upon eliminating one of the coordinates by means of the equation of state, U and H may be expressed as functions of any two of P, V, and T and all the n's. Since entropy is a measure of the molecular disorder of the system, the entropy of a phase that is not in chemical equilibrium must have a meaning. We shall assume that the entropy of a phase, and therefore the Helmholtz and Gibbs functions, also can be expressed as functions of any two of P, V, and T and all the n's.

During a change of state, the n's, which determine the composition of the phase, change either by virtue of a chemical reaction or by virtue of a transport of matter across the boundaries between phases, or both. In general, under given conditions, there is a set of values of the n's for which the phase is in chemical, and therefore in thermodynamic, equilibrium. The functions that express the properties of a phase when it is not in chemical equilibrium must obviously reduce to those for thermodynamic equilibrium when the equilibrium values of the n's are substituted. We are therefore led to assume that *any property of a phase in mechanical and thermal equilibrium can be represented by a function of any two of P, V, T, and the n's of the same form as that used to denote the same property when the phase is in thermodynamic equilibrium.*

Consider, for example, a phase consisting of a mixture of ideal gases. When the gases are inert, the equation of state is

$$PV_t = \Sigma n_i RT,$$

the molar entropy is

$$S = \Sigma[y_i(S_i - R \ln y_i)],$$

and the molar Gibbs function is

$$G = \Sigma[y_i(G_i + RT \ln y_i)].$$

According to the assumption just made, these same equations may be used in connection with an ideal-gas phase in mechanical and thermal equilibrium when the gases are chemically active, when the phase is in contact with other phases, or under both conditions, whether chemical equilibrium exists or not. Under these conditions the y_i's are variables. Whether they are all independent variables or not is a question that cannot be answered until the conditions under which a change of state takes place are specified. It is clear that, if the mass of the phase remains constant and the gases are inert, the y_i's are constants. If the mass of the phase remains constant and the gases are chemically active, it will be shown that each y is a function of only one independent variable, the degree of reaction.

14.9/ Conditions for Chemical Equilibrium

Consider any PVT system of constant mass, either homogeneous or heterogeneous, in mechanical and thermal equilibrium but not in chemical equilibrium. Suppose that the system is in contact with a reservoir at temperature T and undergoes an infinitesimal irreversible process involving an exchange of heat $đQ$ with the reservoir. The process may involve a chemical reaction or a transport of matter between phases or both. Let dS_t denote the total entropy change of the system, and dS_0 the total entropy change of the reservoir. The total entropy change of the universe is therefore $dS_0 + dS_t$, and since the performance of an irreversible process is attended by an increase in the total entropy of the universe, we may write

$$dS_0 + dS_t > 0.$$

Since
$$dS_0 = -\frac{đQ}{T},$$

we have
$$-\frac{đQ}{T} + dS_t > 0,$$

or
$$đQ - T\,dS_t < 0.$$

During the infinitesimal irreversible process the total internal energy of the system changes by an amount dU_t, and an amount of work $P\,dV_t$ is performed. The first law can therefore be written in its usual form,

$$đQ = dU_t + P\,dV_t,$$

and the inequality becomes

$$\boxed{dU_t + P\,dV_t - T\,dS_t < 0.}$$

This inequality holds during any infinitesimal portion and therefore during all infinitesimal portions of the irreversible process. According to the assumption made in the preceding article, U_t, V_t, and S_t may all be regarded as functions of thermodynamic coordinates.

During the irreversible process for which the above inequality holds, some or all of the coordinates may change. If we restrict the irreversible process by imposing the condition that two of the thermodynamic coordinates remain constant, the inequality can be reduced to a simpler form. Suppose, for example, that the total internal energy and the total volume remain constant. Then the inequality reduces to $dS_t > 0$, which means that the total entropy of a system at constant U_t and V_t increases during an irreversible process, approaching a maximum at the final state of equilibrium. This result, however, is obvious from the entropy principle, since a system at constant U_t and V_t is isolated and is therefore, so to speak, its own universe. The most useful set of conditions is that in which T and P remain constant.

If T and P are constant, the inequality reduces to

$$d(U_t + PV_t - TS_t) < 0,$$

or
$$dG_t < 0,$$

expressing the result that *the total Gibbs function of a system at constant T and P decreases during an irreversible process.* Every increment of such a process must result in a decrease in the Gibbs function of the system and must bring the system closer to equilibrium. Hence the equilibrium state, if reached along a path of constant T and P, must be the one having the minimum Gibbs function. Thus, at the equilibrium state,

$$\boxed{d(nG)_{T,P} = 0,}$$

where G is now the *molar* Gibbs function, and n is the total moles of the system. This equation is a general criterion of equilibrium. It is *not* necessary in the application of this criterion that the system considered actually reach the equilibrium state along a path of constant T and P. Once an equilibrium state is established, no further changes occur, and the system exists in this state at a particular T and P. How this state was *actually* attained is not important, and for purposes of calculation one may as well take the path followed in getting there to have been one of constant T and P.

14.10/ Degree of Reaction

If we introduce into a vessel a mixture of any arbitrary number of moles of water vapor, hydrogen, and oxygen, the chemical reaction that is capable of taking place is indicated by the notation

$$H_2O \rightleftharpoons H_2 + \tfrac{1}{2}O_2,$$

where the quantity that is written on the left is called an *initial constituent* and those on the right *final constituents.* The numbers that precede the chemical symbols and that "balance" the equation (it is understood that both H_2O and H_2 are preceded by unity) are called the *stoichiometric coefficients* and are proportional to the numbers of moles of the constituents that *change* during the reaction. Thus, if 1 mole of water vapor dissociates, then 1 mole of hydrogen and 0.5 mole of oxygen are formed; or if 0.1 mole of water vapor dissociates, then 0.1 mole of hydrogen and 0.05 mole of oxygen are formed; or if n_0 moles of water vapor dissociates, n_0 being any number whatever, then n_0 moles of hydrogen and $n_0/2$ moles of oxygen are formed. Similarly, if the reaction proceeds to the left to the extent that n_0' moles of hydrogen combines with $n_0'/2$ moles of oxygen, then n_0' moles of water vapor is formed.

In general, suppose we have a mixture of four substances whose chemical symbols are A_1, A_2, A_3, and A_4. Let A_1 and A_2 be the initial constituents and A_3 and A_4 the final constituents, the reaction being represented by

$$\nu_1 A_1 + \nu_2 A_2 \rightleftharpoons \nu_3 A_3 + \nu_4 A_4.$$

We have chosen four substances only for convenience. The equations to be developed are of such a character that they can easily be applied to reactions in which any number of substances participate. The ν's are the stoichiometric coefficients, which are always positive integers or fractions.

Suppose we start with arbitrary amounts of *both* initial and final constituents. If we imagine the reaction to proceed completely to the right, at least one of the initial constituents, say, A_1, will completely disappear. Then it is possible to find a positive number n_0 such that the original number of moles of each of the initial constituents is expressed in the form

$$n_1(\text{original}) = n_0\nu_1,$$
$$n_2(\text{original}) = n_0\nu_2 + N_2,$$

where N_2 is a constant representing the number of moles of A_2 that cannot combine. If we imagine the reaction to proceed completely to the left, at least one of the final constituents, say, A_3, will completely disappear. In this event, another positive number n_0' may be found such that the original number of moles of each final constituent is expressed in the form

$$n_3(\text{original}) = n_0'\nu_3,$$
$$n_4(\text{original}) = n_0'\nu_4 + N_4.$$

If the reaction is imagined to proceed completely to the left, there is the maximum amount possible of each initial constituent and the minimum amount of each final constituent. Thus

$$n_1(\text{max}) = (n_0 + n_0')\nu_1,$$
$$n_2(\text{max}) = (n_0 + n_0')\nu_2 + N_2,$$
$$n_3(\text{min}) = 0$$
$$n_4(\text{min}) = N_4.$$

If the reaction is imagined to proceed completely to the right, there is the minimum amount possible of each initial constituent and the maximum amount of each final constituent. Thus

$$n_1(\text{min}) = 0,$$
$$n_2(\text{min}) = N_2,$$
$$n_3(\text{max}) = (n_0 + n_0')\nu_3,$$
$$n_4(\text{max}) = (n_0 + n_0')\nu_4 + N_4.$$

Suppose the reaction proceeds partially either to the right or to the left to such an extent that there are n_1 moles of A_1, n_2 moles of A_2, n_3 moles of A_3, and n_4 moles of A_4 present at a given moment. We define the *degree of reaction* ϵ in terms of any one of the *initial* constituents, say,

A_1, as the fraction

$$\epsilon = \frac{n_1(\text{max}) - n_1}{n_1(\text{max}) - n_1(\text{min})}.$$

In terms of a *final* constituent, say, A_3, ϵ is given as

$$\epsilon = \frac{n_3 - n_3(\text{min})}{n_3(\text{max}) - n_3(\text{min})}.$$

It follows that $\epsilon = 0$ when the reaction is completely to the left and $\epsilon = 1$ when the reaction is completely to the right. When the reaction consists in the dissociation of one initial constituent, ϵ is called the *degree of dissociation;* when it consists in the ionization of one initial constituent, ϵ is called the *degree of ionization.* Expressing $n_1(\text{max})$ and $n_1(\text{min})$ in terms of the constants that express the original amounts of the constituents, we get

$$\epsilon = \frac{(n_0 + n_0')\nu_1 - n_1}{(n_0 + n_0')\nu_1},$$

and solving for n_1,

$$n_1 = (n_0 + n_0')\nu_1(1 - \epsilon).$$

The number of moles of each of the constituents is therefore given by the expressions

$$n_1 = (n_0 + n_0')\nu_1(1 - \epsilon),$$
$$n_2 = (n_0 + n_0')\nu_2(1 - \epsilon) + N_2,$$
$$n_3 = (n_0 + n_0')\nu_3\epsilon,$$
$$n_4 = (n_0 + n_0')\nu_4\epsilon + N_4.$$

When a chemical reaction takes place, all the n's change, but not independently. The restrictions imposed upon the n's are given by the above relations. These equations are therefore examples of *equations of constraint.* Since all the n's are functions of ϵ only, it follows that, in a homogeneous system, all the mole fractions are functions of ϵ only.

If the reaction is imagined to proceed to an infinitesimal extent, the degree of reaction changing from ϵ to $\epsilon + d\epsilon$, the various n's will change by the amounts

$$dn_1 = -(n_0 + n_0')\nu_1 \, d\epsilon,$$
$$dn_2 = -(n_0 + n_0')\nu_2 \, d\epsilon,$$
$$dn_3 = (n_0 + n_0')\nu_3 \, d\epsilon,$$
$$dn_4 = (n_0 + n_0')\nu_4 \, d\epsilon.$$

These equations show that the changes in the n's are proportional to the ν's, the factor of proportionality being, for the initial constituents, $-(n_0 + n_0') \, d\epsilon$ and, for the final constituents, $+(n_0 + n_0') \, d\epsilon$. Another way of writing them is as follows:

$$\frac{dn_1}{-\nu_1} = \frac{dn_2}{-\nu_2} = \frac{dn_3}{\nu_3} = \frac{dn_4}{\nu_4} = (n_0 + n_0')\, d\epsilon,$$

which shows clearly that the dn's are proportional to the ν's. The usefulness of these equations is shown by the following examples.

Consider a vessel containing n_0 moles of water vapor only, with no hydrogen or oxygen present. If dissociation occurs according to the reaction

$$H_2O \rightarrow H_2 + \tfrac{1}{2}O_2,$$

we may relate the mole numbers of each constituent present to the degree of dissociation ϵ through the equation

$$\frac{dn_{H_2O}}{-1} = \frac{dn_{H_2}}{1} = \frac{dn_{O_2}}{\tfrac{1}{2}} = (n_0 + n_0')\, d\epsilon.$$

In the initial state $\epsilon = 0$ and $n_{H_2O} = n_0$. If the reaction proceeded to the maximum extent to the right, ϵ would be 1 and n_{H_2O} would be zero. Integrating the expression obtained from the first and last terms of the above set of equalities, we have

$$\int_{n_0}^{0} dn_{H_2O} = (-1)(n_0 + n_0') \int_0^1 d\epsilon,$$

or
$$-n_0 = -(n_0 + n_0').$$
Hence
$$n_0' = 0.$$

We may now write

$$dn_{H_2O} = -n_0\, d\epsilon,$$
$$dn_{H_2} = n_0\, d\epsilon,$$
$$dn_{O_2} = \tfrac{1}{2}n_0\, d\epsilon.$$

Integration from the initial state where $\epsilon = 0$ to a state where $\epsilon = \epsilon$ gives

$$
\begin{aligned}
n_{H_2O} - n_0 &= -n_0\epsilon, &\quad \text{or} \quad& n_{H_2O} = n_0(1 - \epsilon),\\
n_{H_2} - 0 &= n_0\epsilon, &\quad \text{or} \quad& n_{H_2} = n_0\epsilon,\\
n_{O_2} - 0 &= \tfrac{1}{2}n_0\epsilon, &\quad \text{or} \quad& n_{O_2} = \tfrac{1}{2}n_0\epsilon,
\end{aligned}
$$

and
$$\Sigma n = n_0\left(1 + \frac{\epsilon}{2}\right).$$

The various mole fractions are obtained from the expression $y_i = n_i/\Sigma n_i$, and are

$$y_{H_2O} = \frac{1 - \epsilon}{1 + \epsilon/2}, \qquad y_{H_2} = \frac{\epsilon}{1 + \epsilon/2}, \qquad \text{and} \qquad y_{O_2} = \frac{\epsilon/2}{1 + \epsilon/2}.$$

The composition of the mixture is clearly a function of the degree of dissociation ϵ.

Consider the chemical reaction

$$CH_4 + H_2O \rightleftharpoons CO + 3H_2.$$

Assume there are present initially 2 moles CH_4, 1 mole H_2O, 1 mole CO, and 4 moles H_2. We may write

$$\frac{dn_{CH_4}}{-1} = \frac{dn_{H_2O}}{-1} = \frac{dn_{CO}}{1} = \frac{dn_{H_2}}{3} = (n_0 + n_0')\, d\epsilon.$$

Now, in the original state, the degree of reaction ϵ is not zero. It would be zero if the reaction proceeded to the left until the original 1 mole of CO disappeared. This would give $n_{CH_4}(\max) = 3$. If the reaction proceeded as far as possible to the right ($\epsilon = 1$), so that the original 1 mole of H_2O disappeared, we should have $n_{CH_4}(\min) = 1$. Integration of the expression

$$\frac{dn_{CH_4}}{-1} = (n_0 + n_0')\, d\epsilon$$

between these two states gives

$$\int_3^1 dn_{CH_4} = (-1)(n_0 + n_0') \int_0^1 d\epsilon,$$

or
$$n_0 + n_0' = 2.$$

Thus we have, in general,

$$\begin{aligned}
dn_{CH_4} &= -2d\epsilon, \\
dn_{H_2O} &= -2d\epsilon, \\
dn_{CO} &= 2d\epsilon, \\
dn_{H_2} &= 6d\epsilon.
\end{aligned}$$

These expressions may be integrated between any two states of the system, for example, between that for which $\epsilon = 0$ and that for which $\epsilon = \epsilon$. When $\epsilon = 0$, the reaction is displaced to the left as far as possible. In this state there are 3 moles CH_4, 2 moles H_2O, 0 moles CO, and 1 mole H_2. Thus integration gives

$$n_{CH_4} = 3 - 2\epsilon, \qquad y_{CH_4} = \frac{3 - 2\epsilon}{6 + 4\epsilon},$$

$$n_{H_2O} = 2 - 2\epsilon, \qquad y_{H_2O} = \frac{1 - \epsilon}{3 + 2\epsilon},$$

$$n_{CO} = 2\epsilon, \qquad y_{CO} = \frac{\epsilon}{3 + 2\epsilon},$$

$$n_{H_2} = 1 + 6\epsilon, \qquad y_{H_2} = \frac{1 + 6\epsilon}{6 + 4\epsilon},$$

$$\overline{\Sigma n = 6 + 4\epsilon.}$$

14.11/ Chemical-reaction Equilibrium in Ideal Gases

In Sec. 14.9 it was shown that a criterion for equilibrium is

$$d(nG)_{T,P} = 0.$$

In Sec. 14.6 the following equation was derived for a mixture of ideal gases:

$$G = \Sigma[y_i(G_i + RT \ln y_i)].$$

For n moles this becomes

$$nG = \Sigma[n_i(G_i + RT \ln y_i)].$$

We now take the total differential of nG, holding T and P constant. Since the G_i's are for the pure gases at T and P, these also are constant. Thus

$$d(nG)_{T,P} = \Sigma[n_i(RT \, d\ln y_i)] + \Sigma[(G_i + RT \ln y_i) \, dn_i].$$

Consider the first term on the right of this equation. Since $n_i = y_i n$, where $n = \Sigma n_i$, we have

$$\Sigma[n_i(RT \, d\ln y_i)] = \Sigma\left(y_i nRT \frac{dy_i}{y_i}\right) = nRT\Sigma \, dy_i.$$

But $$y_1 + y_2 + y_3 + \cdots = \Sigma y_i = 1.$$

Therefore $d\Sigma y_i = \Sigma \, dy_i = 0$, and the term drops out. As a result we have

$$d(nG)_{T,P} = \Sigma[(G_i + RT \ln y_i) \, dn_i].$$

For equilibrium $$\Sigma[(G_i + RT \ln y_i) \, dn_i] = 0.$$

Consider the application of this equation to a mixture of four ideal gases which are capable of taking part in the reaction

$$\nu_1 A_1 + \nu_2 A_2 \rightleftharpoons \nu_3 A_3 + \nu_4 A_4.$$

For equilibrium at a given temperature and pressure we must have

$$(G_1 + RT \ln y_1) \, dn_1 + (G_2 + RT \ln y_2) \, dn_2 + (G_3 + RT \ln y_3) \, dn_3$$
$$+ (G_4 + RT \ln y_4) \, dn_4 = 0.$$

We showed in the preceding section that for a chemical reaction the dn_i's are all related to the corresponding stoichiometric coefficients according to the equations

$$dn_1 = -(n_0 + n_0')\nu_1 \, d\epsilon,$$
$$dn_2 = -(n_0 + n_0')\nu_2 \, d\epsilon,$$
$$dn_3 = (n_0 + n_0')\nu_3 \, d\epsilon,$$
$$dn_4 = (n_0 + n_0')\nu_4 \, d\epsilon.$$

Substitution for the dn_i's in our equilibrium expression gives

$$- (G_1 + RT \ln y_1)\nu_1 - (G_2 + RT \ln y_2)\nu_2 + (G_3 + RT \ln y_3)\nu_3$$
$$+ (G_4 + RT \ln y_4)\nu_4 = 0.$$

This is the fundamental equation for reaction equilibrium in a mixture of ideal gases. However, it is convenient to put it into quite a different form before using it in numerical calculations. Collection of like terms gives

$$\nu_3 G_3 + \nu_4 G_4 - \nu_1 G_1 - \nu_2 G_2 + RT(\nu_3 \ln y_3 + \nu_4 \ln y_4 - \nu_1 \ln y_1$$
$$- \nu_2 \ln y_2) = 0.$$

Now the G_i's represent the Gibbs function for the pure ideal gases at the temperature and pressure of the mixture. It is convenient to refer these quantities to a *standard state*, which for gases is arbitrarily taken to be the ideal-gas state at 1 atm and at the temperature of the mixture. In Sec. 10.3 the general equation was developed which relates G to T and P:

$$dG = V \, dP - S \, dT.$$

For a change in pressure from the standard-state value of $P° = 1$ atm to the mixture pressure P at constant temperature T for pure ideal gas i,

$$\int_{G°}^{G} dG = \int_{P°}^{P} \frac{RT}{P} \, dP = RT \int_{P°}^{P} \frac{dP}{P},$$

or
$$G - G° = RT \ln \frac{P}{P°},$$

where the superscript ° indicates a value for the standard state. Since $P° = 1$ atm, we may write

$$G_i = G_i° + RT \ln P,$$

where we must remember that P represents the pressure in atmospheres and is understood to be divided by 1 atm. Hence the term $RT \ln P$ has the units of RT only.

We may now substitute for G_1, G_2, G_3, and G_4 in our equilibrium equation:

$$\nu_3(G_3° + RT \ln P) + \nu_4(G_4° + RT \ln P) - \nu_1(G_1° + RT \ln P)$$
$$- \nu_2(G_2° + RT \ln P) + RT(\nu_3 \ln y_3 + \nu_4 \ln y_4 - \nu_1 \ln y_1$$
$$- \nu_2 \ln y_2) = 0.$$

Rearranging,

$$\nu_3 G_3° + \nu_4 G_4° - \nu_1 G_1° - \nu_2 G_2° + RT[(\nu_3 + \nu_4 - \nu_1 - \nu_2) \ln P$$
$$+ \nu_3 \ln y_3 + \nu_4 \ln y_4 - \nu_1 \ln y_1 - \nu_2 \ln y_2] = 0,$$

or
$$\ln \left(\frac{y_3{}^{\nu_3} y_4{}^{\nu_4}}{y_1{}^{\nu_1} y_2{}^{\nu_2}} P^{\nu_3 + \nu_4 - \nu_1 - \nu_2} \right) = \frac{-(\nu_3 G_3° + \nu_4 G_4° - \nu_1 G_1° - \nu_2 G_2°)}{RT}.$$

The right-hand member is a quantity whose value depends only on the temperature. If we denote it by $\ln K$, where K is known as the *equilibrium constant*, we have at equilibrium

$$\frac{y_3{}^{\nu_3} y_4{}^{\nu_4}}{y_1{}^{\nu_1} y_2{}^{\nu_2}} P^{\nu_3 + \nu_4 - \nu_1 - \nu_2} = K.$$

By definition,

$$\ln K = \frac{-(\nu_3 G_3^{\circ} + \nu_4 G_4^{\circ} - \nu_1 G_1^{\circ} - \nu_2 G_2^{\circ})}{RT} = \frac{-\Delta G^{\circ}}{RT}.$$

This is usually written

$$\Delta G^{\circ} = -RT \ln K,$$

where $\qquad \Delta G^{\circ} = (\nu_3 G_3^{\circ} + \nu_4 G_4^{\circ} - \nu_1 G_1^{\circ} - \nu_2 G_2^{\circ})$

is known as the *standard Gibbs-function change of reaction*. Values of this quantity for common reactions are listed in various handbooks and compilations of data.

It should be noted that K is dimensionless. This is evident from examination of the equation $\Delta G^{\circ} = -RT \ln K$, where ΔG° has the dimensions of RT. However, in the preceding equilibrium equation the quantity $P^{\nu_3 + \nu_4 - \nu_1 - \nu_2}$, and hence K, appear to have dimensions of pressure raised to the $(\nu_3 + \nu_4 - \nu_1 - \nu_2)$th power. One must remember that P here represents the pressure in atmospheres divided by 1 atm, and is therefore dimensionless.

The equilibrium expression which we have developed for the case of two initial constituents and two final constituents may obviously be generalized to apply to any number of either. It may be written

$$\frac{\Pi y_f{}^{\nu_f}}{\Pi y_i{}^{\nu_i}} P^{\Sigma \nu_f - \Sigma \nu_i} = K,$$

where Π indicates a continuous product, the subscript f denotes a final constituent, and the subscript i, an initial constituent. The equilibrium constant K is given by

$$-RT \ln K = \Delta G^{\circ},$$
$$\Delta G^{\circ} = \Sigma \nu_f G_f^{\circ} - \Sigma \nu_i G_i^{\circ}.$$

where

The equilibrium equation allows the calculation of the degree of reaction at equilibrium for a given temperature and pressure once the equilibrium constant is known. For example, the value of ΔG° at

298°K (25°C) for the reaction

$$N_2O_4 \rightleftharpoons 2NO_2$$

is 1290 cal.　Thus

$$\ln K = \frac{-\Delta G^\circ}{RT} = \frac{-1290}{(1.987)(298)} = -2.179$$

and
$$K = 0.1133.$$

Assume we start with 1 gm mole of N_2O_4 and allow the system to reach equilibrium according to the above dissociation reaction at 25°C and 2 atm.　The equilibrium mole fractions of N_2O_4 and NO_2 are related to the degree of reaction at equilibrium.　We have

$$\frac{dn_{N_2O_4}}{-1} = \frac{dn_{NO_2}}{2} = (n_0 + n_0')\, d\epsilon.$$

When $\epsilon = 0$, $n_{N_2O_4} = 1$, and when $\epsilon = 1$, $n_{N_2O_4} = 0$.　Thus

$$\int_1^0 dn_{N_2O_4} = -(n_0 + n_0') \int_0^1 d\epsilon,$$

or
$$n_0 + n_0' = 1.$$

As a result we may write the general equations

$$dn_{N_2O_4} = -d\epsilon \quad \text{and} \quad dn_{NO_2} = 2d\epsilon.$$

Integration from $\epsilon = 0$ to $\epsilon = \epsilon_e$, the degree of reaction at equilibrium, gives

$$n_{N_2O_4} = 1 - \epsilon_e, \qquad y_{N_2O_4} = \frac{1 - \epsilon_e}{1 + \epsilon_e},$$

$$n_{NO_2} = 2\epsilon_e, \qquad y_{NO_2} = \frac{2\epsilon_e}{1 + \epsilon_e},$$

$$\overline{\Sigma n = 1 + \epsilon_e.}$$

The equilibrium equation for this particular reaction now becomes

$$\frac{y_{NO_2}^2}{y_{N_2O_4}} P^{2-1} = \frac{\left(\dfrac{2\epsilon_e}{1 + \epsilon_e}\right)^2}{\dfrac{1 - \epsilon_e}{1 + \epsilon_e}} P = \frac{4\epsilon_e^2}{(1 - \epsilon_e)(1 + \epsilon_e)} P = K.$$

Since $P = 2$ and $K = 0.1133$, we have

$$\frac{\epsilon_e^2}{1 - \epsilon_e^2} = \frac{0.1133}{(2)(4)} = 0.01417,$$

or
$$\epsilon_e^2 = \frac{0.01417}{1.01417} = 0.01397.$$

Thus
$$\epsilon_e = 0.1182.$$

$$y_{N_2O_4} = \frac{1 - 0.1182}{1 + 0.1182} = 0.789$$

and
$$y_{NO_2} = 0.211.$$

It should be noted that K is a function of temperature, and therefore the equilibrium composition shifts with changes in temperature. Although the equilibrium constant is itself independent of pressure, the equilibrium *composition* is seen in the preceding example to depend on pressure, because the term $P^{\Sigma\nu_f-\Sigma\nu_i}$ appears in the equilibrium equation. Reactions of ideal gases for which $\Sigma\nu_f = \Sigma\nu_i$ are not influenced by pressure.

14.12/ Standard Heat of Reaction

The equilibrium constant is defined by the equation

$$\ln K = \frac{-(\nu_3 G_3^\circ + \nu_4 G_4^\circ - \nu_1 G_1^\circ - \nu_2 G_2^\circ)}{RT}.$$

Differentiating $\ln K$ with respect to T, we get

$$\frac{d\ln K}{dT} = -\left[\nu_3 \frac{d(G_3^\circ/RT)}{dT} + \nu_4 \frac{d(G_4^\circ/RT)}{dT} - \nu_1 \frac{d(G_1^\circ/RT)}{dT}\right.$$
$$\left. - \nu_2 \frac{d(G_2^\circ/RT)}{dT}\right].$$

Now G_1° is the value of the Gibbs function for the standard state, which for ideal gases is taken to be the state at 1 atm. Thus the pressure of the standard state is constant. The basic differential equation for the Gibbs function,

$$dG = V\,dP - S\,dT,$$

applied to the standard state of pure ideal gas i then becomes

$$dG_i^\circ = -S_i^\circ\,dT,$$

or

$$\frac{dG_i^\circ}{dT} = -S_i^\circ,$$

where S_i° is the entropy of i in the standard state.

The enthalpy H_i° of i in the standard state is related to G_i° and S_i° by the definition

$$G_i^\circ = H_i^\circ - TS_i^\circ.$$

Substituting for S_i°, we get

$$G_i^\circ = H_i^\circ + T\frac{dG_i^\circ}{dT},$$

or

$$-H_i^\circ = T\frac{dG_i^\circ}{dT} - G_i^\circ.$$

But

$$T^2 \frac{d(G_i^\circ/T)}{dT} = T^2\left[\frac{1}{T}\left(\frac{dG_i^\circ}{dT}\right) - \frac{G_i^\circ}{T^2}\right]$$
$$= T\frac{dG_i^\circ}{dT} - G_i^\circ.$$

Therefore
$$-H_i^\circ = T^2 \frac{d(G_i^\circ/T)}{dT},$$

or
$$\frac{d(G_i^\circ/RT)}{dT} = \frac{-H_i^\circ}{RT^2}.$$

Returning now to our expression for $d \ln K/dT$, we see that it becomes

$$\frac{d \ln K}{dT} = \frac{\nu_3 H_3^\circ + \nu_4 H_4^\circ - \nu_1 H_1^\circ - \nu_2 H_2^\circ}{RT^2},$$

or
$$\boxed{\frac{d \ln K}{dT} = \frac{\Delta H^\circ}{RT^2},}$$

where
$$\Delta H^\circ = \nu_3 H_3^\circ + \nu_4 H_4^\circ - \nu_1 H_1^\circ - \nu_2 H_2^\circ$$

is known as the *standard enthalpy change of reaction*, or more commonly, as the *standard heat of reaction*. This latter term arises because of the fact that if ν_1 moles of gas 1 and ν_2 moles of gas 2 were converted at constant temperature and at the standard-state pressure of 1 atm to ν_3 moles of gas 3 and ν_4 moles of gas 4, the heat transferred would be equal to the final enthalpy $\nu_3 H_3^\circ + \nu_4 H_4^\circ$ minus the initial enthalpy $\nu_1 H_1^\circ + \nu_2 H_2^\circ$.

Since the change of the equilibrium constant with temperature depends on the heat of reaction, knowledge of this quantity is most important for reacting systems. If the heat of reaction is positive, that is, if the final enthalpy is greater than the initial enthalpy, heat must be added to the system as the reaction proceeds from left to right to maintain constant temperature. Such a reaction is *endothermic*. If the heat of reaction is negative, heat is given off and the reaction is *exothermic*. Combustion reactions are exothermic.

The standard heat of reaction is a function of temperature. Since the standard-state pressure for ideal gases is always 1 atm, changes in temperature of the standard state produce enthalpy changes according to the equation

$$dH_i^\circ = C_{P_i}^\circ \, dT,$$

or
$$H_i^\circ = H_0 + \int C_{P_i}^\circ \, dT,$$

where H_0 is a constant of integration. Thus

$$\Delta H^\circ = \nu_3 H_{0_3} + \nu_4 H_{0_4} - \nu_1 H_{0_1} - \nu_2 H_{0_2}$$
$$+ \int (\nu_3 C_{P_3}^\circ + \nu_4 C_{P_4}^\circ - \nu_1 C_{P_1}^\circ - \nu_2 C_{P_2}^\circ) \, dT.$$

The constant part of this equation may be denoted by ΔH_0. Thus

$$\Delta H_0 = \nu_3 H_{0_3} + \nu_4 H_{0_4} - \nu_1 H_{0_1} - \nu_2 H_{0_2}.$$

Furthermore, the integrand may be written

$$\Delta C_P^\circ = \nu_3 C_{P_3}^\circ + \nu_4 C_{P_4}^\circ - \nu_1 C_{P_1}^\circ - \nu_2 C_{P_2}^\circ.$$

So we have, finally,

$$\Delta H^\circ = \Delta H_0 + \int (\Delta C_P^\circ)\, dT.$$

This may also be written

$$\frac{d(\Delta H^\circ)}{dT} = \Delta C_P^\circ,$$

from which we see that the standard heat of reaction increases with temperature when the total heat capacity of the final constituents is greater than the total heat capacity of the initial constituents. Conversely, when ΔC_P° is negative, ΔH° decreases with an increase in temperature.

ΔC_P° may be expressed as a function of temperature by substituting for the $C_{P_i}^\circ$'s the empirical equations expressing their temperature dependence. It was pointed out in Art. 5.5 that such equations often take the form

$$C_P^\circ = a + bT + cT^2,$$

and values for the constants in this equation are listed for a number of gases in Table 5.2. Combination of these equations gives

$$\Delta C_P^\circ = \Delta a + (\Delta b)T + (\Delta c)T^2,$$

where Δ has the same significance as it does in ΔG°, ΔH°, etc.

The temperature dependence of the equilibrium constant is given by

$$\frac{d \ln K}{dT} = \frac{\Delta H^\circ}{RT^2}.$$

Integration yields

$$\ln K = \frac{1}{R} \int \frac{\Delta H^\circ}{T^2}\, dT + I,$$

where I is a constant of integration, and ΔH° is given as a function of temperature by

$$\Delta H^\circ = \Delta H_0 + \int (\Delta C_P^\circ)\, dT.$$

Standard heats of reaction for gaseous systems are usually determined calorimetrically, and values of ΔH° at 25°C are listed in standard handbooks for the formation of many compounds from their constituent *elements*. These values are denoted by $\Delta H_{f_{298}}^\circ$, where the subscript f specifies a *heat of formation* and the 298 indicates the Kelvin temperature. Similarly, standard changes of formation for the Gibbs function at 25°C or 298°K, designated by $\Delta G_{f_{298}}^\circ$, are also listed in handbooks and compilations of thermodynamic data. Table 14.2 gives such values for a few common substances.

Table 14.2/ Standard Heats of Formation and Standard Gibbs-function Changes of Formation for Gases at 298°K in the Ideal-gas State at 1 Atm

Gas	Formula	$\Delta H^{\circ}_{f_{298}}$, cal/gm mole	$\Delta G^{\circ}_{f_{298}}$, cal/gm mole
Acetylene	C_2H_2	54,194	50,000
Ammonia	NH_3	−11,040	− 3,976
Benzene	C_6H_6	19,820	30,989
Carbon dioxide	CO_2	−94,052	−94,260
Carbon monoxide	CO	−26,416	−32,808
Ethyl alcohol	C_2H_6O	−56,240	−40,300
Hydrogen chloride	HCl	−22,063	−22,769
Methane	CH_4	−17,889	−12,140
Sulfur dioxide	SO_2	−70,960	−71,790
Water	H_2O	−57,798	−54,635

For example, the formation reaction for ammonia is

$$\tfrac{1}{2}N_2 + \tfrac{3}{2}H_2 \rightarrow NH_3.$$

For this reaction Table 14.2 gives the values

$$\Delta H^{\circ}_{f_{298}} = -11,040 \text{ cal/gm mole } NH_3,$$
$$\Delta G^{\circ}_{f_{298}} = -3,976 \text{ cal/gm mole } NH_3.$$

The heat-capacity data given in Table 5.2 for N_2, H_2, and NH_3 allow the determination of ΔC°_P for this reaction as a function of temperature. Numerical substitution in the defining equation for ΔC°_P yields

$$\Delta C^{\circ}_P = -7.596 + 8.487 \times 10^{-3}T - 2.227 \times 10^{-6}T^2,$$

where T is in degrees Kelvin, and ΔC°_P has the units of calories per °K. Since ΔH° is given as a function of temperature by

$$\Delta H^{\circ} = \Delta H_0 + \int (\Delta C^{\circ}_P)\, dT,$$

we have after integration

$$\Delta H^{\circ} = \Delta H_0 - 7.596T + 4.244 \times 10^{-3}T^2 - 0.742 \times 10^{-6}T^3.$$

At 298°K, we have $\Delta H^{\circ} = -11,040$. Substitution of these values now provides a value for ΔH_0. The result is a general equation for ΔH°:

$$\Delta H^{\circ} = -9140 - 7.596T + 4.244 \times 10^{-3}T^2 - 0.742 \times 10^{-6}T^3.$$

A general equation giving $\ln K$ as a function of T is now obtained by substitution for ΔH° in the equation

$$\ln K = \frac{1}{R} \int \frac{\Delta H^{\circ}}{T^2}\, dT + I.$$

Integration gives

$$\ln K = \frac{4600}{T} - 3.823 \ln T + 2.136 \times 10^{-3}T - 0.187 \times 10^{-6}T^2 + I.$$

At $T = 298°K$, we may calculate K from the given data for $\Delta G°$:

$$\ln K = -\frac{\Delta G°}{RT} = \frac{3976}{(1.987)(298)} = 6.715.$$

The integration constant I is now determined by substitution of this value for $\ln K$ at 298°K into the above equation. The result is an equation for $\ln K$ as a function of T:

$$\ln K = \frac{4600}{T} - 3.823 \ln T + 2.136 \times 10^{-3}T$$
$$- 0.187 \times 10^{-6}T^2 + 12.431.$$

With the aid of this equation we can calculate the degree of reaction at equilibrium for the ammonia synthesis reaction as a function of temperature. Assume that $\frac{1}{2}$ mole of N_2 and $\frac{3}{2}$ mole of H_2 represent the original constitution of the system, which is to come to equilibrium at pressure P and temperature T. We may write

$$\frac{dn_{N_2}}{-\frac{1}{2}} = \frac{dn_{H_2}}{-\frac{3}{2}} = \frac{dn_{NH_3}}{1} = (n_0 + n_0')\, d\epsilon.$$

It is easily shown that $n_0 + n_0' = 1$. Thus, at equilibrium,

$$n_{N_2} = \tfrac{1}{2}(1 - \epsilon_e), \qquad y_{N_2} = \frac{1 - \epsilon_e}{2(2 - \epsilon_e)},$$

$$n_{H_2} = \tfrac{3}{2}(1 - \epsilon_e), \qquad y_{H_2} = \frac{3(1 - \epsilon_e)}{2(2 - \epsilon_e)},$$

$$n_{NH_3} = \epsilon_e, \qquad y_{NH_3} = \frac{\epsilon_e}{2 - \epsilon_e},$$

$$\overline{\Sigma n = 2 - \epsilon_e.}$$

Thus

$$\frac{y_{NH_3}}{y_{N_2}^{\frac{1}{2}} y_{H_2}^{\frac{3}{2}}} P^{-1} = \frac{\epsilon_e(2 - \epsilon_e)}{[\frac{1}{2}(1 - \epsilon_e)]^{\frac{1}{2}}[\frac{3}{2}(1 - \epsilon_e)]^{\frac{3}{2}}P} = K,$$

or

$$\frac{\epsilon_e(2 - \epsilon_e)}{(1 - \epsilon_e)^2} = 1.30KP.$$

Rearrangement gives

$$(1 + 1.30KP)\epsilon_e^2 - 2(1 + 1.30KP)\epsilon_e + 1.30KP = 0.$$

Let

$$r = 1 + 1.30KP.$$

Then

$$r\epsilon_e^2 - 2r\epsilon_e + (r - 1) = 0.$$

Substitution of the proper coefficients in the formula for the roots of a quadratic equation gives, after reduction, the simple expression

$$\epsilon_e = 1 \pm \frac{1}{r^{\frac{1}{2}}}.$$

Table 14.3/ Results of Calculations for the Ammonia Synthesis Reaction

(Reactants Initially in the Stoichiometric Proportion)

T, °K	K	1 atm		100 atm	
		ϵ_e	y_{NH_3}	ϵ_e	y_{NH_3}
300	7.22×10^2	0.968	0.938	0.997	0.994
400	6.37	0.673	0.507	0.964	0.931
500	3.31×10^{-1}	0.164	0.089	0.849	0.738
600	4.31×10^{-2}	0.022	0.01⁴	0.610	0.439
700	9.68×10^{-3}	0.006	0.003	0.336	0.202
800	3.23×10^{-3}			0.155	0.084
900	1.24×10^{-3}			0.072	0.037
1000	5.95×10^{-4}			0.037	0.019

Since ϵ_e must always be less than unity, we need only the smaller root, and

$$\epsilon_e = 1 - \frac{1}{r^{\frac{1}{2}}},$$

or

$$\epsilon_e = 1 - \frac{1}{(1 + 1.3KP)^{\frac{1}{2}}}.$$

We may now evaluate ϵ_e as a function of temperature and pressure. The results of these calculations are shown in Table 14.3. The influence of temperature and pressure on the degree of reaction and on the conversion of reactants to ammonia is clear. It is desirable from the standpoint of the equilibrium conversion to carry out this synthesis at about room temperature. However, at this temperature the reaction rate is negligible, even with the best catalyst yet discovered. At higher temperatures, say 600 or 700°K, rapid reaction can be attained, but the degree of reaction is very small at atmospheric pressure. Therefore the synthesis is carried out at elevated pressures. The assumption of ideal gases is not really justified at 100 atm. However, the calculated results are certainly qualitatively valid.

For reactions that are not formation reactions, the chemical equation may be expressed as a combination of formation reactions. Values of $\Delta H°$ and $\Delta G°$ are then found by a corresponding combination of $\Delta H_f°$ and $\Delta G_f°$ values. For example, the reaction

$$CH_4 + H_2O \rightarrow CO + 3H_2$$

is obtained from the formation reactions

$C + \frac{1}{2}O_2 \rightarrow CO,$	$\Delta H_f° = -26,416,$	$\Delta G_f° = -32,808,$
$-[C + 2H_2 \rightarrow CH_4],$	$-\Delta H_f° = +17,889,$	$-\Delta G_f° = +12,140,$
$-[H_2 + \frac{1}{2}O_2 \rightarrow H_2O],$	$-\Delta H_f° = +57,798,$	$-\Delta G_f° = +54,635,$
$CH_4 + H_2O \rightarrow CO + 3H_2,$	$\Delta H° = \quad 49,271,$	$\Delta G° = \quad 33,967.$

14.13/ Reversible Cells

Equations for a reversible cell composed of solids and liquids only may be obtained from corresponding equations for a PVT system by replacing V by the charge of the cell q and $-P$ by the emf of the cell e.   Thus the first $T\,dS$ equation becomes

$$T\,dS = C_q\,dT - T\left(\frac{\partial e}{\partial T}\right)_q dq,$$

and for a saturated cell whose emf depends on the temperature only, the equation becomes

$$T\,dS = C_q\,dT - T\frac{de}{dT}\,dq.$$

From the equations developed in Secs. 2.8 and 3.9, we have

$$dq = -jF\,dn \qquad \text{and} \qquad \mathchar'26d W = ejF\,dn,$$

where jF is the charge transferred per mole of reacting material, and dn is the moles of material reacted.   It will be recalled that by convention dn is taken as positive for discharging the cell and as negative for charging.

For the *reversible isothermal* transfer of charge dq, $T\,dS$ equals $\mathchar'26d Q$, and the first $T\,dS$ equation becomes

$$\mathchar'26d Q = T\,dS = -T\frac{de}{dT}\,dq$$

$$= jFT\frac{de}{dT}\,dn.$$

By the first law

$$dU = \mathchar'26d Q - \mathchar'26d W.$$

Substitution for $\mathchar'26d Q$ and $\mathchar'26d W$ gives

$$dU = jFT\frac{de}{dT}\,dn - ejF\,dn$$

$$= jF\left(T\frac{de}{dT} - e\right)dn.$$

In the above equations the charge q and the moles of material reacted n are measures of the extent of the chemical reaction which occurs in the cell, and replace the quantity called the degree of reaction employed for gaseous systems.   For cells operating at constant pressure and with negligible volume change, the change of internal energy for a differential amount of reaction is equal to the change of enthalpy. This follows from the definition

$$H = U + PV$$

and
$$dH = dU + P\,dV + V\,dP;$$

whence, under the conditions mentioned,

$$dH = dU.$$

Therefore

$$dH = jF\left(T\frac{de}{dT} - e\right)dn.$$

For the reversible reaction of 1 mole of material having the valence j, this equation integrates to give

$$\Delta H = jF\left(T\frac{de}{dT} - e\right).$$

In order to interpret this change of enthalpy, let us take the particular case of the Daniell cell. The transfer of positive electricity externally from the copper to the zinc electrode is accompanied by the reaction

$$Zn + CuSO_4 \rightarrow Cu + ZnSO_4.$$

When jF coul is transferred, 1 mole of each of the initial constituents disappears and 1 mole of each of the final constituents is formed. The change of enthalpy in this case is equal to the enthalpy of 1 mole of each of the final constituents minus the enthalpy of 1 mole of each of the initial constituents at the same temperature and pressure, and is the heat of reaction. Since

$$F = 96,500 \text{ coul} = 96,500 \text{ joules/volt}$$
$$= \frac{96,500 \text{ joules/volt}}{4.1840 \text{ joules/cal}} = 23,060 \text{ cal/volt},$$

we get, finally,

$$\Delta H = (-23,060 \text{ cal/volt})j\left(e - T\frac{de}{dT}\right).$$

In the case of a saturated reversible cell in which gases are liberated, it can be shown rigorously (see Prob. 14.26) that

$$\boxed{\Delta H = (-23,060 \text{ cal/volt})j\left[e - T\left(\frac{\partial e}{\partial T}\right)_P\right].}$$

The important feature of this equation is that it provides a method of measuring the heat of reaction of a chemical reaction without resorting to calorimetry. If the reaction can be made to proceed in a reversible cell, all that is necessary is to measure the emf of the cell as a function of the temperature at constant atmospheric pressure. The heat of reaction is therefore measured with a potentiometer and a thermometer. Both measurements can be made with great accuracy, and hence this method yields by far the most accurate values of the heat of reaction. It is interesting to compare values of ΔH obtained electrically with those measured calorimetrically. This is shown for a number of cells in Table 14.4.

Table 14.4/ Reversible Cells

Reaction	Temp. T, °K	Va- lence j	Emf e, volts	$\frac{de}{dT}$, volts/°K	ΔH (electric method), cal	ΔH (calori- metric method), cal
$Zn + CuSO_4 = Cu + ZnSO_4$	273	2	1.0934	−0.0004533	−56,090	−55,200
$Zn + 2AgCl = 2Ag + ZnCl_2$	273	2	1.0171	−0.0002103	−49,540	−49,080
$Cd + 2AgCl = 2Ag + CdCl_2$	298	2	0.6753	−0.00065	−40,076	−39,530
$Pb + 2AgI = 2Ag + PbI_2$	298	2	0.2135	−0.000173	−12,230	−12,200
$Ag + \frac{1}{2}Hg_2Cl_2 = Hg + AgCl$	298	1	0.0455	+0.000338	+ 1,300	+ 900
$Pb + Hg_2Cl_2 = 2Hg + PbCl_2$	298	2	0.5356	+0.000145	−22,900	−23,400
$Pb + 2AgCl = 2Ag + PbCl_2$	298	2	0.4900	−0.000186	−25,100	−24,900

By the first $T\,dS$ equation we have, for reversible isothermal operation of a cell,

$$T\,dS = jFT\,\frac{de}{dT}\,dn.$$

The Gibbs function is defined by

$$G = H - TS,$$

and at constant temperature

$$dG = dH - T\,dS.$$

Since

$$dH = jF\left(T\,\frac{de}{dT} - e\right)dn,$$

we have the result

$$dG = -jFe\,dn.$$

For the reversible reaction of 1 mole of material having the valence j, this equation may be integrated, giving

$$\Delta G = -jFe,$$

where ΔG is the Gibbs-function change for the reaction occurring in the cell. The equilibrium constant for the reaction is given by

$$\ln K = -\frac{\Delta G}{RT}.$$

Thus

$$\ln K = \frac{jFe}{RT},$$

or

$$\boxed{\ln K = (23{,}060 \text{ cal/volt})\left(\frac{je}{RT}\right).}$$

This equation provides a most convenient method for the measurement of the equilibrium constant of any reaction that can be made to proceed in a reversible cell.

14.14/ Fuel Cells

A fuel cell is a device, similar in some respects to an electrolytic cell, in which the energy released as the result of a combustion reaction appears, at least in part, directly as electric energy. It has the characteristics of a cell in that it consists of a positive and a negative electrode, separated by an electrolyte. However, the reactants are not stored in the cell, but are fed to it continuously, and the products of reaction are continuously withdrawn. Thus the fuel cell is not given an initial electric charge, and in operation it does not lose an electric charge. It operates as a continuous-flow system, so long as reactants are supplied, and produces a steady electric current.

One electrode is known as the fuel electrode, because fuel, such as hydrogen, methane, propane, etc., is supplied to the cell in such a way as to come into intimate contact with this electrode. The other electrode is known as the oxygen electrode, because oxygen is supplied to it. The cell as a whole acts to effect oxidation of the fuel by means of an electrochemical reaction. The hydrogen-oxygen fuel cell is probably the simplest such device, and will serve to illustrate the principles of operation. A schematic diagram of this cell is shown in Fig. 14.4.

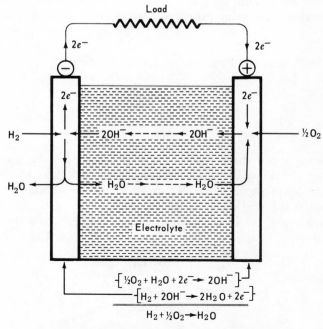

Fig. 14.4   Hydrogen-oxygen fuel cell.

The half-cell reaction occurring at the fuel or hydrogen electrode is

$$H_2 + 2OH^- \rightarrow 2H_2O + 2e^-.$$

and that at the oxygen electrode is

$$\tfrac{1}{2}O_2 + H_2O + 2e^- \rightarrow 2OH^-,$$

The overall cell reaction is

$$H_2 + \tfrac{1}{2}O_2 \rightarrow H_2O$$

and is merely the "combustion" of hydrogen.

Since fuel-cell operation is a steady-flow process, the form taken by the first law is

$$\Delta H = Q - W,$$

where potential- and kinetic-energy terms have been omitted as negligible. If the cell operates *reversibly and isothermally*,

$$Q = T \, \Delta S.$$

Thus $\qquad \Delta H = T \, \Delta S - W,$

or $\qquad W = -(\Delta H - T \, \Delta S) = -\Delta G.$

From this we also see that

$$Q = T \, \Delta S = \Delta H - \Delta G.$$

Now the work done by a reversible fuel cell is given in terms of its emf by exactly the same expression as for an electrolytic cell:

$$dW = ejF \, dn,$$

or for the reaction of 1 mole of material of valence j,

$$W = ejF.$$

In summary,

$$W = ejF = -\Delta G$$

and $\qquad Q = \Delta H - \Delta G.$

We may apply these equations to the hydrogen-oxygen fuel cell operating at atmospheric pressure and 25°C. At these conditions the reactants, hydrogen and oxygen, are gases in their standard states, and the product is liquid water in its standard state. Hence, for ΔH and ΔG, we may use the standard heat of reaction ΔH°_{298} and the standard Gibbs-function change of reaction ΔG°_{298} for the reaction

$$H_2 + \tfrac{1}{2}O_2 \rightarrow H_2O(\text{liquid}).$$

These are

$$\Delta H^\circ_{298} = -68{,}317 \text{ cal}$$

and $\qquad \Delta G^\circ_{298} = -56{,}690 \text{ cal}.$

Thus the reversible work of the hydrogen-oxygen fuel cell under the prescribed conditions for the reaction of 1 gm mole of hydrogen and the production of 1 gm mole of water is

$$W = -\Delta G^{\circ}_{298} = 56,690 \text{ cal.}$$

Since

$$-\Delta G^{\circ}_{298} = ejF,$$

the reversible emf of this cell is calculated to be

$$e = \frac{-\Delta G^{\circ}_{298}}{jF} = \frac{(56,690 \text{ cal})(4.1840 \text{ joules/cal})}{(2)(96,500 \text{ joules/volt})}$$
$$= 1.229 \text{ volts}$$

The heat transfer between cell and surroundings in order to maintain isothermal operation is

$$Q = \Delta H^{\circ}_{298} - \Delta G^{\circ}_{298}$$
$$= -68,317 + 56,690 = -11,627 \text{ cal.}$$

The principles of fuel-cell operation have been understood for many years. However, the intensive research necessary to make them practical engineering devices did not start until after World War II. Considerable effort is still being expended to devise means to make their actual operation approach that which may be predicted on the assumption of reversibility. It is entirely possible that in time fuel cells will become common devices for the generation of electric power.

Problems

14.1 The tension in a steel rod, 10 ft in length and 1 in. square at $300°K$, is increased reversibly and isothermally from 0 to $50,000 \text{ lb}_f/\text{in.}^2$
(a) How much heat in Btu is transferred?
(b) How much work in Btu is done?
(c) What is the change in internal energy?
Assume the following quantities to remain constant:

$$\alpha = 12 \times 10^{-6} °K^{-1},$$
$$E = 30 \times 10^6 \text{ lb}_f/\text{in.}^2,$$
$$C_\sigma = 47 \text{ ft} \cdot \text{lb}_f/\text{in.}^3 \cdot °K.$$

14.2 (a) Write the *first T dS* equation for a simple system consisting of a stressed bar, and show that for an isothermal, reversible extension or compression it becomes

$$dQ = -T \left(\frac{\partial \sigma}{\partial T} \right)_\epsilon d\epsilon,$$

where dQ is for a unit volume. For a total volume V, we have

$$dQ = -VT \left(\frac{\partial \sigma}{\partial T} \right)_\epsilon d\epsilon.$$

(b) The equation of state for an ideal elastomer is (see Prob. 3.6)

$$\sigma = \frac{A_0 K T}{A}\left(\lambda - \frac{1}{\lambda^2}\right),$$

where λ is the extension ratio L/L_0, and L_0 is the no-load length and is a function of temperature only. Using this equation together with the result of (a), show for a sample of no-load volume V_0 that the heat transferred in a reversible, isothermal process is

$$dQ = -V_0 T K \left(\lambda - \frac{1}{\lambda^2}\right) d\lambda.$$

(c) From this result and that of Prob. 3.6, show that for an ideal elastomer, as for an ideal gas, U is a function of temperature only.

14.3 With reference to the problem worked out in Sec. 14.3, how much work is required to form isothermally and reversibly a mist consisting of 1 lb_m of liquid water at 100°C as droplets having a radius of 1 micron? How much heat is transferred?

14.4 Show that the difference between the interior pressure of a spherical liquid drop P_i and the external pressure P_e is given by

$$P_i - P_e = \frac{2\gamma}{r},$$

where r is the drop radius, and γ is the surface tension of the liquid. Calculate this pressure difference for water droplets at 100°C with a radius of 1 micron.

14.5 (a) Prove that, for a dielectric,

$$\left(\frac{\partial U}{\partial \mathcal{E}}\right)_T = T\left(\frac{\partial P}{\partial T}\right)_\mathcal{E} + \mathcal{E}\left(\frac{\partial P}{\partial \mathcal{E}}\right)_T,$$

where U is internal energy per unit volume.

(b) Assuming the equation of state to be

$$P = \chi\mathcal{E},$$

where the susceptibility χ is a function of T only, show that

$$U = f(T) + \frac{\mathcal{E}^2}{2}\left(\chi + T\frac{d\chi}{dT}\right),$$

where $f(T)$ is an undetermined function of temperature.

(c) What is the necessary relation between χ and T in order that U be a function of T only?

14.6 In the case of a dielectric whose equation of state is

$$P = \left(a + \frac{b}{T}\right)\mathcal{E},$$

show that:

(a) The heat transferred per unit volume in a reversible isothermal change of field is

$$Q = -\frac{b}{2T}(\mathscr{E}_2{}^2 - \mathscr{E}_1{}^2).$$

(b) The small temperature change accompanying a reversible adiabatic change of field is

$$\Delta T = \frac{b}{2C_\mathscr{E}T}(\mathscr{E}_2{}^2 - \mathscr{E}_1{}^2).$$

14.7 Show, for a magnetic material, when Curie's law is obeyed, that:

(a) U and C_m are functions of T only.

(b) $S = \int C_m \dfrac{dT}{T} - \dfrac{\mu_0 \mathscr{M}^2}{2C} + \text{const.}$

(c) $C_\mathscr{H} - C_m = \dfrac{\mu_0 \mathscr{M}^2}{C}.$

(d) $\left(\dfrac{\partial C_\mathscr{H}}{\partial \mathscr{H}}\right)_T = \dfrac{\mu_0 C \mathscr{H}}{T^2}.$

14.8 Consider a paramagnetic substance which obeys Curie's equation and for which at low temperatures

$$C_m = \frac{A}{T^2},$$

where A is a constant.

(a) Show from the *first* $T\,dS$ equation for a reversible, adiabatic demagnetization from state 1 to state 2 that

$$\frac{T_2}{T_1} = \sqrt{\frac{(\mu_0 C/A)\mathscr{H}_2{}^2 + 1}{(\mu_0 C/A)\mathscr{H}_1{}^2 + 1}}.$$

(b) If a sample of chromium–potassium alum exists at 1.5°K in a magnetic field of intensity $\mathscr{H}_1 = 450{,}000$ amp/m, what temperature will it attain upon reversible, adiabatic demagnetization to $\mathscr{H}_2 = 0$? For chromium–potassium alum, $\mu_0 C/A = 1.95 \times 10^{-6}$ m²/amp².

14.9 Take a paramagnetic solid obeying Curie's law through a Carnot cycle and verify that

$$\frac{Q_1}{Q_2} = \frac{T_1}{T_2}.$$

14.10 A mixture of 3 lb moles of helium, 4 lb moles of neon, and 5 lb moles of argon is at a pressure of 1 atm and a temperature of 500°R. Calculate:

(a) The volume.

(b) The various mole fractions.

(c) The various partial pressures.

(d) The change of entropy due to mixing.

(e) The change in the Gibbs function due to mixing.

14.11 n_1 moles of an ideal monatomic gas at temperature T_1 and pressure P is in one compartment of an insulated container. In an adjoining compartment, separated by an insulating partition, is n_2 moles of another ideal monatomic gas at temperature T_2 and pressure P. When the partition is removed:

(a) Show that the final pressure of the mixture is P.

(b) Calculate the entropy change when the gases are identical.

(c) Calculate the entropy change when the gases are different.

14.12 n_1 moles of an ideal gas at pressure P_1 and temperature T is in one compartment of an insulated container. In an adjoining compartment, separated by a partition, is n_2 moles of an ideal gas at pressure P_2 and temperature T. When the partition is removed:

(a) Calculate the final pressure of the mixture.

(b) Calculate the entropy change when the gases are identical.

(c) Calculate the entropy change when the gases are different.

(d) Prove that the entropy change in (c) is the same as that which would be produced by two independent free expansions.

14.13 What is the minimum amount of work required to separate 1 lb mole of air at 80°F and 1 atm (21 mole percent O_2 and 79 mole percent N_2) into pure oxygen and pure nitrogen at 80°F and 1 atm?

14.14 For a system made up initially of an equimolar mixture of CO and H_2O and reacting according to the equation

$$CO + H_2O \rightleftharpoons CO_2 + H_2$$

in the gaseous phase, develop general expressions for the mole fractions of the constituents as functions of the degree of reaction.

14.15 For a system made up initially of 3 moles of H_2O for every mole of H_2S and undergoing the reaction

$$H_2S + 2H_2O \rightleftharpoons 3H_2 + SO_2$$

in the gaseous phase, develop general expressions for the mole fractions of the constituents as functions of the degree of reaction.

14.16 Prove that $-\Delta H°/R$ is equal to the slope of a plot of $\ln K$ versus $1/T$.

14.17 Develop general equations giving $\Delta H°$ and $\ln K$ as functions T for the reaction

$$\tfrac{1}{2}N_2 + \tfrac{1}{2}O_2 \rightarrow NO.$$

The molar heat capacities as functions of T are given by (298 to 2500°K)

N_2: $C_P° = 6.66 + 1.02 \times 10^{-3}T$,

O_2: $C_P° = 7.16 + 1.00 \times 10^{-3}T - 0.40 \times 10^5T^{-2}$,

NO: $C_P° = 7.03 + 0.92 \times 10^{-3}T - 0.14 \times 10^5T^{-2}$.

In addition, for NO,

$$\Delta H^{\circ}_{f_{298}} = 21,600 \text{ cal/gm mole,}$$
$$\Delta G^{\circ}_{f_{298}} = 20,720 \text{ cal/gm mole.}$$

Prepare a plot of $\ln K$ versus $1/T$ for T from 300 to 2500°K.

14.18 Starting with n_0 moles of NO, which dissociates according to the equation $NO \rightleftharpoons \frac{1}{2}N_2 + \frac{1}{2}O_2$, show that at equilibrium

$$K = \frac{1}{2}\frac{\epsilon_e}{1 - \epsilon_e}.$$

14.19 Starting with n_0 moles of NH_3, which dissociates according to the equation $NH_3 \rightleftharpoons \frac{1}{2}N_2 + \frac{3}{2}H_2$, show that at equilibrium

$$K = \frac{\sqrt{27}}{4}\frac{\epsilon_e^{\ 2}}{1 - \epsilon_e^{\ 2}}P.$$

14.20 A mixture of $n_0\nu_1$ moles of A_1 and $n_0\nu_2$ moles of A_2 at temperature T and pressure P occupies a volume V_0. When the reaction

$$\nu_1 A_1 + \nu_2 A_2 \rightleftharpoons \nu_3 A_3 + \nu_4 A_4$$

has come to equilibrium at the same T and P, the volume is V_e. Show that

$$\epsilon_e = \frac{V_e - V_0}{V_0}\frac{\nu_1 + \nu_2}{\nu_3 + \nu_4 - \nu_1 - \nu_2}.$$

14.21 (a) Prove that, for a mixture of reacting ideal gases,

$$\frac{d}{d\epsilon}\ln\frac{y_3^{\ \nu_3}y_4^{\ \nu_4}}{y_1^{\ \nu_1}y_2^{\ \nu_2}} = \frac{n_0 + n_0'}{\Sigma n_k}\frac{1}{\psi},$$

where
$$\frac{1}{\psi} = \frac{\nu_1^{\ 2}}{y_1} + \frac{\nu_2^{\ 2}}{y_2} + \frac{\nu_3^{\ 2}}{y_3} + \frac{\nu_4^{\ 2}}{y_4} - (\Delta\nu)^2,$$
$$\Delta\nu = \nu_3 + \nu_4 - \nu_1 - \nu_2.$$

(b) If we start with $n_0\nu_1$ moles of A_1, $n_0\nu_2$ moles of A_2, and no A_3 or A_4, show that

$$\psi = \frac{\epsilon(1 - \epsilon)}{(\nu_1 + \nu_2)(\nu_3 + \nu_4)}.$$

14.22 Prove that, for a mixture of reacting ideal gases *in equilibrium*,

(a) $\left(\dfrac{\partial V}{\partial P}\right)_T = -\dfrac{V}{P} - \dfrac{(n_0 + n_0')RT(\Delta\nu)^2}{P^2\dfrac{d}{d\epsilon_e}\ln\dfrac{y_3^{\ \nu_3}y_4^{\ \nu_4}}{y_1^{\ \nu_1}y_2^{\ \nu_2}}}.$

(b) $\left(\dfrac{\partial V}{\partial T}\right)_P = \dfrac{V}{T} + \dfrac{(n_0 + n_0')\Delta\nu\,\Delta H^{\circ}}{PT\dfrac{d}{d\epsilon_e}\ln\dfrac{y_3^{\ \nu_3}y_4^{\ \nu_4}}{y_1^{\ \nu_1}y_2^{\ \nu_2}}}.$

(c) $\left(\dfrac{\partial P}{\partial T}\right)_{\epsilon_e} = -\dfrac{P\,\Delta H^{\circ}}{RT^2\,\Delta\nu}.$

14.23 Prepare a table similar to that of Table 14.3 for the ammonia synthesis reaction at 100 atm but for the case where the initial constitution of the system is 2 moles of N_2 for each mole of H_2.

14.24 Hydrogen and oxygen are being produced by the continuous electrolysis of a dilute caustic solution at atmospheric pressure. Liquid water is supplied to the cell at 25°C, and gaseous hydrogen and oxygen are removed at the same temperature. A current of 3,000 amp at 2.00 volts is passed through the cell at a current efficiency of 90 percent. At what rate (Btu/hr) must heat be supplied or removed from the cell so that its temperature will be constant at 25°C? Current efficiency is defined as the ratio of actual product to that formed according to Faraday's law of electrolysis.

14.25 The emf of the cell

$$Zn|ZnCl_2(sat)\|Hg_2Cl_2(sat)|Hg$$

is given by the equation

$$e = 1.000 + 0.000094(t - 15),$$

where t is in °C.

Write the reaction, and calculate $\ln K$ and the heat of reaction at 100°C.

14.26 Using the five coordinates P, V, T, e, and q to describe a reversible cell in which gases may be liberated, show that:
(a) $dG = -S\,dT + V\,dP + e\,dq$, where $G = U + PV - TS$.

(b) $-\left(\dfrac{\partial S}{\partial q}\right)_{T,P} = \left(\dfrac{\partial e}{\partial T}\right)_{P,q}$.

(c) $dH = T\,dS + V\,dP + e\,dq$.

(d) $\left(\dfrac{\partial H}{\partial q}\right)_{T,P} = e - T\left(\dfrac{\partial e}{\partial T}\right)_{P,q}$.

(e) For a saturated cell, $\Delta H = -jF\left[e - T\left(\dfrac{\partial e}{\partial T}\right)_P\right]$.

Chapter 15/
The Statistical Interpretation
of Thermodynamics

15.1/ Introduction

In the preceding chapters we invariably adopted the macroscopic point of view of matter. Nowhere was it necessary to appeal to any theory of the constitution of matter. Such considerations need never arise in a treatment of classical thermodynamics.

However, atomic theory is firmly established, and it is clear that the macroscopic properties of matter are manifestations on a gross scale of the positions, velocities, and interactions of the countless atoms that constitute a macroscopic system and its surroundings. It is evident, therefore, that if one seeks understanding of the laws of thermodynamics on a basis more fundamental than empirical observation, he must adopt the microscopic point of view.

One might at first hope to proceed by determining in complete detail the microscopic state of a system at a given instant. That is, one would determine the exact position and velocity of every atom of a system. The laws of mechanics would then be used to compute the microscopic state of the system at any subsequent time. From such information one could calculate the instantaneous properties of the system at various times, and thus the time-averaged properties. All this is impossible, first, in practice, because of the enormous number of atoms which would be involved, and, second, in theory, because of the uncertainty principle. It is for this reason that one must have recourse to a statistical method for averaging over the possible microscopic states of the system.

In this chapter we shall give an elementary treatment of the basic ideas of statistical mechanics for the purpose of providing an insight into the laws of thermodynamics.

15.2/ The Basis of Statistical Mechanics

It is the object of statistical mechanics to predict the macroscopic behavior of matter from a picture or model of the microscopic world. We must therefore start by formulating the microscopic model. Here we make use of atomic theory and quantum theory. First, it is universally accepted that matter consists of atoms of the chemical elements, which interact more or less strongly, depending on conditions. The very strong coupling of atoms through chemical bonds produces larger entities made up of numbers of atoms which are called molecules. Each gram mole of a chemical species consists of about 6×10^{23} molecules.

The atoms and molecules which constitute matter are in continual motion; they translate, rotate, vibrate, and collide. Thus they possess kinetic energy of translation, rotation, and vibration, and furthermore, they exchange energy through collision. In addition, there is potential energy associated with the forces that act between atoms and between molecules. Energy of this form cannot be attributed to single atoms and molecules, but is shared among the interacting particles. Energy is also associated with the electrons and nuclei of atoms. All these forms of energy existing at the microscopic level constitute what in macroscopic thermodynamics is known as internal energy.

A fundamental postulate of quantum theory is that energy is quantized. This means that energy on the atomic or microscopic scale is made up of discrete units, all very small but of many different sizes. Thus the total internal energy of a macroscopic system is the sum of an enormous number of quanta of energy. Because energy is quantized there is a discrete (but very large) set of energy levels allowed for the internal energy of any macroscopic system. The exact expression for these allowed energy levels is provided by quantum mechanics, and is thus outside the realm of statistical mechanics. Each energy level corresponds to one or more *quantum states* of the system. Quantum states are specified by a function which is the solution of a differential equation called the Schrödinger equation. The number of different quantum states possible for a particular energy level is called the *degeneracy* of the level.

These ideas can be made clearer through illustration by means of a numerical example. Quite obviously, we cannot deal with a real macroscopic system because of the enormous number of energy levels

Table 15.1

Level i	Energy E_i	j	k	l	Degeneracy g_i
0	3	1	1	1	1
1	4	1	1	2	3
		1	2	1	
		2	1	1	
2	5	1	2	2	6
		2	1	2	
		2	2	1	
		3	1	1	
		1	3	1	
		1	1	3	
3	6	2	2	2	10
		1	2	3	
		1	3	2	
		2	1	3	
		3	1	2	
		2	3	1	
		3	2	1	
		1	1	4	
		4	1	1	
		1	4	1	

and quantum states associated with a system of some 10^{23} molecules. We must consider a small-scale system which can exist only in the imagination, but which displays the same general behavior as a real system.

Consider, therefore, a system whose energy values are given by the expression

$$E_i = j + k + l,$$

where E_i is the energy of level i, and j, k, and l may independently have any integral value 1, 2, 3, 4, etc. Thus the lowest energy level represents an energy $E_0 = 3$, and there is but one way it may be attained: j, k, and l must each be unity. Thus the degeneracy of the level $g_0 = 1$. The next energy level represents an energy $E_1 = 4$, and it may be attained in three ways, so that the degeneracy of the level $g_1 = 3$. The next energy level represents an energy $E_2 = 5$, attainable in six ways, so that $g_2 = 6$. Table 15.1 illustrates the counting scheme, where each row represents a quantum state. The procedure shown may be continued without limit, but one soon realizes that g_i increases in a systematic way. A general formula for g_i for the particular system considered is found to be

$$g_i = \frac{(i+1)(i+2)}{2},$$

and the degeneracy is seen to increase rapidly as higher energy levels are considered.

An important result of quantum mechanics is that, *for a closed system consisting of N particles, the energy levels "allowed" to the system are entirely determined by the volume of the system.* This does not mean that fixing the volume of a closed system fixes its energy. It just determines a discrete set of energy values that the system can possibly attain or that are allowed to it. If the temperature of the system is raised at constant volume, the energy of the system will change to a higher allowed energy value. If the system is isolated and thus constrained from exchanging energy with its surroundings, its energy remains constant at one of the levels of the allowed set. Even so, the system may exist in any of the g_i degenerate quantum states associated with its particular energy level. In fact, because of the constantly changing positions and velocities of the atoms and molecules, it is presumed that over a period of time the system passes through all its accessible quantum states.

If the system of fixed volume is not isolated, but rather is brought into equilibrium with a heat reservoir, a much larger number of quantum states becomes accessible to it. We now consider such a system in detail, for it is the primary focus of our attention. Take the system to be a gram mole of material, made up of about 6×10^{23} molecules, existing either as solid, liquid, or gas, with a fixed volume and in equilibrium with a heat reservoir at temperature T. From the thermodynamic point of view, we have a closed system with a fixed volume and a fixed temperature. Thus it has a fixed thermodynamic state, characterized by particular values of pressure, internal energy, entropy, etc. On the microscopic scale, however, our picture is one of chaotic motion. Macroscopic equilibrium does not imply a static situation on the microscopic level. The ceaseless motion of the particles and their consequent collision with the walls of their container result in exchanges of energy between the system and the heat reservoir, causing momentary fluctuations in the energy of the system. Thus the macroscopically "constant" internal energy of the system is an average value around which the instantaneous values of the energy fluctuate. Nevertheless, these instantaneous values must be members of the discrete (but very large) set of energy values allowed by quantum theory.

The problem now is to determine a suitable method of averaging over the energy values of the allowed quantum states so as to obtain the correct value of the macroscopic internal energy. For this purpose we imagine that our macroscopic system of volume V and number of particles N is replicated a very large number of times. As a result we have a (mental) collection of a great many macroscopically and thermodynamically identical systems. We further imagine that this collection of systems is arranged in a lattice so that each system, insofar as possible, is intimately in contact with and surrounded by other systems of the collection. The entire collection is allowed to come to equilibrium with a heat reservoir at temperature T. Once equilibrium is attained, the collection is isolated from its surroundings so that the total energy of the collection is fixed. Each individual system is then in thermal contact with the other systems which surround it and which constitute a heat reservoir at temperature T for that system. Such a collection of systems is known as an *ensemble*, and the particular collection just described is called a *canonical ensemble*.

Although the members of the ensemble are always macroscopically and thermodynamically identical, they are not at any given instant microscopically identical. Since all systems have the same volume V and contain the same number of particles N, all have the same set of allowed energy levels and all have the same quantum states accessible to them. But each system in passing through the accessible quantum states is presumed to do so in a random fashion. Thus, if we imagine the ensemble to be "frozen" at a given instant so that we could examine the individual systems, we should find represented a very large number of different quantum states and very many different energy levels. We therefore define the *probability* of occurrence of a particular quantum state P_q to be the number of systems found to be in quantum state q divided by the total number of systems of the ensemble. Clearly,

$$\sum_q P_q = 1,$$

where the summation is over all accessible quantum states.

It is assumed that our original system over a period of time will pass through the same quantum states as are represented in the ensemble, and furthermore, that a probability P_q will represent the fraction of time that the system spends in quantum state q.

Let E_0, E_1, E_2, E_3, etc., represent a list of the energy values for the allowed quantum states of the system, arranged in the order of increasing values of E. E_0 is the lowest allowed energy value, but is not usually zero. Large numbers of the E's may be exactly the same, for, as we have seen, different quantum states may have the same energy. Nevertheless, our list includes an E_q for each quantum state. For each E_q there is a probability P_q, and the corresponding list of probabilities would include P_0, P_1, P_2, P_3, etc. Now, to obtain the thermodynamic internal energy of our original macroscopic system, we need merely take an average of the energies E_q over all accessible quantum states, weighting each E_q according to its probability P_q. Thus

where

$$U = \sum_q P_q E_q,$$
$$\sum_q P_q = 1.$$

(15.1)

We have not yet indicated how the probabilities P_q are to be determined. Indeed, this is the very crux of the problem. Because we cannot appeal to the laws of mechanics for an answer, we are forced to adopt a fundamental postulate with respect to the probabilities. We have nothing to guide us in the formulation of this postulate save common sense and intuition. Yet all results depend on it. Thus its validity can be tested only by the agreement of results based upon statistical mechanical calculations with those obtained experimentally. The postulate which leads to this agreement can be stated as follows: *For a closed system in equilibrium with a heat reservoir at temperature T, P_q is a function of E_q only.* That is,

$$P_q = f(E_q).$$

In other words, for the system as specified, each quantum state has associated with it a particular probability P_q, which depends only on the energy of that quantum state. A corollary of this postulate is that *all quantum states having the same energy have the same probability.* Our postulate could hardly be less restrictive. No limitations whatever have been put on the form of the functional relationship. It is also clearly reasonable, for what is more likely to determine the probability of a particular energy value than the energy itself.

15.3/ Mathematical Formulation

We must now determine the actual functional relationship which connects P_q to E_q. To do this, consider two randomly selected systems of the canonical ensemble described in the preceding section. Exactly the same quantum states are accessible to both systems. However, the two systems are independent of each other and will not pass through these quantum states in the same order. Let P_q be the probability that the first system has the energy value E_q at a given instant and P_k be the probability that the second system has the energy value E_k at the same instant. Now, by our basic postulate, the same functional relationship must apply to each system taken alone and also to the combined system made up of the two considered together. Thus

$$P_q = f(E_q),$$
$$P_k = f(E_k),$$
and
$$P_{qk} = f(E_q + E_k),$$

where P_{qk} is the compound probability that the first system has energy E_q *and* that the second system has the energy E_k. The compound probability of two independent events is the product of their separate probabilities. That is,

$$P_{qk} = P_q \cdot P_k.$$
Thus
$$f(E_q) \cdot f(E_k) = f(E_q + E_k).$$

What sort of function satisfies this relationship?　Let us differentiate partially first with respect to E_q and then with respect to E_k.　The first equation which results is

$$f(E_k)\frac{\partial f(E_q)}{\partial E_q} = \frac{\partial f(E_q + E_k)}{\partial E_q} = \frac{\partial f(E_q + E_k)}{\partial (E_q + E_k)}\frac{\partial (E_q + E_k)}{\partial E_q}$$

$$= \frac{\partial f(E_q + E_k)}{\partial (E_q + E_k)} \times 1,$$

or
$$f(E_k)\frac{df(E_q)}{dE_q} = \frac{\partial f(E_q + E_k)}{\partial (E_q + E_k)}.$$

Similarly, the second equation is

$$f(E_q)\frac{df(E_k)}{dE_k} = \frac{\partial f(E_q + E_k)}{\partial (E_q + E_k)}.$$

From these two equations we see that

$$f(E_k)\frac{df(E_q)}{dE_q} = f(E_q)\frac{df(E_k)}{dE_k}.$$

Separating variables, we have

$$\frac{1}{f(E_q)}\frac{df(E_q)}{dE_q} = \frac{1}{f(E_k)}\frac{df(E_k)}{dE_k}. \qquad (15.2)$$

Since E_q and E_k are independent, the two sides of Eq. (15.2) can be the same only if they are each equal to the same constant.　If we let this constant be $-\beta$, we get

$$\frac{df(E_q)}{f(E_q)} = -\beta\, dE_q \qquad \text{and} \qquad \frac{df(E_k)}{f(E_k)} = -\beta\, dE_k. \qquad (15.3)$$

The use of the minus sign with β is completely arbitrary.　We shall show later that its inclusion makes β a positive number.　It is also to be noted that β must be an intensive rather than an extensive parameter.　That is, if both systems, as characterized by q and k, were doubled in size by doubling both the volume V and the number of particles N (hence keeping the pressure constant), β would be unchanged.　The reason for this is that the two sides of Eq. (15.2) contain exactly analogous terms.　Hence any size factors must necessarily cancel.

Integration of Eqs. (15.3) yields

$$\ln f(E_q) = -\beta E_q + \text{const} \qquad \text{and} \qquad \ln f(E_k) = -\beta E_k + \text{const}.$$

Let us express the integration constants in these equations as $\ln (1/Z')$ and $\ln (1/Z'')$.　In addition, we have

$$f(E_q) = P_q \qquad \text{and} \qquad f(E_k) = P_k.$$

Therefore

$$\ln P_q = -\beta E_q + \ln \frac{1}{Z'} \qquad \text{and} \qquad \ln P_k = -\beta E_k + \ln \frac{1}{Z''}.$$

In exponential form these become

$$P_q = \frac{1}{Z'} e^{-\beta E_q} \qquad \text{and} \qquad P_k = \frac{1}{Z''} e^{-\beta E_k}.$$

It is seen from these equations that β must be positive. If it were negative, increasing E_q or E_k without limit would increase the probabilities without limit, but the probabilities must always be fractions.

If we sum the above equations over all quantum states q and k, respectively, we have

$$\Sigma P_q = \frac{1}{Z'} \Sigma e^{-\beta E_q} \qquad \text{and} \qquad \Sigma P_k = \frac{1}{Z''} \Sigma e^{-\beta E_k}.$$

But $\qquad\qquad\qquad \Sigma P_q = 1 \qquad$ and $\qquad \Sigma P_k = 1.$

Therefore $\qquad Z' = \Sigma e^{-\beta E_q} \qquad$ and $\qquad Z'' = \Sigma e^{-\beta E_k}.$

Now the two systems were taken to be macroscopically identical. In particular, both contain the same number of particles N and have the same volume V. We have already stated the result of quantum mechanics that the energy levels available to a system depend on N and V only. Thus the set of energy values E_q and the set E_k must be identical. Since β has been shown to be the same for both systems, the summations $\Sigma e^{-\beta E_q}$ and $\Sigma e^{-\beta E_k}$ must contain exactly the same terms. Thus

$$Z' = Z'' = Z.$$

The quantity Z plays a central role in the calculation of thermodynamic properties by the methods of statistical mechanics. It is called the *partition function.*† We have shown that it has the same value for all systems containing the same kind and number of particles, having the same volume, and in equilibrium with a heat reservoir at temperature T. *Thus Z is a state function and a thermodynamic property.*

Since

$$Z = \Sigma e^{-\beta E_q} = \Sigma e^{-\beta E_k},$$

it is clear that Z depends on the energies of the quantum states and on β. We have shown that β is the same for our two systems, but we have not suggested how β is related to the macroscopic properties of the systems. The fact that they are taken to be in equilibrium with a heat reservoir at temperature T is clearly of importance. In fact, the basic postulate that the probability P_q depends on just the energy value E_q included the condition that the system be in equilibrium with a heat reservoir at temperature T. Thus we clearly anticipated a dependency of the P_q's and hence of the partition function on T, the temperature of the heat reservoir with which the system is in equilibrium. Such a

† The use of Z to represent this quantity comes from the German word for it, *Zustandssumme,* meaning *sum-over-states.*

dependency can come only through β. It is therefore reasonable to expect that β is to be associated with T. We have already shown that β, like T, is an intensive parameter.

We need consider now only our original system, for which the following equation gives the probabilities of the quantum states q:

$$P_q = \frac{e^{-\beta E_q}}{Z},$$ (15.4)

where

$$Z = \sum_q e^{-\beta E_q}.$$ (15.5)

We have so far dealt with the probabilities of individual quantum states. An alternative is to set up equations in terms of the probabilities of energy levels. These two sets of probabilities are not the same because many quantum states may have the same energy. If the list of energy levels E_0, E_1, E_2, E_3, etc., is now set up so that each energy value appears but once, the subscripts on E then denote energy levels rather than quantum states. Thus the E_i represent the set of energy levels as distinct from the E_q, which represent an enumeration of energies of all quantum states. The same numbers appear in each set, but in the list of energy levels each number appears but once, whereas in a listing of the energies of the quantum states a number may appear over and over again.

The probability of an energy level P_i is simply related to the probability P_q of a quantum state having an energy $E_q = E_i$. Our basic postulate requires that all quantum states having the same energy must have the same probability. If there are g_i quantum states with the same energy E_i, the probability of each of these quantum states is P_q and the probability of the energy level is

$$P_i = g_i P_q.$$

Therefore Eq. (15.4) becomes

$$P_i = g_i P_q = \frac{g_i e^{-\beta E_q}}{Z},$$

or since $E_q = E_i$ for all the g_i quantum states,

$$P_i = \frac{g_i e^{-\beta E_i}}{Z},$$ (15.6)

where

$$Z = \sum_i g_i e^{-\beta E_i}.$$ (15.7)

Equation (15.7) can be obtained from Eq. (15.6) by summing over all energy levels i and noting that $\Sigma P_i = 1$. The quantity g_i, the number of different quantum states having energy E_i, has already been designated as the degeneracy of the energy level.

It is our purpose now to relate the internal energy and entropy of our system to its partition function and to establish the connection between β and T. By Eq. (15.1) we have

$$U = \sum_q P_q E_q.$$

In terms of energy levels this equation becomes

$$U = \sum_i P_i E_i, \tag{15.8}$$

where

$$\sum_i P_i = 1.$$

Combination of Eq. (15.6) with Eq. (15.8) gives

$$U = \frac{\sum_i E_i g_i e^{-\beta E_i}}{Z}. \tag{15.9}$$

Now we substitute Eq. (15.7) for Z in the partial derivative on the right side of the following identity:

$$\left(\frac{\partial \ln Z}{\partial \beta} \right)_V = \frac{1}{Z} \left(\frac{\partial Z}{\partial \beta} \right)_V$$

$$= \frac{1}{Z} \left(\frac{\partial \sum_i g_i e^{-\beta E_i}}{\partial \beta} \right)_V.$$

Constancy of V implies also constancy of the E_i's and g_i's. Therefore

$$\left(\frac{\partial \ln Z}{\partial \beta} \right)_V = \frac{1}{Z} \sum g_i e^{-\beta E_i}(-E_i)$$

$$= \frac{-\Sigma E_i g_i e^{-\beta E_i}}{Z}.$$

Comparison of this result with Eq. (15.9) shows that

$$U = - \left(\frac{\partial \ln Z}{\partial \beta} \right)_V. \tag{15.10}$$

Equation (15.7) shows that Z is a function of β, the g_i's, and the E_i's. But the last two sets of variables depend on V. Thus

$$Z = Z(\beta, V).$$

Hence, at constant volume, we may write with the aid of Eq. (15.10)

$$d \ln Z = \left(\frac{\partial \ln Z}{\partial \beta} \right)_V d\beta = -U \, d\beta \qquad \text{const } V.$$

Now
$$d(U\beta) = U\,d\beta + \beta\,dU,$$
or
$$-U\,d\beta = \beta\,dU - d(U\beta).$$

Therefore

$$d\ln Z = \beta\,dU - d(U\beta) \qquad \text{const } V,$$
or
$$\beta\,dU = d(\ln Z + U\beta) \qquad \text{const } V.$$

From thermodynamics, for a differential change in the equilibrium state of a PVT system,

$$dU = T\,dS - P\,dV.$$

At constant V, $dU = T\,dS$, and therefore

$$\beta T\,dS = d(\ln Z + U\beta) \qquad \text{const } V,$$
or
$$dS = \left(\frac{1}{\beta T}\right) d(\ln Z + U\beta) \qquad \text{const } V. \tag{15.11}$$

Now the differentials on both sides of this expression are exact. They are differentials of state functions. Moreover, both functions are extensive. They double when the system size doubles. On the other hand, both β and T are intensive, independent of the size of the system. Thus β and T must be independent of the state functions whose exact differentials appear in Eq. (15.11). Thus the product βT must be a constant, and we may write

$$\frac{1}{\beta T} = k,$$

or
$$\boxed{\beta = \frac{1}{kT}.} \tag{15.12}$$

Equation (15.11) becomes

$$dS = k\,d\left(\ln Z + \frac{U}{kT}\right)$$
$$= d\left(k\ln Z + \frac{U}{T}\right) \qquad \text{const } V.$$

From this it follows immediately that

$$S = k\ln Z + \frac{U}{T} + S_0,$$

where S_0 is a constant of integration. In most applications of thermodynamics we need only entropy *changes*. Hence the assignment of a value to S_0 can be arbitrary, for it cancels out in any calculation of ΔS. It may therefore be taken as zero. For our purposes this is entirely satisfactory, and we shall take the entropy to be expressed by

$$\boxed{S = k\ln Z + \frac{U}{T}.} \tag{15.13}$$

Equation (15.10) may be written

$$U = -\left(\frac{\partial \ln Z}{\partial T}\right)_V \Big/ \left(\frac{d\beta}{dT}\right).$$

Since
$$\beta = \frac{1}{kT},$$

$$\frac{d\beta}{dT} = \frac{-1}{kT^2}.$$

Therefore
$$U = kT^2\left(\frac{\partial \ln Z}{\partial T}\right)_V. \tag{15.14}$$

The definition of the Helmholtz function given in Sec. 10.2 is

$$A = U - TS.$$

Substitution for S by Eq. (15.13) gives

$$A = -kT \ln Z.$$

Differentiation of A with respect to volume V at constant temperature yields

$$\left(\frac{\partial A}{\partial V}\right)_T = -kT\left(\frac{\partial \ln Z}{\partial V}\right)_T.$$

It was shown in Sec. 10.2 that the system pressure is given by

$$P = -\left(\frac{\partial A}{\partial V}\right)_T.$$

Therefore
$$P = kT\left(\frac{\partial \ln Z}{\partial V}\right)_T. \tag{15.15}$$

Equations (15.13) to (15.15) show that the thermodynamic properties are readily calculated once the partition function for a system is known as a function of the primary variables T and V.

15.4/ Numerical Example

The connection between statistical mechanics and thermodynamics as expressed by the equations just developed can be given greater physical meaning through consideration of a simple numerical example. We return to the hypothetical system treated earlier, for which the allowed energy values are given by the expression

$$E_i = j + k + l$$

and for which the degeneracy of any level is found from the equation

$$g_i = \frac{(i + 1)(i + 2)}{2}.$$

Equation (15.6) may be written

$$P_i Z = g_i e^{-\beta E_i}.$$

Since g_i is now known for each E_i, values of $P_i Z$ are readily calculated for any given value of β.   A set of such computations has been carried out for a value of $\beta = \frac{1}{3}$.   The results are shown in column 4 of Table 15.2.   Column 1 identifies the value of the index i; column 2 gives the energy values E_i; and column 3 shows the calculated values of the degeneracy g_i.   The values of $P_i Z$ may be summed to give

$$\sum_i P_i Z = Z \Sigma P_i = Z,$$

the partition function.   The value of Z so determined is shown at the bottom of column 4.

The number of energy levels which might be considered is infinite, and the summation $\sum_i P_i Z$ contains an infinite number of terms; i.e., it is an infinite series.   However, the series converges, and its sum has a limiting value.   Table 15.2 must obviously terminate after the listing of a limited number of values.   It has been carried only far enough to show that succeeding values of $P_i Z$ are decreasing rapidly.   In determining Z we have included an adequate number of terms, so that the sum of those omitted is entirely negligible.

Having determined Z, we can now divide the values in column 4 by Z to obtain the probabilities P_i of the various energy levels.   Thus

$$P_i = \frac{P_i Z}{Z}.$$

Values of the P_i are listed in column 5.

The probability of an individual quantum state of energy E_i is

$$P_q = \frac{P_i}{g_i}.$$

Values of the P_q for each energy level are listed in column 6.

A comparison of columns 5 and 6 shows clearly that although the probability of a given quantum state P_q is largest for the lowest energy level and decreases rapidly at higher energy levels, the probability of a given energy level goes through a maximum at an energy value $E_i = 7$. This results from the fact that P_i is a product:

$$P_i = P_q g_i,$$

Table 15.2/

$\beta = 1/3$

(1) i	(2) E_i	(3) g_i	(4) $P_iZ = g_ie^{-\frac{1}{3}E_i}$	(5) $P_i = (P_iZ)/Z$	(6) $P_q = P_i/g_i$	(7) P_iE_i	(8) $P_iE_i^2$
0	3	1	0.368	0.0227	0.0227	0.0681	0.20
1	4	3	0.792	0.0489	0.0163	0.196	0.78
2	5	6	1.134	0.0701	0.01167	0.350	1.75
3	6	10	1.350	0.0834	0.00834	0.500	3.00
4	7	15	1.460	0.0901	0.00602	0.630	4.42
5	8	21	1.453	0.0897	0.00427	0.718	5.75
6	9	28	1.393	0.0860	0.00307	0.775	6.96
7	10	36	1.290	0.0796	0.00221	0.796	7.96
8	11	45	1.148	0.0710	0.001573	0.782	8.59
9	12	55	1.007	0.0622	0.001130	0.748	8.96
10	13	66	0.869	0.0537	0.000815	0.699	9.09
11	14	78	0.733	0.0452	0.000580	0.634	8.86
12	15	91	0.614	0.0379	0.000416	0.569	8.57
13	16	105	0.507	0.0313	0.000298	0.501	8.02
14	17	120	0.414	0.0256	0.000213	0.435	7.40
15	18	136	0.338	0.0208	0.000153	0.376	6.75
18	21	190	0.173	0.0107	0.0000563	0.224	4.72
21	24	253	0.0848	0.00523	0.0000207	0.126	3.01
24	27	325	0.0400	0.00247	0.00000760	0.0667	1.80
30	33	496	0.0083	0.000512	0.00000103	0.0169	0.56

$$\sum_i P_iZ = Z = 16.2 \qquad \sum_i P_iE_i = U = 10.55 \qquad \sum_i P_iE_i^2 = 138.3$$

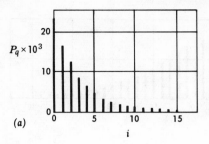

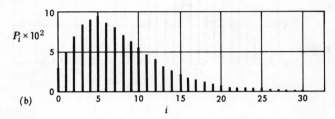

Fig. 15.1   Variation of (a) P_q and (b) P_i with energy level.

and as P_q decreases monotonically, g_i increases monotonically. This causes P_i to pass through a maximum. The change of P_q and P_i with the index i is shown graphically in Fig. 15.1.

From the values of P_i and E_i, we may calculate the product P_iE_i. Results are shown in column 7 of Table 15.2. Since by Eq. (15.8)

$$U = \sum_i P_iE_i,$$

we may determine U for the system by summing the values of P_iE_i over all energy levels. Again the series converges to a limiting value, which is shown at the bottom of column 7 to be 10.55. The variation of the term P_iE_i with the index i is shown graphically in Fig. 15.2a.

It is interesting to consider the deviation of the values E_i from the mean value $\sum_i P_iE_i = U$. Let the deviation be

$$\epsilon_i = E_i - U.$$

Then the mean deviation is

$$\epsilon = \sum_i P_i\epsilon_i = \sum_i P_iE_i - U \sum_i P_i = U - U = 0.$$

Thus the mean deviation is identically zero, because the $+$ and $-$ deviations cancel. This difficulty can be avoided by using the root-

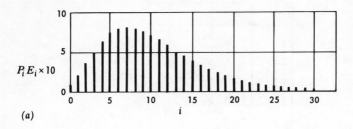

(a)

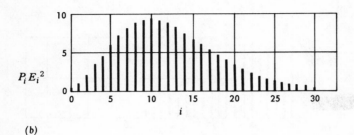

(b)

Fig. 15.2 Variations of (a) P_iE_i and (b) $P_iE_i^2$ with energy level.

mean-square deviation, i.e., the square root of the mean value of the squares of the deviations. Let the deviation be

$$\sigma_i = E_i - U.$$

Then

$$\sigma_i^2 = (E_i - U)^2$$

and

$$\sigma^2 = \sum_i P_i\sigma_i^2 = \sum_i P_i(E_i - U)^2$$

$$= \sum_i P_i(E_i^2 - 2E_iU + U^2)$$

$$= \sum_i P_iE_i^2 - 2U \sum_i P_iE_i + U^2 \sum_i P_i$$

$$= \sum_i P_iE_i^2 - 2U^2 + U^2$$

$$= \sum_i P_iE_i^2 - U^2.$$

Thus

$$\sigma = \sqrt{\sum_i P_iE_i^2 - U^2}. \qquad (15.16)$$

The values necessary for the calculation of σ are listed in Table 15.2. Column .8 lists the values of $P_iE_i^2$ and shows the limiting value of the sum $\Sigma P_iE_i^2$ to be 138.3. The value of U is 10.55. Thus

$$\sigma = \sqrt{138.3 - (10.55)^2} = 5.2.$$

The values of $P_iE_i^2$ are also shown graphically by Fig. 15.2b.

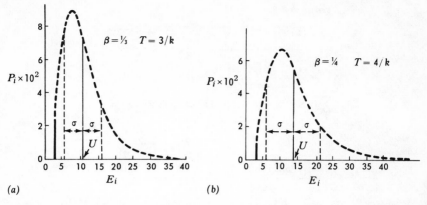

Fig. 15.3 Probabilities P_i **as a function of** E_i**:** (a) **for** $T = 3/k$ **and** (b) **for** $T = 4/k$.

Sufficient information is available in Table 15.2 to allow calculation of the entropy by Eq. (15.13):

$$S = k \ln Z + \frac{U}{T},$$

or

$$\frac{S}{k} = \ln Z + \frac{U}{kT}$$

$$= \ln Z + \beta U.$$

Thus

$$\frac{S}{k} = \ln 16.2 + (\tfrac{1}{3})(10.55) = 6.30.$$

All the calculations just described, made with $\beta = \tfrac{1}{3}$, have been repeated for $\beta = \tfrac{1}{4}$. Since $\beta = 1/kT$, this corresponds to a higher temperature. A summary of results of all calculations, both for $\beta = \tfrac{1}{3}$ and $\beta = \tfrac{1}{4}$, is shown in Table 15.3. The increase in temperature (decrease in β from $\tfrac{1}{3}$ to $\tfrac{1}{4}$) is seen to result in an increase in the partition function Z, in the internal energy U, in the entropy S, and in the root-mean-square deviation σ of the E_i's from U.

In Fig. 15.3 the probabilities P_i of the energy levels are plotted against the energy values E_i for both $\beta = \tfrac{1}{3}$ and $\beta = \tfrac{1}{4}$. It is seen that one effect of increasing temperature (decreasing β) is to broaden the peak and to increase the root-mean-square deviation σ. Clearly, σ is a measure of the broadness of the peak, with larger values of σ corresponding to broader peaks.† It is also seen from Fig. 15.3 that the effect of a temperature increase is to raise the probabilities of finding the system in higher energy levels. If we think of the ensemble of sys-

---

† For real PVT systems it can be shown that σ is extremely small. This means that the peak is very sharp and that it must occur at a value of E_i exceedingly close to the value of U. The significance of this is that the probability of an appreciable fluctuation of the energy of a real PVT system from its average value U is very minute.

Table 15.3

	$\beta = \frac{1}{3}$	$\beta = \frac{1}{4}$
Z	16.2	43.6
$U = \sum_i P_i E_i$	10.55	13.5
$\sum_i P_i E_i{}^2$	138.3	232
U^2	111.4	182
$\sigma^2 = P_i E_i{}^2 - U^2$	26.9	50
σ	5.2	7.1
$S/k = \ln Z + \beta U$	6.30	7.14

tems described in Sec. 15.2, we say that an increase in temperature of the ensemble changes the "populations" of systems in the allowed energy levels, shifting them so that more systems are in higher energy states and fewer are in the lower energy states.

15.5/ Application to Ideal Monatomic Gases

The partition function for an ideal monatomic gas, as provided by quantum mechanics, is given by the expression

$$Z = \frac{V^N}{N!}\left(\frac{2\pi m k T}{h^2}\right)^{\frac{3}{2}N},$$

where N = number of atoms contained in volume V at temperature T,
$\quad m$ = atomic mass,
$\quad h$ = Planck's constant.

The pressure exerted by the system is given by Eq. (15.15):

$$P = kT\left(\frac{\partial \ln Z}{\partial V}\right)_T.$$

Taking the logarithm of Z, we have

$$\ln Z = N \ln V - \ln N! + \tfrac{3}{2}N \ln \frac{2\pi m k T}{h^2}.$$

At constant T and N, the last two terms on the right are constants. Thus

$$\left(\frac{\partial \ln Z}{\partial V}\right)_T = N\left(\frac{\partial \ln V}{\partial V}\right)_T = \frac{N}{V}$$

and

$$P = \frac{NkT}{V}.$$

If the system contains 1 mole, N becomes Avogadro's number N_0, and

$$P = \frac{N_0 k T}{V}.$$

However, for 1 mole of an ideal gas, we know that

$$P = \frac{RT}{V}.$$

Comparison of these two equations shows that

$$\boxed{k = \frac{R}{N_0}.}$$

Thus k, known as Boltzmann's constant, is the gas constant divided by Avogadro's number. It has the value 3.299×10^{-23} cal/°K · molecule.

Equation (15.14) allows us to calculate the internal energy of our system:

$$U = kT^2 \left(\frac{\partial \ln Z}{\partial T} \right)_V.$$

Differentiation of $\ln Z$ at constant V and N gives

$$\left(\frac{\partial \ln Z}{\partial T} \right)_V = \frac{3}{2} \frac{N}{T}.$$

Thus $U = \frac{3}{2} NkT.$

For 1 mole, $U = \frac{3}{2} N_0 kT$
$$= \tfrac{3}{2} RT.$$

By definition of the enthalpy, for 1 mole of an ideal gas,

$$H = U + PV = U + RT.$$

Therefore $H = \tfrac{5}{2} RT.$

Reference to Table 10.1 provides the relations

$$C_V = \left(\frac{\partial U}{\partial T} \right)_V \quad \text{and} \quad C_P = \left(\frac{\partial H}{\partial T} \right)_P.$$

Substitution for U and H yields

$$C_V = \tfrac{3}{2} R \quad \text{and} \quad C_P = \tfrac{5}{2} R$$

for the heat capacities of ideal monatomic gases, in agreement with the observations described in Sec. 5.5.

15.6/ Statistical Interpretation of the First and Second Laws

We have from Eq. (15.8) the basic relation between internal energy and the statistical mechanical coordinates P_i and E_i:

$$U = \sum_i P_i E_i,$$

where $\sum_i P_i = 1.$

We now wish to consider the effects of a differential change in the *equilibrium* state of a system as brought about by changes in its volume and temperature. The thermodynamic state of a closed system in equilibrium with a heat reservoir is established by its volume and by the temperature of the heat reservoir. If either changes, the state of the system will change, and the change of internal energy is given by the total differential of U:

$$dU = \sum_i E_i \, dP_i + \sum_i P_i \, dE_i. \tag{15.17}$$

From the viewpoint of statistical mechanics, the properties of the system are seen to depend on the P_i and the E_i.

Again we make use of the result of quantum mechanics that, for a closed system, the E_i's depend only on the volume of the system. Thus changes in volume produce changes in the energy levels E_i and influence U through the term $\sum_i P_i \, dE_i$ as shown by Eq. (15.17). Since volume changes of the system involve work, we may associate the term $\sum_i P_i \, dE_i$ with dW. Thus, from the point of view of statistical mechanics, work is done on a system when the surroundings interact with the system in such a way as to change its set of allowed energy levels to higher values, that is, to increase the values of the E_i.

Consider now a differential increase in temperature of the heat reservoir. This change causes heat to flow to the system until it once again comes to thermal equilibrium with the heat reservoir. If this process occurs at constant volume, we have, from Eq. (15.17) and the first law of thermodynamics,

$$dQ = dU = \sum_i E_i \, dP_i \qquad \text{const } V.$$

Thus changes in temperature influence U through the term $\sum_i E_i \, dP_i$, and this term is clearly to be associated with dQ. We have already seen that an increase in temperature of a system results in a redistribution of the probabilities associated with the energy levels, increasing the P_i's for the higher levels and decreasing those for the lower levels. Thus heat is interpreted as an interaction between the system and surroundings which alters the probabilities associated with the various energy levels.

We turn now to the statistical interpretation of entropy and the second law of thermodynamics. By Eq. (15.13) we have

$$S = k \ln Z + \frac{U}{T}.$$

Since $\sum_i P_i = 1$ and $U = \sum_i P_i E_i$, we may write

$$S = k \sum_i P_i \ln Z + \frac{1}{T} \sum_i P_i E_i.$$

Equation (15.6) may be rearranged as follows:

$$e^{-\beta E_i} = \frac{P_i Z}{g_i},$$

which in logarithmic form is

$$E_i = -\frac{1}{\beta} \ln \frac{P_i Z}{g_i} = -\frac{1}{\beta} \ln e^{-\beta E_i},$$

or
$$E_i = -kT \ln e^{-\beta E_i}.$$

Incorporating this in the equation for S, we have

$$S = k \sum_i P_i \ln Z - k \sum_i P_i \ln e^{-\beta E_i}$$

$$= -k \sum_i P_i \ln \frac{e^{-\beta E_i}}{Z}$$

$$= -k \sum_i P_i \ln \frac{P_i}{g_i}.$$

Since $P_i/g_i = P_q$, the probability of a quantum state having energy E_i, we may equally well write

$$S = -k \sum_i (P_i \ln P_q),$$

or
$$\boxed{S = -k \sum_q (P_q \ln P_q).} \qquad (15.18)$$

We have arrived at an expression which relates the thermodynamic entropy to the microscopic probabilities of the quantum states.

Consider now the application of this equation to an *isolated* system, i.e., a system which can exchange neither mass nor energy with its surroundings, and is therefore a system of constant mass and energy. Such a system can exist at but a single energy level, an energy level equal to the internal energy of the system. The number of quantum states accessible to the system must equal the degeneracy of the energy level at which the system exists. Let the number of such states be g. Since each has the same energy, all have the same probability, $P_q = 1/g$. The entropy as given by Eq. (15.18) is

$$S = -k \sum_q P_q \ln P_q.$$

Setting $P_q = 1/g$ and summing over the g quantum states gives

$$S = -kg \left(\frac{1}{g} \ln \frac{1}{g} \right),$$

or

$$\boxed{S = k \ln g.}$$

(15.19)

According to the second law of thermodynamics, an irreversible change in an isolated system must result in an increase in the entropy of the system. Equation (15.19) indicates that this increase in entropy results from an increase in the number of quantum states accessible to the system. This is entirely reasonable, for a system which undergoes a change of state at constant mass and energy has available to it all the quantum states accessible to it in its initial state plus additional states that were not accessible in the initial state but which become accessible in the final state. Consider, for example, a system consisting of an insulated vessel partitioned into two equal parts and containing 1 mole of helium on one side of the partition and 1 mole of argon on the other side. Removal of the partition permits the mixing of the helium and argon to form quantum states not accessible to the partitioned system, but does not disallow those states accessible to the partitioned system.

Since any system plus its surroundings is an isolated system, the most general form of the second law, which states that the total entropy change in a system plus its surroundings must be positive when irreversible changes occur, has as its counterpart in statistical mechanics the statement that the accessible quantum states of the system plus its surroundings must increase.

Problems

15.1 Equation (15.9) may be written

$$UZ = \sum_i g_i e^{-\beta E_i} E_i.$$

Differentiate this equation partially with respect to β at constant volume (and hence constant g_i and E_i). Using this result together with Eqs. (15.6), (15.10), and (15.16), show that, for a real material,

$$\sigma = T \sqrt{kC_V}.$$

For a monatomic gas at 300°K, what is the value of σ? What is the value of σ/U?

15.2 Prepare a table similar to Table 15.2, but for $\beta = \frac{1}{4}$, and confirm the results of the last column of Table 15.3.

Appendix A/
Conversion Factors

	In one:	There are:
Length	angstrom	10^{-8} cm.
	micron	10^{-4} cm.
	meter	100 cm.
	inch (U.S.)	2.5400 cm.
	foot (U.S.)	12 in., or
		30.48 cm.
	yard (U.S.)	3 ft, or
		0.9144 m.
	mile (U.S.)	5,280 ft, or
		1.609 km.
Mass	kilogram	1,000 gm.
	pound mass	0.4535924 kg.
	slug	32.1740 lb_m, or
		14.594 kg.
	ton (short)	2,000 lb_m.
Force	poundal	0.13825 newton.
	newton	10^5 dynes.
	pound force	32.1740 poundals, or
		4.44804 newtons.
Pressure	standard atmosphere	14.696 $lb_f/in.^2$, or
		10.1325 newtons/cm^2.
	standard atmosphere	29.921 in. Hg (0°C), or
		760 mm Hg (0°C).
	bar	0.9869 atm, or
		10 newtons/cm^2.
Volume	liter	1,000 cm^3.
	gallon (U.S.)	3.7853 liters.
	cubic foot	7.4805 gal.
Density	gram/cm^3	62.428 lb_m/ft^3, or
		8.3454 lb_m/gal.

Conversion Factors/ (Continued)

	In one:	There are:
Energy	joule	1 newton-m, or
		1 volt-coul, or
		1 watt-sec.
	joule	10^7 ergs, or 10^7 dyne · cm.
	calorie	4.1840 joules.
	I.T. calorie	4.18674 joules.
	Btu	1055.04 joules, or
		252.161 cal, or
		251.996 I.T. cal.
	Btu	778.156 ft · lb_f.
	kilowatt-hour	3412.19 Btu, or
		2.655×10^6 ft · lb_f.
	horsepower-hour	2544.48 Btu, or
		1.980×10^6 ft · lb_f, or
		0.7457 kwhr.
	calorie/gram	1.7988 Btu/lb_m.
	I.T. calorie/gram	1.8000 Btu/lb_m.
	Btu/lb_m · °R	1.000 I.T. cal/gm · °K, or
		1.00065 cal/gm · °K.
Power	horsepower	33,000 ft · lb_f/min, or
		550 ft · lb_f/sec, or
		42.408 Btu/min.
	kilowatt	44,253 ft · lb_f/min, or
		735.55 ft · lb_f/sec, or
		56.869 Btu/min.

Notes: Joule = absolute joule; watt = absolute watt; calorie = thermochemical calorie; and I.T. calorie = International Table calorie.

Appendix B/
Steam Tables and Mollier Diagram

Table B-1/ Saturated Steam†

Absolute pressure = atmospheric pressure − vacuum.

Barometer and vacuum columns may be corrected to mercury at 32°F by subtracting $0.00009 \times (t - 32) \times$ column height, where t is the column temperature in degrees Fahrenheit.

1 in. of mercury at 32°F = $0.4912 \ \text{lb}_f/\text{in.}^2$

Example

Barometer reads 30.17 in. at 70°F.

Vacuum column reads 28.26 in. at 80°F.

Absolute pressure = $(30.17 - 0.00009 \times 38 \times 30.17) - (28.26 - 0.00009 \times 48 \times 28.26) = 1.93$ in. Hg at 32°F.

Saturation temperature (from table) = 100°F.

V = specific volume, ft^3/lb_m

H = specific enthalpy, Btu/lb_m

S = specific entropy, $\text{Btu}/\text{lb}_m \cdot °\text{R}$

Temp. t, °F	Absolute pressure P		Specific volume			Enthalpy			Entropy		
	Psia	In. Hg (32°F)	Sat. liquid V_f	Evap. V_{fg}	Sat. vapor V_g	Sat. liquid H_f	Evap. H_{fg}	Sat. vapor H_g	Sat. liquid S_f	Evap. S_{fg}	Sat. vapor S_g
32	0.0886	0.1806	0.01602	3305.7	3305.7	0	1075.1	1075.1	0	2.1865	2.1865
34	0.0961	0.1957	0.01602	3060.4	3060.4	2.01	1074.0	1076.0	0.0041	2.1755	2.1796
36	0.1041	0.2120	0.01602	2836.6	2836.6	4.03	1072.9	1076.9	0.0082	2.1645	2.1727
38	0.1126	0.2292	0.01602	2632.2	2632.2	6.04	1071.7	1077.7	0.0122	2.1533	2.1655
40	0.1217	0.2478	0.01602	2445.1	2445.1	8.05	1070.5	1078.6	0.0162	2.1423	2.1585

42	0.1315	0.2677	0.01602	2271.8	2271.8	10.06	1069.3	0.0203	1079.4	2.1314	2.1517
44	0.1420	0.2891	0.01602	2112.2	2112.2	12.06	1068.2	0.0242	1080.3	2.1207	2.1449
46	0.1532	0.3119	0.01602	1965.5	1965.5	14.07	1067.1	0.0282	1081.2	2.1102	2.1384
48	0.1652	0.3364	0.01602	1829.9	1829.9	16.07	1065.9	0.0322	1082.0	2.0995	2.1317
50	0.1780	0.3624	0.01602	1704.9	1704.9	18.07	1064.8	0.0361	1082.9	2.0891	2.1252
52	0.1918	0.3905	0.01603	1588.4	1588.4	20.07	1063.6	0.0400	1083.7	2.0786	2.1186
54	0.2063	0.4200	0.01603	1482.4	1482.4	22.07	1062.5	0.0439	1084.6	2.0684	2.1123
56	0.2219	0.4518	0.01603	1383.5	1383.5	24.07	1061.4	0.0478	1085.5	2.0582	2.1060
58	0.2384	0.4854	0.01603	1292.7	1292.7	26.07	1060.2	0.0517	1086.3	2.0479	2.0996
60	0.2561	0.5214	0.01603	1208.1	1208.1	28.07	1059.1	0.0555	1087.2	2.0379	2.0934
62	0.2749	0.5597	0.01604	1129.7	1129.7	30.06	1057.9	0.0594	1088.0	2.0278	2.0872
64	0.2949	0.6004	0.01604	1057.1	1057.1	32.06	1056.8	0.0632	1088.9	2.0180	2.0812
66	0.3162	0.6438	0.01604	989.6	989.6	34.06	1055.7	0.0670	1089.8	2.0082	2.0752
68	0.3388	0.6898	0.01605	927.0	927.0	36.05	1054.5	0.0708	1090.6	1.9983	2.0691
70	0.3628	0.7387	0.01605	868.9	868.9	38.05	1053.4	0.0745	1091.5	1.9887	2.0632
72	0.3883	0.7906	0.01606	814.9	814.9	40.04	1052.3	0.0783	1092.3	1.9792	2.0575
74	0.4153	0.8456	0.01606	764.7	764.7	42.04	1051.2	0.0820	1093.2	1.9697	2.0517
76	0.4440	0.9040	0.01607	718.0	718.0	44.03	1050.1	0.0858	1094.1	1.9603	2.0461
78	0.4744	0.9659	0.01607	674.4	674.4	46.03	1048.9	0.0895	1094.9	1.9508	2.0403
80	0.5067	1.032	0.01607	633.7	633.7	48.02	1047.8	0.0932	1095.8	1.9415	2.0347
82	0.5409	1.101	0.01608	595.8	595.8	50.02	1046.6	0.0969	1096.6	1.9321	2.0290
84	0.5772	1.175	0.01608	560.4	560.4	52.01	1045.5	0.1006	1097.5	1.9230	2.0236
86	0.6153	1.253	0.01609	527.6	527.6	54.01	1044.4	0.1042	1098.4	1.9139	2.0181
88	0.6555	1.335	0.01609	497.0	497.0	56.00	1043.2	0.1079	1099.2	1.9047	2.0126
90	0.6980	1.421	0.01610	468.4	468.4	58.00	1042.1	0.1115	1100.1	1.8958	2.0073

Table B-1/ Saturated Steam (Continued)

Temp. t, °F	Absolute pressure P		Specific volume			Enthalpy			Entropy		
	Psia	In. Hg (32°F)	Sat. liquid V_f	Evap. V_{fg}	Sat. vapor V_g	Sat. liquid H_f	Evap. H_{fg}	Sat. vapor H_g	Sat. liquid S_f	Evap. S_{fg}	Sat. vapor S_g
92	0.7429	1.513	0.01611	441.7	441.7	59.99	1040.9	1100.9	0.1151	1.8867	2.0018
94	0.7902	1.609	0.01611	416.7	416.7	61.98	1039.8	1101.8	0.1187	1.8779	1.9966
96	0.8403	1.711	0.01612	393.2	393.2	63.98	1038.7	1102.7	0.1223	1.8692	1.9915
98	0.8930	1.818	0.01613	371.3	371.3	65.98	1037.5	1103.5	0.1259	1.8604	1.9863
100	0.9487	1.932	0.01613	350.8	350.8	67.97	1036.4	1104.4	0.1295	1.8517	1.9812
102	1.0072	2.051	0.01614	331.5	331.5	69.96	1035.2	1105.2	0.1330	1.8430	1.9760
104	1.0689	2.176	0.01614	313.5	313.5	71.96	1034.1	1106.1	0.1366	1.8345	1.9711
106	1.1338	2.308	0.01615	296.5	296.5	73.95	1033.0	1107.0	0.1401	1.8261	1.9662
108	1.2020	2.447	0.01616	280.7	280.7	75.94	1032.0	1107.9	0.1436	1.8179	1.9615
110	1.274	2.594	0.01617	265.7	265.7	77.94	1030.9	1108.8	0.1471	1.8096	1.9567
112	1.350	2.749	0.01617	251.6	251.6	79.93	1029.7	1109.6	0.1506	1.8012	1.9518
114	1.429	2.909	0.01618	238.5	238.5	81.93	1028.6	1110.5	0.1541	1.7930	1.9471
116	1.512	3.078	0.01619	226.2	226.2	83.92	1027.5	1111.4	0.1576	1.7848	1.9424
118	1.600	3.258	0.01620	214.5	214.5	85.92	1026.4	1112.3	0.1610	1.7767	1.9377
120	1.692	3.445	0.01620	203.45	203.47	87.91	1025.3	1113.2	0.1645	1.7687	1.9332
122	1.788	3.640	0.01621	193.16	193.18	89.91	1024.1	1114.0	0.1679	1.7606	1.9285
124	1.889	3.846	0.01622	183.44	183.46	91.90	1023.0	1114.9	0.1714	1.7526	1.9240
126	1.995	4.062	0.01623	174.26	174.28	93.90	1021.8	1115.7	0.1748	1.7446	1.9194
128	2.105	4.286	0.01624	165.70	165.72	95.90	1020.7	1116.6	0.1782	1.7368	1.9150
130	2.221	4.522	0.01625	157.55	157.57	97.89	1019.5	1117.4	0.1816	1.7289	1.9105

132	2.343	4.770	0.01626	149.83	149.85	99.89	1018.3	1118.2	0.1849	1.7210	1.9059
134	2.470	5.029	0.01626	142.59	142.61	101.89	1017.2	1119.1	0.1883	1.7134	1.9017
136	2.603	5.300	0.01627	135.73	135.75	103.88	1016.0	1119.9	0.1917	1.7056	1.8973
138	2.742	5.583	0.01628	129.26	129.28	105.88	1014.9	1120.8	0.1950	1.6980	1.8930
140	2.887	5.878	0.01629	123.16	123.18	107.88	1013.7	1121.6	0.1984	1.6904	1.8888
142	3.039	6.187	0.01630	117.37	117.39	109.88	1012.5	1122.4	0.2017	1.6828	1.8845
144	3.198	6.511	0.01631	111.88	111.90	111.88	1011.3	1123.2	0.2050	1.6752	1.8802
146	3.363	6.847	0.01632	106.72	106.74	113.88	1010.2	1124.1	0.2083	1.6678	1.8761
148	3.536	7.199	0.01633	101.82	101.84	115.87	1009.0	1124.9	0.2116	1.6604	1.8720
150	3.716	7.566	0.01634	97.18	97.20	117.87	1007.8	1125.7	0.2149	1.6530	1.8679
152	3.904	7.948	0.01635	92.79	92.81	119.87	1006.7	1126.6	0.2181	1.6458	1.8639
154	4.100	8.348	0.01636	88.62	88.64	121.87	1005.5	1127.4	0.2214	1.6384	1.8598
156	4.305	8.765	0.01637	84.66	84.68	123.87	1004.4	1128.3	0.2247	1.6313	1.8560
158	4.518	9.199	0.01638	80.90	80.92	125.87	1003.2	1129.1	0.2279	1.6241	1.8520
160	4.739	9.649	0.01639	77.37	77.39	127.87	1002.0	1129.9	0.2311	1.6169	1.8480
162	4.970	10.12	0.01640	74.00	74.02	129.88	1000.8	1130.7	0.2343	1.6098	1.8441
164	5.210	10.61	0.01642	70.79	70.81	131.88	999.7	1131.6	0.2376	1.6029	1.8405
166	5.460	11.12	0.01643	67.76	67.78	133.88	998.5	1132.4	0.2408	1.5958	1.8366
168	5.720	11.65	0.01644	64.87	64.89	135.88	997.3	1133.2	0.2439	1.5888	1.8327
170	5.990	12.20	0.01645	62.12	62.14	137.89	996.1	1134.0	0.2471	1.5819	1.8290
172	6.272	12.77	0.01646	59.50	59.52	139.89	995.0	1134.9	0.2503	1.5751	1.8254
174	6.565	13.37	0.01647	57.01	57.03	141.89	993.8	1135.7	0.2535	1.5683	1.8218
176	6.869	13.99	0.01648	54.64	54.66	143.90	992.6	1136.5	0.2566	1.5615	1.8181
178	7.184	14.63	0.01650	52.39	52.41	145.90	991.4	1137.3	0.2598	1.5547	1.8145
180	7.510	15.29	0.01651	50.26	50.28	147.91	990.2	1138.1	0.2629	1.5479	1.8108

Table B-1/ Saturated Steam (Continued)

Temp. t, °F	Absolute pressure P		Specific volume			Enthalpy			Entropy		
	Psia	In. Hg (32°F)	Sat. liquid V_f	Evap. V_{fg}	Sat. vapor V_g	Sat. liquid H_f	Evap. H_{fg}	Sat. vapor H_g	Sat. liquid S_f	Evap. S_{fg}	Sat. vapor S_g
182	7.849	15.98	0.01652	48.22	48.24	149.92	989.0	1138.9	0.2661	1.5412	1.8073
184	8.201	16.70	0.01653	46.28	46.30	151.92	987.8	1139.7	0.2692	1.5346	1.8038
186	8.566	17.44	0.01654	44.43	44.45	153.93	986.6	1140.5	0.2723	1.5280	1.8003
188	8.944	18.21	0.01656	42.67	42.69	155.94	985.3	1141.3	0.2754	1.5213	1.7967
190	9.336	19.01	0.01657	40.99	41.01	157.95	984.1	1142.1	0.2785	1.5147	1.7932
192	9.744	19.84	0.01658	39.38	39.40	159.95	982.8	1142.8	0.2816	1.5081	1.7897
194	10.168	20.70	0.01659	37.84	37.86	161.96	981.5	1143.5	0.2847	1.5015	1.7862
196	10.605	21.59	0.01661	36.38	36.40	163.97	980.3	1144.3	0.2877	1.4951	1.7828
198	11.057	22.51	0.01662	34.98	35.00	165.98	979.0	1145.0	0.2908	1.4885	1.7793
200	11.525	23.46	0.01663	33.65	33.67	167.99	977.8	1145.8	0.2938	1.4822	1.7760
202	12.010	24.45	0.01665	32.37	32.39	170.01	976.6	1146.6	0.2969	1.4759	1.7728
204	12.512	25.47	0.01666	31.15	31.17	172.02	975.3	1147.3	0.2999	1.4695	1.7694
206	13.031	26.53	0.01667	29.99	30.01	174.03	974.1	1148.1	0.3029	1.4633	1.7662
208	13.568	27.62	0.01669	28.88	28.90	176.04	972.8	1148.8	0.3059	1.4570	1.7629
210	14.123	28.75	0.01670	27.81	27.83	178.06	971.5	1149.6	0.3090	1.4507	1.7597
212	14.696	29.92	0.01672	26.81	26.83	180.07	970.3	1150.4	0.3120	1.4446	1.7566
215	15.591	....	0.01674	25.35	25.37	183.10	968.3	1151.4	0.3165	1.4352	1.7517
220	17.188	....	0.01677	23.14	23.16	188.14	965.2	1153.3	0.3239	1.4201	1.7440
225	18.915	....	0.01681	21.15	21.17	193.18	961.9	1155.1	0.3313	1.4049	1.7362

230	20.78	.....	0.01684	19.371	19.388	198.22	958.7	1156.9	0.3386	1.3900	1.7286
235	22.80	.....	0.01688	17.761	17.778	203.28	955.3	1158.6	0.3459	1.3751	1.7210
240	24.97	.....	0.01692	16.307	16.324	208.34	952.1	1160.4	0.3531	1.3607	1.7138
245	27.31	.....	0.01696	15.010	15.027	213.41	948.7	1162.1	0.3604	1.3462	1.7066
250	29.82	.....	0.01700	13.824	13.841	218.48	945.3	1163.8	0.3675	1.3320	1.6995
255	32.53	.....	0.01704	12.735	12.752	223.56	942.0	1165.6	0.3747	1.3181	1.6928
260	35.43	.....	0.01708	11.754	11.771	228.65	938.6	1167.3	0.3817	1.3042	1.6859
265	38.54	.....	0.01713	10.861	10.878	233.74	935.3	1169.0	0.3888	1.2906	1.6794
270	41.85	.....	0.01717	10.053	10.070	238.84	931.8	1170.6	0.3958	1.2770	1.6728
275	45.40	.....	0.01721	9.313	9.330	243.94	928.2	1172.1	0.4027	1.2634	1.6661
280	49.20	.....	0.01726	8.634	8.651	249.06	924.6	1173.7	0.4096	1.2500	1.6596
285	53.25	.....	0.01731	8.015	8.032	254.18	921.0	1175.2	0.4165	1.2368	1.6533
290	57.55	.....	0.01735	7.448	7.465	259.31	917.4	1176.7	0.4234	1.2237	1.6471
295	62.13	.....	0.01740	6.931	6.948	264.45	913.7	1178.2	0.4302	1.2107	1.6409
300	67.01	.....	0.01745	6.454	6.471	269.60	910.1	1179.7	0.4370	1.1980	1.6350
305	72.18	.....	0.01750	6.014	6.032	274.76	906.3	1181.1	0.4437	1.1852	1.6289
310	77.68	.....	0.01755	5.610	5.628	279.92	902.6	1182.5	0.4505	1.1727	1.6232
315	83.50	.....	0.01760	5.239	5.257	285.10	898.8	1183.9	0.4571	1.1587	1.6158
320	89.65	.....	0.01765	4.897	4.915	290.29	895.0	1185.3	0.4637	1.1479	1.6116
325	96.16	.....	0.01771	4.583	4.601	295.49	891.1	1186.6	0.4703	1.1356	1.6059
330	103.03	.....	0.01776	4.292	4.310	300.69	887.1	1187.8	0.4769	1.1234	1.6003
335	110.31	.....	0.01782	4.021	4.039	305.91	883.2	1189.1	0.4835	1.1114	1.5949
340	117.99	.....	0.01788	3.771	3.789	311.14	879.2	1190.3	0.4900	1.0994	1.5894
345	126.10	.....	0.01793	3.539	3.557	316.38	875.1	1191.5	0.4966	1.0875	1.5841
350	134.62	.....	0.01799	3.324	3.342	321.64	871.0	1192.6	0.5030	1.0757	1.5787

Table B-1/ Saturated Steam (Continued)

Temp. t, °F	Absolute pressure P		Specific volume			Enthalpy			Entropy		
	Psia	In. Hg (32°F)	Sat. liquid V_f	Evap. V_{fg}	Sat. vapor V_g	Sat. liquid H_f	Evap. H_{fg}	Sat. vapor H_g	Sat. liquid S_f	Evap. S_{fg}	Sat. vapor S_g
355	143.58	...	0.01805	3.126	3.144	326.91	866.8	1193.7	0.5094	1.0640	1.5734
360	153.01	...	0.01811	2.940	2.958	332.19	862.5	1194.7	0.5159	1.0522	1.5681
365	162.93	...	0.01817	2.768	2.786	337.48	858.2	1195.7	0.5223	1.0406	1.5629
370	173.33	...	0.01823	2.607	2.625	342.79	853.8	1196.6	0.5286	1.0291	1.5577
375	184.23	...	0.01830	2.458	2.476	348.11	849.4	1197.5	0.5350	1.0176	1.5526
380	195.70	...	0.01836	2.318	2.336	353.45	844.9	1198.4	0.5413	1.0062	1.5475
385	207.71	...	0.01843	2.189	2.207	358.80	840.4	1199.2	0.5476	0.9949	1.5425
390	220.29	...	0.01850	2.064	2.083	364.17	835.7	1199.9	0.5540	0.9835	1.5375
395	233.47	...	0.01857	1.9512	1.9698	369.56	831.0	1200.6	0.5602	0.9723	1.5325
400	247.25	...	0.01864	1.8446	1.8632	374.97	826.2	1201.2	0.5664	0.9610	1.5274
405	261.67	...	0.01871	1.7445	1.7632	380.40	821.4	1201.8	0.5727	0.9499	1.5226
410	276.72	...	0.01878	1.6508	1.6696	385.83	816.6	1202.4	0.5789	0.9390	1.5179
415	292.44	...	0.01886	1.5630	1.5819	391.30	811.7	1203.0	0.5851	0.9280	1.5131
420	308.82	...	0.01894	1.4806	1.4995	396.78	806.7	1203.5	0.5912	0.9170	1.5082
425	325.91	...	0.01902	1.4031	1.4221	402.28	801.6	1203.9	0.5974	0.9061	1.5035
430	343.71	...	0.01910	1.3303	1.3494	407.80	796.5	1204.3	0.6036	0.8953	1.4989
435	362.27	...	0.01918	1.2617	1.2809	413.35	791.2	1204.6	0.6097	0.8843	1.4940
440	381.59	...	0.01926	1.1973	1.2166	418.91	785.9	1204.8	0.6159	0.8735	1.4894
445	401.70	...	0.01934	1.1367	1.1560	424.49	780.4	1204.9	0.6220	0.8626	1.4846
450	422.61	...	0.01943	1.0796	1.0990	430.11	774.9	1205.0	0.6281	0.8518	1.4799

455	444.35	.....	0.0195	1.0256	1.0451	435.74	769.3	1205.0	0.6342	0.8410	1.4752
460	466.97	.....	0.0196	0.9745	0.9941	441.42	763.6	1205.0	0.6403	0.8303	1.4706
465	490.43	.....	0.0197	0.9262	0.9459	447.10	757.8	1204.9	0.6463	0.8195	1.4658
470	514.70	.....	0.0198	0.8808	0.9006	452.84	751.9	1204.7	0.6524	0.8088	1.4612
475	539.90	.....	0.0199	0.8379	0.8578	458.59	745.9	1204.5	0.6585	0.7980	1.4565
480	566.12	.....	0.0200	0.7972	0.8172	464.37	739.8	1204.2	0.6646	0.7873	1.4519
485	593.28	.....	0.0201	0.7585	0.7786	470.18	733.6	1203.8	0.6706	0.7766	1.4472
490	621.44	.....	0.0202	0.7219	0.7421	476.01	727.3	1203.3	0.6767	0.7658	1.4425
495	650.59	.....	0.0203	0.6872	0.7075	481.90	720.8	1202.7	0.6827	0.7550	1.4377
500	680.80	.....	0.0204	0.6544	0.6748	487.80	714.2	1202.0	0.6888	0.7442	1.4330
505	712.19	.....	0.0206	0.6230	0.6436	493.8	707.5	1201.3	0.6949	0.7334	1.4283
510	744.55	.....	0.0207	0.5932	0.6139	499.8	700.6	1200.4	0.7009	0.7225	1.4234
515	777.96	.....	0.0208	0.5651	0.5859	505.8	693.6	1199.4	0.7070	0.7116	1.4186
520	812.68	.....	0.0209	0.5382	0.5591	511.9	686.5	1198.4	0.7132	0.7007	1.4139
525	848.37	.....	0.0210	0.5128	0.5338	518.0	679.2	1197.2	0.7192	0.6898	1.4090
530	885.20	.....	0.0212	0.4885	0.5097	524.2	671.9	1196.1	0.7253	0.6789	1.4042
535	923.45	.....	0.0213	0.4654	0.4867	530.4	664.4	1194.8	0.7314	0.6679	1.3993
540	962.80	.....	0.0214	0.4433	0.4647	536.6	656.7	1193.3	0.7375	0.6569	1.3944
545	1003.6	.....	0.0216	0.4222	0.4438	542.0	648.9	1191.8	0.7436	0.6459	1.3895
550	1045.6	.....	0.0218	0.4021	0.4239	549.3	640.9	1190.2	0.7498	0.6347	1.3845
555	1088.8	.....	0.0219	0.3830	0.4049	555.7	632.6	1188.3	0.7559	0.6234	1.3793
560	1133.4	.....	0.0221	0.3648	0.3869	562.2	624.1	1186.3	0.7622	0.6120	1.3742
565	1179.3	.....	0.0222	0.3472	0.3694	568.8	615.4	1184.2	0.7684	0.6006	1.3690
570	1226.7	.....	0.0224	0.3304	0.3528	575.4	606.5	1181.9	0.7737	0.5890	1.3627
575	1275.7	.....	0.0226	0.3143	0.3369	582.1	597.4	1179.5	0.7810	0.5774	1.3584

Table B-1 / Saturated Steam (Continued)

Temp. t, °F	Absolute pressure P		Specific volume			Enthalpy			Entropy		
	Psia	In. Hg (32°F)	Sat. liquid V_f	Evap. V_{fg}	Sat. vapor V	Sat. liquid H_f	Evap. H_{fg}	Sat. vapor H_g	Sat. liquid S_f	Evap. S_{fg}	Sat. vapor S_g
580	1326.1	....	0.0228	0.2989	0.3217	588.9	588.1	1177.0	0.7872	0.5656	1.3528
585	1378.1	....	0.0230	0.2840	0.3070	595.7	578.6	1174.3	0.7936	0.5538	1.3474
590	1431.5	....	0.0232	0.2699	0.2931	602.6	568.8	1171.4	0.8000	0.5419	1.3419
595	1486.5	....	0.0234	0.2563	0.2797	609.7	558.7	1168.4	0.8065	0.5297	1.3362
600	1543.2	....	0.0236	0.2432	0.2668	616.8	548.4	1165.2	0.8130	0.5175	1.3305
605	1601.5	....	0.0239	0.2306	0.2545	624.1	537.7	1161.8	0.8196	0.5050	1.3246
610	1661.6	....	0.0241	0.2185	0.2426	631.5	526.6	1158.1	0.8263	0.4923	1.3186
615	1723.4	....	0.0244	0.2068	0.2312	638.9	515.3	1154.2	0.8330	0.4795	1.3125
620	1787.0	....	0.0247	0.1955	0.2202	646.5	503.7	1150.2	0.8398	0.4665	1.3063
625	1852.4	....	0.0250	0.1845	0.2095	654.3	491.5	1145.8	0.8467	0.4531	1.2998
630	1919.8	....	0.0253	0.1740	0.1993	662.2	478.8	1141.0	0.8537	0.4394	1.2931
635	1989.0	....	0.0256	0.1638	0.1894	670.4	465.5	1135.9	0.8609	0.4252	1.2861
640	2060.3	....	0.0260	0.1539	0.1799	678.7	452.0	1130.7	0.8681	0.4110	1.2791
645	2133.5	....	0.0264	0.1441	0.1705	687.3	437.6	1124.9	0.8756	0.3961	1.2717
650	2208.8	....	0.0268	0.1348	0.1616	696.0	422.7	1118.7	0.8832	0.3809	1.2641
655	2286.4	....	0.0273	0.1256	0.1529	705.2	407.0	1112.2	0.8910	0.3651	1.2561
660	2366.2	....	0.0278	0.1167	0.1445	714.4	390.5	1104.9	0.8991	0.3488	1.2479
665	2448.0	....	0.0283	0.1079	0.1362	724.5	372.1	1096.6	0.9074	0.3308	1.2382
670	2532.4	....	0.0290	0.0991	0.1281	734.6	353.3	1087.9	0.9161	0.3127	1.2288
675	2619.2	....	0.0297	0.0904	0.1201	745.5	332.8	1078.3	0.9253	0.2933	1.2186

680	2708.4	....	0.0305	0.0810	0.1115	757.2	310.0	1067.2	0.9352	0.2720	1.2072
685	2800.4	....	0.0316	0.0716	0.1032	770.1	284.5	1054.6	0.9459	0.2485	1.1944
690	2895.0	....	0.0328	0.0617	0.0945	784.2	254.9	1039.1	0.9579	0.2217	1.1796
695	2992.7	....	0.0345	0.0511	0.0856	801.3	219.1	1020.4	0.9720	0.1897	1.1617
700	3094.1	....	0.0369	0.0389	0.0758	823.9	171.7	995.6	0.9904	0.1481	1.1385
705	3199.1	....	0.0440	0.0157	0.0597	870.2	77.6	947.8	1.0305	0.0661	1.0966
705.34‡	3206.2	....	0.0541	0	0.0541	910.3	0	910.3	1.0645	0	1.0645

‡ Critical temperature.

Table B-2/ Superheated Steam†

Abs press., psia (sat. temp.)	V H S	Sat. water	Sat. steam	Temperature, °F													
				200	250	300	350	400	450	500	600	700	800	900	1000	1100	1200
1 (101.76)	V	0.0161	333.79	392.5	422.5	452.1	482.1	511.7	541.8	571.3	630.9	690.6	750.2	809.8	869.4	929.1	988.7
	H	69.72	1105.2	1149.2	1171.9	1194.4	1217.3	1240.2	1263.5	1286.7	1333.9	1382.1	1431.0	1480.8	1531.4	1583.0	1635.4
	S	0.1326	1.9769	2.0491	2.0822	2.1128	2.1420	2.1694	2.1957	2.2206	2.2673	2.3107	2.3512	2.3892	2.4251	2.4592	2.4918
5 (162.25)	V	0.0164	73.600	78.17	84.24	90.21	96.26	102.19	108.23	114.16	126.11	138.05	149.99	161.91	173.83	185.80	197.72
	H	130.13	1130.8	1148.3	1171.1	1193.6	1216.6	1239.8	1263.0	1286.1	1333.5	1381.8	1430.8	1480.6	1531.3	1582.9	1635.3
	S	0.2347	1.8437	1.8710	1.9043	1.9349	1.9642	1.9920	2.0182	2.0429	2.0898	2.1333	2.1738	2.2118	2.2478	2.2820	2.3146
10 (193.21)	V	0.0166	38.462	38.88	41.96	44.98	48.02	51.01	54.04	57.02	63.01	68.99	74.96	80.92	86.89	92.88	98.85
	H	161.17	1143.3	1146.7	1170.2	1192.8	1216.0	1239.3	1262.5	1285.8	1333.3	1381.6	1430.6	1480.5	1531.2	1582.8	1635.2
	S	0.2834	1.7876	1.7928	1.8271	1.8579	1.8875	1.9154	1.9416	1.9665	2.0135	2.0570	2.0975	2.1356	2.1716	2.2058	2.2384
14.696 (212.00)	V	0.0167	26.828	......	28.44	30.52	32.61	34.65	36.73	38.75	42.83	46.91	50.97	55.03	59.09	63.19	67.25
	H	180.07	1150.4	......	1169.2	1192.0	1215.4	1238.9	1262.1	1285.4	1333.0	1381.4	1430.5	1480.4	1531.1	1582.7	1635.1
	S	0.3120	1.7566	......	1.7838	1.8148	1.8446	1.8727	1.8989	1.9238	1.9709	2.0145	2.0551	2.0932	2.1292	2.1634	2.1960
15 (213.03)	V	0.0167	26.320	......	27.86	29.90	31.94	33.95	35.98	37.97	41.98	45.97	49.95	53.93	57.91	61.91	65.89
	H	181.11	1150.7	......	1169.2	1192.0	1215.4	1238.9	1262.1	1285.4	1333.0	1381.4	1430.5	1480.4	1531.1	1582.7	1635.1
	S	0.3135	1.7548	......	1.7816	1.8126	1.8424	1.8705	1.8967	1.9216	1.9687	2.0123	2.0529	2.0910	2.1270	2.1612	2.1938
20 (227.96)	V	0.0168	20.110	......	20.81	22.36	23.91	25.43	26.95	28.45	31.46	34.46	37.44	40.43	43.42	46.43	49.41
	H	196.16	1156.1	......	1168.0	1191.1	1214.8	1238.4	1261.8	1285.0	1332.7	1381.2	1430.3	1480.2	1531.0	1582.6	1635.1
	S	0.3356	1.7315	......	1.7485	1.7799	1.8101	1.8384	1.8646	1.8896	1.9368	1.9805	2.0211	2.0592	2.0952	2.1294	2.1620
25 (240.07)	V	0.0169	16.321	......	16.58	17.84	19.08	20.30	21.53	22.73	25.15	27.55	29.94	32.33	34.73	37.14	39.52
	H	208.41	1160.4	......	1166.3	1190.2	1214.1	1237.9	1261.1	1284.6	1332.4	1381.0	1430.1	1480.0	1530.9	1582.5	1635.0
	S	0.3532	1.7137	......	1.7221	1.7570	1.7875	1.8160	1.8422	1.8673	1.9146	1.9584	1.9990	2.0371	2.0732	2.1074	2.1400
30 (250.34)	V	0.0170	13.763	......	......	14.82	15.87	16.89	17.91	18.92	20.94	22.94	24.94	26.93	28.93	30.94	32.93
	H	218.83	1164.0	......	......	1189.2	1213.4	1237.4	1260.6	1284.2	1332.1	1380.8	1429.9	1479.9	1530.8	1582.4	1634.9
	S	0.3680	1.6992	......	......	1.7335	1.7643	1.7930	1.8192	1.8444	1.8918	1.9357	1.9763	2.0145	2.0506	2.0848	2.1174

Abs. Press. (Sat. Temp.)		Sat. Liq.	Sat. Vap.	1	2	3	4	5	6	7	8	9	10	11	12
35 (259.28)	V	0.0171	11.907	12.66	13.57	14.45	15.33	16.20	17.94	19.66	21.36	23.08	24.79	26.52	28.22
	H	227.92	1167.0	1188.2	1212.7	1236.9	1260.1	1283.8	1331.9	1380.6	1429.8	1479.8	1530.7	1582.3	1634.8
	S	0.3807	1.6869	1.7156	1.7468	1.7758	1.8020	1.8274	1.8750	1.9189	1.9596	1.9978	2.0339	2.0681	2.1007
40 (267.24)	V	0.0172	10.506	11.04	11.84	12.62	13.40	14.16	15.68	17.19	18.69	20.18	21.68	23.20	24.69
	H	236.02	1169.7	1187.1	1211.9	1236.4	1259.6	1283.4	1331.6	1380.4	1429.6	1479.7	1530.6	1582.2	1634.8
	S	0.3919	1.6763	1.6997	1.7313	1.7606	1.7868	1.8123	1.8600	1.9040	1.9447	1.9829	2.0191	2.0533	2.0860
45 (274.45)	V	0.0172	9.408	9.785	10.50	11.20	11.89	12.57	13.93	15.27	16.60	17.94	19.27	20.62	21.95
	H	243.38	1172.0	1185.9	1211.1	1235.8	1259.1	1283.0	1331.3	1380.1	1429.4	1479.4	1530.5	1582.1	1634.7
	S	0.4019	1.6668	1.6854	1.7175	1.7471	1.7734	1.7990	1.8468	1.8908	1.9315	1.9697	2.0059	2.0401	2.0728
50 (281.01)	V	0.0173	8.522	8.777	9.430	10.06	10.69	11.30	12.53	13.74	14.93	16.14	17.34	18.55	19.75
	H	250.09	1174.0	1184.6	1210.3	1235.2	1258.6	1282.6	1331.0	1379.9	1429.3	1479.3	1530.4	1582.0	1634.6
	S	0.4110	1.6583	1.6724	1.7051	1.7349	1.7613	1.7870	1.8349	1.8790	1.9198	1.9580	1.9942	2.0284	2.0611
55 (287.07)	V	0.0173	7.792	7.950	8.553	9.180	9.703	10.26	11.38	12.48	13.57	14.67	15.76	16.86	17.95
	H	256.30	1175.8	1183.2	1209.4	1234.6	1258.2	1282.2	1330.7	1379.7	1429.1	1479.2	1530.3	1581.9	1634.5
	S	0.4193	1.6506	1.6604	1.6938	1.7240	1.7507	1.7764	1.8244	1.8685	1.9093	1.9475	1.9837	2.0179	2.0512
60 (292.71)	V	0.0174	7.179	7.260	7.821	8.353	8.882	9.398	10.42	11.44	12.44	13.44	14.44	15.45	16.45
	H	262.10	1177.5	1181.8	1208.5	1234.0	1257.7	1281.8	1330.4	1379.5	1428.9	1479.0	1530.2	1581.8	1634.4
	S	0.4271	1.6437	1.6494	1.6834	1.7139	1.7407	1.7665	1.8146	1.8588	1.8996	1.9378	1.9741	2.0083	2.0410
65 (297.97)	V	0.0174	6.654	6.674	7.202	7.696	8.187	8.665	9.614	10.55	11.48	12.40	13.33	14.26	15.19
	H	267.51	1179.1	1180.4	1207.6	1233.4	1257.2	1281.0	1330.1	1379.3	1428.8	1478.9	1530.1	1581.7	1634.4
	S	0.4342	1.6374	1.6391	1.6738	1.7047	1.7316	1.7575	1.8057	1.8500	1.8909	1.9291	1.9654	1.9996	2.0323
70 (302.92)	V	0.0175	6.210	...	6.671	7.132	7.592	8.036	8.920	9.791	10.65	11.51	12.37	13.24	14.10
	H	272.61	1180.5	...	1206.7	1232.8	1256.7	1281.0	1329.9	1379.0	1428.6	1478.7	1530.0	1581.6	1634.3
	S	0.4409	1.6314	...	1.6647	1.6960	1.7230	1.7490	1.7974	1.8416	1.8826	1.9208	1.9572	1.9914	2.0241
75 (307.60)	V	0.0175	5.820	...	6.210	6.644	7.076	7.492	8.319	9.133	9.938	10.74	11.54	12.36	13.16
	H	277.44	1181.9	...	1205.8	1232.2	1256.2	1280.7	1329.6	1378.8	1428.4	1478.6	1529.8	1581.5	1634.2
	S	0.4472	1.6260	...	1.6563	1.6879	1.7150	1.7411	1.7896	1.8339	1.8749	1.9132	1.9495	1.9837	2.0184

Table B-2/ Superheated Steam (Continued)

Temperature, °F

Abs press., psia (sat. temp.)		Sat. water	Sat. steam	340	360	380	400	420	450	500	600	700	800	900	1000	1100	1200
80 (312.03)	V	0.0176	5.476	5.720	5.889	6.055	6.217	6.384	6.623	7.015	7.793	8.558	9.313	10.07	10.82	11.58	12.33
	H	282.02	1183.1	1200.0	1211.0	1221.2	1231.5	1240.3	1255.7	1280.2	1329.3	1378.5	1428.2	1478.4	1529.7	1581.4	1634.1
	S	0.4532	1.6209	1.6424	1.6560	1.6683	1.6804	1.6905	1.7077	1.7339	1.7825	1.8268	1.8679	1.9062	1.9426	1.9768	2.0095
85 (316.25)	V	0.0176	5.169	5.368	5.528	5.685	5.839	5.995	6.226	6.594	7.329	8.050	8.762	9.472	10.18	10.90	11.61
	H	286.40	1184.3	1198.5	1210.0	1220.5	1230.7	1239.7	1255.1	1279.7	1329.0	1378.3	1428.0	1478.2	1529.6	1581.3	1634.0
	S	0.4587	1.6159	1.6339	1.6481	1.6608	1.6728	1.6831	1.7003	1.7266	1.7754	1.8198	1.8609	1.8992	1.9357	1.9699	2.0026
90 (320.27)	V	0.0177	4.898	5.055	5.208	5.357	5.504	5.653	5.869	6.220	6.916	7.599	8.272	8.943	9.626	10.29	10.96
	H	290.57	1185.4	1197.3	1209.0	1219.8	1230.0	1239.1	1254.5	1279.3	1328.7	1378.1	1427.9	1478.1	1529.5	1581.2	1634.0
	S	0.4641	1.6113	1.6264	1.6408	1.6538	1.6658	1.6763	1.6935	1.7200	1.7689	1.8134	1.8546	1.8929	1.9294	1.9636	1.9964
95 (324.13)	V	0.0177	4.653	4.773	4.921	5.063	5.205	5.346	5.552	5.886	6.547	7.195	7.834	8.481	9.117	9.751	10.38
	H	294.58	1186.4	1196.0	1208.0	1219.0	1229.3	1238.6	1254.0	1278.9	1328.4	1377.8	1427.7	1478.0	1529.4	1581.1	1633.9
	S	0.4692	1.6070	1.6191	1.6339	1.6472	1.6593	1.6700	1.6872	1.7138	1.7628	1.8073	1.8485	1.8869	1.9234	1.9576	1.9904
100 (327.83)	V	0.0177	4.433	4.520	4.663	4.801	4.936	5.070	5.286	5.589	6.217	6.836	7.448	8.055	8.659	9.262	9.862
	H	298.43	1187.3	1194.9	1207.0	1218.3	1228.4	1238.6	1253.7	1278.6	1327.9	1377.5	1427.5	1478.0	1529.2	1581.0	1633.7
	S	0.4741	1.6028	1.6124	1.6273	1.6409	1.6528	1.6645	1.6814	1.7080	1.7568	1.8015	1.8428	1.8814	1.9177	1.9520	1.9847
105 (331.38)	V	0.0178	4.232	4.292	4.429	4.562	4.691	4.820	5.007	5.316	5.916	6.507	7.090	7.670	8.245	8.819	9.391
	H	302.13	1188.2	1193.5	1205.9	1217.2	1227.6	1237.5	1252.9	1278.0	1327.6	1377.4	1427.3	1477.7	1529.2	1580.9	1633.7
	S	0.4787	1.5988	1.6055	1.6208	1.6344	1.6466	1.6580	1.6752	1.7020	1.7511	1.7960	1.8372	1.8757	1.9122	1.9464	1.9791
110 (334.79)	V	0.0178	4.050	4.084	4.217	4.345	4.469	4.592	4.773	5.069	5.643	6.208	6.765	7.319	7.869	8.417	8.963
	H	305.69	1189.0	1192.2	1204.9	1216.4	1226.9	1236.9	1252.4	1277.5	1327.4	1377.1	1427.1	1477.5	1529.1	1580.8	1633.6
	S	0.4832	1.5950	1.5990	1.6147	1.6286	1.6410	1.6525	1.6698	1.6966	1.7460	1.7908	1.8321	1.8706	1.9072	1.9414	1.9742
115 (338.08)	V	0.0179	3.882	....	4.022	4.146	4.266	4.384	4.558	4.843	5.393	5.935	6.469	6.999	7.525	8.049	8.572
	H	309.13	1189.8	....	1203.8	1215.6	1226.2	1236.3	1251.9	1277.1	1327.1	1376.9	1427.0	1477.4	1528.9	1580.7	1633.6
	S	0.4875	1.5915	....	1.6088	1.6230	1.6355	1.6471	1.6645	1.6915	1.7410	1.7859	1.8273	1.8658	1.9023	1.9366	1.9695

120 (341.26)	V	0.0179		3.728		3.845	3.963	4.079	4.194	4.361	4.635	5.165	5.685	6.197	6.705	7.210	7.713	8.215
	H	312.46		1190.6		1202.7	1214.7	1225.4	1235.7	1251.4	1276.7	1326.8	1376.7	1426.8	1477.2	1528.8	1580.6	1633.5
	S	0.4916		1.5879		1.6028	1.6173	1.6299	1.6417	1.6592	1.6863	1.7359	1.7809	1.8223	1.8608	1.8974	1.9317	1.9646
125 (344.34)	V	0.0179		3.586		3.680	3.796	3.908	4.019	4.181	4.445	4.954	5.454	5.947	6.435	6.920	7.403	7.885
	H	315.69		1191.3		1201.6	1213.7	1224.5	1235.0	1250.8	1276.3	1326.5	1376.4	1426.6	1477.1	1528.7	1580.5	1633.4
	S	0.4956		1.5846		1.5973	1.6119	1.6246	1.6367	1.6544	1.6817	1.7314	1.7764	1.8179	1.8565	1.8931	1.9274	1.9603
130 (347.31)	V	0.0180		3.455		3.528	3.641	3.750	3.857	4.013	4.268	4.760	5.242	5.716	6.186	6.653	7.117	7.581
	H	318.81		1192.0		1200.4	1212.7	1223.6	1234.3	1250.3	1275.8	1326.1	1376.1	1426.4	1476.9	1528.6	1580.4	1633.3
	S	0.4995		1.5815		1.5918	1.6066	1.6194	1.6317	1.6496	1.6769	1.7267	1.7718	1.8134	1.8520	1.8887	1.9230	1.9559
135 (350.21)	V	0.0180		3.333		3.388	3.497	3.603	3.707	3.859	4.105	4.580	5.045	5.502	5.955	6.405	6.853	7.303
	H	321.86		1192.7		1199.2	1211.7	1222.7	1233.6	1249.7	1275.4	1325.8	1375.9	1426.2	1476.8	1528.5	1580.3	1633.2
	S	0.5032		1.5784		1.5864	1.6015	1.6144	1.6269	1.6449	1.6724	1.7223	1.7674	1.8090	1.8476	1.8843	1.9186	1.9515
140 (353.03)	V	0.0180		3.220		3.258	3.364	3.467	3.567	3.715	3.954	4.413	4.862	5.303	5.741	6.175	6.607	7.037
	H	324.83		1193.7		1198.0	1210.6	1221.8	1232.9	1249.1	1275.0	1325.5	1375.7	1426.0	1476.6	1528.4	1580.2	1633.1
	S	0.5069		1.5755		1.5813	1.5965	1.6097	1.6225	1.6406	1.6683	1.7183	1.7635	1.8051	1.8437	1.8804	1.9147	1.9476
145 (355.76)	V	0.0181		3.114		3.136	3.240	3.340	3.438	3.581	3.812	4.257	4.692	5.119	5.541	5.961	6.378	6.794
	H	327.71		1193.9		1196.7	1209.5	1220.9	1232.2	1248.5	1274.5	1325.1	1375.4	1425.8	1476.5	1528.3	1580.1	1633.1
	S	0.5104		1.5726		1.5760	1.5914	1.6048	1.6178	1.6360	1.6638	1.7139	1.7592	1.8009	1.8396	1.8763	1.9106	1.9435
150 (358.43)	V	0.0181		3.016			3.124	3.221	3.317	3.456	3.681	4.112	4.533	4.946	5.355	5.761	6.164	6.567
	H	330.53		1194.4			1208.4	1220.0	1231.4	1248.0	1274.1	1324.9	1375.1	1425.6	1476.3	1528.1	1580.0	1633.0
	S	0.5138		1.5698			1.5865	1.6002	1.6133	1.6319	1.6598	1.7101	1.7553	1.7970	1.8357	1.8724	1.9068	1.9397
155 (361.02)	V	0.0181		2.921			3.015	3.110	3.203	3.340	3.558	3.976	4.384	4.785	5.181	5.574	5.964	6.354
	H	333.27		1195.0			1207.2	1219.1	1230.7	1247.5	1273.6	1324.5	1374.9	1425.4	1476.2	1528.0	1579.9	1632.9
	S	0.5172		1.5671			1.5818	1.5958	1.6091	1.6279	1.6558	1.7062	1.7516	1.7933	1.8321	1.8688	1.9032	1.9361
160 (363.55)	V	0.0182		2.834			2.913	3.006	3.097	3.230	3.443	3.849	4.245	4.633	5.018	5.398	5.777	6.155
	H	335.95		1195.5			1206.0	1218.3	1230.0	1246.9	1273.2	1324.1	1374.7	1425.2	1476.0	1527.9	1579.8	1632.8
	S	0.5204		1.5646			1.5772	1.5917	1.6052	1.6241	1.6522	1.7026	1.7482	1.7899	1.8287	1.8655	1.8999	1.9328

Table B-2/ Superheated Steam (Continued)

Abs press., psia (sat. temp.)	V H S	Sat. water	Sat. steam	Temperature, °F 400	420	440	460	480	500	550	600	700	800	900	1000	1100	1200
165 (366.01)	V	0.0182	2.752	2.909	2.997	3.084	3.170	3.251	3.334	3.533	3.729	4.114	4.491	4.864	5.234	5.601	5.967
	H	338.55	1195.9	1217.4	1229.3	1241.1	1251.8	1262.4	1272.8	1298.5	1323.8	1374.5	1425.0	1475.9	1527.8	1579.7	1632.7
	S	0.5236	1.5619	1.5874	1.6011	1.6144	1.6262	1.6376	1.6486	1.6747	1.6991	1.7448	1.7865	1.8254	1.8622	1.8966	1.9295
170 (368.42)	V	0.0182	2.674	2.816	2.903	2.988	3.071	3.151	3.232	3.426	3.617	3.991	4.357	4.720	5.079	5.436	5.791
	H	341.11	1196.3	1216.5	1228.4	1240.5	1251.3	1261.8	1272.3	1298.2	1323.5	1374.2	1424.9	1475.7	1527.6	1579.6	1632.7
	S	0.5266	1.5593	1.5832	1.5969	1.6105	1.6224	1.6337	1.6448	1.6711	1.6955	1.7412	1.7831	1.8219	1.8587	1.8931	1.9261
175 (370.77)	V	0.0182	2.601	2.730	2.814	2.897	2.979	3.057	3.136	3.325	3.510	3.875	4.231	4.584	4.932	5.279	5.625
	H	343.61	1196.7	1215.6	1227.6	1239.9	1250.8	1261.3	1271.9	1297.8	1323.2	1374.0	1424.7	1475.6	1527.5	1579.5	1632.6
	S	0.5296	1.5569	1.5793	1.5931	1.6069	1.6189	1.6302	1.6414	1.6677	1.6922	1.7380	1.7799	1.8185	1.8553	1.8897	1.9227
180 (373.08)	V	0.0183	2.532	2.648	2.731	2.812	2.892	2.968	3.045	3.229	3.410	3.765	4.112	4.455	4.794	5.132	5.468
	H	346.07	1197.2	1214.6	1226.6	1239.2	1250.2	1260.8	1271.5	1297.4	1322.8	1373.7	1424.5	1475.5	1527.4	1579.4	1632.5
	S	0.5325	1.5545	1.5751	1.5891	1.6030	1.6151	1.6265	1.6378	1.6641	1.6886	1.7345	1.7765	1.8154	1.8522	1.8866	1.9196
185 (375.34)	V	0.0183	2.466	2.570	2.651	2.731	2.809	2.884	2.958	3.139	3.315	3.661	3.999	4.333	4.664	4.992	5.319
	H	348.47	1197.6	1213.7	1226.0	1238.4	1249.6	1260.3	1271.0	1297.1	1322.4	1373.4	1424.3	1475.3	1527.3	1579.3	1632.4
	S	0.5354	1.5522	1.5712	1.5853	1.5992	1.6115	1.6230	1.6343	1.6611	1.6853	1.7312	1.7733	1.8122	1.8491	1.8835	1.9165
190 (377.55)	V	0.0183	2.404	2.496	2.576	2.654	2.731	2.804	2.877	3.053	3.225	3.563	3.893	4.218	4.540	4.860	5.179
	H	350.83	1198.0	1212.7	1225.1	1237.7	1249.0	1259.8	1270.5	1296.6	1322.1	1373.1	1424.1	1475.2	1527.1	1579.2	1632.3
	S	0.5382	1.5501	1.5674	1.5817	1.5959	1.6083	1.6199	1.6312	1.6577	1.6823	1.7282	1.7703	1.8093	1.8461	1.8806	1.9136
195 (379.70)	V	0.0184	2.344	2.426	2.505	2.581	2.656	2.728	2.799	2.972	3.140	3.470	3.791	4.109	4.423	4.735	5.046
	H	353.13	1198.4	1211.7	1224.2	1237.0	1248.3	1259.3	1270.0	1296.2	1321.8	1372.9	1423.9	1475.0	1527.0	1579.1	1632.2
	S	0.5409	1.5479	1.5636	1.5780	1.5924	1.6048	1.6166	1.6279	1.6545	1.6792	1.7252	1.7673	1.8063	1.8432	1.8777	1.9107
200 (381.82)	V	0.0184	2.288	2.360	2.437	2.512	2.585	2.656	2.726	2.895	3.059	3.381	3.697	4.005	4.311	4.616	4.919
	H	355.40	1198.7	1210.8	1223.7	1236.3	1247.9	1258.7	1269.4	1295.6	1321.4	1372.5	1423.9	1474.9	1526.6	1579.0	1632.1
	S	0.5436	1.5457	1.5599	1.5748	1.5889	1.6017	1.6133	1.6245	1.6511	1.6761	1.7221	1.7646	1.8035	1.8402	1.8749	1.9079

205 (383.89)	V	0.0184	2.235	2.297	2.372	2.446	2.518	2.587	2.656	2.821	2.982	3.297	3.604	3.906	4.205	4.502	4.798
	H	357.61	1199.0	1209.7	1222.5	1235.4	1247.1	1258.2	1269.0	1295.4	1321.0	1372.4	1423.5	1474.7	1526.8	1578.9	1632.1
	S	0.5462	1.5436	1.5562	1.5709	1.5854	1.5983	1.6102	1.6216	1.6484	1.6731	1.7194	1.7616	1.8007	1.8377	1.8722	1.9052
210 (385.93)	V	0.0184	2.183	2.237	2.311	2.384	2.454	2.522	2.589	2.751	2.909	3.216	3.516	3.812	4.104	4.395	4.683
	H	359.80	1199.4	1208.8	1221.8	1234.7	1246.5	1257.7	1268.5	1295.0	1320.7	1372.1	1423.3	1474.6	1526.6	1578.8	1632.0
	S	0.5488	1.5417	1.5527	1.5676	1.5821	1.5951	1.6071	1.6185	1.6454	1.6702	1.7165	1.7588	1.7980	1.8349	1.8695	1.9025
215 (387.93)	V	0.0185	2.134	2.179	2.252	2.324	2.393	2.460	2.526	2.685	2.839	3.140	3.433	3.722	4.008	4.292	4.574
	H	361.95	1199.6	1207.8	1221.0	1234.0	1245.9	1257.0	1268.0	1294.6	1320.4	1371.9	1423.1	1474.4	1526.5	1578.7	1631.9
	S	0.5513	1.5395	1.5491	1.5643	1.5789	1.5920	1.6042	1.6156	1.6426	1.6675	1.7139	1.7562	1.7954	1.8324	1.8670	1.9000
220 (389.89)	V	0.0185	2.086	2.124	2.196	2.267	2.335	2.400	2.465	2.621	2.772	3.067	3.354	3.637	3.916	4.193	4.469
	H	364.05	1199.9	1206.8	1220.1	1233.2	1245.2	1256.7	1267.5	1294.1	1320.0	1371.6	1422.9	1474.2	1526.4	1578.6	1631.8
	S	0.5538	1.5376	1.5457	1.5610	1.5757	1.5889	1.6013	1.6127	1.6397	1.6647	1.7112	1.7536	1.7928	1.8298	1.8644	1.8974
225 (391.81)	V	0.0185	2.042	2.072	2.142	2.212	2.279	2.344	2.407	2.560	2.708	2.997	3.278	3.555	3.828	4.100	4.369
	H	366.11	1200.2	1205.8	1219.2	1232.3	1244.5	1256.2	1267.1	1293.7	1319.6	1371.4	1422.7	1474.1	1526.3	1578.5	1631.7
	S	0.5562	1.5358	1.5423	1.5577	1.5724	1.5858	1.5984	1.6099	1.6369	1.6619	1.7086	1.7510	1.7902	1.8272	1.8618	1.8948
230 (393.70)	V	0.0186	1.9989	2.021	2.091	2.160	2.226	2.289	2.352	2.502	2.647	2.930	3.205	3.477	3.744	4.010	4.274
	H	368.16	1200.4	1204.9	1218.3	1231.6	1243.8	1255.6	1266.7	1293.3	1319.3	1371.1	1422.5	1474.0	1526.2	1578.4	1631.6
	S	0.5585	1.5337	1.5390	1.5544	1.5693	1.5827	1.5954	1.6071	1.6341	1.6592	1.7059	1.7484	1.7877	1.8247	1.8593	1.8923
235 (395.56)	V	0.0186	1.9573	1.973	2.042	2.110	2.175	2.237	2.298	2.446	2.589	2.866	3.136	3.402	3.664	3.924	4.182
	H	370.17	1200.7	1203.9	1217.5	1230.8	1243.2	1255.0	1266.2	1292.9	1319.0	1370.9	1422.3	1473.8	1526.0	1578.3	1631.6
	S	0.5609	1.5320	1.5357	1.5513	1.5662	1.5798	1.5925	1.6043	1.6314	1.6566	1.7034	1.7459	1.7852	1.8222	1.8568	1.8899
240 (397.40)	V	0.0186	1.9176	.....	1.995	2.062	2.126	2.187	2.247	2.392	2.532	2.805	3.069	3.330	3.586	3.841	4.095
	H	372.16	1200.9	.....	1216.6	1230.0	1242.5	1254.4	1265.7	1292.5	1318.6	1370.5	1422.1	1473.6	1525.9	1578.2	1631.5
	S	0.5632	1.5301	.....	1.5482	1.5633	1.5770	1.5898	1.6017	1.6289	1.6541	1.7009	1.7435	1.7828	1.8199	1.8545	1.8876
245 (399.20)	V	0.0186	1.8797	.....	1.950	2.015	2.078	2.139	2.198	2.341	2.479	2.746	3.006	3.261	3.513	3.762	4.011
	H	374.11	1201.1	.....	1215.6	1229.1	1241.8	1253.8	1265.2	1292.0	1318.3	1370.3	1421.9	1473.5	1525.8	1578.1	1631.4
	S	0.5654	1.5283	.....	1.5450	1.5602	1.5742	1.5871	1.5991	1.6263	1.6517	1.6985	1.7411	1.7805	1.8176	1.8522	1.8853

Table B-2/ Superheated Steam (Continued)

Temperature, °F

Abs press., psia (sat. temp.)	V H S	Sat. water	Sat. steam	420	440	460	480	500	520	550	600	700	800	900	1000	1100	1200
250 (400.97)	V	0.0187	1.8431	1.9065	1.9711	2.0334	2.0932	2.1515	2.2085	2.2920	2.4272	2.6897	2.9444	3.1949	3.4416	3.6867	3.9299
	H	376.04	1201.4	1214.6	1228.3	1241.0	1253.2	1264.7	1274.5	1291.6	1317.9	1370.0	1421.7	1473.3	1525.6	1578.0	1631.3
	S	0.5677	1.5287	1.5419	1.5573	1.5713	1.5844	1.5965	1.6066	1.6238	1.6492	1.6961	1.7388	1.7782	1.8153	1.8500	1.8831
255 (402.71)	V	0.0187	1.8079	1.8686	1.9286	1.9899	2.0489	2.1065	2.1626	2.2447	2.3776	2.6354	2.8855	3.1313	3.3733	3.6138	3.8524
	H	377.91	1201.6	1213.7	1227.5	1240.3	1252.6	1264.2	1274.2	1291.2	1317.5	1369.8	1421.5	1473.2	1525.5	1577.9	1631.2
	S	0.5698	1.5249	1.5388	1.5543	1.5684	1.5816	1.5938	1.6041	1.6212	1.6466	1.6937	1.7364	1.7759	1.8130	1.8477	1.8808
260 (404.43)	V	0.0187	1.7742	1.8246	1.8876	1.9482	2.0063	2.0631	2.1185	2.1991	2.3299	2.5833	2.8289	3.0701	3.3077	3.5437	3.7778
	H	379.78	1201.8	1212.8	1226.6	1239.5	1252.0	1263.6	1273.8	1290.8	1317.1	1369.5	1421.3	1473.0	1525.4	1577.8	1631.1
	S	0.5720	1.5233	1.5359	1.5514	1.5656	1.5790	1.5912	1.6017	1.6188	1.6442	1.6914	1.7342	1.7737	1.8109	1.8456	1.8787
265 (406.12)	V	0.0187	1.7416	1.7858	1.8481	1.9080	1.9654	2.0213	2.0759	2.1554	2.2840	2.5331	2.7744	3.0114	3.2446	3.4761	3.7061
	H	381.62	1202.0	1211.9	1225.7	1238.7	1251.2	1263.0	1273.4	1290.4	1316.8	1369.3	1421.1	1472.9	1525.3	1577.7	1631.1
	S	0.5741	1.5217	1.5330	1.5485	1.5628	1.5762	1.5886	1.5993	1.6164	1.6419	1.6892	1.7320	1.7715	1.8087	1.8434	1.8765
270 (407.79)	V	0.0188	1.7101	1.7486	1.8101	1.8692	1.9259	1.9810	2.0350	2.1131	2.2399	2.4847	2.7219	2.9548	3.1838	3.4112	3.6370
	H	383.43	1202.2	1211.0	1224.9	1238.0	1250.6	1262.5	1273.0	1290.0	1316.4	1369.0	1420.9	1472.7	1525.1	1577.6	1631.0
	S	0.5761	1.5200	1.5301	1.5457	1.5601	1.5736	1.5861	1.5969	1.6140	1.6395	1.6869	1.7298	1.7693	1.8065	1.8413	1.8744
275 (409.44)	V	0.0188	1.6798	1.7127	1.7735	1.8318	1.8879	1.9422	1.9956	2.0725	2.1973	2.4382	2.6714	2.9002	3.1253	3.3486	3.5704
	H	385.22	1202.3	1210.0	1224.1	1237.3	1250.0	1262.0	1272.6	1289.5	1316.1	1368.7	1420.7	1472.6	1525.0	1577.5	1630.9
	S	0.5782	1.5183	1.5271	1.5429	1.5574	1.5711	1.5837	1.5946	1.6116	1.6373	1.6847	1.7277	1.7673	1.8045	1.8393	1.8724
280 (411.06)	V	0.0188	1.6504	1.6780	1.7381	1.7957	1.8512	1.9048	1.9575	2.0334	2.1562	2.3932	2.6226	2.8475	3.0688	3.2883	3.5062
	H	386.99	1202.5	1209.0	1223.2	1236.5	1249.4	1261.5	1272.2	1289.1	1315.7	1368.5	1420.5	1472.4	1524.9	1577.4	1630.8
	S	0.5802	1.5167	1.5241	1.5401	1.5547	1.5686	1.5813	1.5923	1.6093	1.6350	1.6826	1.7256	1.7652	1.8024	1.8372	1.8703
285 (412.66)	V	0.0188	1.6232	1.6446	1.7040	1.7610	1.8157	1.8687	1.9207	1.9955	2.1165	2.3499	2.5756	2.7968	3.0143	3.2300	3.4443
	H	388.74	1202.7	1208.0	1222.3	1235.6	1248.7	1260.9	1271.8	1288.6	1315.4	1368.2	1420.3	1472.2	1524.7	1577.3	1630.7
	S	0.5822	1.5153	1.5214	1 5375	1.5521	1.5662	1.5790	1.5902	1.6071	1.6330	1.6806	1.7237	1.7633	1.8005	1.8353	1.8684

290 (414.24)	V	0.0189	1.5947	1.6122	1.6710	1.7273	1.7815	1.8338	1.8853	1.9590	2.0783	2.3080	2.5302	2.7478	2.9616	3.1738	3.3844
	H	390.47	1202.9	1207.0	1221.4	1234.8	1248.0	1260.4	1271.4	1288.2	1315.0	1367.9	1420.1	1472.1	1524.6	1577.2	1630.6
	S	0.5841	1.5137	1.5184	1.5346	1.5493	1.5635	1.5766	1.5879	1.6048	1.6307	1.6784	1.7215	1.7612	1.7994	1.8332	1.8663
295 (415.80)	V	0.0189	1.5684	1.5809	1.6391	1.6948	1.7484	1.8001	1.8510	1.9236	2.0413	2.2677	2.4863	2.7004	2.9108	3.1195	3.3267
	H	392.17	1203.0	1206.1	1220.5	1234.0	1247.4	1259.8	1271.0	1287.8	1314.7	1367.6	1419.9	1472.0	1524.5	1577.1	1630.5
	S	0.5861	1.5122	1.5157	1.5319	1.5467	1.5611	1.5742	1.5857	1.6026	1.6286	1.6763	1.7195	1.7593	1.7965	1.8313	1.8644
300 (417.33)	V	0.0189	1.5426	1.5506	1.6082	1.6634	1.7164	1.7677	1.8172	1.8896	2.0056	2.2286	2.4447	2.6547	2.8634	3.0670	3.2707
	H	393.85	1203.2	1205.2	1219.5	1233.4	1246.6	1259.2	1270.5	1287.4	1314.4	1367.4	1419.7	1471.8	1524.4	1577.0	1630.4
	S	0.5879	1.5107	1.5130	1.5291	1.5443	1.5585	1.5718	1.5834	1.6004	1.6265	1.6742	1.7175	1.7572	1.7945	1.8294	1.8625
310 (420.35)	V	0.0189	1.4938	......	1.5495	1.6036	1.6555	1.7054	1.7546	1.8246	1.9375	2.1541	2.3631	2.5675	2.7682	2.9671	3.1645
	H	397.16	1203.5	......	1217.8	1231.5	1245.3	1258.0	1269.6	1286.4	1313.5	1366.9	1419.3	1471.5	1524.1	1576.8	1630.3
	S	0.5917	1.5079	......	1.5240	1.5391	1.5539	1.5673	1.5793	1.5962	1.6224	1.6705	1.7138	1.7536	1.7909	1.8258	1.8590
320 (423.29)	V	0.0190	1.4479	......	1.4943	1.5473	1.5982	1.6472	1.6954	1.7637	1.8737	2.0844	2.2874	2.4857	2.6804	2.8735	3.0648
	H	400.40	1203.8	......	1216.0	1229.9	1244.0	1256.8	1268.6	1285.6	1312.8	1366.3	1418.9	1471.2	1523.8	1576.6	1630.1
	S	0.5953	1.5052	......	1.5189	1.5342	1.5494	1.5629	1.5751	1.5922	1.6185	1.6667	1.7102	1.7501	1.7874	1.8224	1.8556
330 (426.16)	V	0.0190	1.4048	......	1.4424	1.4944	1.5445	1.5925	1.6397	1.7064	1.8138	2.0189	2.2163	2.4090	2.5981	2.7855	2.9712
	H	403.56	1204.0	......	1214.1	1228.2	1242.5	1255.5	1267.6	1284.7	1312.1	1365.8	1418.4	1470.8	1523.6	1576.4	1630.0
	S	0.5988	1.5023	......	1.5136	1.5291	1.5445	1.5582	1.5707	1.5879	1.6144	1.6628	1.7063	1.7463	1.7837	1.8187	1.8520
340 (428.96)	V	0.0191	1.3640	......	1.3935	1.4446	1.4936	1.5409	1.5872	1.6525	1.7573	1.9572	2.1493	2.3368	2.5206	2.7027	2.8831
	H	406.65	1204.2	......	1212.2	1226.5	1241.0	1254.2	1266.6	1283.8	1311.4	1365.2	1418.0	1470.5	1523.3	1576.2	1629.8
	S	0.6023	1.4997	......	1.5086	1.5243	1.5399	1.5538	1.5666	1.5839	1.6106	1.6591	1.7027	1.7428	1.7802	1.8152	1.8485
350 (431.71)	V	0.0191	1.3255	......	1.3472	1.3976	1.4460	1.4923	1.5377	1.6016	1.7041	1.8991	2.0863	2.2687	2.4475	2.6246	2.8000
	H	409.70	1204.4	......	1210.3	1224.8	1239.5	1252.9	1265.5	1282.9	1310.6	1364.7	1417.6	1470.2	1523.0	1576.0	1629.6
	S	0.6057	1.4972	......	1.5038	1.5197	1.5355	1.5496	1.5626	1.5801	1.6069	1.6556	1.6993	1.7395	1.7769	1.8120	1.8453
360 (434.39)	V	0.0192	1.2889	......	1.3035	1.3532	1.4008	1.4463	1.4909	1.5536	1.6538	1.8441	2.0266	2.2044	2.3784	2.5506	2.7213
	H	412.67	1204.5	......	1208.5	1223.1	1238.0	1251.5	1264.5	1282.0	1309.9	1364.1	1417.2	1469.9	1522.8	1575.8	1629.4
	S	0.6090	1.4946	......	1.4991	1.5151	1.5311	1.5453	1.5587	1.5763	1.6033	1.6521	1.6960	1.7362	1.7737	1.8088	1.8421

Table B-2/ Superheated Steam (Continued)

Temperature, °F

Abs press., psia (sat. temp.)	V H S	Sat. water	Sat. steam	460	480	500	520	540	560	580	600	700	800	900	1000	1100	1200
370 (437.01)	V	0.0192	1.2545	1.3111	1.3579	1.4028	1.4466	1.4881	1.5286	1.5675	1.6063	1.7921	1.9703	2.1435	2.3131	2.4809	2.6471
	H	415.58	1204.6	1221.4	1236.5	1250.2	1263.4	1275.2	1286.7	1298.3	1309.1	1363.6	1410.8	1469.6	1522.5	1575.6	1629.2
	S	0.6122	1.4921	1.5106	1.5268	1.5412	1.5548	1.5667	1.5781	1.5894	1.5997	1.6488	1.6928	1.7331	1.7706	1.8058	1.8391
380 (439.59)	V	0.0193	1.2217	1.2711	1.3173	1.3614	1.4045	1.4452	1.4850	1.5232	1.5612	1.7428	1.9168	2.0859	2.2512	2.4148	2.5768
	H	418.45	1204.7	1219.8	1235.0	1248.8	1262.3	1274.2	1286.0	1297.5	1308.4	1363.0	1416.4	1469.2	1522.2	1575.4	1629.1
	S	0.6154	1.4897	1.5063	1.5226	1.5371	1.5510	1.5630	1.5747	1.5859	1.5963	1.6455	1.6896	1.7299	1.7675	1.8027	1.8361
390 (442.11)	V	0.0193	1.1904	1.2332	1.2788	1.3222	1.3647	1.4046	1.4436	1.4812	1.5184	1.6961	1.8661	2.0311	2.1925	2.3521	2.5101
	H	421.27	1204.8	1218.0	1233.4	1247.4	1261.2	1273.2	1285.1	1296.7	1307.7	1362.5	1416.0	1468.9	1522.0	1575.2	1628.9
	S	0.6184	1.4872	1.5017	1.5183	1.5330	1.5472	1.5593	1.5711	1.5824	1.5929	1.6423	1.6865	1.7269	1.7646	1.7998	1.8332
400 (444.58)	V	0.0193	1.1609	1.1972	1.2422	1.2849	1.3269	1.3660	1.4042	1.4413	1.4777	1.6522	1.8179	1.9796	2.1367	2.2926	2.4475
	H	424.02	1204.9	1216.5	1231.6	1245.9	1259.9	1272.1	1284.3	1295.8	1307.0	1362.1	1415.5	1468.6	1521.5	1574.8	1628.8
	S	0.6215	1.4850	1.4977	1.5140	1.5290	1.5434	1.5561	1.5678	1.5790	1.5897	1.6393	1.6835	1.7240	1.7615	1.7968	1.8304
410 (447.00)	V	0.0194	1.1327	1.1628	1.2071	1.2494	1.2906	1.3291	1.3669	1.4033	1.4390	1.6095	1.7722	1.9297	2.0837	2.2359	2.3864
	H	426.74	1205.0	1214.6	1230.2	1244.5	1258.8	1271.2	1283.5	1295.1	1306.2	1361.4	1415.1	1468.3	1521.4	1574.8	1628.6
	S	0.6244	1.4828	1.4933	1.5101	1.5252	1.5399	1.5524	1.5646	1.5759	1.5865	1.6362	1.6806	1.7212	1.7589	1.7943	1.8277
420 (449.38)	V	0.0194	1.1058	1.1300	1.1738	1.2156	1.2561	1.2942	1.3312	1.3671	1.4021	1.5693	1.7285	1.8826	2.0332	2.1819	2.3290
	H	429.42	1205.0	1213.0	1228.6	1243.1	1257.5	1270.2	1282.6	1294.3	1305.5	1360.8	1414.6	1468.0	1521.2	1574.6	1628.4
	S	0.6273	1.4805	1.4892	1.5060	1.5213	1.5361	1.5489	1.5612	1.5726	1.5832	1.6331	1.6776	1.7184	1.7561	1.7915	1.8249
430 (451.72)	V	0.0195	1.0800	1.0986	1.1419	1.1834	1.2233	1.2607	1.2972	1.3326	1.3670	1.5309	1.6889	1.8377	1.9850	2.1305	2.2742
	H	432.05	1205.0	1211.2	1227.0	1241.7	1256.3	1269.1	1281.8	1293.5	1304.6	1360.3	1414.2	1467.6	1520.9	1574.4	1628.2
	S	0.6302	1.4782	1.4850	1.5020	1.5175	1.5326	1.5455	1.5581	1.5695	1.5801	1.6303	1.6748	1.7156	1.7534	1.7888	1.8222
440 (454.01)	V	0.0195	1.0554	1.0688	1.1116	1.1524	1.1918	1.2288	1.2648	1.2996	1.3334	1.4943	1.6472	1.7949	1.9390	2.0814	2.2220
	H	434.63	1205.0	1209.6	1225.3	1240.2	1255.0	1268.0	1280.9	1292.6	1303.9	1359.7	1413.8	1467.3	1520.6	1574.1	1628.0
	S	0.6330	1.4762	1.4812	1.4981	1.5138	1.5291	1.5422	1.5550	1.5664	1.5772	1.6275	1.6722	1.7130	1.7508	1.7862	1.8197

Abs. Press. (Sat. Temp.)																	
450 (456.27)	V	0.0195	1.0318	1.0401	1.0824	1.1230	1.1617	1.1982	1.2337	1.2681	1.3013	1.4593	1.6092	1.7539	1.8951	2.0345	2.1720
	H	437.18	1205.0	1207.9	1223.7	1238.7	1253.8	1266.9	1280.0	1291.8	1303.1	1359.1	1413.4	1467.0	1520.3	1573.9	1627.8
	S	0.6357	1.4739	1.4771	1.4941	1.5099	1.5255	1.5387	1.5517	1.5632	1.5740	1.6245	1.6694	1.7103	1.7481	1.7836	1.8171
460 (458.48)	V	0.0196	1.0092	....	1.0545	1.0946	1.1329	1.1690	1.2039	1.2379	1.2706	1.4258	1.5729	1.7147	1.8530	1.9896	2.1243
	H	439.69	1205.0	....	1222.0	1237.2	1252.5	1265.8	1279.0	1291.0	1302.3	1358.6	1413.0	1466.6	1520.0	1573.7	1627.7
	S	0.6384	1.4719	....	1.4902	1.5062	1.5220	1.5354	1.5485	1.5602	1.5710	1.6217	1.6667	1.7076	1.7455	1.7811	1.8146
470 (460.66)	V	0.0196	0.9875	....	1.0278	1.0676	1.1053	1.1410	1.1755	1.2091	1.2412	1.3937	1.5381	1.6772	1.8127	1.9466	2.0785
	H	442.17	1205.0	....	1220.2	1235.7	1251.2	1264.7	1278.0	1290.0	1301.5	1358.0	1412.5	1466.3	1519.8	1573.5	1627.5
	S	0.6411	1.4699	....	1.4862	1.5025	1.5185	1.5321	1.5453	1.5570	1.5680	1.6189	1.6639	1.7050	1.7429	1.7785	1.8120
480 (462.80)	V	0.0197	0.9668	....	1.0021	1.0416	1.0789	1.1141	1.1482	1.1813	1.2131	1.3630	1.5049	1.6413	1.7742	1.9054	2.0347
	H	444.60	1205.0	....	1218.6	1234.2	1249.9	1263.5	1277.0	1289.1	1300.8	1357.5	1412.1	1466.0	1519.5	1573.3	1627.3
	S	0.6436	1.4679	....	1.4825	1.4989	1.5151	1.5288	1.5422	1.5539	1.5650	1.6161	1.6612	1.7023	1.7402	1.7758	1.8093
490 (464.91)	V	0.0197	.9466	....	0.9774	1.0166	1.0535	1.0884	1.1220	1.1548	1.1860	1.3335	1.4729	1.6067	1.7371	1.8659	1.9927
	H	447.00	1205.0	....	1217.0	1232.7	1248.4	1262.3	1276.0	1288.3	1300.0	1356.9	1411.7	1465.6	1519.2	1573.1	1627.1
	S	0.6462	1.4659	....	1.4789	1.4954	1.5116	1.5256	1.5392	1.5511	1.5622	1.6135	1.6588	1.6999	1.7379	1.7736	1.8071
500 (467.00)	V	0.0197	0.9274	....	0.9538	0.9926	1.0290	1.0636	1.0969	1.1292	1.1600	1.3051	1.4417	1.5735	1.7016	1.8280	1.9532
	H	449.40	1204.9	....	1215.3	1231.4	1246.6	1261.1	1275.0	1287.3	1299.3	1356.3	1411.2	1465.1	1518.8	1572.9	1626.9
	S	0.6488	1.4641	....	1.4752	1.4922	1.5079	1.5225	1.5363	1.5482	1.5596	1.6110	1.6564	1.6975	1.7356	1.7714	1.8052
510 (469.05)	V	0.0198	0.9090	....	0.9310	0.9695	1.0056	1.0397	1.0727	1.1046	1.1350	1.2780	1.4127	1.5418	1.6675	1.7915	1.9135
	H	451.75	1204.8	....	1213.5	1229.6	1245.6	1259.9	1274.0	1286.6	1298.4	1355.7	1410.9	1465.0	1518.7	1572.6	1626.8
	S	0.6513	1.4621	....	1.4714	1.4883	1.5048	1.5192	1.5332	1.5454	1.5566	1.6082	1.6538	1.6951	1.7332	1.7689	1.8026
520 (471.07)	V	0.0198	0.8912	....	0.9091	0.9472	0.9829	1.0169	1.0494	1.0810	1.1110	1.2519	1.3844	1.5113	1.6347	1.7565	1.8763
	H	454.07	1204.7	....	1211.8	1228.1	1244.2	1258.6	1272.9	1285.6	1297.6	1355.1	1410.4	1464.6	1518.4	1572.4	1626.6
	S	0.6537	1.4601	....	1.4677	1.4849	1.5015	1.5160	1.5302	1.5425	1.5539	1.6057	1.6514	1.6928	1.7310	1.7668	1.8005
530 (473.05)	V	0.0199	0.8741	....	0.8879	0.9258	0.9612	0.9948	1.0269	1.0582	1.0878	1.2267	1.3571	1.4818	1.6031	1.7228	1.8402
	H	456.35	1204.6	....	1210.0	1226.5	1242.8	1257.3	1271.8	1284.8	1296.8	1354.6	1410.0	1464.3	1518.1	1572.2	1626.4
	S	0.6562	1.4584	....	1.4642	1.4816	1.4984	1.5130	1.5274	1.5400	1.5514	1.6035	1.6493	1.6908	1.7290	1.7648	1.7985

Table B-2/ Superheated Steam (Continued)

Abs press., psia (sat. temp.)	V H S	Sat. water	Sat. steam	500	520	540	560	580	600	650	700	750	800	900	1000	1100	1200
540 (475.02)	V	0.0199	0.8576	0.9051	0.9401	0.9736	1.0054	1.0363	1.0655	1.1356	1.2025	1.2671	1.3309	1.4535	1.5727	1.6903	1.8056
	H	458.62	1204.5	1225.0	1241.4	1256.1	1270.7	1283.8	1296.0	1325.6	1354.0	1382.1	1409.6	1463.9	1517.8	1572.0	1626.2
	S	0.6585	1.4565	1.4781	1.4950	1.5098	1.5243	1.5370	1.5486	1.5759	1.6009	1.6246	1.6469	1.6884	1.7266	1.7625	1.7962
550 (476.94)	V	0.0199	0.8416	0.8851	0.9198	0.9530	0.9846	1.0151	1.0441	1.1132	1.1791	1.2428	1.3055	1.4262	1.5434	1.6590	1.7724
	H	460.83	1204.4	1223.4	1240.0	1254.8	1269.6	1282.9	1295.2	1324.9	1353.5	1381.6	1409.2	1463.6	1517.5	1571.7	1626.0
	S	0.6609	1.4548	1.4748	1.4919	1.5068	1.5215	1.5344	1.5461	1.5735	1.5987	1.6224	1.6447	1.6862	1.7244	1.7603	1.7940
560 (478.85)	V	0.0200	0.8263	0.8658	0.9003	0.9332	0.9644	0.9947	1.0233	1.0917	1.1566	1.2193	1.2810	1.3998	1.5151	1.6289	1.7403
	H	463.04	1204.3	1221.8	1238.5	1253.5	1268.5	1282.0	1294.4	1324.2	1352.9	1381.1	1408.7	1463.2	1517.2	1571.5	1625.8
	S	0.6632	1.4530	1.4714	1.4886	1.5038	1.5187	1.5318	1.5436	1.5711	1.5964	1.6202	1.6425	1.6841	1.7224	1.7584	1.7921
570 (480.73)	V	0.0200	0.8114	0.8472	0.8814	0.9141	0.9450	0.9749	1.0033	1.0708	1.1348	1.1966	1.2575	1.3744	1.4879	1.5998	1.7093
	H	465.22	1204.1	1220.2	1236.9	1252.2	1267.3	1281.0	1293.5	1323.5	1352.3	1380.6	1408.3	1462.9	1517.0	1571.3	1625.6
	S	0.6655	1.4512	1.4681	1.4853	1.5008	1.5156	1.5291	1.5410	1.5686	1.5940	1.6179	1.6403	1.6820	1.7204	1.7564	1.7901
580 (482.58)	V	0.0201	0.7968	0.8291	0.8631	0.8956	0.9263	0.9558	0.9839	1.0506	1.1137	1.1747	1.2347	1.3498	1.4618	1.5714	1.6794
	H	467.37	1204.0	1218.6	1235.5	1250.9	1266.1	1280.0	1292.6	1322.8	1351.6	1380.0	1407.8	1462.5	1516.7	1571.0	1625.4
	S	0.6677	1.4494	1.4648	1.4822	1.4978	1.5128	1.5264	1.5384	1.5662	1.5916	1.6156	1.6381	1.6799	1.7183	1.7543	1.7881
590 (484.41)	V	0.0201	0.7831	0.8116	0.8455	0.8778	0.9082	0.9373	0.9653	1.0310	1.0934	1.1535	1.2128	1.3262	1.4360	1.5442	1.6505
	H	469.50	1203.8	1217.0	1234.0	1249.6	1265.0	1278.9	1291.8	1322.1	1351.1	1379.5	1407.4	1462.2	1516.4	1570.8	1625.3
	S	0.6699	1.4477	1.4616	1.4791	1.4949	1.5101	1.5236	1.5359	1.5638	1.5894	1.6134	1.6360	1.6778	1.7162	1.7522	1.7861
600 (486.21)	V	0.0201	0.7695	0.7945	0.8284	0.8605	0.8907	0.9194	0.9471	1.0123	1.0738	1.1332	1.1915	1.3032	1.4115	1.5179	1.6224
	H	471.59	1203.6	1215.6	1232.5	1248.3	1263.7	1278.1	1290.9	1321.4	1350.5	1379.0	1407.0	1461.8	1516.0	1570.5	1625.0
	S	0.6721	1.4460	1.4586	1.4760	1.4920	1.5072	1.5212	1.5334	1.5615	1.5871	1.6112	1.6339	1.6757	1.7141	1.7502	1.7841
610 (487.99)	V	0.0202	0.7565	0.7781	0.8120	0.8436	0.8736	0.9022	0.9296	0.9942	1.0548	1.1135	1.1708	1.2809	1.3878	1.4928	1.5964
	H	473.67	1203.5	1213.8	1230.9	1246.9	1262.5	1276.8	1290.0	1320.6	1350.0	1378.5	1406.5	1461.5	1515.8	1570.3	1624.9
	S	0.6743	1.4444	1.4552	1.4728	1.4890	1.5044	1.5183	1.5309	1.5591	1.5850	1.6091	1.6318	1.6738	1.7123	1.7484	1.7823

Temperature, °F

Abs. Press. lb/sq in. (Sat. Temp.)																
620 (489.75)	V	0.0202		0.7622	0.7960	0.8275	0.8572	0.8856	0.9127	0.9765	1.0364	1.0943	1.1505	1.2596	1.3648	1.4677	1.5707
	H	475.72		1212.2	1229.5	1245.5	1261.3	1275.8	1289.1	1319.9	1349.2	1377.9	1406.1	1461.2	1515.5	1570.5	1624.7
	S	0.6764		1.4520	1.4698	1.4860	1.5016	1.5157	1.5284	1.5568	1.5827	1.6068	1.6296	1.6717	1.7102	1.7464	1.7803
630 (491.49)	V	0.0202		0.7466	0.7802	0.8117	0.8413	0.8694	0.8963	0.9595	1.0187	1.0757	1.1312	1.2387	1.3423	1.4445	1.5449
	H	477.75		1210.6	1227.8	1244.1	1260.1	1274.7	1288.3	1319.2	1348.7	1377.4	1405.7	1460.8	1515.2	1569.9	1624.5
	S	0.6785		1.4488	1.4665	1.4830	1.4988	1.5130	1.5260	1.5545	1.5805	1.6047	1.6276	1.6697	1.7083	1.7445	1.7784
640 (493.21)	V	0.0203		0.7317	0.7651	0.7963	0.8258	0.8537	0.8804	0.9429	1.0015	1.0578	1.1124	1.2187	1.3210	1.4213	1.5193
	H	479.79		1209.0	1226.3	1242.7	1258.9	1273.6	1287.4	1318.5	1348.2	1376.8	1405.2	1460.5	1515.0	1569.7	1624.3
	S	0.6806		1.4458	1.4636	1.4802	1.4962	1.5105	1.5236	1.5523	1.5785	1.6026	1.6256	1.6678	1.7065	1.7427	1.7766
650 (494.90)	V	0.0203		0.7171	0.7504	0.7816	0.8107	0.8384	0.8648	0.9269	0.9846	1.0404	1.0944	1.1988	1.2999	1.3987	1.4958
	H	481.73		1207.3	1224.8	1241.3	1257.6	1272.5	1286.5	1317.8	1347.6	1376.3	1404.7	1460.1	1514.7	1569.4	1624.1
	S	0.6826		1.4427	1.4607	1.4774	1.4935	1.5080	1.5213	1.5501	1.5764	1.6006	1.6236	1.6659	1.7046	1.7408	1.7748
660 (496.58)	V	0.0204	0.6969	0.7031	0.7361	0.7672	0.7962	0.8237	0.8499	0.9113	0.9686	1.0234	1.0769	1.1803	1.2797	1.3774	1.4727
	H	483.77	1202.5	1205.7	1223.2	1240.0	1256.4	1271.4	1285.5	1317.1	1347.0	1375.8	1404.3	1459.7	1514.4	1569.2	1624.0
	S	0.6847	1.4363	1.4396	1.4576	1.4746	1.4908	1.5054	1.5188	1.5479	1.5742	1.5985	1.6216	1.6639	1.7027	1.7390	1.7730
670 (498.23)	V	0.0204	0.6861	0.6892	0.7224	0.7531	0.7820	0.8093	0.8354	0.8963	0.9527	1.0072	1.0599	1.1617	1.2600	1.3560	1.4503
	H	485.61	1202.3	1204.0	1221.7	1238.7	1255.1	1270.2	1284.5	1316.3	1346.3	1375.3	1403.9	1459.4	1514.1	1569.0	1623.8
	S	0.6867	1.4349	1.4367	1.4549	1.4721	1.4883	1.5030	1.5166	1.5459	1.5723	1.5968	1.6200	1.6624	1.7012	1.7376	1.7716
680 (499.87)	V	0.0204	0.6757	....	0.7089	0.7397	0.7683	0.7954	0.8212	0.8814	0.9375	0.9912	1.0432	1.1440	1.2408	1.3357	1.4283
	H	487.64	1202.1	....	1220.2	1237.3	1253.9	1269.1	1283.6	1315.6	1345.8	1374.7	1403.4	1459.0	1513.8	1568.7	1623.6
	S	0.6886	1.4332	....	1.4519	1.4692	1.4856	1.5004	1.5142	1.5437	1.5703	1.5947	1.6179	1.6603	1.6992	1.7356	1.7697
690 (501.49)	V	0.0205	0.6652	....	0.6956	0.7263	0.7549	0.7818	0.8075	0.8675	0.9225	0.9758	1.0272	1.1267	1.2223	1.3162	1.4075
	H	489.56	1201.8	....	1218.5	1235.8	1252.5	1268.0	1282.7	1314.9	1345.1	1374.2	1402.8	1458.7	1513.6	1568.5	1623.4
	S	0.6906	1.4316	....	1.4488	1.4663	1.4828	1.4978	1.5118	1.5415	1.5681	1.5927	1.6159	1.6586	1.6975	1.7339	1.7680
700 (503.09)	V	0.0205	0.6552	....	0.6830	0.7133	0.7419	0.7687	0.7941	0.8534	0.9084	0.9608	1.0117	1.1096	1.2043	1.2965	1.3870
	H	491.49	1201.6	....	1217.1	1234.7	1251.3	1266.8	1281.9	1314.3	1344.6	1373.7	1402.5	1458.2	1513.4	1568.2	1623.3
	S	0.6925	1.4301	....	1.4461	1.4638	1.4803	1.4953	1.5097	1.5396	1.5663	1.5908	1.6141	1.6567	1.6958	1.7321	1.7663

Table B-2/ Superheated Steam (Continued)

Abs press., psia (sat. temp.)		Sat. water	Sat. steam	520	540	560	580	600	620	650	700	750	800	900	1000	1130	1200
725 (507.01)	V	0.0206	0.6314	0.6524	0.6827	0.7109	0.7373	0.7624	0.7864	0.8203	0.8740	0.9250	0.9745	1.0697	1.1612	1.2511	1.3383
	H	496.2	1200.9	1212.8	1230.9	1248.0	1264.0	1279.1	1293.8	1312.3	1343.0	1372.3	1401.3	1457.4	1512.5	1567.7	1622.7
	S	0.6973	1.4263	1.4385	1.4568	1.4737	1.4892	1.5036	1.5173	1.5342	1.5612	1.5859	1.6094	1.6522	1.6913	1.7279	1.7621
750 (510.83)	V	0.0207	0.6091	0.6237	0.6538	0.6818	0.7080	0.7326	0.7561	0.7896	0.8419	0.8918	0.9399	1.0326	1.1212	1.2078	1.2928
	H	500.8	1200.2	1208.8	1227.4	1244.9	1261.0	1276.6	1291.4	1310.5	1341.5	1371.0	1400.2	1456.5	1511.8	1567.1	1622.3
	S	0.7019	1.4225	1.4313	1.4501	1.4674	1.4830	1.4979	1.5117	1.5291	1.5564	1.5813	1.6049	1.6479	1.6871	1.7237	1.7580
775 (514.57)	V	0.0208	0.5882	0.5969	0.6268	0.6545	0.6803	0.7047	0.7278	0.7607	0.8119	0.8606	0.9073	0.9977	1.0838	1.1676	1.2505
	H	505.3	1199.5	1204.7	1223.7	1241.5	1258.2	1271.9	1289.0	1308.6	1340.0	1369.7	1399.0	1455.6	1511.1	1566.6	1621.8
	S	0.7064	1.4189	1.4242	1.4434	1.4610	1.4772	1.4902	1.5062	1.5241	1.5518	1.5769	1.6006	1.6438	1.6832	1.7200	1.7543
800 (518.20)	V	0.0209	0.5685	0.5714	0.6013	0.6288	0.6545	0.6785	0.7013	0.7336	0.7838	0.8313	0.8770	0.9648	1.0486	1.1302	1.2105
	H	509.7	1198.8	1200.3	1220.0	1238.2	1255.3	1271.4	1286.5	1306.6	1338.4	1368.5	1397.8	1454.9	1510.5	1566.0	1621.4
	S	0.7108	1.4155	1.4170	1.4369	1.4549	1.4715	1.4888	1.5009	1.5195	1.5473	1.5727	1.5964	1.6400	1.6794	1.7162	1.7506
825 (521.75)	V	0.0210	0.5500		0.5774	0.6046	0.6300	0.6539	0.6763	0.7081	0.7573	0.8038	0.8483	0.9338	1.0155	1.0950	1.1727
	H	514.0	1198.0		1216.1	1234.9	1252.1	1268.5	1284.0	1304.8	1336.8	1367.0	1396.6	1453.8	1509.7	1565.4	1620.8
	S	0.7152	1.4121		1.4304	1.4490	1.4657	1.4813	1.4958	1.5148	1.5430	1.5685	1.5925	1.6362	1.6758	1.7127	1.7471
850 (525.23)	V	0.0210	0.5326		0.5545	0.5817	0.6070	0.6306	0.6528	0.6841	0.7323	0.7779	0.8213	0.9048	0.9845	1.0619	1.1375
	H	518.3	1197.2		1212.4	1231.5	1249.1	1265.7	1281.4	1302.9	1335.2	1365.7	1395.4	1452.8	1509.0	1564.8	1620.4
	S	0.7194	1.4087		1.4240	1.4429	1.4600	1.4758	1.4905	1.5101	1.5386	1.5643	1.5883	1.6321	1.6720	1.7090	1.7435
875 (528.62)	V	0.0211	0.5162		0.5327	0.5601	0.5851	0.6085	0.6305	0.6615	0.7087	0.7535	0.7960	0.8773	0.9554	1.0306	1.1045
	H	522.4	1196.4		1208.4	1228.0	1246.0	1263.0	1279.0	1300.9	1333.5	1364.4	1394.2	1451.9	1508.3	1564.3	1619.9
	S	0.7236	1.4056		1.4177	1.4371	1.4546	1.4708	1.4858	1.5058	1.5345	1.5606	1.5847	1.6287	1.6687	1.7058	1.7403
900 (531.94)	V	0.0212	0.5006		0.5123	0.5394	0.5644	0.5876	0.6094	0.6399	0.6866	0.7304	0.7720	0.8516	0.9277	1.0010	1.0727
	H	526.6	1195.6		1204.0	1224.2	1242.6	1260.0	1276.5	1298.5	1331.8	1363.0	1392.9	1451.1	1507.8	1563.7	1619.3
	S	0.7276	1.4022		1.4106	1.4306	1.4484	1.4649	1.4803	1.5004	1.5296	1.5559	1.5801	1.6245	1.6647	1.7017	1.7362

Temperature, °F

925 (535.20)	V	0.0213	0.4858	0.4927	0.5199	0.5448	0.5678	0.5894	0.6196	0.6655	0.7085	0.7494	0.8272	0.9014	0.9731	1.0432
	H	530.6	1194.7	1200.0	1220.8	1239.6	1257.0	1273.9	1296.7	1330.2	1361.7	1391.7	1450.7	1506.9	1563.1	1618.9
	S	0.7316	1.3991	1.4044	1.4250	1.4433	1.4599	1.4757	1.4965	1.5260	1.5526	1.5769	1.6214	1.6618	1.6990	1.7337
950 (538.38)	V	0.0214	0.4717	0.4741	0.5014	0.5262	0.5491	0.5705	0.6003	0.6456	0.6877	0.7277	0.8039	0.8766	0.9465	1.0148
	H	534.6	1193.8	1195.8	1217.0	1236.4	1254.1	1271.3	1294.5	1328.5	1360.3	1390.5	1449.1	1506.1	1562.6	1618.5
	S	0.7355	1.3960	1.3980	1.4190	1.4378	1.4547	1.4708	1.4920	1.5220	1.5488	1.5733	1.6180	1.6584	1.6958	1.7305
975 (541.50)	V	0.0215	0.4583	....	0.4835	0.5083	0.5311	0.5524	0.5820	0.6266	0.6680	0.7073	0.7820	0.8533	0.9214	0.9880
	H	538.5	1192.9	....	1213.0	1233.0	1251.2	1268.7	1292.1	1326.7	1358.8	1389.2	1448.2	1505.2	1562.0	1618.0
	S	0.7393	1.3929	....	1.4128	1.4322	1.4495	1.4659	1.4873	1.5178	1.5449	1.5695	1.6145	1.6551	1.6926	1.7274
1000 (544.56)	V	0.0216	0.4456	....	0.4665	0.4914	0.5141	0.5351	0.5639	0.6085	0.6492	0.6879	0.7611	0.8306	0.8974	0.9626
	H	542.4	1191.9	....	1208.8	1229.4	1248.2	1265.8	1289.6	1324.9	1357.2	1388.0	1447.3	1504.7	1561.3	1617.5
	S	0.7468	1.3899	....	1.4066	1.4266	1.4445	1.4610	1.4827	1.5138	1.5411	1.5660	1.6113	1.6520	1.6895	1.7244
1025 (547.57)	V	0.0217	0.4334	....	0.4498	0.4751	0.4978	0.5188	0.5479	0.5913	0.6314	0.6695	0.7413	0.8095	0.8746	0.9384
	H	546.1	1191.0	....	1204.5	1225.9	1245.2	1263.0	1287.6	1323.1	1355.7	1386.8	1446.6	1504.1	1560.6	1617.0
	S	0.7431	1.3871	....	1.4004	1.4212	1.4396	1.4562	1.4787	1.5100	1.5375	1.5627	1.6082	1.6491	1.6866	1.7216
1050 (550.52)	V	0.0218	0.4219	....	0.4345	0.4596	0.4822	0.5031	0.5320	0.5749	0.6143	0.6519	0.7223	0.7892	0.8531	0.9154
	H	550.0	1190.0	....	1200.5	1222.4	1241.9	1260.2	1285.1	1321.3	1354.2	1385.6	1445.4	1503.6	1560.0	1616.5
	S	0.7504	1.3839	....	1.3942	1.4155	1.4341	1.4512	1.4739	1.5058	1.5336	1.5590	1.6047	1.6458	1.6833	1.7184
1075 (553.42)	V	0.0219	0.4108	....	0.4195	0.4446	0.4672	0.4879	0.5169	0.5592	0.5980	0.6349	0.7042	0.7696	0.8322	0.8933
	H	553.7	1188.9	....	1196.3	1218.7	1238.8	1257.2	1282.8	1319.4	1352.6	1384.1	1444.3	1502.5	1559.3	1615.9
	S	0.7540	1.3810	....	1.3883	1.4100	1.4292	1.4464	1.4698	1.5020	1.5300	1.5555	1.6015	1.6428	1.6804	1.7156
1100 (556.26)	V	0.0219	0.4002	....	0.4054	0.4304	0.4530	0.4736	0.5027	0.5445	0.5828	0.6190	0.6871	0.7511	0.8125	0.8724
	H	557.4	1187.8	....	1192.3	1214.9	1235.6	1254.5	1280.6	1317.8	1351.3	1383.0	1443.6	1501.7	1558.7	1615.4
	S	0.7575	1.3780	....	1.3824	1.4044	1.4241	1.4418	1.4656	1.4984	1.5287	1.5523	1.5986	1.6398	1.6776	1.7128
1125 (559.07)	V	0.0220	0.3902	....	....	0.4167	0.4392	0.4598	0.4883	0.5301	0.5678	0.6036	0.6706	0.7333	0.7938	0.8524
	H	561.0	1186.7	....	....	1211.3	1232.2	1251.5	1277.7	1315.9	1349.6	1381.7	1442.6	1500.8	1558.2	1614.9
	S	0.7610	1.3752	....	....	1.3991	1.4190	1.4370	1.4610	1.4946	1.5231	1.5491	1.5956	1.6369	1.6749	1.7101

Table B-2/ Superheated Steam (Continued)

Temperature, °F

Abs press., psia (sat. temp.)	V H S	Sat. water	Sat. steam	580	600	620	640	660	680	700	720	750	800	900	1000	1100	1200
1150 (561.81)	V	0.0221	0.3804	0.4035	0.4259	0.4468	0.4659	0.4839	0.5005	0.5165	0.5317	0.5537	0.5889	0.6549	0.7166	0.7760	0.8333
	H	564.6	1185.6	1207.4	1228.7	1248.6	1266.9	1284.4	1299.5	1314.1	1327.9	1348.1	1380.4	1441.7	1500.2	1557.8	1614.5
	S	0.7644	1.3723	1.3934	1.4137	1.4323	1.4491	1.4649	1.4783	1.4910	1.5028	1.5197	1.5458	1.5926	1.6341	1.6723	1.7075
1175 (564.54)	V	0.0222	0.3710	0.3911	0.4133	0.4339	0.4530	0.4708	0.4874	0.5032	0.5183	0.5400	0.5747	0.6396	0.7005	0.7586	0.8149
	H	568.2	1184.4	1203.6	1225.4	1245.4	1264.6	1281.5	1297.3	1312.1	1326.1	1346.4	1379.0	1440.6	1499.4	1557.0	1614.0
	S	0.7678	1.3694	1.3880	1.4088	1.4275	1.4451	1.4603	1.4743	1.4872	1.4991	1.5161	1.5425	1.5896	1.6313	1.6694	1.7048
1200 (567.19)	V	0.0223	0.3620	0.3793	0.4013	0.4219	0.4408	0.4585	0.4750	0.4907	0.5056	0.5271	0.5613	0.6251	0.6853	0.7423	0.7975
	H	571.7	1183.2	1200.2	1222.1	1242.6	1261.5	1279.2	1295.3	1310.3	1324.4	1345.0	1377.7	1439.5	1499.0	1556.6	1613.6
	S	0.7712	1.3667	1.3831	1.4040	1.4232	1.4405	1.4565	1.4707	1.4838	1.4958	1.5131	1.5395	1.5867	1.6289	1.6671	1.7025
1225 (569.82)	V	0.0224	0.3534	0.3669	0.3895	0.4102	0.4290	0.4466	0.4631	0.4786	0.4934	0.5146	0.5483	0.6113	0.6702	0.7264	0.7806
	H	575.1	1182.0	1195.6	1218.6	1239.7	1258.8	1276.7	1293.3	1308.3	1322.7	1343.3	1376.4	1438.6	1498.0	1556.0	1613.0
	S	0.7745	1.3640	1.3771	1.3990	1.4188	1.4363	1.4524	1.4671	1.4802	1.4925	1.5097	1.5365	1.5840	1.6262	1.6646	1.7000
1250 (572.39)	V	0.0225	0.3453	0.3549	0.3782	0.3991	0.4177	0.4354	0.4517	0.4672	0.4817	0.5027	0.5360	0.5980	0.6558	0.7113	0.7644
	H	578.6	1180.8	1190.9	1215.0	1236.7	1256.0	1274.5	1291.2	1306.6	1321.0	1341.9	1375.2	1437.7	1497.1	1555.4	1612.6
	S	0.7777	1.3612	1.3710	1.3939	1.4142	1.4319	1.4486	1.4634	1.4768	1.4891	1.5066	1.5335	1.5813	1.6235	1.6620	1.6975
1275 (574.93)	V	0.0226	0.3371	0.3437	0.3672	0.3881	0.4068	0.4244	0.4406	0.4560	0.4705	0.4912	0.5241	0.5852	0.6420	0.6966	0.7488
	H	582.0	1179.5	1186.5	1211.2	1233.5	1253.3	1272.0	1289.0	1304.6	1319.4	1340.3	1373.9	1436.7	1496.3	1554.7	1612.0
	S	0.7809	1.3584	1.3651	1.3887	1.4095	1.4277	1.4445	1.4596	1.4732	1.4858	1.5033	1.5305	1.5785	1.6207	1.6594	1.6950
1300 (577.43)	V	0.0227	0.3294	0.3329	0.3567	0.3776	0.3965	0.4140	0.4301	0.4453	0.4598	0.4803	0.5127	0.5730	0.6290	0.6826	0.7340
	H	585.4	1178.3	1182.0	1207.7	1230.3	1250.6	1269.6	1287.0	1302.8	1317.8	1338.9	1372.6	1435.8	1495.7	1554.2	1611.6
	S	0.7840	1.3557	1.3593	1.3837	1.4049	1.4235	1.4406	1.4560	1.4698	1.4826	1.5002	1.5275	1.5758	1.6183	1.6570	1.6926
1325 (579.89)	V	0.0228	0.3220	....	0.3463	0.3673	0.3863	0.4037	0.4200	0.4350	0.4493	0.4696	0.5016	0.5611	0.6162	0.6689	0.7195
	H	588.7	1177.0	....	1203.8	1227.0	1247.8	1267.0	1285.0	1300.8	1315.9	1337.3	1371.2	1434.8	1494.9	1553.4	1611.0
	S	0.7871	1.3530	....	1.3785	1.4002	1.4193	1.4366	1.4525	1.4663	1.4792	1.4971	1.5246	1.5731	1.6158	1.6545	1.6903

Press. (°F)		P1	P2	P3	P4	P5	P6	P7	P8	P9	P10	P11	P12	P13	P14	P15	P16
1350 (582.32)	V	0.0229	0.3147	....	0.3363	0.3576	0.3766	0.3940	0.4105	0.4252	0.4393	0.4594	0.4911	0.5497	0.6042	0.6559	0.7057
	H	592.1	1175.8	....	1200.0	1223.8	1245.0	1264.6	1283.2	1299.1	1314.2	1335.8	1370.0	1433.8	1494.3	1552.8	1610.6
	S	0.7902	1.3504	....	1.3734	1.3957	1.4151	1.4328	1.4492	1.4631	1.4760	1.4941	1.5218	1.5705	1.6134	1.6521	1.6881
1375 (584.71)	V	0.0230	0.3078	....	0.3266	0.3480	0.3670	0.3847	0.4007	0.4154	0.4295	0.4494	0.4808	0.5387	0.5922	0.6432	0.6922
	H	595.3	1174.5	....	1195.8	1220.2	1242.0	1262.1	1280.7	1296.8	1312.3	1334.1	1368.6	1432.8	1493.2	1552.0	1609.9
	S	0.7932	1.3477	....	1.3680	1.3908	1.4108	1.4289	1.4453	1.4593	1.4726	1.4908	1.5188	1.5678	1.6107	1.6496	1.6856
1400 (587.07)	V	0.0231	0.3011	....	0.3172	0.3388	0.3581	0.3760	0.3914	0.4063	0.4203	0.4401	0.4711	0.5283	0.5811	0.6313	0.6795
	H	598.6	1173.2	....	1191.8	1216.9	1239.2	1260.1	1278.2	1294.9	1310.6	1332.8	1367.4	1431.9	1492.7	1551.7	1609.6
	S	0.7963	1.3452	....	1.3629	1.3863	1.4068	1.4256	1.4416	1.4562	1.4696	1.4882	1.5162	1.5654	1.6086	1.6476	1.6836
1425 (589.40)	V	0.0232	0.2947	....	0.3081	0.3297	0.3491	0.3668	0.3825	0.3972	0.4112	0.4308	0.4616	0.5180	0.5701	0.6195	0.6671
	H	601.8	1171.8	....	1187.7	1213.2	1236.2	1257.2	1275.8	1292.9	1308.9	1331.1	1366.1	1431.0	1491.8	1551.0	1609.1
	S	0.7992	1.3425	....	1.3576	1.3814	1.4025	1.4215	1.4379	1.4528	1.4665	1.4850	1.5134	1.5629	1.6061	1.6453	1.6814
1450 (591.70)	V	0.0233	0.2885	....	0.2991	0.3211	0.3405	0.3580	0.3739	0.3885	0.4025	0.4220	0.4524	0.5082	0.5597	0.6083	0.6552
	H	605.0	1170.5	....	1183.2	1209.7	1233.1	1254.3	1273.5	1290.6	1307.0	1329.7	1364.8	1430.1	1491.3	1550.4	1608.6
	S	0.8022	1.3401	....	1.3521	1.3769	1.3994	1.4175	1.4345	1.4493	1.4634	1.4824	1.5108	1.5606	1.6041	1.6432	1.6794
1475 (593.97)	V	0.0234	0.2824	....	0.2903	0.3126	0.3318	0.3495	0.3654	0.3801	0.3939	0.4129	0.4435	0.4986	0.5493	0.5973	0.6439
	H	608.2	1169.1	....	1178.7	1206.2	1229.7	1251.5	1271.0	1288.8	1305.0	1327.4	1363.5	1429.1	1490.3	1549.8	1608.4
	S	0.8052	1.3375	....	1.3466	1.3723	1.3939	1.4135	1.4308	1.4463	1.4601	1.4789	1.5081	1.5582	1.6016	1.6410	1.6774
1500 (596.20)	V	0.0235	0.2765	....	0.2817	0.3044	0.3236	0.3413	0.3573	0.3721	0.3856	0.4042	0.4349	0.4894	0.5396	0.5869	0.6332
	H	611.4	1167.7	....	1174.2	1202.5	1226.4	1248.5	1268.6	1286.8	1303.0	1325.4	1362.1	1428.1	1489.8	1549.3	1608.4
	S	0.8081	1.3350	....	1.3411	1.3676	1.3895	1.4094	1.4272	1.4431	1.4569	1.4757	1.5054	1.5558	1.5995	1.6390	1.6757
1525 (598.41)	V	0.0236	0.2708	....	....	0.2962	0.3158	0.3335	0.3495	0.3642	0.3777	0.3965	0.4265	0.4804	0.5299	0.5766	0.6218
	H	614.5	1166.2	....	....	1198.6	1223.5	1245.8	1266.2	1284.7	1301.2	1324.1	1360.7	1427.0	1488.9	1548.6	1607.4
	S	0.8109	1.3323	....	....	1.3626	1.3855	1.4055	1.4236	1.4397	1.4538	1.4730	1.5026	1.5532	1.5971	1.6367	1.6732
1550 (600.59)	V	0.0237	0.2653	....	....	0.2883	0.3084	0.3261	0.3420	0.3567	0.3702	0.3891	0.4185	0.4719	0.5208	0.5669	0.6113
	H	617.7	1164.8	....	....	1194.5	1220.5	1243.3	1264.0	1282.7	1299.6	1323.0	1359.4	1426.2	1488.3	1548.2	1607.0
	S	0.8138	1.3298	....	....	1.3576	1.3814	1.4020	1.4203	1.4365	1.4510	1.4706	1.5001	1.5511	1.5951	1.6348	1.6713

Table B-2/ Superheated Steam (Continued)

Temperature, °F

Abs press., psia (sat. temp.)	V H S	Sat. water	Sat. steam	620	640	660	680	700	720	740	760	780	800	900	1000	1100	1200
1575 (602.74)	V	0.0238	0.2599	0.2804	0.3008	0.3186	0.3345	0.3492	0.3627	0.3755	0.3877	0.3993	0.4105	0.4633	0.5117	0.5573	0.6010
	H	620.8	1163.4	1190.3	1216.9	1240.3	1261.3	1280.5	1297.6	1313.5	1328.8	1343.5	1357.8	1424.9	1487.3	1547.4	1606.2
	S	0.8166	1.3273	1.3524	1.3768	1.3979	1.4165	1.4332	1.4478	1.4612	1.4738	1.4858	1.4972	1.5485	1.5927	1.6325	1.6691
1600 (604.87)	V	0.0239	0.2548	0.2730	0.2935	0.3114	0.3274	0.3421	0.3555	0.3682	0.3802	0.3919	0.4031	0.4554	0.5032	0.5482	0.5914
	H	623.9	1161.9	1186.3	1213.7	1237.6	1258.9	1278.4	1295.7	1311.8	1327.3	1342.2	1356.7	1424.1	1486.8	1547.0	1605.8
	S	0.8195	1.3249	1.3477	1.3728	1.3943	1.4132	1.4302	1.4449	1.4585	1.4713	1.4834	1.4950	1.5465	1.5909	1.6308	1.6674
1625 (606.97)	V	0.0240	0.2497	0.2656	0.2864	0.3044	0.3203	0.3348	0.3484	0.3610	0.3729	0.3845	0.3957	0.4474	0.4948	0.5391	0.5816
	H	627.0	1160.4	1182.1	1210.2	1234.5	1256.2	1275.9	1293.5	1310.0	1325.5	1340.6	1355.2	1423.0	1486.0	1546.3	1605.2
	S	0.8222	1.3223	1.3425	1.3683	1.3902	1.4094	1.4266	1.4416	1.4555	1.4683	1.4806	1.4923	1.5440	1.5887	1.6287	1.6652
1650 (609.05)	V	0.0241	0.2448	0.2583	0.2794	0.2976	0.3136	0.3280	0.3417	0.3542	0.3661	0.3776	0.3887	0.4399	0.4867	0.5305	0.5724
	H	630.0	1158.8	1177.6	1206.8	1231.7	1253.7	1273.6	1291.8	1308.4	1324.1	1339.3	1354.0	1422.1	1485.3	1545.7	1604.7
	S	0.8250	1.3198	1.3373	1.3641	1.3865	1.4060	1.4233	1.4389	1.4528	1.4658	1.4782	1.4899	1.5420	1.5867	1.6268	1.6634
1675 (611.10)	V	0.0242	0.2401	0.2511	0.2726	0.2909	0.3069	0.3214	0.3350	0.3474	0.3592	0.3706	0.3817	0.4324	0.4787	0.5220	0.5634
	H	633.1	1157.2	1173.1	1203.2	1228.7	1251.0	1271.5	1289.7	1306.4	1322.2	1337.5	1352.5	1420.9	1484.4	1545.0	1604.1
	S	0.8278	1.3173	1.3321	1.3597	1.3827	1.4024	1.4203	1.4358	1.4499	1.4629	1.4754	1.4874	1.5396	1.5846	1.6248	1.6615
1700 (613.12)	V	0.0243	0.2354	0.2441	0.2659	0.2844	0.3006	0.3152	0.3286	0.3411	0.3528	0.3641	0.3750	0.4254	0.4711	0.5139	0.5549
	H	636.1	1155.7	1168.1	1199.4	1225.7	1248.4	1269.4	1287.8	1304.7	1320.7	1336.2	1351.2	1420.1	1483.7	1544.4	1603.9
	S	0.8304	1.3147	1.3262	1.3549	1.3786	1.3987	1.4170	1.4327	1.4469	1.4602	1.4728	1.4848	1.5374	2.5825	1.6227	1.6597
1725 (615.13)	V	0.0244	0.2309	0.2384	0.2593	0.2780	0.2943	0.3088	0.3222	0.3346	0.3463	0.3575	0.3684	0.4183	0.4636	0.5058	0.5464
	H	639.1	1154.1	1165.2	1195.6	1222.4	1245.8	1266.8	1285.5	1302.7	1318.9	1334.5	1349.5	1419.0	1482.9	1543.7	1603.4
	S	0.8332	1.3123	1.3226	1.3505	1.3747	1.3954	1.4136	1.4296	1.4441	1.4575	1.4702	1.4822	1.5352	1.5806	1.6208	1.6579
1750 (617.11)	V	0.0245	0.2265	0.2329	0.2529	0.2718	0.2882	0.3028	0.3162	0.3285	0.3402	0.3514	0.3622	0.4116	0.4564	0.4982	0.5383
	H	642.1	1152.5	1162.0	1191.7	1219.2	1243.1	1264.5	1283.6	1300.9	1317.4	1333.1	1348.3	1418.1	1481.2	1543.3	1603.0
	S	0.8359	1.3099	1.3187	1.3460	1.3708	1.3919	1.4105	1.4269	1.4414	1.4550	1.4678	1.4800	1.5333	1.5780	1.6192	1.6562

Year (value)		V/H/S																
1775 (619.07)	V	0.0246		0.2222	0.2466	0.2657	0.2822	0.2968	0.3102	0.3225	0.3340	0.3452	0.3559	0.4049	0.4493	0.4906	0.5302
	H	645.0		1150.9	1187.6	1216.0	1240.4	1262.1	1281.5	1299.0	1315.5	1331.5	1346.8	1416.9	1481.3	1542.5	1602.3
	S	0.8386		1.3076	1.3413	1.3669	1.3885	1.4074	1.4239	1.4387	1.4523	1.4653	1.4775	1.5311	1.5767	1.6173	1.6544
1800 (621.00)	V	0.0247		0.2180	0.2405	0.2598	0.2764	0.2912	0.3045	0.3168	0.3283	0.3393	0.3499	0.3986	0.4425	0.4834	0.5224
	H	648.0		1149.3	1183.7	1212.7	1237.6	1259.8	1279.6	1297.4	1313.9	1329.9	1345.3	1416.0	1480.6	1542.0	1601.8
	S	0.8412		1.3051	1.3367	1.3628	1.3848	1.4041	1.4211	1.4360	1.4497	1.4627	1.4750	1.5290	1.5748	1.6155	1.6526
1825 (622.92)	V	0.0248		0.2139	0.2345	0.2540	0.2708	0.2855	0.2991	0.3112	0.3225	0.3335	0.3441	0.3924	0.4357	0.4763	0.5147
	H	650.9		1147.7	1179.5	1209.4	1234.9	1257.3	1277.8	1295.6	1312.2	1328.3	1343.9	1415.0	1479.6	1541.3	1601.1
	S	0.8439		1.3028	1.3319	1.3589	1.3815	1.4009	1.4185	1.4334	1.4471	1.4602	1.4727	1.5270	1.5728	1.6137	1.6508
1850 (624.82)	V	0.0249		0.2099	0.2285	0.2482	0.2651	0.2799	0.2936	0.3056	0.3170	0.3279	0.3384	0.3863	0.4293	0.4695	0.5075
	H	653.9		1145.9	1175.1	1205.8	1231.8	1254.8	1275.6	1293.5	1310.5	1326.7	1342.4	1413.9	1479.0	1540.8	1600.8
	S	0.8465		1.3002	1.3269	1.3546	1.3776	1.3976	1.4154	1.4305	1.4445	1.4577	1.4703	1.5248	1.5710	1.6120	1.6492
1875 (626.69)	V	0.0251		0.2060	0.2225	0.2427	0.2597	0.2746	0.2882	0.3003	0.3115	0.3224	0.3328	0.3804	0.4229	0.4626	0.5003
	H	656.9		1144.2	1170.5	1202.3	1229.0	1252.3	1273.5	1291.8	1308.7	1325.2	1340.8	1412.9	1478.0	1540.2	1600.3
	S	0.8491		1.2977	1.3218	1.3504	1.3741	1.3943	1.4124	1.4278	1.4418	1.4552	1.4677	1.5227	1.5689	1.6101	1.6475
1900 (628.55)	V	0.0252		0.2022	0.2165	0.2371	0.2543	0.2694	0.2828	0.2950	0.3063	0.3171	0.3274	0.3747	0.4170	0.4562	0.4934
	H	659.9		1142.4	1165.6	1198.8	1225.9	1249.8	1271.0	1289.7	1307.0	1323.5	1339.4	1411.9	1477.5	1539.7	1599.8
	S	0.8517		1.2951	1.3163	1.3462	1.3702	1.3910	1.4091	1.4249	1.4392	1.4526	1.4653	1.5207	1.5672	1.6084	1.6457
1925 (630.38)	V	0.0253		0.1985	0.2107	0.2317	0.2491	0.2642	0.2776	0.2898	0.3010	0.3118	0.3221	0.3690	0.4109	0.4497	0.4864
	H	662.8		1140.6	1160.9	1195.0	1223.1	1247.5	1268.7	1287.7	1305.1	1321.8	1337.8	1410.7	1476.6	1538.9	1599.0
	S	0.8543		1.2926	1.3111	1.3419	1.3667	1.3878	1.4061	1.4221	1.4364	1.4500	1.4628	1.5185	1.5652	1.6065	1.6438
1950 (632.20)	V	0.0254		0.1949	0.2049	0.2264	0.2440	0.2591	0.2726	0.2848	0.2960	0.3067	0.3170	0.3636	0.4052	0.4436	0.4800
	H	665.7		1138.8	1155.8	1191.3	1220.0	1244.8	1266.5	1285.8	1303.4	1320.2	1336.3	1409.7	1476.0	1538.4	1598.8
	S	0.8569		1.2901	1.3056	1.3376	1.3630	1.3846	1.4031	1.4194	1.4339	1.4476	1.4604	1.5165	1.5635	1.6048	1.6424
1975 (634.00)	V	0.0256		0.1913	0.1992	0.2212	0.2391	0.2544	0.2678	0.2798	0.2910	0.3016	0.3117	0.3581	0.3994	0.4376	0.4737
	H	668.7		1137.0	1150.5	1187.5	1217.0	1242.4	1264.4	1283.6	1301.5	1318.3	1334.4	1408.4	1475.1	1537.8	1598.4
	S	0.8595		1.2877	1.3000	1.3334	1.3595	1.3816	1.4004	1.4165	1.4313	1.4450	1.4579	1.5144	1.5617	1.6032	1.6409

Table B-2/ Superheated Steam (Continued)

Temperature, °F

Abs press., psia (sat. temp.)	V H S	Sat. water	Sat. steam	660	680	700	720	740	760	780	800	820	850	900	1000	1100	1200
2000 (635.78)	V	0.0257	0.1879	0.2162	0.2344	0.2498	0.2633	0.2752	0.2862	0.2966	0.3067	0.3165	0.3305	0.3528	0.3940	0.4319	0.4678
	H	671.7	1135.2	1183.7	1214.3	1240.0	1262.4	1281.8	1299.6	1316.4	1332.7	1348.6	1371.1	1407.2	1473.5	1537.4	1598.6
	S	0.8620	1.2851	1.3289	1.3560	1.3783	1.3975	1.4138	1.4285	1.4422	1.4552	1.4677	1.4851	1.5122	1.5592	1.6015	1.6395
2025 (637.54)	V	0.0258	0.1845	0.2112	0.2296	0.2452	0.2587	0.2707	0.2816	0.2919	0.3020	0.3116	0.3257	0.3478	0.3887	0.4262	0.4617
	H	674.7	1133.3	1179.9	1211.1	1237.5	1260.3	1280.1	1297.9	1314.8	1331.3	1347.1	1370.1	1406.2	1473.8	1537.0	1598.1
	S	0.8646	1.2826	1.3246	1.3523	1.3752	1.3947	1.4114	1.4261	1.4398	1.4530	1.4654	1.4832	1.5103	1.5552	1.6001	1.6380
2050 (639.29)	V	0.0259	0.1812	0.2062	0.2248	0.2405	0.2541	0.2661	0.2769	0.2872	0.2972	0.3067	0.3208	0.3428	0.3833	0.4205	0.4556
	H	677.6	1131.4	1175.7	1207.7	1234.6	1257.9	1278.0	1295.9	1313.0	1329.5	1345.3	1368.6	1405.1	1472.8	1536.2	1597.4
	S	0.8671	1.2800	1.3199	1.3483	1.3717	1.3916	1.4085	1.4233	1.4372	1.4504	1.4628	1.4808	1.5082	1.5562	1.5982	1.6362
2075 (641.02)	V	0.0261	0.1780	0.2013	0.2200	0.2358	0.2494	0.2615	0.2724	0.2828	0.2927	0.3022	0.3161	0.3374	0.3782	0.4151	0.4499
	H	680.5	1129.5	1171.5	1204.3	1231.6	1255.2	1275.7	1294.0	1311.5	1328.1	1344.0	1367.3	1403.1	1472.1	1535.7	1597.0
	S	0.8697	1.2776	1.3154	1.3445	1.3682	1.3884	1.4056	1.4208	1.4350	1.4483	1.4608	1.4788	1.5056	1.5546	1.5967	1.6348
2100 (642.73)	V	0.0262	0.1748	0.1964	0.2152	0.2310	0.2447	0.2568	0.2679	0.2783	0.2882	0.2977	0.3114	0.3319	0.3730	0.4096	0.4441
	H	683.4	1127.6	1167.3	1200.4	1228.2	1252.2	1273.0	1292.0	1309.6	1326.4	1342.6	1365.8	1400.8	1471.0	1534.8	1596.4
	S	0.8722	1.2751	1.3108	1.3401	1.3643	1.3848	1.4023	1.4180	1.4323	1.4458	1.4585	1.4764	1.5027	1.5525	1.5947	1.6330
2125 (644.43)	V	0.0263	0.1716	0.1918	0.2108	0.2268	0.2406	0.2527	0.2637	0.2739	0.2838	0.2933	0.3070	0.3280	0.3682	0.4045	0.4386
	H	686.3	1125.6	1163.0	1197.3	1225.7	1250.2	1271.3	1290.2	1307.8	1324.8	1341.2	1364.7	1400.8	1470.5	1534.5	1596.0
	S	0.8747	1.2726	1.3060	1.3364	1.3611	1.3820	1.3994	1.4151	1.4294	1.4430	1.4559	1.4740	1.5011	1.5505	1.5929	1.6311
2150 (646.11)	V	0.0265	0.1685	0.1872	0.2064	0.2225	0.2364	0.2485	0.2594	0.2695	0.2793	0.2889	0.3026	0.3240	0.3633	0.3993	0.4331
	H	689.2	1123.5	1158.6	1193.7	1222.7	1247.7	1269.1	1288.1	1305.7	1322.7	1339.4	1363.2	1400.5	1469.4	1533.8	1595.3
	S	0.8773	1.2700	1.3015	1.3326	1.3578	1.3792	1.3972	1.4129	1.4272	1.4408	1.4540	1.4723	1.5003	1.5492	1.5918	1.6300
2175 (647.77)	V	0.0266	0.1655	0.1828	0.2018	0.2182	0.2321	0.2442	0.2552	0.2654	0.2752	0.2847	0.2983	0.3196	0.3587	0.3943	0.4279
	H	692.0	1121.5	1154.3	1189.7	1219.8	1244.9	1266.5	1286.1	1304.0	1321.3	1338.0	1361.9	1399.4	1468.9	1533.1	1595.0
	S	0.8798	1.2676	1.2971	1.3284	1.3546	1.3760	1.3942	1.4104	1.4250	1.4388	1.4519	1.4704	1.4985	1.5478	1.5903	1.6288

2200 (649.42)	V	0.0267	0.1626	0.1773	0.1972	0.2138	0.2277	0.2399	0.2509	0.2612	0.2710	0.2804	0.2939	0.3151	0.3540	0.3893	0.4226
	H	695.0	1119.4	1148.0	1185.8	1216.2	1241.8	1263.8	1283.6	1302.9	1319.5	1336.2	1360.3	1398.1	1467.9	1532.3	1594.3
	S	0.8823	1.2649	1.2906	1.3239	1.3504	1.3723	1.3907	1.4072	1.4229	1.4362	1.4494	1.4679	1.4962	1.5458	1.5884	1.6269
2225 (651.06)	V	0.0269	0.1597	0.1727	0.1931	0.2097	0.2237	0.2360	0.2471	0.2574	0.2671	0.2765	0.2900	0.3109	0.3495	0.3847	0.4175
	H	697.9	1117.4	1142.7	1182.1	1213.3	1239.1	1261.7	1282.0	1300.5	1318.0	1335.2	1359.2	1397.0	1467.0	1531.9	1593.7
	S	0.8848	1.2625	1.2852	1.3201	1.3472	1.3693	1.3883	1.4051	1.4201	1.4341	1.4476	1.4661	1.4944	1.5441	1.5871	1.6255
2250 (652.67)	V	0.0270	0.1569	0.1680	0.1889	0.2055	0.2197	0.2320	0.2432	0.2535	0.2632	0.2726	0.2860	0.3066	0.3449	0.3800	0.4125
	H	700.8	1115.3	1137.0	1178.0	1209.7	1236.5	1259.2	1279.8	1298.6	1316.3	1333.5	1357.3	1395.5	1465.8	1531.2	1593.1
	S	0.8873	1.2599	1.2795	1.3156	1.3432	1.3661	1.3852	1.4022	1.4175	1.4317	1.4452	1.4640	1.4922	1.5421	1.5854	1.6239
2275 (654.27)	V	0.0272	0.1542	0.1630	0.1848	0.2018	0.2159	0.2281	0.2393	0.2496	0.2594	0.2688	0.2821	0.3026	0.3407	0.3755	0.4077
	H	703.8	1113.2	1130.8	1174.3	1207.1	1233.9	1256.7	1277.6	1296.6	1314.8	1332.1	1356.5	1394.4	1465.1	1530.7	1592.8
	S	0.8898	1.2573	1.2731	1.3116	1.3401	1.3630	1.3822	1.3995	1.4151	1.4295	1.4431	1.4619	1.4903	1.5405	1.5839	1.6225
2300 (655.87)	V	0.0274	0.1514	0.1580	0.1807	0.1980	0.2120	0.2241	0.2353	0.2457	0.2556	0.2649	0.2781	0.2986	0.3365	0.3709	0.4029
	H	706.7	1111.0	1124.2	1169.9	1204.0	1230.9	1253.9	1275.0	1294.5	1312.9	1330.3	1354.9	1393.2	1464.3	1529.9	1592.2
	S	0.8923	1.2547	1.2665	1.3070	1.3366	1.3596	1.3790	1.3964	1.4123	1.4270	1.4407	1.4597	1.4884	1.5388	1.5823	1.6210
2325 (657.74)	V	0.0275	0.1488	0.1530	0.1766	0.1941	0.2083	0.2207	0.2319	0.2423	0.2520	0.2613	0.2744	0.2948	0.3324	0.3665	0.3983
	H	709.7	1108.8	1117.1	1165.7	1200.4	1228.2	1252.0	1273.3	1293.0	1311.5	1329.0	1353.6	1392.1	1463.5	1529.2	1591.7
	S	0.8948	1.2521	1.2595	1.3025	1.3327	1.3565	1.3765	1.3941	1.4101	1.4249	1.4387	1.4577	1.4866	1.5372	1.5807	1.6196
2350 (659.00)	V	0.0277	0.1462	0.1479	0.1725	0.1901	0.2046	0.2172	0.2285	0.2389	0.2484	0.2576	0.2706	0.2910	0.3282	0.3621	0.3936
	H	712.6	1106.5	1109.7	1161.2	1196.6	1225.2	1249.8	1271.7	1291.6	1309.8	1327.3	1352.1	1391.0	1462.3	1528.3	1590.9
	S	0.8974	1.2495	1.2524	1.2980	1.3287	1.3532	1.3739	1.3920	1.4082	1.4227	1.4365	1.4557	1.4848	1.5354	1.5791	1.6180
2375 (660.55)	V	0.0278	0.1436	......	0.1686	0.1863	0.2010	0.2137	0.2250	0.2353	0.2450	0.2541	0.2671	0.2873	0.3244	0.3580	0.3892
	H	715.6	1104.0	......	1156.9	1193.0	1222.4	1247.5	1269.5	1289.6	1308.3	1325.8	1350.8	1389.8	1461.7	1527.8	1590.4
	S	0.9000	1.2467	......	1.2935	1.3249	1.3501	1.3712	1.3893	1.4057	1.4207	1.4344	1.4537	1.4830	1.5340	1.5777	1.6166
2400 (662.09)	V	0.0280	0.1410	......	0.1646	0.1824	0.1974	0.2101	0.2214	0.2317	0.2415	0.2506	0.2636	0.2836	0.3205	0.3538	0.3848
	H	718.5	1101.4	......	1152.2	1189.1	1219.4	1244.7	1267.1	1287.3	1306.5	1324.2	1349.6	1388.5	1460.8	1526.9	1589.8
	S	0.9025	1.2438	......	1.2887	1.3208	1.3467	1.3680	1.3865	1.4030	1.4183	1.4323	1.4519	1.4810	1.5323	1.5761	1.6152

Table B-2/ Superheated Steam (Continued)

Abs press., psia (sat. temp.)		Sat. water	Sat. steam	680	700	720	740	760	780	800	820	850	900	950	1000	1100	1200
2450 (665.12)	V	0.0283	0.1360	0.1567	0.1750	0.1902	0.2032	0.2147	0.2250	0.2347	0.2440	0.2569	0.2766	0.2954	0.3130	0.3458	0.3764
	H	724.6	1096.3	1142.3	1181.3	1212.9	1239.5	1262.8	1283.5	1302.9	1321.4	1347.1	1386.3	1423.8	1459.0	1525.6	1588.9
	S	0.9076	1.2381	1.2787	1.3127	1.3397	1.3620	1.3813	1.3981	1.4136	1.4282	1.4481	1.4774	1.5045	1.5290	1.5732	1.6125
2500 (668.10)	V	0.0287	0.1313	0.1488	0.1680	0.1834	0.1967	0.2083	0.2188	0.2285	0.2375	0.2503	0.2700	0.2884	0.3058	0.3381	0.3683
	H	730.7	1091.0	1131.9	1173.9	1206.8	1234.5	1258.6	1280.1	1299.9	1318.3	1344.2	1384.3	1421.8	1457.3	1524.2	1587.9
	S	0.9127	1.2322	1.2683	1.3048	1.3329	1.3562	1.3761	1.3936	1.4095	1.4240	1.4440	1.4740	1.5011	1.5258	1.5701	1.6097
2550 (671.03)	V	0.0291	0.1264	0.1408	0.1606	0.1766	0.1902	0.2020	0.2125	0.2223	0.2315	0.2440	0.2634	0.2817	0.2989	0.3308	0.3604
	H	736.7	1085.6	1120.0	1164.7	1199.8	1228.9	1254.0	1276.0	1296.5	1315.6	1341.5	1381.8	1419.8	1455.6	1522.9	1586.7
	S	0.9179	1.2265	1.2568	1.2957	1.3257	1.3502	1.3709	1.3888	1.4052	1.4202	1.4402	1.4704	1.4979	1.5228	1.5674	1.6070
2600 (673.91)	V	0.0295	0.1219	0.1323	0.1541	0.1706	0.1842	0.1961	0.2066	0.2164	0.2256	0.2380	0.2573	0.2754	0.2924	0.3237	0.3530
	H	743.1	1080.1	1106.0	1157.0	1194.0	1223.9	1249.7	1272.2	1293.1	1312.6	1338.9	1379.7	1418.1	1454.2	1521.6	1585.8
	S	0.9232	1.2205	1.2433	1.2877	1.3193	1.3444	1.3657	1.3840	1.4008	1.4161	1.4364	1.4670	1.4947	1.5199	1.5645	1.6044
2650 (676.75)	V	0.0300	0.1173	0.1235	0.1469	0.1640	0.1782	0.1903	0.2009	0.2108	0.2200	0.2322	0.2514	0.2691	0.2859	0.3169	0.3458
	H	749.5	1074.5	1090.1	1146.8	1186.4	1218.3	1245.1	1268.3	1289.9	1309.9	1336.6	1377.5	1415.9	1452.2	1520.2	1584.7
	S	0.9287	1.2147	1.2284	1.2777	1.3116	1.3384	1.3606	1.3794	1.3967	1.4125	1.4328	1.4637	1.4914	1.5167	1.5618	1.6018
2700 (679.54)	V	0.0305	0.1123	....	0.1402	0.1581	0.1725	0.1846	0.1954	0.2053	0.2147	0.2269	0.2458	0.2632	0.2798	0.3105	0.3389
	H	756.1	1068.3	....	1137.5	1179.7	1213.0	1240.3	1264.5	1286.5	1307.2	1334.0	1375.7	1414.0	1450.6	1519.2	1583.8
	S	0.9342	1.2082	....	1.2684	1.3045	1.3325	1.3550	1.3747	1.3923	1.4086	1.4293	1.4606	1.4882	1.5137	1.5592	1.5993
2750 (682.28)	V	0.0310	0.1077	....	0.1335	0.1520	0.1670	0.1794	0.1902	0.2000	0.2094	0.2215	0.2402	0.2576	0.2740	0.3043	0.3322
	H	763.0	1061.8	....	1127.1	1172.2	1207.4	1236.0	1260.8	1283.0	1304.2	1331.4	1373.3	1412.2	1449.2	1518.0	1582.8
	S	0.9399	1.2016	....	1.2583	1.2969	1.3265	1.3501	1.3703	1.3881	1.4048	1.4258	1.4572	1.4853	1.5110	1.5566	1.5969
2800 (684.98)	V	0.0316	0.1032	....	0.1267	0.1461	0.1615	0.1741	0.1851	0.1950	0.2045	0.2166	0.2351	0.2521	0.2685	0.2983	0.3258
	H	770.0	1054.6	....	1115.9	1164.5	1201.5	1231.3	1257.0	1279.8	1301.7	1329.3	1371.5	1410.4	1447.9	1517.0	1581.9
	S	0.9458	1.1944	....	1.2476	1.2892	1.3203	1.3449	1.3658	1.3840	1.4013	1.4226	1.4542	1.4823	1.5084	1.5542	1.5945

Temperature, °F

Sat. press. (temp.)																
2850 (687.65)	V	0.0322	0.0986	0.1198	0.1404	0.1563	0.1690	0.1801	0.1903	0.1995	0.2117	0.2298	0.2469	0.2629	0.2925	0.3197
	H	777.5	1046.6	1103.5	1156.6	1195.8	1226.5	1252.9	1276.9	1298.4	1326.8	1368.9	1408.7	1446.0	1515.8	1581.1
	S	0.9521	1.1866	1.2359	1.2813	1.3143	1.3397	1.3611	1.3803	1.3973	1.4192	1.4507	1.4795	1.5055	1.5517	1.5923
2900 (690.26)	V	0.0329	0.0941	0.1126	0.1348	0.1511	0.1641	0.1754	0.1855	0.1949	0.2069	0.2250	0.2418	0.2578	0.2870	0.3138
	H	785.2	1038.1	1089.2	1148.3	1189.5	1221.6	1249.1	1273.3	1295.7	1324.2	1367.1	1406.9	1444.8	1514.8	1580.2
	S	0.9586	1.1785	1.2228	1.2733	1.3080	1.3345	1.3569	1.3762	1.3939	1.4159	1.4480	1.4767	1.5032	1.5495	1.5902
2950 (692.83)	V	0.0337	0.0895	0.1052	0.1292	0.1460	0.1593	0.1708	0.1809	0.1902	0.2023	0.2202	0.2369	0.2527	0.2815	0.3081
	H	793.6	1028.9	1073.2	1139.5	1183.1	1216.6	1245.1	1269.8	1292.5	1321.7	1364.9	1405.1	1443.2	1513.5	1579.4
	S	0.9655	1.1697	1.2080	1.2647	1.3014	1.3290	1.3522	1.3720	1.3898	1.4124	1.4448	1.4738	1.5004	1.5469	1.5879
3000 (695.37)	V	0.0346	0.0849	0.0972	0.1236	0.1410	0.1546	0.1661	0.1763	0.1856	0.1978	0.2155	0.2322	0.2478	0.2763	0.3027
	H	802.6	1019.3	1054.0	1130.3	1176.4	1211.4	1240.6	1266.0	1289.0	1319.0	1362.5	1403.4	1441.7	1512.4	1578.9
	S	0.9731	1.1607	1.1907	1.2559	1.2947	1.3236	1.3474	1.3677	1.3858	1.4090	1.4416	1.4711	1.4978	1.5447	1.5860
3050 (697.84)	V	0.0357	0.0804	0.0868	0.1183	0.1361	0.1499	0.1617	0.1719	0.1812	0.1935	0.2111	0.2275	0.2431	0.2712	0.2973
	H	812.9	1007.7	1025.0	1121.2	1169.6	1205.9	1236.3	1262.4	1285.7	1316.4	1360.4	1401.3	1440.2	1511.1	1577.9
	S	0.9818	1.1501	1.1650	1.2472	1.2879	1.3179	1.3437	1.3635	1.3819	1.4056	1.4386	1.4681	1.4952	1.5422	1.5837
3100 (700.29)	V	0.0372	0.0752	……	0.1128	0.1312	0.1456	0.1576	0.1680	0.1771	0.1891	0.2068	0.2231	0.2385	0.2663	0.2921
	H	824.6	994.0	……	1110.8	1162.4	1200.9	1232.5	1259.4	1282.7	1313.4	1358.2	1399.5	1438.7	1509.9	1577.0
	S	0.9916	1.1376	……	1.2374	1.2808	1.3126	1.3383	1.3599	1.3782	1.4019	1.4355	1.4653	1.4926	1.5398	1.5815
3150 (702.69)	V	0.0392	0.0691	……	0.1075	0.1266	0.1410	0.1532	0.1636	0.1729	0.1850	0.2024	0.2187	0.2341	0.2615	0.2871
	H	841.3	976.3	……	1100.3	1155.3	1194.7	1227.6	1254.9	1279.2	1310.5	1355.5	1397.5	1437.2	1508.6	1576.1
	S	1.0056	1.1217	……	1.2276	1.2738	1.3064	1.3331	1.3550	1.3741	1.3983	1.4320	1.4623	1.4900	1.5373	1.5792
3200 (705.04)	V	0.0443	0.0596	……	0.1024	0.1217	0.1368	0.1493	0.1596	0.1687	0.1810	0.1985	0.2145	0.2296	0.2570	0.2822
	H	871.4	946.6	……	1089.8	1146.9	1189.3	1223.4	1251.1	1275.2	1307.7	1353.8	1395.7	1435.2	1507.6	1575.3
	S	1.0311	1.0958	……	1.2180	1.2660	1.3011	1.3288	1.3510	1.3699	1.3950	1.4296	1.4598	1.4874	1.5353	1.5774
3206.2‡ (705.34)	V	0.0541	0.0541	……	0.1018	0.1211	0.1363	0.1488	0.1591	0.1682	0.1805	0.1980	0.2140	0.2290	0.2564	0.2816
	H	910.3	910.3	……	1088.5	1145.8	1188.5	1222.9	1250.6	1274.8	1307.3	1353.4	1395.3	1434.8	1507.3	1575.1
	S	1.0645	1.0645	……	1.2170	1.2652	1.3005	1.3284	1.3506	1.3696	1.3947	1.4293	1.4596	1.4872	1.5351	1.5773

‡ Critical pressure.